Empirical Implications of Theoretical Models in Political Science

Tension has long existed in the political and social sciences between quantitative and qualitative approaches on one hand, and theory-minded and empirical techniques on the other. The latter divide has grown sharper in the wake of new behavioral and experimental perspectives that draw on both sides of these modeling schemes. This book works to address this disconnect by establishing a framework for methodological unification: empirical implications of theoretical models (EITM). This framework connects behavioral and applied statistical concepts, develops analogues of these concepts, and links and evaluates these analogues. The authors offer detailed explanations of how these concepts may be framed to assist researchers interested in incorporating EITM into their own research. They go on to demonstrate how EITM can be put into practice for a range of political and social science questions.

JIM GRANATO is Associate Dean in the Hobby School of Public Affairs at the University of Houston.

MELODY LO is the Endowed Dean in the Neil Griffin College of Business at Arkansas State University.

M. C. SUNNY WONG is a professor in the Hobby School of Public Affairs at the University of Houston.

Empirical Implications of Theoretical Models in Political Science

JIM GRANATO
University of Houston

MELODY LO
Arkansas State University

M. C. SUNNY WONG
University of Houston

CAMBRIDGE
UNIVERSITY PRESS

University Printing House, Cambridge CB2 8BS, United Kingdom

One Liberty Plaza, 20th Floor, New York, NY 10006, USA

477 Williamstown Road, Port Melbourne, VIC 3207, Australia

314–321, 3rd Floor, Plot 3, Splendor Forum, Jasola District Centre, New Delhi – 110025, India

79 Anson Road, #06-04/06, Singapore 079906

Cambridge University Press is part of the University of Cambridge.

It furthers the University's mission by disseminating knowledge in the pursuit of education, learning, and research at the highest international levels of excellence.

www.cambridge.org
Information on this title: www.cambridge.org/9780521193863
DOI: 10.1017/9781139026819

© Cambridge University Press 2021

This publication is in copyright. Subject to statutory exception and to the provisions of relevant collective licensing agreements, no reproduction of any part may take place without the written permission of Cambridge University Press.

First published 2021

A catalogue record for this publication is available from the British Library.

Library of Congress Cataloging-in-Publication Data
Names: Granato, Jim, 1960– author. | Lo, Melody, author. |
  Wong, M. C. Sunny, 1976– author.
Title: Empirical implications of theoretical models in political, social and
  economic sciences / Jim Granato, Melody Lo, M.C. Sunny Wong.
Description: New York : Cambridge University Press, [2021] |
  Includes bibliographical references and index.
Identifiers: LCCN 2020041346 (print) | LCCN 2020041347 (ebook) |
  ISBN 9780521193863 (hardback) | ISBN 9780521122801 (paperback) |
  ISBN 9781139026819 (epub)
Subjects: LCSH: Political science–Research–Methodology. |
  Social science–Research–Methodology. | Economics–Research–Methodology.
Classification: LCC JA86 .G73 2021 (print) | LCC JA86 (ebook) | DDC 300.1/1–dc23
LC record available at https://lccn.loc.gov/2020041346
LC ebook record available at https://lccn.loc.gov/2020041347

ISBN 978-0-521-19386-3 Hardback
ISBN 978-0-521-12280-1 Paperback

Cambridge University Press has no responsibility for the persistence or accuracy of URLs for external or third-party internet websites referred to in this publication and does not guarantee that any content on such websites is, or will remain, accurate or appropriate.

To John and Frank

Contents

List of Figures   *page* xiii
List of Tables   xv
Preface   xvii
Acknowledgments   xxxv

PART I EITM: BACKGROUND AND FRAMEWORK

1   Modeling Insights and Pathbreaking Institutions: A Sketch   3
    1.1   *The Utility of Models and Modeling*   4
    1.2   *Institutional Developments*   5
       1.2.1   *The SSRC*   6
       1.2.2   *The Econometric Society and the Cowles Commission*   7
       1.2.3   *The Political Science Department at the University of Rochester*   9
       1.2.4   *The Society for Political Methodology*   10
    1.3   *Summary*   10

2   Contemporary Methodological Practices   12
    2.1   *Scientific Research Methods: A Dialogue between Theory and Empirics*   12
    2.2   *Noncumulative Research Practices*   14
       2.2.1   *Assessment*   18
    2.3   *Noncumulative Practices: An Example of What Can Go Wrong*   19
    2.4   *Summary*   24

3   The EITM Framework   26
    3.1   *The EITM Framework*   27
    3.2   *Examples of Methodological Unification*   30
       3.2.1   *Example 1: The Solow Model*   30

		3.2.2 Example 2: Ostrom's Social Dilemma Research	36
	3.3	EITM Criticisms	38
		3.3.1 Motivation Criticisms	39
		3.3.2 EITM and the Hypothetico-Deductive (H-D) Method	44
		3.3.3 EITM Limitations	49
	3.4	Summary	50
	3.5	Appendix: The Derivation of the Conditional Convergence Hypothesis	51

PART II EITM IN PRACTICE

4	Economic Voting		57
	4.1	Background	57
	4.2	Step 1: Relating Expectations, Uncertainty, and Measurement Error	59
	4.3	Step 2: Analogues for Expectations, Uncertainty, and Measurement Error	59
	4.4	Step 3: Unifying and Evaluating the Analogues	61
	4.5	Summary	62
	4.6	Appendix	67
		4.6.1 Empirical Analogues	67
		4.6.2 Formal Analogues	69
		4.6.3 Signal-Extraction Problems	74
5	Strategists and Macropartisanship		78
	5.1	Background	78
	5.2	Step 1: Relating Expectations and Persistence	80
	5.3	Step 2: Analogues for Expectations and Persistence	81
	5.4	Step 3: Unifying and Evaluating the Analogues	82
	5.5	Summary	84
	5.6	Appendix	84
		5.6.1 The Clarke and Granato (2004) MSV Solution	84
		5.6.2 The Concept of Persistence: An EITM Perspective	86
		5.6.3 Empirical Analogues	87
		5.6.4 Formal Analogues	90
6	Macro Policy		108
	6.1	Background	108
	6.2	Step 1: Relating Expectations, Learning, and Persistence	110
	6.3	Step 2: Analogues for Expectations, Learning, and Persistence	110
	6.4	Step 3: Unifying and Evaluating the Analogues	112
	6.5	Summary	114
	6.6	Appendix	115
		6.6.1 Formal Analogues	116
		6.6.2 Adaptive Learning	117

Contents ix

7	Information Diffusion	124
	7.1 Background	124
	7.2 Step 1: Relating Social Interaction, Expectations, and Learning to Simultaneity and Prediction Error	126
	7.3 Step 2: Analogues for Social Interaction, Expectations, Learning, Simultaneity, and Prediction Error	127
	7.4 Step 3: Unifying and Evaluating the Analogues	132
	7.5 Summary	138
	7.6 Appendix	138
8	Political Parties and Representation	150
	8.1 Background	150
	8.2 Step 1: Relating Decision Making and Nominal Choice	151
	8.3 Step 2: Analogues for Decision Making and Nominal Choice	151
	8.4 Step 3: Unifying and Evaluating the Analogues	154
	8.5 Summary	155
	8.6 Appendix	157
	8.6.1 Empirical Analogues	157
	8.6.2 Formal Analogues	161
	8.6.3 Details on the Kedar (2005) Application	163
9	Voter Turnout	164
	9.1 Background	164
	9.2 Step 1: Relating Decision Making, Learning, and Discrete Choice	165
	9.3 Step 2: Analogues for Decision Making, Learning, and Discrete Choice	166
	9.4 Step 3: Unifying and Evaluating the Analogues	168
	9.5 Summary	170
	9.6 Appendix	171
	9.6.1 Empirical Analogues	171
	9.6.2 Formal Analogues	172
10	International Political Economy	174
	10.1 Background	174
	10.2 Step 1: Relating Decision Making, Bargaining, Strategic Interaction, and Nominal Choice	175
	10.3 Step 2: Analogues for Decision Making, Bargaining, Strategic Interaction, and Nominal Choice	176
	10.4 Step 3: Unifying and Evaluating the Analogues	177
	10.5 Summary	179
	10.6 Appendix	181
	10.6.1 Formal Analogues	181
11	Macro Political Economy	195
	11.1 Background	195
	11.2 Step 1: Relating Decision Making to Prediction	197
	11.3 Step 2: Analogues for Decision Making and Prediction	197

	11.3.1	Household Utility Maximization	197
	11.3.2	Firm Profit Maximization	199
	11.3.3	Governmental Approval Target Deviation Minimization	199
11.4	Step 3: Unifying and Evaluating the Analogues		201
11.5	Summary		204
11.6	Appendix		206
	11.6.1	The Derivation of Optimal Household Behavior	206
	11.6.2	General Equilibrium Modeling	208
	11.6.3	An introduction to Dynamic Optimization	225

12 Social Behavior and Evolutionary Dynamics — 247

- 12.1 Background — 247
- 12.2 Example I: ABM and Voter Turnout — 248
- 12.3 Step 1: Relating Decision Making and Learning to Prediction — 248
- 12.4 Step 2: Analogues for Decision Making, Learning, and Prediction — 249
- 12.5 Step 3: Unifying and Evaluating the Analogues — 252
- 12.6 Summary — 253
- 12.7 Example II: GA and Firm Price Setting — 255
- 12.8 Step 1: Relating Elements of Social Interaction (Imitation, Invention, Communication, and Examination) to Prediction — 256
- 12.9 Step 2: Analogues for Social Interaction and Prediction — 256
- 12.10 Step 3: Unifying and Evaluating the Analogues — 259
- 12.11 Summary — 262
- 12.12 Appendix — 263
  - 12.12.1 The Derivation of Optimal Firm Behavior — 264
  - 12.12.2 Formal Analogues: GA Operations — 266
  - 12.12.3 MATLAB Simulations — 270

13 Competition and Reward Valuation — 277

- 13.1 Background — 277
- 13.2 Step 1: Relating Decision Making and Prediction — 279
- 13.3 Step 2: Analogues for Decision Making and Prediction — 279
- 13.4 Step 3: Unifying and Evaluating the Analogues — 284
- 13.5 Summary and Extension — 290
- 13.6 Appendix — 293

14 An Alternative Unification Framework — 298

- 14.1 Background — 298
- 14.2 Jasso's Tripartite Structure: A Summary — 299
  - 14.2.1 Element I: The Framework — 300
  - 14.2.2 Element II: Theoretical Analysis — 303
  - 14.2.3 Element III: Empirical Analysis — 304
- 14.3 An Illustration of Extratheoretical Research: The Justice Index and Gender Gaps — 305
  - 14.3.1 Justice Indexes — 306
  - 14.3.2 Results — 308

14.4	*Summary*	311
14.5	*Appendix*	311
	14.5.1 *Linking Instruments to Outcomes: The Case of Monetary Aggregates*	311
	14.5.2 *Relating Theory to Measurement*	313
	14.5.3 *Aggregation Theory*	314
	14.5.4 *Index Number Theory*	318
15 Conclusion		321
15.1	*Current and Future Implementation Challenges*	322
	15.1.1 *Instruction: A Reorientation*	322
	15.1.2 *Supporting Science, Policy, and Society*	323
Bibliography		325
Index		347

Figures

2.1	Summary dialogue between theory and empirics	page 13
2.2	Noncumulative practices	19
2.3	Simulation results	23
5.1	Macropartisanship persistence (Π_2) and willingness to maintain a macropartisanship target (c_2)	83
5.2	A random walk process	89
5.3	An autoregressive process	90
5.4	Cobweb model with static expectation formation	92
5.5	Price movements in the cobweb model	94
6.1	Taylor rule parameters and inflation persistence	114
6.2	E-stability versus E-instability	122
6.3	Simulation with E-stable condition ($b < 1$)	122
6.4	Simulation with E-unstable condition ($b > 1$)	123
8.1	Estimated results of the compensational-voting model	155
9.1	Normal PDF and CDF	172
10.1	Extensive-form game of currency attacks	175
10.2	Extensive-form game with true utility	176
10.3	Leblang (2003) Model with regressors and parameters	178
10.4	Two-player, three-outcome game	182
10.5	Subgame perfect equilibrium in a two-player, three-outcome game	183
10.6	A two-player, three-outcome game with utility functions	183
10.7	The case of agent error	185
10.8	The case of private information	187
10.9	Identified model with regressors and parameters	189
10.10	Leblang (2003) data set in **STATA**	190
10.11	Leblang (2003) data set in **R**	191
10.12	Leblang's (2003) results in **R**	192

List of Figures

10.13	R codes for Leblang's (2003) results	194
11.1	Baseline model simulated data and actual data (Freeman and Houser 1998)	203
11.2	Simulated data for baseline and LAS models and actual data (Freeman and Houser 1998)	204
11.3	Simulated data for baseline and HAT models and actual data (Freeman and Houser 1998)	204
11.4	Calibration of the RBC model	222
11.5	Actual versus simulated volatilities of macro-variables (Prescott 1986)	224
11.6	Actual versus simulated correlations of macro-variables with GNP (Prescott 1986)	224
11.7	The optimal path of pie consumption	237
11.8	The function of $\dot{c}$	244
11.9	The function of $\dot{k}$	245
11.10	Phase diagram of the Ramsey Model	245
12.1	Simulations of adaptive rational model (BDT 2003)	252
12.2	Frequency distribution of voting turnout in South Bend, Indiana (*Source*: Fowler 2006)	254
12.3	Simulations of habitual voting model (Fowler 2006)	255
12.4	GA simulations (Stable case: $\lambda/\beta = 0.95 < 1$)	261
12.5	GA simulations (Unstable case: $\lambda/\beta = 1.05 > 1$)	263
12.6	An example of crossover	269
12.7	An example of mutation	269
12.8	The structure of the genetic algorithm process	271
12.9	The output level over time	271
12.10	The standard deviation of the output level over time	272
13.1	Nash equilibrium effort level for player i	281
13.2	Nash equilibrium effort level for player i by varying V_i and V_j	282
13.3	Player i's expected payoff level in Nash equilibrium	283
13.4	Player i's expected payoff value by varying V_i and V_j	284
13.5	Estimated effects of own-value, getting-deterred, and doing-the-deterring on efforts in the asymmetric information contest experiment	287
13.6	Percentage difference across treatments	288
13.7	Estimated effects of information treatments	289
13.8	Optimal effort levels for player i in a modified asymmetric contest model	292
14.1	Jasso's tripartite structure	299
14.2	Affine transformation	318
14.3	Gradient	319

Tables

7.1	Granger causality test results: Group H, Group L1, and Group L2	page 134
7.2	Unit root test results for MSE_H, $\sigma^2_{\tilde{e},L1}$, and $\sigma^2_{\tilde{e},L2}$	136
7.3	Johansen cointegration tests and Granger causality tests: MSE_H, $\sigma^2_{\tilde{e},L1}$, and $\sigma^2_{\tilde{e},L2}$	137
10.1	Leblang's (2003) results	180
11.1	Parameter values (Freeman and Houser 1998)	202
11.2	Shock values and corresponding transition probabilities (Freeman and Houser 1998)	202
11.3	The complete RBC model	216
11.4	The linearized RBC model	222
11.5	Parameter values	222
11.6	The dynamic optimal consumption of a pie	236
12.1	Adaptively rational voting model parameters	252
12.2	Cobweb model parameters	260
12.3	Crossover and mutation rates	260
13.1	Subjective values, equilibrium effort levels and expected payoffs	285
14.1	Justice indexes and gender gaps: US sample, ISJP 1991 (Jasso 2004, 426)	309

Preface

On July 9 and 10, 2001, the Political Science Program of the National Science Foundation (NSF) convened a workshop seeking ways to improve technical-analytical proficiency in Political Science. This workshop, termed the Empirical Implications of Theoretical Models (hereafter EITM) Workshop, suggested constructive approaches the NSF Political Science Program could employ to foster linkages between formal and empirical modeling.

Workshop members acknowledged a schism existed between those who engage in formal modeling focusing on quantifying abstract concepts mathematically, and those employing empirical modeling emphasizing applied statistics. As a consequence, a good deal of research in political science is competent in one technical area but lacking in another. To put this another way, and in more technical language, the impaired competency is reflected by either a formal approach with substandard (or no) empirical tests or an empirical approach without formal clarity. This "siloed" research contributes to a failure to identify the proximate causes explicated in a theory and, in turn, increases the difficulty of achieving a meaningful increase in scientific knowledge.

EITM was also thought to combat a particular set of applied statistical practices that had developed to the point where many statistical procedures were not intended to fix inaccuracies in specification. Rather, they were used to improve the significance levels of estimated parameters – regardless of the structural failure of a model. An emphasis on the t-statistic displaced emphasis on whether a model had systematic (as opposed to random) error.

In this book we extend and address these initial Workshop concerns – and more.

MOTIVATION, PROBLEM DIAGNOSIS, AND REMEDIES

There were several motivating factors contributing to the EITM initiative at NSF, ranging from reputational to matters of basic research design and competitiveness of grant submissions.[1] EITM was believed to be one way to reverse or at least address the following issues:

- Change the negative image of the political science discipline at NSF.
- Address old methodological antagonisms that negatively influence methodology training.
- Address fundamental reasons that lead to noncompetitive NSF proposals.

Motivation 1: Perceived Weakness of the Political Science Discipline at NSF

Granato and Scioli (2004) cite the following report relating how political science was perceived at NSF:

The recent Report of the APSA Ad Hoc Committee on the National Science Foundation found that political science had been characterized as, "not very exciting, not on the cutting edge of the research enterprise, and in certain quarters as journalistic and reformist." We disagree with this statement and believe there has been considerable improvement in political science in the past 40 years through the use of formal models, case studies, and applied statistical modeling (page 313).

This negative perception also led to skepticism as to whether the political science discipline (i.e., its current training practices) was technically equipped to improve on the existing methodological status quo. Social and Economic Sciences (SES) Division Director Bill Butz stated all was not certain about the outcome:

Sometimes that works and sometimes you're just pushing on a string because the field isn't ready for it yet...And getting you all here and I judge from the papers it resonated with you, too. And we'll see in the succeeding year or 2 or 3 whether this is pushing on a string or whether it's really lighting a fire (EITM Workshop Transcript 2001, 18).

Motivation 2: Old Antagonisms and the Methodological Status Quo

Workshop participants were from varied methodological backgrounds where long antagonisms had existed and led to splits in departments as well as various subfields. But, EITM workshop panelist Dina Zinnes expressed hope that these old antagonisms between formal and empirical modelers could be overcome and lead to some meaningful advice.

First let me just say what a pleasure it is to be amongst this group of people. I have to admit that when I got those initial memos I sort of put them on the side burners, thinking, well, okay, I'll look at them eventually, because I was worried about the fights

---

[1] This section draws directly from Granato et al. (2015, 372–376).

Preface

and the antagonisms that I thought would emerge. And it was with great delight that I read those and discovered, my gosh, there really is a consensus going on here. And listening to people this morning confirms that. I find that it's wonderful to see that both the empirical and statistical side and the modeling side really all sort of agree on certain things. And I think that's a fabulous beginning (EITM Workshop Transcript 2001, 113–114).

Motivation 3: Weaknesses in Research Design for NSF Competitions

In his role as SES Division Director over a six-year period, Director Butz reviewed and approved over 16,000 proposals. He stated:

And of those 16,000, about 2 years ago I formulated just a sort of a stylized FAQ what the principal ways are to be sure that you don't get money from NSF. And out of all the possible reasons, there were three that came to the front…Now, it varies some across fields. And I don't mean to say that this is particularly true of political science, but I want to show it to you because it may give you an additional context for the reasons why scientific proposals fail in the social and behavioral sciences – how to get zero money (EITM Workshop Transcript 2001, 13).

One reason for noncompetitive proposals – in Director Butz's survey – is that they are vague in conceptualization. There is "no sense of how what this person is doing fits into what came before conceptually or how the results, if they're confirmed or not confirmed, will feed some kind of a general conceptual sense of what's going on" (EITM Workshop Transcript 2001, 14).

A second reason is even though basic conceptualization exists, there is still a failure to connect theories to tests:

there will be a well-developed deductive theory at the beginning, and then the next section will be data, the next section will be empirical equations, and you'll look at the empirical stuff and it's just – it's not connected, or it's only connected in the vaguest sense (EITM Workshop Transcript 2001, 14–15).

A final reason in his summary was inadequate specification:

I don't know how many panels I've sat in where people say, well, you know, we can't really tell how they're going to form this proxy from these variables, or we can't really tell how they're going to get over the statistical problem with such and such (EITM Workshop Transcript 2001, 17).

In concluding his presentation Director Butz states:

There are many other things that are wrong with proposals, but these two – something wrong with the theory and something wrong with the data or the statistical methods are two of the three most common ones across – and I really don't think there are very many exceptions to this – across the 18, I think now 19, programs in the social, behavioral, and economic sciences here. So I thought I would just point that out (EITM Workshop Transcript 2001, 16–17).

PROBLEM DIAGNOSIS: SILOED TRAINING AND THINKING IN METHODOLOGY

Against this backdrop it was clear social science methodology and the attendant research designs based on said methodology played an important role in the negative outcomes above, not only for political science but for other social and behavioral sciences. While research methodology encompasses many elements, the EITM workshop focused on the state of quantitative methodology and whether it was a source of the problems cited above.

In diagnosing the factors, workshop participants reflected on the natural division of labor and specialization but also the cost of this natural division:

> Isolation – compartmentalization – of fields and sub-fields is the status quo in political science...This current field and sub-field structure exacerbates the separation between formal and empirical modeling. For example, focusing on a question that is particular to American Politics increases specialization and, turn, discourages integrating approaches and theories that would best come about from studying a particular research question in many countries (EITM Report 2002, 6).

Moreover, field and subfield isolation reinforces separation between formal and empirical analysis, including the belief that an:

> outdated perspective about formal and empirical analysis is the assertion that these technical-analytical approaches are simply interesting intellectual enterprises that lack political and social relevance (EITM Report 2002, 6).

The consequence of this divide is not neutral in its effect; indeed the effect can be negative. In particular:

> a good deal of research in political science is competent in one technical area, but lacking in another, that is, a formal approach with substandard (or no) empirical tests or an empirical approach without formal clarity. Such impaired competency contributes to a failure to identify the proximate causes explicated in a theory and, in turn, increases the difficulty of achieving a meaningful increase in scientific knowledge (EITM Report 2002, 1).

Siloed Training: Consequences for Formal and Empirical Modeling

In sum, a "siloed" research program contributes to a failure to identify the proximate causes explicated in a theory and, in turn, increases the difficulty to achieve a meaningful increase in scientific knowledge. Researchers limit themselves to the strengths and weaknesses of a single or narrow methodological approach. For formal modelers, this manifests itself in not respecting the facts; for researchers who rely exclusively on applied statistics, we find data mining, garbage-can regressions, and statistical patches (i.e., omega matrices) (Granato and Scioli 2004).

Siloed training in formal modeling can be sourced to basic comfort levels in approach:

Preface

Many formal modelers feel uncomfortable with powerful empirical concepts such as social norms, limited rationality, and psychological factors such as personality and identity. The usual argument is that formal models are not meant to fit data, or should not be. While there is much to be learned from pure theory and abstract formal arguments, the formal modeling isolation reinforces distance from basic circumstances that these abstract models could help to illuminate. This isolation also contributes to the basic misunderstanding noted above about the great attributes formal modeling brings to the scientific process (EITM Report 2002, 6–7).

Empirical modelers face their own limitations:

Empirical modeling isolation, on the other hand, is equally guilty of not advancing scientific understanding when it fails to incorporate their "more complex and general assumptions" into a mathematically identified model with direct and testable implications. Instead "errors" or "confounding variables" that derail the inferential process are treated as statistical problems that require only statistical fixes (EITM Report 2002, 7).

Factors Reinforcing the Status Quo

The resistance to unify formal and empirical modeling is due to several factors. These obstacles are not only contained in the 2002 EITM Report but also stated in Poteete, Janssen, and Ostrom (2010, 3–27). Among those factors are intellectual investment, training differences, and research practice.

THE INTELLECTUAL INVESTMENT Scholars have to invest in different skill sets. The intellectual investment needed for formal modeling is different than the knowledge needed for empirical modeling. But, given the greater mathematical demands in formal modeling the tendency is for students and scholars not to have sufficient training in formal modeling. This deficit is compounded since there are few incentives to motivate tenured faculty to try new methods, including using formal modeling as part of their tool kit.

TRAINING DIFFERENCES Empirical modelers devote their energies to data collection, measurement, and statistical matters, and formal modelers focus on mathematical rigor. This divide is reinforced in departments having a strong tradition in either formal or empirical analysis but not both.

RESEARCH PRACTICE For empirical modelers, model failures lead to emphasis on additional statistical training or more sophisticated uses of statistics to "correct" model breakdown. Formal modelers, on the other hand, deal with model controversies by considering alternative mathematical formulations, but this is usually done piecemeal while not engaging empirics. These research practices – by both modeling camps – can be reinforced in the publication realm since the review process and journal editors are in the same area of specialization and typically share similar methodological traditions.

These implementation challenges are deeply rooted in the academic community – fostered by career incentives – taking years to overcome (Poteete, Janssen, and Ostrom 2010, 18–24). Consequently, "old habits" learned in graduate school inhibit the desire to make the changes in skill development.

But, the situation is worse since many things learned in graduate school tend to become out-of-date by mid-career.

When methodological instruction reflects these status quo forces, successive generations will only repeat the shortcomings. Indeed, disciplines failing to provide incentives for this type of risk taking and re-tooling increase the occurrence of an:

assembly-line model of research production that imperils innovative theories and methodologies and, in turn, scientific breakthroughs. One could make the argument that EITM or initiatives like it are unnecessary because the unfettered marketplace of ideas expedites best scientific practices and progress. But, it is precisely because there are significant rigidities (training and otherwise) in the current academic setting (imperfect competition) which makes EITM-type initiatives not only necessary – but imperative (EITM Report 2002, 8).

We now see, and have repeatedly seen, practices unsuitable for addressing complex issues. The failure to build coherent research areas is not the only consequence either. Invalid policy prescriptions take place: Prediction without basic understanding of how a system under study works is of little scientific or social value.

PROPOSED REMEDIES: ENCOURAGING METHODOLOGICAL UNIFICATION

In both written and spoken commentaries, EITM Workshop participants recommended the NSF Political Science Program address the technical-analytical divide between formal and empirical approaches in three priority areas:

- Education: Training and Retraining.
- Dissemination of Knowledge: Conferences and Workshops.
- Research: Establishment of Research Work Groups.

The EITM initiative, then, was viewed as using these priority areas to expose students to integrating formal and empirical approaches. Students (and faculty) gain a vantage point and a means to escape the destructive practices resulting from siloed training and research. By integrating the two approaches students would be exposed to the strengths of both:

At the most basic level, formal modeling assists in the "construction of valid arguments such that the fact or facts to be explained can be derived from the premises that constitute the explanation." An important virtue of formal modeling is that it often yields surprising implications that would not have been considered had they not emerged from formal analysis. Conversely, if practiced correctly, applied statistical and case study analysis shows researchers where a model went wrong and leaves open the possibility that a more accurate model can be constructed (Granato and Scioli 2004, 314).

Preface

Deliverables from the 2001 EITM Workshop

The proposed remedies were circulated – in the form of a "Dear Colleague Letter" – approximately three weeks after the Workshop concluded and covered a call for establishing EITM summer training institutes, workshops, and assembling research work teams. The call was answered and the first competition was completed in March 2002 with the first EITM activities underway in the summer of 2002. There have been subsequent competitions for the summer training institutes and a one-time only EITM graduate fellowship program that was competed in fiscal year 2003.

A key outcome of the EITM initiative has been the EITM Summer Institutes. The Summer Institutes have taken place at:

- Harvard University (2002)
- University of Michigan (2003, 2006, 2009, 2015, 2018)
- Washington University, St. Louis (2003–2009)
- Duke University (2004, 2008, 2014, 2016)
- UC-Berkeley (2005, 2010, 2013, 2017)
- UCLA (2007)
- University of Chicago (2011)
- Princeton University (2012)
- Emory University (2019)
- University of Houston (2012–2017, 2019)

Generally, the EITM Summer Institutes cover two to four weeks of intensive training (the two- and three-week institutes often provide training six days per week) with morning and afternoon instructional presentations, and evening laboratories or workshops where participants complete their daily assignments.[2]

SCIENTIFIC PURPOSE

This book provides a framework for demonstrating how to unify formal and empirical analysis not only for political science questions but also for questions in the social sciences. By arguing for the scientific benefits of methodological unification, it is shown that the linkage between formal and empirical analysis

---

[2] Since the inception of the EITM initiative, hundreds of students have participated in the Summer Institutes, both stipend and non-stipend. If the data are broken down further the reach of the program may be understated. For example, Washington University reported that, for the 2003–2009 period, there were 163 stipend participants, and at least 75 non-stipend. The latter included about a dozen from European universities as well as a large number of Washington University Ph.D. students, some of whom only participated in certain sessions but some of whom completed the whole program.

assists in the process of uncovering causal mechanisms. We hasten to add that methodological unification in the social and behavioral sciences is not new and can be traced primarily to the accomplishments of the Cowles Commission in the 1930s.

With these potential scientific benefits in mind, EITM is also a response – as mentioned earlier – to some current methodological practices (see Achen 2002, 2005 for a review). These practices, for example, borrow applied statistical tools to improve on older techniques, but this largely comes at the expense of the search for identified and invariant relations. Indeed, with this current mindset, the creation of methodologies isolating structural parameters is secondary to the use of applied statistical techniques that end up manipulating standard errors and associated t-statistics. There is no use of formal modeling to aid in this process of identifying causal relations. Moreover, there is little effort to seek unification between formal and empirical approaches.

Some political scientists did see the shortcomings associated with disjointed quantitative work. For example, Aldrich argued in 1980:

Empirical observation, in the absence of a theoretical base, is at best descriptive. It tells one what happened, but not why it has the pattern one perceives. Theoretical analysis, in the absence of empirical testing, has a framework more noteworthy for its logical or mathematical elegance than for its utility in generating insights into the real world. The first exercise has been described as "data dredging," the second as building "elegant models of irrelevant universes." My purpose is to try to understand what I believe to be a problem of major importance. This understanding cannot be achieved merely by observation, nor can it be attained by the manipulation of abstract symbols. Real insight can be gained only by their combination (page 4).

More than a decade later, Bartels and Brady (1993) echoed these sentiments, arguing that, in the field of political methodology, "there is still far too much data analysis without formal theory – and far too much formal theory without data analysis" (page 148). In her important treatment on the subject, Morton (1999) discusses these issues in the following terms:

Political Scientists have become adept at applying – from economics and other disciplines – exciting new statistical methods to analyze data...Yet this increase in complexity is not without costs. As the use of methodological techniques in political science has advanced, researchers have found that often their empirical study leads to more questions, questions that need theoretical input. However, because little existing theory is relevant or because the well-developed theory that does exist seems unconnected to the empirical issues, typically the response is to use more sophisticated methods or data gathering to answer the questions without reference to a fully developed theory. But these new methods often lead to still more questions, which in turn result in the use of more sophisticated methods to gather or analyze the data. The connection to theory seems to get lost in the methodological discussion. Rarely do researchers take the empirical results and rework the theoretical framework that began the discussion (page 3).

These concerns emerged in the 2001 NSF EITM Workshop. The NSF EITM Report concluded the sources for the methodological status quo were deep and would be difficult to overcome:

There are at least two reasons for this state of research competency. One is that rigorous formal and empirical training is a somewhat recent development in political science. Another is that there are significant obstacles in the current political science training environment. The first obstacle is time. Students who desire training in both formal and empirical modeling will take longer to get a Ph.D. and most graduate programs do not have the resources to support students for more than four or five years. Consequently, students take the sequence of formal or empirical modeling classes but seldom both sequences. In addition to classes in formal or empirical modeling, students must take classes in their substantive area. For students in comparative politics there are field work and language requirements. What normally is sacrificed, then, is either the formal or empirical modeling sequence. Taking a single course in formal and empirical modeling is not nearly enough to develop competency to do research. The second obstacle to establishing formal and empirical modeling competency centers on the training itself (EITM Report 2002, 7).

IDEAS

To change the current methodological emphasis an EITM framework is presented in this book. Several ideas provide a foundation. The first idea is the ultimate focus of a model and test is to support a coherent and cumulative scientific process. The ability of a researcher to parse out specific causal linkages, among the many factors, is fundamental to the scientific enterprise. But, it also should be noted that no one engaged in the scientific enterprise would call finding causal mechanisms easy. What makes methodological unification useful in this process is that specifying a model linking both formal and empirical approaches alerts researchers to outcomes when specific conditions are in place.

To be clear, then, prediction and predictive accuracy are important aspects of scientific inquiry and scientific cumulation, but they do not exist in a vacuum. Understanding the workings of a system (particularly through formalization), which can sometimes occur long before tests and data are available, is a coequal partner in the process. As Coase (1994) argues:

The view that the worth of a theory is to be judged solely by the extent and accuracy of its predictions seems to me wrong. Of course, any theory has implications. It tells us that if something happens, something else will follow, and it is true that most of us would not value the theory if we did not think these implications corresponded to happenings in the ... system. But, a theory is not like an airline or bus timetable. We are not interested simply in the accuracy of it predictions. A theory also serves as a base for thinking. It helps us to understand what is going on by enabling us to organize our thoughts. Faced with a choice between a theory which predicts well but gives us little insight into how the system works and one which gives us this insight but predicts badly, I would choose the latter...No doubt...that ultimately theory would enable us to make predictions about what would happen in the real world; but since these predictions would emerge at a later date ... to assert that the choice between theories depends on their predictive powers becomes completely ambiguous (pages 16–17).

In sum, the EITM framework is a means – via the dialogue it creates between theory and test – to attain a valid understanding of the workings of a system and assessing a theory's predictive accuracy. EITM is not a sufficient condition for cumulation but it is a necessary one. Cumulation over time can ultimately be upended by alternative theories that lay far outside the current literature. A new cumulative process would then be built around the new and novel theory. In acknowledging this reality, we make the weaker claim that methodological unification fosters a coherent evolving process where successive research builds on prior research and where the linkage between theory and test directs successive research to alternative measures, theoretical assumptions, and new formal and empirical analogues (Granato et al. 2010a, 784). More to the point, using the EITM framework supports cumulation because the formal model, informed by various empirical tests (i.e., fitting facts, predictive accuracy), can reveal how the covariates relate to each other (i.e., understanding the inner-workings of the system). The other strength is that these covariates can be investigated ex ante and prior to doing any testing.[3]

A second idea is that the methodological isolation of fields and subfields in political and social sciences is the status quo. Among the consequences of this isolation is the schism between formal and empirical modeling and the concomitant weaknesses in how social science researchers specify and test their models. An objective of this book is to select examples from various subfields or disciplines for creating an awareness of EITM-type research and breaking down the barriers to achieving methodological unification.

The third idea follows the second where EITM collaborations in education, knowledge dissemination, and research result in promoting interdisciplinary interactions. The EITM framework presented here originates in political science, but it is based, in part, on the original work of the Cowles Commission – a group of quantitatively inclined economists. The contributions of the Cowles Commission rest on a scientific vision involving the merging of formal and applied statistical analysis. The basis for this linkage is the notion that random samples are governed by a latent and probabilistic law of motion (Haavelmo

---

[3] On this latter issue, Granato et al. (2010a) point out:

> Even scholars who are sensitive to establishing robustness in their applied statistical results find the available tools inadequate when used in isolation. For example, augmenting applied statistical tests with Extreme Bounds Analysis (EBA) provides a check on parameter stability (Leamer 1983), but the test is performed ex-post and therefore does not allow for ex-ante prediction... This should not be surprising when one considers the effects of previously unspecified covariates in this procedure. Each time an applied statistical model is respecified, the entire model is subject to change. But without a priori use of equilibrium conditions (e.g., stability conditions) in a formal model, the parameter "changes" in a procedure such as EBA are of ambiguous origin (page 784).

1944; Morgan 1990). Further, this view argues that formal models, related to an applied statistical model, could be interpreted as creating a sample drawn from the underlying law of motion. A well-grounded test of a theory could be accomplished then by relating a formal model to an applied statistical model and testing the applied statistical model.

A fourth idea is that EITM extends the Cowles Commission approach. As noted earlier, the Cowles Commission contributed to the rise of quantitative methodology in many ways. The Cowles methodology created new research aimed at determining valid inference by highlighting issues such as identification and invariance. For the first issue, identification, rules (i.e., rank and order conditions) were devised so that an equation of a model could reveal one and only one set of parameters consistent with both the model and the observations (see, for example, Koopmans 1949a,b). A second issue involved the invariance of a (structural) relation. If an underlying mechanism is constant in the past and future, then the path of the relevant variable(s) will be predictable from the past, apart from random disturbances (see, for example, Marschak 1947, 1953). There was no concerted attempt assuring this latter condition obtained and this failure invited both theoretical and empirical criticisms.

These criticisms were fundamental and they figure prominently in social science progress. Consider that if one were to strictly adhere to the Cowles Commission approach we would, for example, forego the chance of modeling new uncertainty created by shifts in behavioral traits (e.g., public tastes, attitudes, expectations, communication, and learning). The scientific consequence of this omission directly affects the issues of identification and invariance because these unaccounted behavioral shifts of variables would not be linked with the other variables and specified parameters. The EITM framework is devised to deal with these dynamic behavioral concerns. It also takes a more expansive view on the modeling enterprise. Not only does the EITM framework make use of structural equation modeling associated with the Cowles Commission but it also includes alternative probability approaches, computational methods, and experimental methods (see Poteete et al. 2010).

In sum, the EITM framework builds on the Cowles Commission approach. This framework takes advantage of the mutually reinforcing properties of formal and empirical analysis while addressing the challenge(s) above. Moreover, this framework focuses on general behavioral concepts integral to many fields of research but seldom modeled and tested in a direct way. EITM emphasizes discovering ways to model human behavior and action and, thereby, aids in creating realistic representations improving on simple socioeconomic categorization. Numerous social science disciplines focus a good deal of research effort on the interactions between agent behavior and public policies. Yet, current research practices can fail to develop formal models analyzing these interactions. Our approach emphasizes modeling behavior so new uncertainty created by shifts in behavioral traits such as public tastes, attitudes, expectations, learning, and the like are properly studied.

FEATURES

This book has several distinctive features. The first is a review of some current methodological practices and how they undermine cumulative scientific progress. We then discuss how EITM combats the overemphasis on the t-statistic and the nonfalsifiable statistical practices it engenders.

A second feature emphasizes the analytical and technical approach. Formal analysis is merged directly with empirical analysis (*using data or possessing testable implications or both*). The EITM framework builds on the concepts and vision of the Cowles Commission but it also relies on other background literature and approaches.

A third feature focuses on mechanism operationalization. Operationalizing mechanisms involves creating measurable devices (what we term analogues) on the formal and behavioral side but also on the empirical side. Behavioral concepts include (but are not limited to) expectations, learning, social interaction, decision making, strategic interaction, and more. Empirical concepts include (but are not limited to) persistence, measurement error, simultaneity, prediction, nominal choice, and more. Traditional operationalization involves finding measures for behavioral concepts. These measures are usually a variable of some sort. Operationalizing mechanisms encompasses this tradition but also extends it to include the use of operators, frameworks (that can include variables), and tools to represent both behavioral and empirical concepts.

A fourth feature is that this book is self-contained. The examples we use are quite varied and, at times, require a working knowledge of tools with which you may be unfamiliar. This is due to the EITM emphasis on operationalizing mechanisms noted above. We are also aware of the sometimes daunting task of learning new technical material when the details are unclear. Indeed, we share the frustration with many readers who, when reading technically challenging material, find authors leave out important steps in demonstrating a solution – or the tools used. To deal with this issue we use examples and tools that are blended together (relying on the original sources) so readers can learn how to apply the EITM framework. This effort is reinforced by the use of appendices accompanying each chapter. They provide even greater detail on the tools used and, when possible, provide original sources for an even more expanded reading and understanding.

WHAT THE MATERIAL IN THIS BOOK MEANS FOR YOUR RESEARCH AND INSTRUCTION

Who benefits from mastering the material in this book? By its very nature, this book mixes formal analysis and applied statistical analysis. The book is designed first to account for the differences between formal and empirical approaches, and their respective intellectual outlook, skills, and training. In terms of outlook, formal modelers typically emphasize, in minute detail,

Preface

linkages between concepts, whereas empirical modelers rarely spend their time parsing through minute details that may not add to their understanding. Formal modeling also requires analytical, logical, and mathematical modeling skills, while empirical modeling is inductive and, therefore, places emphasis on descriptive and statistical skills. Empirical modelers devote their energies to data collection, measurement, and statistical matters, but formal modelers focus on mathematical rigor.

These differences are eliminated because the tools are merged in accordance with the EITM framework. It is likely that a person using this book will have knowledge with one technical tradition (formal or empirical), but they will also be given the appropriate steps to solve parts less familiar. This task is accomplished by not only presenting the various tools and solution procedures but in also featuring examples that may be applied to a variety of social science questions.

The book is presented at a technical level similar to econometric texts. The markets it is geared toward are primarily academic and policy. People most comfortable with this material will be graduate students and academics. Policy analysts may strengthen their analyses by applying this approach. This book is also useful as a capstone course for students who have taken both formal and empirical courses.

As a final thought, and if we were to sum up the EITM framework, we would argue it is a guide to unification. But, there is no set formula for what tools to use. What dictates the tools to use is how you characterize your idea. At that point you will need to look in a tool box and use the specific formal and empirical techniques available and appropriate. Our appendices serve this latter purpose. They are certainly not the last word on what the mix is or should be. Competing characterizations are appropriate and should be evaluated on their ability to represent accurately the workings of the system as well as their predictive power.

THE PLAN OF THE BOOK

The book has two parts. Part I provides the background and framework. Chapter 1 gives an overview of how methodology and modeling are integral to the scientific process. We discuss the fundamental scientific ideas – *order, cause, and chance* – and how models can be used to attain these ideas. The discussion also includes various and select academic institutions that gave rise to the development of formal and applied statistical modeling. These institutions (a sample) are the precursors to methodological unification – and EITM.

Chapter 2 lays out, in nontechnical terms, how the dialogue between formal and empirical analysis can advance science. This chapter also provides readers with an analysis of some contemporary methodological practices. Some of these practices (data mining, overparameterization, and statistical patching ["omega matrices"]) contribute to noncumulation. An example is provided on how these practices fail to support a valid understanding of a system or predictive power.

The EITM framework is presented in Chapter 3. For illustration – and as a precursor to examples in Part II of the book – we then present two well-know examples that separately demonstrate methodological unification but also the dialogue manifested in these research efforts. The first example – the Solow (1956) economic growth model – is related to the Cowles Commission's approach. The second – Ostrom's (2010) work on social dilemmas – relies on experimental design. The remainder of the chapter focuses on criticisms (rebuttals) and limitations of EITM.

Part II of the book provides several examples from a variety of research areas in political science, political economy, economics, and sociology. Each example provides a brief background (targeting a small slice of the existing literature) of the research topic, the details of the model unification process, and a brief summary. Recall, each chapter is self-contained: Each chapter provides an appendix giving a thorough description (and source literature or both) of the formal and empirical tools used in the specific example. The tool sections provide the basis for creating an analogue for each concept.

In the first four chapters, we focus on the techniques for modeling and testing behavioral traits. A fundamental difference between social sciences (such as economics and political science) and the natural sciences is that human beings make forward-looking decisions (Evans and Honkapohja 2001). People's expectations of future events affect their current behavior and numerous researchers study how people form expectations and make forecasts. In the next four chapters, we discuss the integration of expectation formation with four distinctive behavioral traits: (1) uncertainty, (2) persistence (habit formation), (3) learning, and (4) communication (social interaction).

Chapter 4 focuses on economic voting. Using Alesina and Rosenthal's (1995) model it is demonstrated how the model can be extended (see Suzuki and Chappell 1996; Lin 1999). From an EITM perspective this involves the linkage of the behavioral concepts of expectations and uncertainty with the empirical concept of measurement error. The tools in this chapter include the theory of rational expectations (use of linear projections) solution procedures and the technique of signal extraction. The empirical tools include error-in-variables regression and the relation between signal extraction and error-in-variables regression.

Chapter 5 presents an example of macropartisanship and EITM. The EITM linkage cements the relation between the behavioral concept of expectations and the empirical concept of persistence. An example of party identification that provides a linkage between expectations and persistence is Clarke and Granato (2004). The appendix in this chapter includes an extended discussion of expectations modeling, including the use of difference equations (various orders), their solution procedures, and stability conditions. Along with these

Preface

relevant formal modeling tools is a comprehensive discussion of the empirical estimation and properties of autoregressive processes.

Chapter 6 presents a macro policy example, relating monetary policy to inflation. The example used in this chapter is Granato and Wong's (2006) real wage contract model. As with Chapter 5, the EITM linkage offers a relation between the behavioral concept of expectations and the empirical concept of persistence. The appendix in this chapter provides an extension of the uses of difference equations and adaptive learning procedures.

In Chapter 7, the focus is on social interaction and learning. The EITM linkage involves relating and unifying the behavioral concepts of expectations, learning, and social interaction with the empirical concept of simultaneity. The example used is Granato et al. (2011). The tools in this chapter include discussions of techniques in modeling expectations and learning (Evans and Honkapohja 2001). The empirical tools include time series econometrics and multi-equation estimation.

A second focus is on how citizens (voters or economic agents) respond to incentives and make decisions to maximize their utility. Chapters 8–10 present research studies connecting the theoretical concept of utility-maximization with various statistical concepts, such as discrete choice estimation, Bayesian learning/updating mechanism, and strategic choice modeling – quantal response equilibrium (QRE), respectively.

Chapter 8 gives an example of the relation between political parties and political representation. One well-researched area in the literature centers on when and why voters choose one party over the others based on the relative political positions of parties. The work of Kedar (2005) is used in this chapter. The EITM linkage in this example is between decision-theoretic models with discrete outcomes. The tools in this chapter include an introduction to discrete choice modeling and decision theory.

Voter turnout is the topic in Chapter 9. Here the EITM linkage is the behavioral concept of learning combined with the empirical concept of discrete choice. The example we use is Achen (2006). The tools in this chapter include Bayesian learning and discrete choice statistical models.

An EITM approach to international conflict and cooperation is the subject of Chapter 10. The EITM linkage includes the behavioral concept of bargaining and strategic interaction combined with the empirical concept of discrete choice. This linkage is captured using quantal response equilibrium (QRE). QRE – which merges game theory and discrete choice models – was developed by McKelvey and Palfrey (1995, 1996, 1998). In this chapter we use Leblang's (2003) application to currency crises. The tools introduced in this chapter involve the elements of game theory, discrete choice modeling, and how these inform QRE.

In the next three chapters, we show that implementing EITM framework is not limited to solving closed-form solutions in a formal model and estimating the empirical model with secondary data sources. Other techniques, such as numerical solution procedures and experiments, are widely used in social science research. Chapter 11 illustrates the use of simulations and calibration in macro political economy. The EITM linkage is between the behavioral concept of decision making with the empirical concept of prediction. We present Freeman and Houser's (1998) work. They use a dynamic stochastic general equilibrium (DSGE) model to examine the relation between economic performance and presidential approval. The formal tools introduced in this chapter include basic optimization – in both discrete- and continuous-time – and model calibration. These tools are described (with examples) in the appendix.

In Chapter 12, we turn our focus from mimicking observable macro-level political-economic structures (again via calibration and simulation) to imitating micro-level electoral and economic decisions. These computationally generated tools provide an expansion in analogue development. Agent-based modeling (ABM) is a case in point. The first example is Fowler (2006), who uses an agent-based model to study voting patterns and turnout. The EITM linkage is between the behavioral concepts of learning and uncertainty with the empirical concept of prediction (discrete outcomes). We then include an alternative ABM tool – the genetic algorithm (GA) – and use the work of Arifovic (1994) as the second example. The EITM linkage in her example is the behavioral concept of learning and social interaction (e.g., imitation, invention, communication, and examination) with the empirical concept of prediction (discrete choice outcomes). The tools we introduce in this chapter involve the elements of GA simulations and adaptive learning simulations. The appendix provides extensive background on GA programming and overall ABM implementation.

Researchers can benefit from computational simulations to understand micro-level decisions. They also adopt simulation techniques to assess policy effectiveness by systematically varying parameter values in the simulated model (including counterfactual analysis). This computational exercise is particularly valuable when closed-form solutions cannot be solved, or actual data are challenging to obtain. However, we may not be able to understand individuals' decisions and behavior entirely with a system of logically consistent equations since human reasoning is significantly more complicated. Chapter 13 provides an EITM application using an experimental design driven by human subjects, rather than by artificial agents in a computational setting. In this case, researchers construct a laboratory experiment – a simulated setting – with a set of restrictive conditions, which are comparable to the assumptions imposed in a theoretical model. Human subject reactions to exogenous events are then examined. We select Chaudoin and Woon (2018) as an example of conducting laboratory experiments for social science research. The EITM linkage is the behavioral concept of strategic decision making with the empirical concept of prediction (choice outcomes). The appendix in this chapter includes a discussion on basic experimental design elements, but also their background literature.

Preface

An alternative unification framework is presented in Chapter 14. This example also highlights theoretically and unified driven approaches to measurement. Jasso's (2004) Tripartite Structure of Social Science Analysis provides a framework that shares similarities to EITM but also provides a unique perspective. One important emphasis in Jasso's framework is her focus on probability distributions – and the linkage between formalization with known distribution functions. In addition, and as mentioned above, Jasso's unification method extends to measurement issues. The example we use in this chapter focuses on a theoretically motivated index measure of justice and relates this index to gender gaps in earnings. The appendix in this chapter differs from others. We deal with the linkage of behavioral theory and measurement, but the example is from economics. Specifically, we describe how monetary aggregates are based on decision theory, aggregation theory, and index number theory.

Chapter 15 concludes the book. An overview of the obstacles in implementation, as well as how training can be reoriented, is discussed. The chapter ends with a discussion of how future developments in methodological unification can assist both basic and applied research.

Acknowledgments

We thank Marianne Stewart and Harold Clarke for early conversations on the EITM initiative. We also thank Cong Huang, Pablo Pinto, Kwok Wai Wan, Ching-Hsing Wang, and Erika Zuloaga for their careful and thoughtful review of the manuscript. We owe a special thanks to the participants of the Hobby School of Public Affairs EITM Summer Institute. They were the first to use the materials and their insightful feedback proved invaluable. Thanks also to the folks at Cambridge University Press – Robert Dreesen, Catherine Smith, and Erika Walsh – for their assistance throughout the entire process. A final thanks to both Monica Mendez and EMC Design for their work on the book cover design.

This book is dedicated to two individuals who stand out most because their involvement marks the time – from beginning to end. First, John Aldrich encouraged a graduate student to think about methodological questions in different ways and also provided support for the added training required: His early guidance set the foundation for EITM. And Frank Scioli, who saw the potential value in EITM and made numerous suggestions pertaining to its intellectual and scientific merit: He was the driving force in seeing its ultimate implementation. This book was made possible because of them.

PART I

EITM

Background and Framework

1

Modeling Insights and Pathbreaking Institutions

A Sketch

EITM is a natural outgrowth of prior modeling and testing approaches – research methods – aimed at fostering social scientific cumulation.[1] The enduring effort – instituting the ideas – to create modeling and testing methods is of vital importance to the social sciences since it "provides a shared language so that even scholars thinking problems with little substantive overlap... can communicate efficiently and productively. It means that we begin with common first principles, and proceed with our research in a way that is commonly understood" (Gerber 2003, 3). Or, as Pearson (1957, 2004) states: "the unity of all science consists alone in its method, not in its material... It is not the facts themselves which make science, but the method by which they are dealt with" (page 12).[2]

With the attributes of shared (and improving) standards, language, and technical-analytical competence, research methods allow us to find ways to implement the fundamental scientific ideas of *order, cause, and chance* (Bronowski 1978).[3]

---

[1] This chapter borrows from sources such as: Gow (1985), Landreth and Colander (2002), Morgan (1990), Poteete et al. (2010, 3–27), Schumpeter (1954, 1994), Sowell (1974, 2006), Worcester (2001), and Zellner (1984).

[2] The American Heritage Dictionary definition of science is "[t]he observation, identification, description, experimental investigation, and theoretical explanation of phenomena."

[3] *Order* is defined as "the selection of one set of appearances rather than another because it gives a better sense of the reality behind the appearances" (Bronowski 1978, 48). Order can require devices that depict relations and predictions. Abstract models and the use of mathematics are natural devices. *Cause* – determining what brings about an effect – was thought by early social scientists (or more accurately political economists) to be a sequential process (see Hoover 2001a, 1–28 for a review of David Hume's influence). For an extensive treatment see Pearl (2000), but see also Kellstedt and Whitten (2009, 45–66) and Zellner (1984, 35–74) for a discussion of causality in applied statistics and econometrics, respectively. As for the concept of *chance*, Bronowski (1978) is critical of what he believes is the misuse of the term "cause" and prefers to link it with probabilistic statements – "chance" – which "replaces the concept of the inevitable effect by that of the probable trend" (page 87). Modern conceptions on the utility of mathematics also point to how applied statistical analysis aids in the idea of chance (e.g., statistical significance).

1.1 THE UTILITY OF MODELS AND MODELING

Order, cause, and chance can be effectuated by the use of models describing hypothetical worlds whose predictions have testable potential and assist in the systematization of knowledge.[4] With models one may "put all these effects together, and, from what they are separately ... collect what would be the effect of all these causes acting at once" (Sowell 1974, 137–138). As Gabaix and Laibson (2008) argue:

> Models that make quantitatively precise predictions are the norm in other sciences. Models with predictive precision are easy to empirically test, and when such models are approximately empirically accurate, they are likely to be useful. (page 299)[5]

If models possess attributes that enhance the scientific process, then how do we go about constructing them? Valid models make use of both deductive and inductive inference. Deductive inference, where "the conclusion is obtained by deducing it from other statements, known as premises of the argument. The argument is so constructed that if the premises are true the conclusion must also be true" (Reichenbach 1951, 37).

Inductive inference – because it relies on making inferences from the past to predict the future:

> ... enables us to associate probabilities – cause and chance – with propositions and to manipulate them in a consistent, logical way to take account of new information. Deductive statements of proof and disproof are then viewed as limiting cases of inductive logic wherein probabilities approach one or zero, respectively. (Zellner 1984, 5)

Abstract modeling in the social sciences traces its origins to the early political economists.[6] The initial modeling efforts were deductive in orientation. Mathematics and mathematical models were argued as an attribute for determining order and cause because their logical consistency can be verified using the available operations of mathematics.[7] David Ricardo was one of the first to make use of "abstract models, rigid and artificial definitions, syllogistic reasoning," and applied the conclusions from the highly restrictive models

---

[4] See Granato (2005) for a discussion of these issues.

[5] The EITM framework can be applied to either observational designs or more controlled settings (See Freedman et al. 1998, 3–28 and Shively 2017). For a review of some of the more important developments on research design issues (e.g., counterfactuals) and causality see Morgan and Winship (2007) and Brady (2008). An example of multiple designs and multiple methods can be found in Poteete et al. (2010).

[6] There are numerous discussions on the utility of formal analysis and modeling. In political science, see Wagner (2001) and Wagner (2007, 1–52) for a review of the ongoing debate over modeling and an application to theories of international relations. See Clarke and Primo (2012), Krugman (1994, 1998), Wolpin (2013), and Jasso (2002) for discussions in the fields of political science, economics, and sociology, respectively.

[7] See Sowell (1974) and Landreth and Colander (2002), but for subsequent changes in the use of mathematics (see Weintraub 2002).

directly to the complexities of the real world (see Sowell 1974, 113; Landreth and Colander 2002, 113–115).

These early modeling efforts were not without detractors.[8] Richard Jones, for example, argued modeling generalizations were invalid if they ignored things that exist in the world including institutions, history, and statistics. Robert Malthus, Jean Baptiste Say, and J. C. L. Sismonde also criticized attempts at premature generalization (Sowell 1974, 114–116).

These critics gave no consideration that mathematics might be used to contribute to conceptual clarity rather than to derive numerical predictions. Antoine Augustin Cournot pointed out that mathematical analysis was used "not simply to calculate numbers" but to find "relations" (Sowell 1974, 117–118). Yet, the criticisms endured. More than a century later Kenneth Arrow (1948) provided the following defense of mathematical modeling:

> It is true that there are certain limitations of mathematical methods in the social sciences. However, it must be insisted that the advantages are equally apparent and may frequently be worth a certain loss of realism. In the first place, clarity of thought is still a pearl of great price. In particular, the multiplicity of values of verbal symbols may be a great disadvantage when it comes to drawing the logical consequences of a proposition. (page 131)[9]

In the early 1920s, inductive inference – and linking cause to chance and providing a basis for regression analysis and econometrics – was given important support when the sampling distribution(s) for regression coefficients were established (Fisher 1922). This latter contribution was an important precursor to what has been called the "probability approach" to statistical inference (Haavelmo 1944) – and efforts to link deductive and inductive approaches using formal analysis and applied statistical tools.

1.2 INSTITUTIONAL DEVELOPMENTS

While EITM draws inspiration from the Cowles Commission, it would be a mistake to limit it only to Cowles. The EITM framework builds on a variety of formal institutions and organizations in the social sciences. These institutions – ranging from research organizations to university departments – developed and supported the antecedents to EITM.[10] The entities supporting the creation

---

[8] In the seventeenth and eighteenth centuries a break occurred between those who believed political economy should base its method on rigor and precision versus those who emphasized the certainty of the results. The debate focused in part on whether political economic principles should be founded on abstract assumptions or factual premises (Sowell 1974, 117–118).

[9] There are numerous examples where the use of mathematical models uncover logical inconsistencies that would be more difficult to find using verbal argument(s). Viner (1958), for instance, discusses how the aid of mathematics leads to clarification on the uses of average and marginal cost.

[10] An expanded sample can be found in Mitchell (1930, 1937, 58–71).

and development of formal and applied statistical analysis include (but are not limited to):

- The Social Science Research Council (SSRC).
- The Econometric Society and the Cowles Commission.
- The Political Science Department at the University of Rochester.
- The Society for Political Methodology.

1.2.1 The SSRC

The 1920s saw movement in the social sciences toward improving quantitative methods of study.[11] One leading figure was Charles Merriam who worked to alter the methods of political study (Merriam 1921, 1923, 1924; Merriam et al. 1923). At that time, he believed the existing methods of analysis failed on a fundamental level – identifying underlying mechanisms:

> The difficulty of isolating political phenomena sufficiently to determine precisely the causal relations between them. We know that events occur, but we find so many alternate causes that we are not always able to indicate a specific cause. For the same reason we are unable to reach an expert agreement upon the proper or scientific policy to pursue and by the same logic we are unable to predict the course of events in future situations. (Merriam 1923, 288)

Merriam stressed the need to examine and use multiple methods from numerous social science disciplines (i.e., economics, statistics, history, anthropology, geography, psychology).

> In place of literature Merriam favored a better organized and more consciously scientific and social psychological approach to the study of human behavior. Statistics and other empirical tools would play a critical role in shifting the political and social sciences closer to the "hard sciences." (Worcester 2001, 16–17)

To accomplish these goals, Merriam proposed an interdisciplinary institution to help promote his vision – the SSRC. In the 1920s, the SSRC was considered the first national organization of all the social sciences, and from the outset its goal has been to improve the quality of, and infrastructure for, research in the social sciences.[12] Among the contributions of the SSRC has been its multidisciplinary outlook and emphasis on creating and using data.

---

[11] Early political science examples can be found in Mayo-Smith (1890), Ogburn and Peterson (1916), and Ogburn and Goltra (1919).
[12] Another important research institution, the National Bureau of Economic Research (NBER), was founded in 1920. The NBER had a narrower disciplinary focus (economics), but in many ways shared the same basic vision as the SSRC.

1.2.2 The Econometric Society and the Cowles Commission

The creation of the SSRC was followed by two other significant institutional developments.

The Econometric Society was established in 1930...The Society greatly facilitated academic exchanges between European and American scholars not only in the young econometrics profession but also in mathematical statistics. It thus rapidly promoted the growth of econometrics into a separate discipline. (Duo 1993, 5)

The Econometric Society sought to use mathematics and statistics to increase the level of rigor in the formulation and testing of economic theory. The society initially featured scholarly meetings and the creation of the journal *Econometrica*.

The Cowles Commission followed in 1932. It was a:

research institution which contributed uniquely to the formalization of econometrics (see Christ 1952; Hildreth 1986). The Commission had a close connection with the Econometric Society from its beginning. (Duo 1993, 5)

The Cowles Commission advanced the rise and adoption of econometric methodology in two ways.[13] Recall that it developed the *probability approach*. This approach highlighted the issues of *identification and invariance*.[14] Identification was central since a goal of econometrics is to determine the true values of the parameters among all the possible sets of values consistent with the data and with the known or assumed properties of the model.[15]

The second issue was the invariance of a relation. If structure is known to remain in the future what it was in the past, and if the auxiliary variables have constant values through both periods, the path of each variable will be predictable from the past, apart from random disturbances. By addressing the

---

[13] Econometric research associated with the Cowles Commission includes (but is not limited to): Cooper (1948), Haavelmo (1943, 1944), Hood and Koopmans (1953), Klein (1947), Koopmans (1945, 1949a,b, 1950), Koopmans and Reiersol (1950), Marschak (1947, 1953), Vining (1949), Christ (1994), and Heckman (2000). For further background on the Cowles Commission consult the following URL: http://cowles.econ.yale.edu/.

[14] The intuition behind the terms identify (i.e., identification) and invariant (i.e., invariance) are as follows. For applied statistical models identification relates to model parameters (e.g., $\widehat{\beta}$) and whether they indicate the magnitude of the effect for that particular independent variable. Or, in more technical terms, "A parameter is identifiable if different values for the parameter produce different distributions for some observable aspect of the data" (Brady and Collier 2004, 290).

In applied statistical practice, invariance refers to the constancy of the parameters of interest. More generally, "the distinctive features of causal models is that each variable is determined by a set of other variables through a relationship (known as 'mechanism') that remains invariant (constant) when those other variables are subjected to external influences. Only by virtue of its invariance do causal models allow us to predict the effect of changes and interventions ..." (Pearl 2000, 63).

[15] An equation of a model is declared to be identifiable in that model if, given a sufficient (possibly infinite) number of observations of the variables, it would be possible to find one and only one set of parameters for it that is consistent with both the model and the observations.

issues of identification and invariance, the probability approach – and the linkage of formal and empirical analysis – provides a connection to falsifiability, predictive precision, and the workings of a system.[16] We would add those models that have these properties also facilitate comparison between rival and competing theories over the same phenomena – and can enhance scientific cumulation (Kuhn 1979).

The Cowles approach also drew criticisms. These criticisms for the most part focused on measurement and inferences issues (Keynes 1940) and questions about predictive accuracy (Christ 1951). Despite the criticisms, the Cowles Commission approach was widely adopted and by the mid-1960s was standard in quantitative economics. However, during the 1970s more fundamental criticisms – regarding invariance and identification – arose.

In 1976, Robert Lucas questioned the robustness of invariance when the Cowles approach is used. His formal analysis demonstrated that models based on the Cowles approach were fundamentally flawed in their ability to evaluate the outcomes of alternative economic policies. The reason, he argued, is that in-sample estimation provides little guidance in predicting the effects of policy changes because the parameters of the applied statistical models are unlikely to remain stable under alternative stimuli.[17]

Sims (1980) later challenged the identification procedures inspired by the Cowles Commission. Sims argued against the reliance on "incredible restrictions" to identify structural models. These restrictions had the effect of undermining an understanding of the system. Sims offered a change in emphasis from focusing on individual coefficients, as the structural modeling approach did, to

---

[16] Gabaix and Laibson (2008) argue that falsifiability and predictive precision are among the key properties of useful models (see Gabaix and Laibson 2008). "A model is falsifiable if and only if the model makes nontrivial predictions that can in principle be empirically falsified" (page 295). "Models have *predictive precision* when they make precise – or "strong" – predictions. Strong predictions are desirable because they facilitate model evaluation and model testing. When an incorrect model makes strong predictions, it is easy to empirically falsify the model, even when the researcher has access only to a small amount of data. A model with predictive precision also has greater potential to be practically useful if it survives empirical testing. Models with predictive precision are useful tools for decision makers who are trying to forecast future events or the consequences of new policies" (page 295).

In the language of econometrics, falsification and predictive precision require the mechanisms relating cause and effect be identified. There is a large literature devoted to identification problems (see, for example, Koopmans 1949a,b; Fisher 1966; and Manski 1995), but we use identification in the broadest sense for purposes of attaining some order and underlying cause as well. Since we as social scientists do not have controlled environments to conduct our inquiry, our efforts to achieve order and cause in our models can only come about probabilistically – by chance.

[17] The Lucas critique is based on the following intuition: "…given that the structure of an econometric model consists of optimal decision rules … and that optimal decision rules vary systematically with changes in the structure of series relevant to the decision maker, it follows that any change in policy will systematically alter the structure of econometric models" (Lucas 1976, 41).

Modeling Insights and Pathbreaking Institutions: A Sketch

vector autoregressive (VAR) modeling with attention given on the dynamic time series properties of an unrestricted (by theory) system of equations.[18]

Despite these challenges, some of the basic tools and procedures of the probability approach remain. One extension of the structural approach, in part a response to Lucas' criticisms, is "real business cycle modeling" (RBC).[19] Here the focus is on isolating parameters and on making greater explicit use of theory at both the individual and aggregate levels of analysis. Where RBCs especially differ from the Cowles Commission is in the use of standard statistical significance testing (see Chapter 11).[20]

1.2.3 The Political Science Department at the University of Rochester

Thanks in part to the SSRC, there was a clear tendency in political science to promote statistical methods.[21] Methodological emphasis was placed on statistical correlation and empirical testing and generally focused on psychological attitudes to derive empirical generalizations. During the late 1950s and early 1960s William Riker and later – the Department of Political Science at the University of Rochester – developed positive political theory.[22]

The goal of positive political theorists is to make positive statements about political phenomena, or descriptive generalizations that can be subjected to empirical verification. This commitment to scientifically explaining political processes involves the use of formal language, including set theory, mathematical models, statistical analysis, game

---

[18] Sims' methodology is grounded in probabilistic inference, imposing only enough economic theory to identify the statistical models and carry out analyses of policy effectiveness. See Freeman et al. (1989) for an application of VAR to political science questions.

[19] See Freeman and Houser (1998) for an application in political economy (see Chapter 11 as well). For a critique of RBCs see Sims (1996).

[20] The method involves computational experiments. These experiments rely on a sequence of steps including: deriving the equilibrium laws of motion for the model economy from "well-tested theory," "calibrating" the model using parameter values derived from historical data, generating simulated realizations of the equilibrium processes, determining the sampling distributions of the statistics computed from the simulated data, and comparing these statistics to those computed for data from actual economies. Kydland and Prescott's (1982) "computational experiments" are often referred to as "calibration" because of the use of parameter values derived from simple measures (such as averages) of historical time series to "calibrate" the theoretical models.

[21] See Von Neumann et al. (1944), Black (1948), Arrow (1951) and Downs (1957) for the start of formal approaches to the study of politics by nonpolitical scientists.

[22] A parallel development, in the early 1960s, was the creation of the Public Choice Society (https://publicchoicesociety.org). This society's statement of purpose (https://publicchoicesociety.org/about) is to:

... facilitate the exchange of research and ideas across disciplines in the social sciences, particularly economics, political science, sociology, law and related fields. It started when scholars from all these groups became interested in the application of essentially economic methods to problems normally dealt with by political theorists. It has retained strong traces of economic methodology, but new and fruitful directions have developed that transcend the boundaries of any self-contained discipline.

theory, and decision theory, as well as historical narrative and experiments. (Amadae and Bueno de Mesquita 1999, 270)

Riker, while not averse to inductive reasoning, put an emphasis on the deductive approach. In particular,

> The Rochester school has emphasized deriving hypotheses from axioms. Doing so reduces the risk that hypotheses are restatements of already observed patterns in the data. Even when models are constructed specifically to account for known empirical regularities, they are likely to produce new propositions that have not previously been tested. These new propositions, of course, create demand tests of the theory. Historical and statistical analyses tend not to hold the relations among variables constant from study to study and so are less likely to test inductively derived hypotheses against independent sources of evidence. (Amadae and Bueno de Mesquita 1999, 289)[23]

The advent of positive political theory (and later game theory) provided another social science discipline – political science – the basis for a graduate training and research regimen that continues to grow to this day.

1.2.4 The Society for Political Methodology

In the early 1970s, political scientists began a process of enhancing the usage of applied statistical procedures.[24] John Sullivan, George Marcus, and Gerald Dorfman created the journal *Political Methodology* (Lewis-Beck 2008). The journal was announced in 1972 and by 1974 the first issue was published. This journal was followed by the creation of the Society for Political Methodology in the early 1980s. Like the Econometric Society, the Society for Political Methodology developed annual meetings and a journal – *Political Analysis* – which succeeded the earlier *Political Methodology*.

The methodological improvements in political science have accelerated since the early 1970s and 1980s. Bartels and Brady (1993) noted political science had started a series of rigorous literatures in topics ranging from parameter variation and nonrandom measurement error to dimensional models. A summary of the increasing breadth of this society can be found in Box-Steffensmeier et al. (2008).

1.3 SUMMARY

The chapter briefly describes ideas and institutions that provide both the direction and a basis for EITM. These predecessors, while they have some similarities, also have distinct identities ranging from data analysis, multidisciplinarity, applied statistical analysis, formal analysis, and the linkage of the

---

[23] See Amadae and Bueno de Mesquita (1999) for a list of publications associated, in part, with the Rochester School.
[24] We thank Christopher Achen and Elinor Ostrom for the background information.

latter two. EITM builds on this foundation and in addressing the scientific ideas – order, cause, and chance – brings "deduction and induction, hypothesis generation and hypothesis testing close together" (Aldrich et al. 2008, 840).

Recall also the EITM framework builds on the Cowles Commission's contributions. However, methodological unification is broader than standard econometric tools. We fully expect innovations beyond what we know today to be consistent with the EITM framework and its aim to facilitate a dialogue between theory and test.

2

Contemporary Methodological Practices

2.1 SCIENTIFIC RESEARCH METHODS: A DIALOGUE BETWEEN THEORY AND EMPIRICS

EITM is intended to encourage a dialogue that supports a cumulative scientific research process. Nobel laureate Richard Feynman provides the elements of a dialogue between theory and test. In his lecture at Cornell University in 1964, he states:[1]

> In general, we look for a new law by the following process. First, we guess it... Then we compute the consequences of the guess, to see what, if this is right, if this law we guess is right, to see what it would imply and then we compare the computation results to nature or we say compare to experiment or experience, compare it directly with observations to see if it works.
>
> If it disagrees with experiment, it's wrong. In that simple statement is the key to science. It doesn't make any difference how beautiful your guess is, it doesn't matter how smart you are who made the guess, or what his name is. If it disagrees with experiment, it's wrong. That's all there is to it.

In his statement, there are two essential elements in the research process: (1) computational results derived from a new law; and (2) observations from experiments or experience. To develop a new theoretical relation – a new law – Feynman argues it is necessary to compute "the consequences" of the new law (predictions), which can be compared with "the observations" from experiments or experience. He stressed that the new law is wrong if the experiments cannot validate the computational results.

How does this ideal process relate to EITM? For Feynman, the consistency between predictions and observational validation is the key to scientific progress (see Figure 2.1). To understand a particular social or behavioral

---

[1] We thank Jonathan Woon for this quote. A video is available at https://youtu.be/0KmimDq4cSU.

Contemporary Methodological Practices

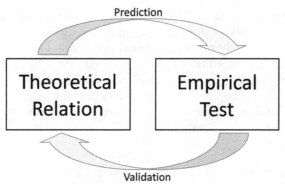

FIGURE 2.1. Summary dialogue between theory and empirics

pattern – and when theoretical models are formalized – researchers develop a formal model based on a "guess," which helps the researcher derive "computational results" predicted from the model. The researcher then validates the accuracy of the theoretical model based on empirical observations. If empirical observations are consistent with predictions from the model, we conclude the model is not rejected and remains valid at that point in time. However, it does not mean that the model is the true model, but it is a not-yet-proven-wrong model. Feynman argues this point as follows:

> Now you see, of course, that with this method we can disprove any definite theories. You have a definite theory and a real guess from which we can clearly compute consequences which could be compared with experiments that in principle you can get rid of any theory. We can always prove any definite theory wrong. Notice, however, we never prove it right. Suppose that you invent a good guess, calculate the consequences to discover that big consequence that you calculate agrees with experiment. The theory is right? No! It is simply not proved wrong because, in the future, there could be a wider range of experiment to compute a wider range of consequences, and you may discover then that this thing is wrong.
>
> That's why laws, like Newton's laws for the motion of planets lasts such a long time. He guessed the law of gravitation calculate all the kinds of consequences for the solar system and so on, and compared them to experiment. And it took several hundred years before the slight error of the motion of mercury was developed during all that time the theory had been failed to be proved wrong and could be taken to be temporarily right, but it can never be proved right because tomorrow's experiment may succeed in proving what you thought was right wrong. So we never are right, we can be only be sure we're wrong.

As described by Feynman, if empirical observations are inconsistent with the model predictions, we have sufficient evidence to believe that the model is invalid for particular predictions. This dialogue necessitates new guesses and revised theories and the process repeats itself.

Again, we hasten to add that Figure 2.1 represents an ideal set of circumstances. One complication is the quality of data used in a test and even the appropriateness of the data. Unlike the natural sciences, in which data can be obtained from repeated experiments and measurement standardization, the social sciences often rely on observational designs and secondary data. It is a major challenge to reproduce social science data in a laboratory setting or an experiment. However, some social scientists conduct experiments in social science studies (see Chapter 13). In that case the use of multiple tests with different data and in different settings provides a safeguard against invalid theory rejection.[2]

2.2 NONCUMULATIVE RESEARCH PRACTICES

While there has been improvement in quantitative social science, there is also cause for concern that social scientists are not absorbing the scientific lessons and emphasis of prior social scientists. The fear is these past contributions have been marginalized and the situation today is one in which so-called technical work is only loosely connected to order, cause, and chance. The dialogue is being lost.

In more technical language, the creation of methodologies that isolated structural parameters – to identify these parameters – became secondary to the use of hand-me-down applied statistical techniques that end up manipulating standard errors and their associated t-statistics. The reliance on statistically significant results means virtually nothing when a researcher makes very little attempt to identify the precise origin of the parameters in question. Absent this identification effort, it is not evident where the model is wrong. The dialogue between theory (model) and test is weakened.

We have now reached the point where some contemporary methodological practices contribute to noncumulation. Borrowing and applying statistical tools did seem to improve upon the use of older techniques. But, as this process of replacing old with new techniques took place, the search for causal mechanisms

---

[2] An additional complication is the ongoing philosophical debate regarding observable and nonobservable phenomena and how these phenomena relate to valid empirical practice. A point of contention between so-called realists and anti-realists is the criteria for a "successful" theory. On the one hand, realists argue successful scientific theories support claims about unobservables, which are true or approximately true (e.g., Boyd 1973; Putnam 1975; Musgrave 1988; Devitt 2008). Anti-realists and later, constructive empiricists, on the other hand, assert that science is aiming for empirical adequacy – the truth about observables only (e.g., Duhem 1954; van Fraassen 1980, 2007; Hausman 1998; Kitcher 2001; Wray 2008, 2013). We refer interested readers to Chakravartty (2017) and Monton and Mohler (2017) for further explanation concerning concepts of scientific realism and constructive empiricism. We also suggest Okasha (2002), Ladyman et al. (2007), and Shaw (2018) for philosophical discussions on contemporary science in detail. What is the relation between these schools of thought and the dialogue between theory and test? Recall that EITM supports a dialogue between theory and test and it is recognized theory can be ahead of data or data can be ahead of theory (see Section 3.4). From this perspective, the goal is to sustain and enhance a cumulative dialogue.

was largely ignored. These practices have not gone unnoticed. Achen (2002) has argued that:

> Dozens of estimators might be used in any of our empirical applications. Too often, applied researchers choose the standard ones because they believe methodologists approve of them, whereas methodologists prefer some new, complicated untested alternative because they know that the standard estimators are often ungrounded in substantive theory, and they hope that the new one might stumble onto something better. Few researchers in either group make a convincing case that their estimator is humming rather than clanking on their dataset. Even the creators of estimators usually do not prove that the supporting assumptions would make rational sense or common sense for the political actors being studied. Nor do they carry out the patient data analysis required to show that their estimator, an arbitrary selection from among dozens that might have been proposed, is more than just computable and plausible, but that its assumptions really match up in detail to the data for which it is intended. If the thing might work on some planet, we think our job is done. (page 436)

Three common practices – data mining, overparameterization, and the use of statistical weighting and patching (e.g., "Omega Matrices") – impair scientific cumulation (Granato and Scioli 2004; Granato et al. 2010a). To demonstrate the consequences of separating theory and test consider how these practices affect a widely used test indicator, the t-statistic – which is defined as the ratio of an estimated coefficient (b) to its standard error $(s.e.(b))$, that is, $b/s.e.(b)$. In the case of a t-statistic, this means linking the formal model to the test and focusing on the identification of the parameter b.

A brief description is presented here of these three common practices and whether they bear any relation to identifying b and by extension falsifiability, predictive precision, and understanding the inner workings of a system:

DATA MINING Data mining involves putting data into a standard statistical package with minimal theory. Regressions (likelihoods) are then estimated until either statistically significant coefficients or coefficients the researcher uses in their "theory" are found. This step-wise search is not random and has little relation to identifying causal mechanisms (see Lovell 1983; Deaton 1985).

An example of the consequences of data mining is found in Friedman and Schwartz (1991).[3] The case Friedman describes occurred while he was working for the Columbia University's Statistical Research Group during World War II. Friedman "was to serve as a statistical consultant to a number of projects to develop an improved alloy for use in airplane turbo-chargers and as a lining for jet engines" (page 48). Friedman's task was to determine the amount of time it took for a blade made of an alloy to fracture.

Friedman relied on data from a variety of lab experiments to assist him in addressing this problem. He then used the data to estimate a single equation linear regression. Standard statistical indicators suggested his approach was valid. The analysis predicted that the blade would rupture in "several hundred

---

[3] This example was originally drawn from Granato and Scioli (2004, 317–318).

hours." However, the results of actual laboratory tests indicated that a rupture occurred in "something like 1–4 hours" (page 49). Because of the lab results – and not the linear regression or the data mining – the alloy was discarded. Since Friedman relied primarily on data mining he could not know the various stresses or conditions in which ruptures would occur. He concluded:

> Ever since, I have been extremely skeptical of relying on projections from a multiple regression, however well it performs on the body of data from which it is derived; and the more complex the regression, the more skeptical I am. In the course of decades, that skepticism has been justified time and again. In my view, regression analysis is a good tool for deriving hypotheses. But any hypothesis must be treated with data or nonquantitative evidence other than that used in deriving the regression or available when the regression is derived. Low standard errors of estimate, high t values, and the like are often tributes to the ingenuity and tenacity of the statistician rather than reliable evidence of the ability of the regression to predict data not used in constructing it. (page 49)

OVERPARAMETERIZATION   This practice, related to data mining, involves a researcher including, absent any systematic specification search, a plethora of independent variables into a statistical package and obtains significant t-statistics. Efforts to identify an underlying causal mechanism are also ineffectual.[4] As Achen (2005) notes:

> …big, mushy linear regression and probit equations seem to need a great many control variables precisely because they are jamming together all sorts of observations that do not belong together. Countries, wars, racial categories, religious preferences, education levels, and other variables that change people's coefficients are "controlled" with dummy variables that are completely inadequate to modeling their effects. The result is a long list of independent variables, a jumbled bag of nearly unrelated observations, and often a hopelessly bad specification with meaningless (but statistically significant with several asterisks!) results. (page 227)[5]

OMEGA MATRICES   Data mining and overparameterized approaches are virtually guaranteed to break down statistically. The question is what to do when these failures occur (e.g., Friedman and Schwartz 1991). There are elaborate ways of using (error) weighting techniques to correct model misspecifications or to use other statistical patches that influence $s.e.(b)$. Many intermediate econometric textbooks contain chapters containing the Greek symbol: Omega (Ω) (e.g., Johnston and DiNardo 1997, 162–164). This symbol is representative of the procedure whereby a researcher weights the arrayed (in matrix form)

---

[4] In the absence of formal models, purely applied statistical procedures relying on systematic rules in a specification search can potentially be cumulative (Leamer 1983). See Clarke et al. (2004, 79–129) for an example of building composite empirical models. Composite models can be useful in the process of methodological unification.

[5] Gabaix and Laibson (2008) label this practice *overfitting*, which "occurs when a model works very well in a given situation but fails to make accurate out-of-sample predictions" (page 293). When the "researcher can combine the myriad elements to match almost any given set of facts…[it becomes] easy to explain in-sample data, producing the false impression that the model will have real (out-of-sample) explanatory power" (page 294).

data so that the statistical errors, ultimately the standard error noted previously, is altered and the *t*-statistic is manipulated.

By way of example (using ordinary least squares (OLS)), consider the following model in scalar form (we drop the constant for simplicity):

$$y_t = \beta x_t + \eta_t,$$

and assume there is first-order serial correlation:

$$\eta_t = \rho \eta_{t-1} + v_t,$$

where v_t is a white noise process. With this estimate of ρ a researcher "removes" the serial correlation:

$$y_t - \rho y_{t-1} = \beta \left(x_t - \rho x_{t-1} \right) + v_t.$$

Alternatively, in matrix form, we express this transformation as:

$$\beta^{GLS} = \left(X' \Omega^{-1} X \right) X' \Omega^{-1} Y,$$

as opposed to the OLS estimator:

$$\beta^{OLS} = \left(X'X \right)^{-1} X'Y.$$

The difference is the Ω matrix, which is represented as:

$$\Omega = \begin{bmatrix} 1 & \rho & \rho^2 & \cdots \\ \rho & 1 & \cdots & \cdots \\ \rho^2 & \cdots & 1 & \cdots \\ \cdots & \cdots & \cdots & 1 \end{bmatrix},$$

and taking the inverse with the "ρ" correction:

$$\Omega^{-1} = \begin{bmatrix} 1 & \rho & \cdots & \cdots \\ -\rho & 1+\rho^2 & \cdots & \cdots \\ \cdots & \cdots & 1+\rho^2 & \cdots \\ \cdots & \cdots & \cdots & \cdots \end{bmatrix} \frac{1}{1-\rho^2}.$$

In principle, there is nothing wrong with knowing the Omega matrix for a particular statistical model. The standard error(s) produced by an Omega matrix can serve as a check on whether inferences have been confounded to such an extent that a Type I or Type II error has been committed. Far too often, however, researchers treat the Omega weights (or alternative statistical patches) as the result of a true model. Given that the parameter of "ρ" is based on estimating the error of the regression, researchers that decide to use this weight are taking the mistakes of their model to "fix" their standard errors. It is akin to painting over a crack on a bridge (Hendry 1995). This activity hampers scientific progress because it uses a model's mistakes to obscure flaws.[6]

---

[6] See Leamer (2010) for an additional critique.

Similarly, when using a ρ-restriction, researchers are imposing a restriction on variables in the estimation system. For time series data, researchers assume all variables in the system have the same level of persistence. Matters are worse when data are time series and cross section. The restriction becomes even more severe as researchers assume all the cases and all the independent variables have the same level of persistence.

A final scientific problem with ρ-restrictions is that they fundamentally alter the original model so there is no longer any relation between the theory and the test. A theory assuming, for example, a certain level of persistence (i.e., regularity) in behavior (e.g., party identification) is altered by tools used to "filter out" persistence (Mizon 1995).

2.2.1 Assessment

To summarize, these current practices can also be evaluated in relation to how they fail to contribute to a modeling dialogue between theory and test. What we see in Figure 2.2 is that the process of theoretical development (understanding the workings of the system), prediction, and validation are never directly applied. Instead, the empirical test(s) remains in a loop or dialogue with itself. An iterative process of data mining, overparameterization, and the use of statistical patches (Omega matrices) replaces prediction, validation (falsification), and an understanding of the process.[7] This consequence inevitably follows because current practice does not attempt to identify model parameters b's with the more general effect to impair scientific progress.[8]

One lesson from this admittedly simplified depiction in Figure 2.2 is applied statistical practices, when used in isolation, lack power since they are not linked to a formal model.[9] Of course, formal models are simplifications of what is studied. Nevertheless, they systematically sort rival arguments and confounding

---

[7] Note when we use the word validation this is not simply a process of a single theory being tested by the accuracy of its predictions but also in comparison to competing theories on the same phenomena. As Kuhn (1979) states:

> Anomalous observations ... cannot tempt [a scientist] to abandon his theory until another one is suggested to replace it ... In scientific practice the real confirmation questions always involve the comparison of two theories with each other and with the world, not the comparison of a single theory with the world (page 211).

[8] While this example uses linear procedures, nonlinear procedures are subject to many of the same weaknesses. Achen (2002), for example, raises questions about the forms of statistical patching in various likelihood procedures and how these practices obscure identification.

[9] This criticism extends to progressive applied statistical research strategies (see Hendry 1995). Despite their rigor, specification searches relying on diagnostics, goodness-of-fit metrics, and comparisons to rival models fail to account for ex-ante changes in parameters that a formal model can provide. These applied statistical approaches succeed in improving in-sample accuracy, but lack power out-of-sample, particularly where behavioral responses to policy interventions or various shocks occur. Ultimately, the most powerful tests of formal models reside in predictions for other cases and over earlier or future periods.

Contemporary Methodological Practices

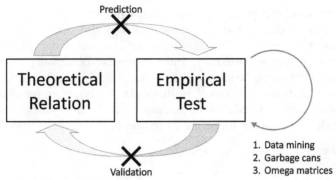

FIGURE 2.2. Noncumulative practices

factors. If formalized predictions, and the underlying system interactions, are inconsistent with empirical tests, then the theory – as represented in the formal model – needs adjustment and the dialogue is maintained.[10]

2.3 NONCUMULATIVE PRACTICES: AN EXAMPLE OF WHAT CAN GO WRONG

The problem with noncumulative practice is demonstrated in the following macro political economy illustration. We employ a structural model to show a relation between parameters and predictions.[11] This is contrary to current practice, which typically ignores structural equation systems (and reduced forms), let alone identification conditions. Then, via simulation, we show how the weaknesses of current practices lead to serious scientific consequences such as incorrect inference and misleading policy advice.

Now consider the relation between a particular macroeconomic policy and outcome: countercyclical monetary policy and inflation. To keep things simple we have left out various political and social influences on the policy rule. While

---

[10] Experiments serve as empirical tests too (see Chapter 13). See Ostrom (2010, 71) for a discussion on how empirical results in experiments contributed to the development of an alternative preference function. Zellner (1984, 9–10) provides other robustness tests, some of which involve the linkage of formal and empirical analysis. These tests include: (a) Studying incorrect predictions; (b) Studying implications of various equations (alter them); (c) Simulating a model's properties; (d) Pushing theories to their extreme; (e) Observing unusual historical periods; (f) Cross level inference; and (g) Experiments.

[11] Classic work in macro political economy by political scientists does not generally rely on structural models (e.g., Hibbs 1977), but see Chappell and Keech (1983), Alesina and Rosenthal (1995), and Freeman and Houser (1998) as exceptions. For a more general overview of macro political economy see Drazen (2000a) and Persson and Tabellini (2002).

this research area holds great potential for explaining why policymakers behave in certain ways, it does not affect the methodological point.[12]

The model incorporates a lagged expectations-augmented Phillips curve, an IS curve (aggregate demand), and an interest rate policy rule (Taylor 1993). Each of these structural equations is a behavioral relation and can be derived from microfoundations.[13] In this example, however, we abstract out the microfoundations since they are not central to the demonstration.

The model contains the following structure:

$$y_t = y_t^n + \gamma \left(\pi_t - E_{t-1}\pi_t\right) + u_{1t}, \qquad \gamma > 0, \tag{2.1}$$

$$y_t = \lambda_1 + \lambda_2 \left(i_t - E_t\pi_{t+1}\right) + \lambda_3 E_t y_{t+1} + u_{2t}, \quad \lambda_1 > 0, \ \lambda_2 < 0, \lambda_3 > 0, \tag{2.2}$$

$$i_t = \pi_t + \alpha_y(y_t - y_t^n) + \alpha_\pi \left(\pi_t - \pi_t^*\right) + r_t^*, \tag{2.3}$$

where y_t is the log of output, y_t^n is the natural rate of output which follows a linear trend: $\alpha + \beta t$, and π_t is price inflation. E_t is a conditional expectations operator such that $E_{t-1}\pi_t$ is expected inflation for period t given the information available up to period $t-1$, $E_t\pi_{t+1}$ is expected inflation one period ahead, and $E_t y_{t+1}$ is expected output one period ahead.[14] The variable i_t is a nominal interest rate that the policymaker can influence, π_t^* is the inflation target, r_t^* is the real interest rate, u_{1t} is an iid shock (demand shock), and u_{2t} is an iid shock (supply shock).

At issue is the relation between policy and inflation. The model posits aggregate supply and demand depend on the expectations over the course of policy and this policy follows some stable probability. Furthermore, agents understand the policy rule and augment their behavior to include the expected gains or losses implied by the policy rule and policymakers' behavior (Lucas 1976).

The coefficients α_y and α_π represent the aggressiveness policymakers possess in stopping inflationary pressures. Positive values of α_y and α_π indicate an aggressive inflation-stabilizing policy tack. These positive parameter values reflect policymakers' willingness to raise nominal interest rates in response to excess demand (inflation), whether it is when output is above its natural rate ($y_t > y_t^n$), or when inflation exceeds its prespecified target ($\pi_t > \pi_t^*$). The coefficients typically range between $[0, 2]$ (Clarida et al. 2000).[15]

---

[12] See Chappell and Keech (1983) for an application of a structural model that incorporates the length of a presidential term.

[13] See Achen and Shively (1995, 23–25) for an example of the importance of linking individual and aggregate levels of analysis.

[14] See Sargent (1979) for the detailed discussion on the rational expectations operator.

[15] Clarida et al. (2000) refer to (2.3) as a "backward looking" rule. They estimate α_y and α_π in (2.3) for the United States (1960:1–1996:4). They find α_y ranges between 0.0 to 0.39 and α_π ranges between 0.86 to 2.55. They conclude the US monetary authority moved to nearly an exclusive focus on stabilizing inflation.

With the relation between countercyclical monetary policy and inflation stated, we now solve for inflation using the method of undetermined coefficients. The minimum state variable solution (MSV) is:[16]

$$\pi_t = \left(\frac{J_0}{1-J_1-J_2} + \frac{J_2 J_3 \beta}{(1-J_1-J_2)^2}\right) + \left(\frac{J_3}{1-J_1-J_2}\right) y_t^n + X_t,$$

where:

$$J_0 = \left(\lambda_1 - \lambda_2 \alpha_\pi \pi_t^* + \lambda_2 r_t^* + \lambda_3 \beta\right) \Theta^{-1},$$
$$J_1 = \left(\gamma - \lambda_2 \alpha_y \gamma\right) \Theta^{-1},$$
$$J_2 = \lambda_2 \Theta^{-1},$$
$$J_3 = (\lambda_3 - 1) \Theta^{-1},$$
$$X_t = \left[(\lambda_2 \alpha_y - 1) u_{1t} + u_{2t}\right] \Theta^{-1}, \text{ and}$$
$$\Theta = \gamma \left(1 - \lambda_2 \alpha_y\right) - \lambda_2 (1 + \alpha_\pi).$$

In more compact form the solution is:

$$\pi_t = \Xi + \Psi y_t^n + X_t, \tag{2.4}$$

where:

$$\Xi = \frac{J_0}{1-J_1-J_2} + \frac{J_2 J_3 \beta}{(1-J_1-J_2)^2}, \text{ and}$$

$$\Psi = \frac{J_3}{1-J_1-J_2}.$$

Equation (2.4) relates parameters (α_y, α_π) with π_t. The problem, however, is – absent added information – it is impossible to explicitly relate policy and treatment changes to outcomes.

There are important scientific consequences when we fail to link formal modeling and applied statistical analysis for purposes of deriving structural parameters. First, consider the utility of a reduced form – which is usually not derived in the current methodological environment. A reduced form such as Eq. (2.4) possesses weaknesses when it comes to making inferences. The reduced form parameters (Ξ, Ψ) cannot strictly identify the parameters relating cause and effect (i.e., α_y, α_π). Where reduced forms have power is not in making inferences but in making predictions: Reduced form estimates provide some assistance in ex-ante forecasts.

How useful then are reduced forms in making predictions based on specific values of the independent variables – the so-called conditional forecast? With

---

[16] The MSV solution is the simplest parameterization one can choose using the method of undetermined coefficients (see McCallum 1983). We discuss these tools in Chapters 5 and 6.

a reduced form a researcher cannot make conditional forecasts. The reason is the system (described in Eqs. (2.1)–(2.3)) depends on the behavior of the agents and whether responses from agents are invariant. If agents' behavior is not invariant, the parameters (in Eqs. (2.1)–(2.3)) are not invariant. Without a mechanism detailing how structural parameters (and behavior) remain (in)variant as independent variables change, an applied statistical model fails in assessing alternative independent variable shifts.

While reduced forms lack inferential power necessary to make conditional forecasts, they still have a linkage to theoretical foundations. Things can be far worse, however, if we use a single empirical equation similar to Eq. (2.4), with no formal-theoretical linkage, and rely on current applied statistical practices – data mining, garbage cans, and "omega matrices." These applied statistical practices lack overall robustness as they obscure fundamental specification error. The parameter(s) "identified" by these current practices lack any real meaning or use.

To see the flaws associated with these contemporary practices more straightforwardly consider Eq. (2.5) as a single equation estimate of π_t:

$$\pi_t = d_0 + d_1 y_t^n + v_{1t}, \tag{2.5}$$

where v_{1t} is the error term. If we contrast the similarly situated parameters in Eq. (2.4) with Eq. (2.5), note that d_0 would serve the purpose of Ξ, and d_1 serves the purpose of Ψ. But, already Eq. (2.5) fails to make any structural statement about the relation between the policy rule in Eq. (2.3) and inflation in Eq. (2.5). There is no explicit relation between d_0 or d_1 and α_y or α_π.

Now, assume the researcher chooses to ignore any process of methodological unification. Instead the analyst tries to estimate a shift in policy regime and reestimates Eq. (2.5) with new variables. A typical way is to add dummy variables signifying policy shifts due to factors such as partisanship and other factors (e.g., Hibbs 1977). We keep the empirical model small and rewrite Eq. (2.5) with just one added variable, a policy shift dummy variable (SHIFT$_t$) signifying a change in the intercept or the level of inflation:

$$\pi_t = \tilde{d}_0 + \tilde{d}_1 y_t^n + \tilde{d}_2 \text{SHIFT}_t + v_{2t}, \tag{2.6}$$

where v_{2t} is the error term.

Does this really assist in achieving identification, predictive precision, falsification, and understanding the working of the system? Notice that the parameter $\tilde{d}_2$ in Eq. (2.6) does not reflect actual policy shifts relating policy parameters to inflation (one such as Eq. (2.3)). This shortcoming is severe. It means we do not know what parameters in the system can lead to counterintuitive results and, ultimately, incorrect policy or treatment recommendations.

Consider the following simulation of the system expressed in Eqs. (2.1), (2.2), and (2.3). In this simulation the structural explanation, relating parameters in the system, shows that aggregate demand, as represented by Eq. (2.2),

Contemporary Methodological Practices

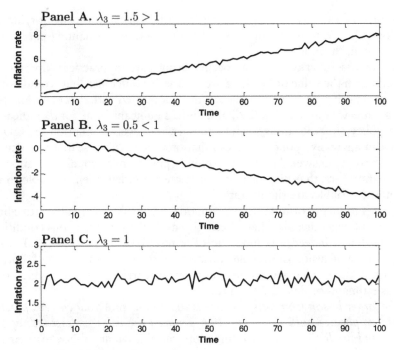

FIGURE 2.3. Simulation results

must respond in a certain way to changes in real interest rates and the expected output level. The relation is represented by the parameter λ_3 in Eq. (2.2). What happens to the relation between inflation-stabilizing policy and inflation if λ_3 is not invariant and contains alternative responses?

In Figure 2.3, Panels A, B, and C report the results in a simulation of the system.[17] Changes in inflation are represented in each panel, given changes to λ_3. In Panel A, when $\lambda_3 > 1$, an aggressive policy ($\alpha_y, \alpha_\pi = 0.5 > 0$) does not reduce inflation. On the other hand, in Panel B, when $0 < \lambda_3 < 1$, inflation falls. It is only in the third case, when $\lambda_3 = 1$, we find that an aggressive policy keeps inflation roughly around a 2 percent target (see Panel C).

The implication of these simulations has direct significance for both reduced form estimation and current practice – with the consequences being especially direct for current practice. If a researcher were to estimate the reduced form of inflation as represented in Eq. (2.4), she would find instability in the forecast and/or forecast error. However, the researcher would have difficulty finding

---

[17] The simulation parameter values are the following for the AS, IS, and policy rule:

- AS: $\alpha = 5; \beta = 0.05; y_0^n = 1; \gamma = 10; \sigma_{u_1} = 1$.
- IS: $\lambda_1 = 3; \lambda_2 = -1; \lambda_3 = (0.5, 1, 1.5); \pi^* = 2; \sigma_{u_2} = 1$.
- Policy rule: $\alpha_y = 0.5; \alpha_\pi = 0.5; r^* = 3$.

the source of the instability given the lack of information in identifying the relation(s) between the parameters in Eq. (2.2) and the remaining parameters (variables) in the model.

Yet, this is superior to what occurs using current practices. Specifically, depending on the value of λ_3, there are alternative outcomes that would not be illuminated using Eq. (2.6) and the practices associated with that equation. But, now assume we estimate Eq. (2.6) and find a significant value for d_2 indicating when policy shifts in an aggressive manner, the level of inflation falls. Does this mean aggressive policy reduces inflation? Using this research practice we do not have an answer. Absent an explicitly posited relation, all we can say is some parameters, that may or may not relate the independent variable to the dependent variable, are significant.

What is more important is a formal model would show the substantive findings are not generalizable when alternative and relevant exogenous conditions are considered. Indeed, the indeterminacy result shown in Figure 2.3 is not robust to the inclusion of nominal variables to the interest rate rule.[18] But, we would not know what we do not know under current practices, which only give us estimates of Eqs. (2.5) and (2.6).

The larger lesson from this exercise is to demonstrate how current practice fails to emphasize both the connection between the valid understanding of a system and predictive power. Adding more variables in an ad-hoc manner will not arrest the specification and theoretical challenges.

2.4 SUMMARY

Some contemporary methodological practices have become acts of preemptive scientific surrender. These practices fail to provide the necessary steps in attaining valid inference and prediction. Embedded in *data mining, overparameterization, and omega matrices* is the general view a researcher will:

Gather the data, run the regression/MLE with the usual linear list of control variables, report the significance tests, and announce that one's pet variable "passed." This dreary hypothesis-testing framework is sometimes seized upon by beginners. Being purely mechanical, it saves a great deal of thinking and anxiety, and cannot help being popular. But obviously, it has to go. Our best empirical generalizations do not derive from that kind of work. (Achen 2002, 442–443)

This scientific weakness is all the clearer when we consider the challenge a social scientist faces. If we simply specify that variable B is a function of variable A, the statistical "tests" estimating a correlation between B and A cannot determine causation between the two even when their correlation is statistically significant. Without unifying formal and empirical analysis we lack

---

[18] Alternatively, McCallum and Nelson (1999) demonstrate that when output is not modeled as a constant, an IS curve of the form (2.2) can produce indeterminacies.

a basic analytical attribute suitable for identifying the following possibilities defining the relation between A and B. As Shively (2017) notes:

> Whenever two variables vary together (are related, coincide), there are four causal sequences that might account for their doing so. A might cause B, B might cause A, both A and B might be caused by something else, or there might be no causation involved. Our task is to eliminate all but one of these, thus leaving an observed relationship, together with a single causal interpretation of it. (page 81)

Yet, as we have seen, too often researchers, using the methods described here, predetermine the significant correlation indicates causation.[19] While EITM does not guarantee a model is correct, it does promote a dialogue between theory and test so that *"causation"* is not the default choice.

---

[19] See Hoover (2001a,b) for a review of these issues and specific methodologies.

3

The EITM Framework

The scientific consequences of the current methodological status quo are far reaching. A significant scientific problem with decoupling formal analysis from applied statistical procedures centers on a failure to *identify invariant* parameter estimates. Developing a basic understanding of how a system operates is a distant hope. This, in turn, impairs falsification of theories and hypotheses as well as the comparison of rival theories and hypotheses. Predictive precision in the policy realm is also negatively affected: Effective policies in the social, political, and economic sphere often require a valid understanding of agent response. Without that acumen policy failure and unintended consequences are virtually assured.[1]

We have been arguing that linking mutually reinforcing properties of formal and empirical analysis provides the necessary transparency between theory and test to aid in valid hypothesis testing. This linkage also contributes to the identification of invariant parameter estimates suitable for improving the accuracy of both ex-ante and ex-post predictions and directly addresses the ideas of order, cause, and chance.[2]

In this chapter we first present the EITM framework to bring some coherence to the idea of methodological unification. We then provide two examples to highlight how methodological unification is achieved. The first – the Solow's economic growth model – is an example more in the Cowles tradition (i.e., structural model and tests with secondary data). The second example – Ostrom's

---

[1] We will use the word "inference" to refer to a parameter in a regression or likelihood (b). We use the word prediction to refer to a model's forecast of a dependent variable ($\hat{y}$). For a technical treatment of these two concepts see Engle et al. (1983).

[2] There is a large literature devoted to identification problems (see, for example, Fisher 1966; Manski 1995). Some researchers treat the issue of simultaneity and identification as one and the same. We consider identification in a broader sense that includes simultaneity, but not limited to simultaneity.

The EITM Framework

work on social dilemmas – highlights the dialogue between theories and tests using experimental designs. Criticisms and limitations of the framework round out this chapter.

3.1 THE EITM FRAMEWORK

In demonstrating the EITM framework, Granato et al. (2015) argue:

> EITM is a method – even a mindset – where researchers treat formal and empirical analysis as linked entities intended to create a dialogue between theory and test. We have already demonstrated the motivation for EITM as a means to counter destructive training and research practices due to compartmentalization. We agree specialization and the division of labor are necessary to begin training processes, but it is also clear that integration is an important next step in the training process and eventually for research practice. (page 376)

Yet, Granato et al. (2015) also recognize it is not enough to criticize existing practices and the current state of methodology:

> But, these motivations are not enough if we want to implement EITM. Implementation involves defining the elements of EITM – a framework – and showing how one does EITM research and how one trains students to do such research. The development of a framework is important since "without a framework to organize relevant variables identified in theories and empirical research, isolated knowledge acquired from studies... by... social and behavioral scientists is not likely to cumulate. (Ostrom 2009: 420)" (page 376)

Recall this EITM framework builds on the Cowles Commission approach and then places an emphasis on developing behavioral and applied statistical analogues and linking these analogues.[3] And while we build on the Cowles Commission approach, there do exist analytical frameworks in other disciplines as well.[4]

EITM includes the following attributes:[5]

- EITM places emphasis on modeling human behavior so new uncertainty created by shifts in behavioral traits such as public tastes, attitudes, expectations, and learning are properly accounted for and studied.
- The Cowles Commission is associated with building a system of equations and then following rules (rank and order conditions) for identification that count on equations and unknowns. In contrast, our EITM framework is

---

[3] Analogues are related to operationalizing a concept. An analogue is a device represented by variable – and measurable – quantities. Analogues include variables, operators, or an estimation process that mimic the concept of interest. They serve as analytical devices – not categorical indicators – for behavior and, therefore, provide for changes in behavior as well as a more transparent interpretation of the formal and applied statistical model.

[4] Jasso's (2004) *Tripartite Framework* will be reviewed in Chapter 14.

[5] See Granato (2005) and Granato et al. (2010a,b, 2011).

agnostic on the choice to build and relate a system or to partition the system (via assumption) into a smaller set of equations, even a single equation.[6] We place emphasis on the mutually reinforcing properties of formal and empirical analysis.

- A final and related point on model specification relates to the critiques of the structural approach leveled by Sims (1980). It is well known that structural parameters are not identified from reduced form estimates. The practice of finding ways to identify models can lead to "incredible" theoretical specifications (Sims 1980; Freeman et al. 1989). The proposed EITM framework, by adding behavioral concepts and analogues, can address Sims' criticisms in a theoretically meaningful way. Analogues, in particular, have important scientific importance since they hold the promise of operationalizing mechanisms.[7]

This EITM framework contains three steps:

STEP 1. RELATE AND UNIFY THEORETICAL CONCEPTS AND APPLIED STATISTICAL CONCEPTS The goal of this first step in EITM is to transform the focus from the substantive topic to the underlying behavioral process. We start, however, not with the development of mathematical structures but with the identification of concepts. It is, of course, standard to suggest that research begin with concepts. We have in mind, however, not the substantive concepts central to a discipline, but instead to the general behavioral attributes of the thing being researched.[8]

---

[6] This debate about general and partial equilibrium model building can be traced back to at least the 1800s. See Friedman (1953) for descriptions and evaluation of "Walrasian" and "Marshallian" model building practice.

[7] Operationalizing causal mechanisms, as opposed to operationalizing variables, involves the creation of measurable devices (i.e., analogues) on both the formal side and the empirical side. An early example of operationalizing a mechanism can be seen in the work of Converse (1969). He advanced the theory that strength of party identification (and voting behavior) is primarily a function of intergenerational transmission plus the number of times one had voted in free elections. To operationalize his proposed mechanism – intergenerational transmission – he made use of the following analogue: the Markov chain. This particular analogue allowed for a particular dynamic prediction he tested with data.

[8] In political science, for example, a student of democracy might focus on *choice*: How do demographic and attitudinal variables drive individual selection over political parties? Another student might focus on *uncertainty and learning*: Given the lack of a "track record" among political parties in newly democratizing states, how do individuals come to form expectations regarding those parties, and how do those expectations shift in response to political and economic changes? A third student might concentrate on the idea of *bargaining*: How do the various party leaders face the trade-offs between maximizing their potential influence in the political system and maintaining the promise to democratize? The idea is not to ignore the substantive aspects, but to look at substance from a different perspective, one that not only helps clarify the focus of the research but also suggests common behavioral concerns that make it easier to communicate across subfields and find common elements and approaches. We thank Douglas Dion for this set of examples.

The EITM Framework

Concepts of particular concern in this framework reflect many overarching social and behavioral processes. Examples include (but are not limited to):

- decision making
- bargaining
- expectations
- learning
- elements of social interaction (strategic and nonstrategic)

It is also important to find an appropriate statistical concept to match with the theoretical concept. Examples of applied statistical concepts include (but are not limited to):

- persistence
- measurement error
- discrete/nominal choice
- simultaneity
- prediction
- prediction error

STEP 2. DEVELOP BEHAVIORAL (FORMAL) AND APPLIED STATISTICAL ANALOGUES   To link concepts with tests, we need analogues. An analogue is a device representing a concept via a continuous and measurable variable or set of variables. Examples of analogues for the behavioral (formal) concepts such as decision making, expectations, learning, and strategic interaction include (but are not limited to):

- decision theory (e.g., utility maximization)
- conditional expectations (forecasting) procedures
- adaptive and Bayesian learning (information updating) procedures
- game theory

Examples of applied statistical analogues for the applied statistical concepts of persistence,[9] measurement error, nominal choice, simultaneity, prediction, and prediction error include (respectively):

- autoregressive estimation
- error-in-variables regression
- discrete/nominal choice modeling
- multi-stage estimation (e.g., two-stage least squares)
- point estimates and distributions
- mean square error

---

[9] Consider, for example, the concept of persistence. Theoretically, this conjures up a host of potential analogues: coordination equilibria, Markov chain steady-states, locally and globally stable solutions to systems of differential equations, or still lifes in cellular automata models. Similarly, persistence can be tied to a number of statistical models, including autoregressive estimation and attendant asymptotic theory.

STEP 3. UNIFY AND EVALUATE THE ANALOGUES The third step unifies the mutually reinforcing properties of the formal and empirical analogues. By starting with the concept and then moving to the theoretical and applied statistical analogues, we guarantee that there must be something in common between the theory and the empirical analysis. The idea, then, is to locate the parameters of interest in each that reflect the underlying concept, and then use those to build clearer and stronger links between the mechanisms of the theoretical model and the specification of the statistical methods. The specified linkage not only draws theory and empirics closer but also provides a way for research to build by showing potential sources of inaccuracies and model failure.

3.2 EXAMPLES OF METHODOLOGICAL UNIFICATION

3.2.1 Example 1: The Solow Model

We first use the well-known Solow (1956) economic growth (development) model as an example of model unification.[10] This example demonstrates how the traditional approach to methodological unification (similar to the Cowles Commission) provides a basis for a modeling dialogue and scientific cumulation. In his seminal paper, Solow (1956) argues capital accumulation and exogenous technological progress are fundamental mechanisms in economic development.

Using a simple Cobb–Douglas production function with a dynamic process for capital accumulation, Solow concludes a country experiences a higher transitory growth rate when the country increases its national savings (to stimulate capital accumulation). One important prediction from the Solow model is the conditional convergence hypothesis, which states that countries with lower initial level output per worker tend to grow faster when the countries' characteristics are held constant.

The formal model has the following structure and outlines this process:

$$Y_t = (A_t K_t)^\alpha L_t^{1-\alpha}, \tag{3.1}$$

$$K_{t+1} - K_t = sY_t - \delta K_t, \tag{3.2}$$

$$L_{t+1} = (1 + \lambda) L_t, \text{ and} \tag{3.3}$$

$$A_{t+1} = (1 + \tau) A_t, \tag{3.4}$$

---

[10] In the language of the EITM framework, the theoretical concepts in the Solow (1956) model are related to decision making. In the model, a representative household owns capital stock and she attempts to maximize her income by leasing all her capital to the firms at the market rental rate. The household also decides on the consumption and saving levels based on her intertemporal budget constraint, where the change in capital stock depends on the difference between saving and depreciation. The empirical concept of the model is prediction. The formal and empirical analogues include decision theory (profit maximization) and point estimation.

The EITM Framework

where $0 < \alpha < 1$. Equation (3.1) is a production function where aggregate production (output) Y_t is determined by capital K_t, labor L_t, and technological progress A_t^α in year t. We also note that the production function is in Cobb–Douglas specification, where α represents the capital share of output, and $(1 - \alpha)$ the labor share of output.[11] Equation (3.2) represents the capital accumulation $(K_{t+1} - K_t)$, which equals the domestic savings sY_t minus capital depreciation δK_t, where $s \in (0, 1)$ is a constant savings rate and δ is the depreciation rate. Equations (3.3) and (3.4) show both labor and technological progress are exogenously increasing at the rates of λ and τ, respectively.

STEADY STATE EQUILIBRIUM To derive the equilibrium (or the steady state) of the model, we first define $k_t = K_t/(A_t L_t)$ and $y_t = Y_t/(A_t L_t)$ as capital per effective unit of worker and output per effective unit of worker, respectively ($A_t L_t$ is known as the effective number of workers). The effective number of workers can be interpreted as the number of typical workers in the production process when the workers are equipped with the existing technology A_t.[12] Now we convert the Cobb–Douglas production function (3.1) into a per-effective-worker production function as follows:

$$y_t = \frac{Y_t}{A_t L_t} = \frac{(A_t K_t)^\alpha L_t^{1-\alpha}}{A_t L_t}$$

$$y_t = k_t^\alpha. \tag{3.5}$$

Equation (3.5) suggests that the level of output per effective worker y_t is determined by the capital stock per effective worker k_t. A larger amount of capital stock (per effective worker) available leads to a higher output (GDP) level.

Next we derive the dynamic process of capital per effective unit of labor using Eq. (3.2):

$$K_{t+1} - K_t = sY_t - \delta K_t$$
$$\Rightarrow K_{t+1} = sY_t + (1 - \delta) K_t. \tag{3.6}$$

According to Eqs. (3.3) and (3.4), we have $A_{t+1} L_{t+1} = (1 + \lambda)(1 + \tau) A_t L_t$. Now divide $A_{t+1} L_{t+1}$ on the left-hand side of Eq. (3.6) and $(1 + \lambda)(1 + \tau) A_t L_t$ on the right-hand side of (3.6):

$$\frac{K_{t+1}}{A_{t+1} L_{t+1}} = \frac{sY_t + (1 - \delta) K_t}{(1 + \lambda)(1 + \tau) A_t L_t}$$

$$\Rightarrow k_{t+1} = \frac{1}{(1 + \lambda)(1 + \tau)} \left[sk_t^\alpha + (1 - \delta) k_t \right] \tag{3.7}$$

$$k_{t+1} = F(k_t), \tag{3.8}$$

---

[11] See Chapter 11, FN 14 for further discussion.
[12] For example, if the current level of technology is $A = 1$ (basic technology) and there are $L = 10$ workers in the production process, then $AL = 10$ effective workers in the production process. Now assuming the technology advances where $A = 2$ (e.g., better tools, equipment or machinery), these 10 actual workers with advanced technology are simply equivalent to 20 typical (or effective) workers without advanced technology ($AL = 2 \times 10$).

where $F(k_t) = [(1+\lambda)(1+\tau)]^{-1}[sk_t^\alpha + (1-\delta)k_t]$. Equation (3.8) shows k_{t+1} is a function of k_t over time. This is a fundamental equation. It depicts how the capital stock k_t accumulates over time. Note, an equilibrium (steady state) exists when the capital stock (per effective unit of labor) is constant over time (i.e., $k_{t+1} = k_t = k^*$). We can solve for the steady state k^* using Eq. (3.7):

$$k^* = \left(\frac{s}{\delta + \lambda + \tau + \lambda\tau}\right)^{1/(1-\alpha)}. \tag{3.9}$$

Next, if we substitute Eq. (3.9) into Eq. (3.5), we obtain the steady state level of output per effective worker:

$$y^* = (k^*)^\alpha = \left(\frac{s}{\delta + \lambda + \tau + \lambda\tau}\right)^{\alpha/(1-\alpha)}. \tag{3.10}$$

Since $y_t = Y_t/(A_t L_t)$, the output level Y_t^* in steady state at time t can be expressed as follows:

$$Y_t^* = A_t L_t y^*$$

$$= A_t L_t \left(\frac{s}{\delta + \lambda + \tau + \lambda\tau}\right)^{\alpha/(1-\alpha)}. \tag{3.11}$$

Equation (3.11) demonstrates that the steady state output level Y_t^* depends on technological level A_t, labor L_t, and a set of exogenous parameters: s, δ, λ, τ, and α. In the economic growth literature, researchers generally focus on the parameters of saving rate s and population growth rate λ. A key implication from Eq. (3.11) is that an increase in national saving rate s stimulates capital accumulation, which in turn raises the output (income) level in an economy. On the other hand, the equation also indicates that income levels tend to be lower in the countries with higher population growth rates λ.

CONDITIONAL CONVERGENCE HYPOTHESIS   Another key finding in the Solow model is known as the conditional convergence hypothesis. The conditional convergence hypothesis states that low-income countries tend to grow at a faster rate than high-income countries, controlling for certain economic characteristics, such as, the saving (or investment) rate, and population and technological growth rates.

To derive the hypothesis of conditional convergence, we begin with the production function (3.5). We can show the growth rate of output per effective worker depends on the growth rate of capital accumulation by taking log-difference of Eq. (3.5):

$$\ln y_t - \ln y_{t-1} = \alpha \left(\ln k_t - \ln k_{t-1}\right),$$

$$g_{y,t} = \alpha g_{k,t} \tag{3.12}$$

where $g_{y,t} = \ln y_t - \ln y_{t-1}$ is the growth rate of output per effective worker y_t from $t-1$ to t, and $g_{k,t} = \ln k_t - \ln k_{t-1}$ is the growth rate of capital per

The EITM Framework

effective worker k_t from $t-1$ to t.[13] Equation (3.12) shows the growth rate of output per effective worker $g_{y,t}$ is simply the growth rate of capital per effective worker $g_{k,t}$ weighted by the capital share of output α. The implication here is that an increase in the growth rate of capital accumulation leads to a higher economic growth rate.

The final element of showing the conditional convergence hypothesis is the growth rate of capital accumulation $g_{k,t}$. Using Eq. (3.7) first subtract k_t on both sides of the equation:

$$k_{t+1} - k_t = \frac{1}{(1+\lambda)(1+\tau)} \left[sk_t^\alpha + (1-\delta)k_t \right] - k_t.$$

Then multiply both sides by $1/k_t$:

$$\frac{k_{t+1} - k_t}{k_t} = \frac{1}{(1+\lambda)(1+\tau)} \left\{ \frac{\left[sk_t^\alpha + (1-\delta)k_t \right] - k_t}{k_t} \right\}$$

$$\Rightarrow g_{k,t+1} = \frac{1}{(1+\lambda)(1+\tau)} \left[sk_t^{\alpha-1} - (\delta + \lambda + \tau + \lambda\tau) \right], \quad (3.13)$$

where $g_{k,t+1} = (k_{t+1} - k_t)/k_t$ represents the growth rate of capital accumulation (per effective unit of labor) from t to $t+1$. Equation (3.13) indicates the level of capital per effective worker k_t affects its growth rate $g_{k,t+1}$ at $t+1$. More specifically, given α is between zero and one, the growth rate of capital accumulation $g_{k,t+1}$ is asymptotically decreasing in its level k_t. In other

---

[13] Note the log-difference is commonly used as the approximation of percentage change or growth rate. To illustrate this transformation, consider the following equation:

$$y_t = \ln x_t.$$

By taking a time derivative, we have:

$$\frac{dy}{dt} = \frac{d \ln x_t}{dt} = \frac{1}{x_t} \frac{dx_t}{dt} = \frac{1}{x_t} \lim_{\Delta t \to 0} \frac{x_{t+\Delta t} - x_t}{\Delta t}, \quad (3.14)$$

or:

$$\frac{dy}{dt} = \frac{d \ln x_t}{dt} = \lim_{\Delta t \to 0} \frac{\ln x_{t+\Delta t} - \ln x_t}{\Delta t}, \quad (3.15)$$

in continuous time. Similarly, for discrete time, we assume that $\Delta t = 1$, then we can first rewrite Eq. (3.14) as follows:

$$\left. \frac{dy}{dt} \right|_{\Delta t = 1} = \frac{\Delta y}{\Delta t} = \frac{1}{x_t} \cdot \frac{x_{t+1} - x_t}{1} = \frac{x_{t+1} - x_t}{x_t}, \quad (3.16)$$

for $\Delta t = 1$. Also, Eq. (3.14) can also be written in discrete form:

$$\left. \frac{dy}{dt} \right|_{\Delta t = 1} = \frac{\Delta y}{\Delta t} = \frac{\ln x_{t+1} - \ln x_t}{1} = \ln x_{t+1} - \ln x_t. \quad (3.17)$$

for $\Delta t = 1$. As a result, the growth rate of x presented in Eq. (3.16) (i.e., $(x_{t+1} - x_t)/x_t$) can be approximated in the form of log differences (i.e., $\ln x_{t+1} - \ln x_t$) presented in (3.17).

words, the value of k_t is inversely related to its growth rate $g_{k,t+1}$. A lower level of capital k_t implies a higher growth rate of capital accumulation. On the other hand, a higher level of k_t presupposes a lower growth rate of capital accumulation.

This result can be extended to the relation between the output level and its growth rate. Note that the per-effective-worker production function (3.5) can be rewritten as follows:

$$y_t = k_t^{\alpha}$$
$$\Rightarrow y_t^{1/\alpha} = k_t. \quad (3.18)$$

Then we divide Eq. (3.5) by Eq. (3.18):

$$y_t^{\frac{\alpha-1}{\alpha}} = k_t^{\alpha-1}. \quad (3.19)$$

Now we move Eq. (3.12) one period forward:

$$g_{y,t+1} = \alpha g_{k,t+1}. \quad (3.20)$$

Finally, by inserting Eqs. (3.13) and (3.19) into Eq. (3.20), we have:

$$g_{y,t+1} = \frac{\alpha}{(1+\lambda)(1+\tau)} \left[s y_t^{\frac{\alpha-1}{\alpha}} - (\delta + \lambda + \tau + \lambda\tau) \right]. \quad (3.21)$$

The interpretation of Eq. (3.21) is similar to that of Eq. (3.13). Equation (3.21) shows that the growth rate of output (per effective worker) $g_{y,t+1}$ is asymptotically decreasing in its output level y_t, $y_t < y^*$. A lower output level y_t tends to have a higher growth rate of output $g_{y,t+1}$. Inversely, a higher level of y_t is associated with a lower output growth rate.

Lastly, using the technique of linear approximation, we derive the average growth rate for output per labor (also known as the labor productivity, Y_t/L_t):[14]

$$g_y = g_A + \frac{1 - F'(k^*)^T}{T} \left[\ln A_0 + \frac{\alpha}{1-\alpha} Z - \ln\left(\frac{Y_0}{L_0}\right) \right], \quad (3.22)$$

where $g_y = [\ln(Y_T/L_T) - \ln(Y_0/L_0)]/T$, $g_A = (\ln A_T - \ln A_0)/T$, $Z = \ln s - \ln(\delta + \lambda + \tau + \lambda\tau)$, and A_0 and Y_0/L_0 are the respective technological level and labor productivity for the initial period, $t = 0$. The dependent variable g_y represents the average (annual) growth rate of labor productivity between $t = 0$ and $t = T$. Equation (3.22) shows the log level of initial output per labor level $\ln(Y_0/L_0)$ is negatively associated with its growth rate. This is the conditional convergence hypothesis, where low-income countries tend to grow at a faster rate than high-income countries, again controlling for certain economic characteristics.

[14] See the Appendix of this chapter (Section 3.5) for the detailed derivation of Eq. (3.22).

MODEL UNIFICATION   To test the theoretical prediction in Eq. (3.22) researchers estimate the following regression model:

$$g_y^j = \beta_0 + \beta_1 \ln\left(\frac{Y_0^j}{L_0^j}\right) + \beta_2 Z^j + \epsilon^j, \qquad (3.23)$$

where g_y^j represents the average of the annual growth rate in country j, $\ln(Y_0^j/L_0^j)$ the initial level of real GDP per capital, Z^j is a set of control variables suggested in Eq. (3.22), and ϵ^j is a stochastic error term that captures other unobservable factors.[15]

The correspondence to EITM is illustrated by linking the empirical model (3.23) to the theoretical model (3.22): The variables g_y^j and Z^j correspond to $\left[\ln(Y_T^j/L_T^j) - \ln(Y_0^j/L_0^j)\right]/T$ and $\ln s_j - \ln(\delta + \lambda + \tau + \lambda\tau)$, respectively, and the coefficients β_0, β_1 and β_2 correspond to: $g_A + \{[1 - F'(k^*)^T]/T\}\ln A_0$, = $-[1 - F'(k^*)^T]/T$, and $[\alpha(1 - F'(k^*)^T)]/[(1-\alpha)T]$, respectively.

In the economic development literature, a common empirical finding is the initial level of GDP per capita possesses a significant negative correlation with a country's economic growth rate (that is, $\hat{\beta}_1 < 0$). This finding supports the conditional convergence hypothesis: A country with a lower level of real GDP per capita tends to grow faster (Barro and Sala-i-Martin 1992; Mankiw et al. 1992).

What role, then, does the Solow model play in cumulation? The typical estimated coefficient of initial real GDP per capita is significantly less than the Solow model prediction. In other words, the Solow model overestimates the speed of convergence. To address the inaccuracy on the speed of convergence, some researchers revised the theoretical model by relaxing the assumption of homogeneous labor and capital in the production process. Mankiw et al. (1992) builds on and modifies the Solow model by introducing the stock of human capital in the production function. Human capital stock is represented as the sum of education and training that workers receive. By controlling for the level of human capital (education), the authors find the rate of convergence

---

[15] Stochastic elements are not included in the theoretical model. In the Solow model setup, we assume the production function depends on two factor inputs only: labor L and capital K. However, we can expand the set of factor inputs, such as raw materials and entrepreneurial management. Or, we can simply make the production function stochastic by including a random error term (with a finite distribution), which covers all other potential factors. We argue that either type of modification does not alter the conditional convergence hypothesis. The reason is the theoretical model provides a minimal set of variables showing a negative relation between initial levels of income $\ln(Y_0/L_0)$ and economic growth rates g_y. However, when estimating for the presence of conditional convergence, we certainly include a stochastic term in the regression model to capture all other unobservable disturbances.

Since EITM encourages a dialogue between theory and test, it certainly is natural for one to consider adding a theoretically justified stochastic term to the theoretical model. We thank the reviewer for the comment.

is approximately 2 percent per year, which is closer to the prediction in the modified Solow model.

The Solow model and the extensions of it provide an example of a cumulative research process. The modifications in the theoretical model were due to the empirical tests, but this is feasible due to methodological unification. The modeling dialogue here gives researchers a better understanding of the regularities in economic development. If researchers did not consider the Solow model (i.e., ignored the inner workings of the system) and solely applied an empirical procedure by regressing the average growth rate on the initial real GDP per capita, they could misinterpret the empirical results and fail to understand the mechanism(s) that influence economic development. On the other hand, if the researchers only set up a theoretical model but do not test it empirically, they would not know the model is actually inconsistent with the empirical observations.

3.2.2 Example 2: Ostrom's Social Dilemma Research

Another example of the dialogue we are describing is Elinor Ostrom's (2010) work, *Revising Theory in Light of Experimental Findings*.[16] In her article, Ostrom explains how the empirical findings from experiments improve social dilemma research. Game theory provides a clear theoretical pathway that can be tested not only by secondary data but also carefully designed experiments. Furthermore, making changes in the experimental design allows examination of game theoretic predictions to support further revisions to the model. As Ostrom (2010, 69) states: "behavior in social dilemma experiments varies dramatically from being consistent with game theory predictions to being inconsistent, depending on the design of the experiment." Ostrom (2010) shows more specific examples of how feedback from experimental tests supports revision of the conventional self-regarding model in social dilemmas.[17]

Scholars find diverse experimental environments bring an immense variety of outcomes related to social dilemmas rather than conforming to theoretical predictions simply from a model of the individuals who maximize their own short-term payoffs (Ostrom 2010, 70). For instance, Ostrom and Walker (1991) allow face-to-face communication in the experiment, which leads to a substantial reduction in subjects' overharvesting. David Sally (1995), in his meta-analysis of 35 years of published experiments related to prisoner's dilemma games, finds communication among the subjects significantly changes their degree of cooperation in repeated experiments. Schmitt et al. (2000) find

---

[16] This section draws directly from Granato et al. (2015: 385–386).

[17] In the language of the EITM framework, Ostrom is working with theoretical concepts related to decision making, learning, and social interaction. The empirical concept centers on prediction. The formal and empirical analogues include game theory and simple numerical and qualitative outcomes.

the influence of communication depends on decision makers' involvement in the discussion after a common-pool resources (CPRs) experiment and also letting the subjects in the subgroup be party to the discussion.[18]

The experimental results – the empirical tests – also challenge the presumption that only externally imposed regulations can make people overcome social dilemmas. Lopez et al. (2009) find informal sanctions and subjective knowledge of the group in a framed field experiment are more effective than external rules. Similarly, Ostrom et al. (1992) find subjects punish those who keep overharvesting if opportunities for engaging in costly punishment were given in CPR lab experiments.[19]

In sum, these empirical findings and tests from diverse experiments indicate the experimental environment and context can change behavior related to social dilemmas, and this is inconsistent with the predictions based on the self-regarding model. It is inadvisable to use the conventional model for predicting outcomes in experiments. Moving forward we need to consider changing the behavioral theory.

What do various empirical tests offer as new information? Numerous studies of social dilemmas have proposed a variety of alternative models of individual behavior that expand the potential factors individuals consider during the decision process (Fehr and Schmidt 1999; Bolton and Ockenfels 2000; Camerer 2003; Cox 2004; Cox and Deck 2005; Camerer and Fehr 2006; Cox et al. 2007).

Individuals in social dilemmas tend to value returns to others rather than solely seeking their own immediate benefits. And how much individuals value returns to others depends on who the others are, their joint history, and information available about past behavior. Individuals apply norms of behavior in a variety of settings besides material interests (Crawford and Ostrom 1995).

It is unsurprising when different individuals behave differently in distinct experiments, but what is also clear is the self-regarding assumption is inconsistent across experiments and field settings. In addition, individuals do learn norms of behavior and are affected by these norms. A different theoretical model would be based on a behavioral theory of the self-regarding individual who possesses "other-regarding" preferences and internal norms. The results indicate a higher level of cooperation than predicted by the conventional theory (Ostrom 2010, 70).

---

[18] Participants in the CPR experiment are asked to make decisions about the investment of an endowment of tokens between two markets. Market 1 yields a certain, private return while the return from tokens invested in Market 2 is dependent on both individual and aggregate token investments in that market. For more detailed information about the CPR experiment, please refer to Ostrom et al. (1994).

[19] Challenges can be found in other motivation sources. Findings from 40 laboratory and field experiments conducted around the world challenge the theoretical assumption that people only focus on material interests for self (Bowles 2008).

An additional point to note is the role of "context" and the importance qualitative attributes such as this play in model and test revision and improvement. First, context refers to the experimental environment designed by the researcher to test theory. Second, it also represents the broader context outside affecting preferences and actions. However, this is not the end of the story. As Ostrom (2010, 70) asserts:

> [w]hen a careful design repeatedly does not produce the predicted outcomes, we have to ask, is it the design? Or, is the theory of the individual being used? I am arguing that we need to assume a more complex theory of the individual when we study social dilemmas.

Indeed, thinking further, we find individuals are likely to revert to their own immediate benefits (self-regarding) when there is no chance to know those with whom they interact, no information available about their past behavior, or no communication in the experiments. Alternatively, individuals tend to cooperate more if trust and reciprocity are well developed because of the two contextual aspects, and the role repetition plays in reputation acquisition.[20]

Theory, then, can be modified to take into account the role of reputation, trust, and reciprocity affecting outcomes in repeated social dilemmas (Ostrom 2010, 71). It is possible that when facing social dilemmas, a cooperator will not be a sucker who contributes while others continue to free ride because individuals can be trustworthy reciprocators. This can help us understand and extend experimental findings related to the governance of natural resources (Arnason et al. 2006).

Ostrom (2010) provides an important example of testing and consistency evaluation. She explains how empirical findings from experiments assist in testing the game theoretic model of the self-regarding individual with no cooperation and how the testing feedback works to revise the theory for social dilemmas: from self-regarding to other-regarding, adding context, reputation, trust, and reciprocity.

3.3 EITM CRITICISMS

Various criticisms have been leveled at the EITM initiative.[21] The criticisms center on the motivation for EITM and the degree to which EITM is related

---

[20] Increasing evidence from neuroeconomics is that some individuals gain real pleasure from norms of behavior such as trustworthy action (McCabe and Smith 2001; Rilling et al. 2002; Fehr et al. 2005), which is consistent with Crawford and Ostrom's (1995) inclusion of the concept of norms in the preference functions of individuals making a cooperative move. As Ostrom (2010) discusses, norms affect individual behavior because people appear to treat positive actions with positive responses and vice versa. Gaining a reputation for being trustworthy and reciprocating cooperation help enhance cooperation to achieve substantial long-run interests and increase individual net benefits substantially.

[21] This section borrows heavily from Granato et al. (2015, 380–387). A more extensive review of these issues can be found there.

The EITM Framework

to the hypothetico-deductive (H-D) approach. At this point in time we find no criticisms leveled at the EITM framework. Rather, criticisms have been leveled at statements in Granato and Scioli (2004) and the documents related to the 2001 NSF EITM Workshop (EITM Report 2002).

3.3.1 Motivation Criticisms

Motivation criticisms of EITM have appeared in Clarke and Primo (2012). Earlier we discussed three motivations for EITM, but here we present Clarke and Primo's arguments and their quotes of various EITM sources. We respond using the same sources.

Clarke and Primo's criticisms on the motivation for EITM can be found in this quote:

> For all the discussion of science in Granato and Scioli's article, there is no actual argument or justification for pursuing an EITM strategy. We are told, for instance, that "by thinking about the empirical implications of theoretical models scholars develop clear-cut empirical tests (Granato and Scioli 2004, 314). Although the statement may or may not be true, it is not an argument that scientific progress results from developing clear-cut empirical tests. That conclusion is simply assumed. (Clarke and Primo 2012, 50)

This statement is incorrect. There are many motivations for "pursuing an EITM strategy," but further explanation can be found as to whether conclusions to motivate EITM are "simply assumed." Consider the following as it pertains to formal modeling practices (Granato and Scioli 2004, 315):

> The assumptions on which some formal modeling rests are often so at variance with empirical reality that model results are dismissed out of hand by those familiar with the facts. The problem is not just unreal assumptions, for one way to build helpful models is to begin with stylized and perhaps overly simple assumptions, test the model's predictions, and then modify the assumptions consistent with a progressively more accurate model of reality. Yet these follow-up steps are too often not taken or left unfinished, with the result being a model that does little to enhance understanding or to advance the discipline.

It is recognized also that abstract modeling is useful – indeed it is fundamental to the EITM framework. The point of departure is whether data exist to force changes in simplifying assumptions:[22]

---

[22] On this matter, Robert Solow (1956, 65) maintains:

> [a]ll theory depends on assumptions which are not quite true. That is what makes it theory. The art of successful theorizing is to make the inevitable simplifying assumptions in such a way that the final results are not very sensitive. A "crucial" assumption is one on which the conclusions do depend sensitively, and it is important that crucial assumptions be reasonably realistic. When the results of a theory seem to flow specifically from a special crucial assumption, then if the assumption is dubious, the results are suspect.

One justification for "theories of unreality" is that realistic models are often so complex as to be of limited value. There is merit to this defense. An important function of formal modeling is to assist in identifying crucial quantitative and qualitative effects from those that are of minimal importance. However, the drive for simplicity can be taken too far. (page 315)

Moreover, it matters to respect and explain well understood empirical generalizations:

The use of simplifying assumptions is in principle a virtue and remains so when such simplifications do no harm to overall predictive accuracy. However, this does not mean that formal modeling should proceed without regard to glaring factual contradictions in its foundational or situation-specific assumptions. Rather, formal modelers must be especially careful to make sure that they test their models in situations that go beyond the circumstances that suggested the models, for it is there that simplifying assumptions are likely to lead to difficulties. (page 315)

Recall from Chapter 2 poor current empirical modeling practices are equally at fault and again serve as motivation. As Granato and Scioli (2004) point out:

...the following ratio is the subject of much attention by applied statistical analysts because it is the basis for which "theories" survive or perish:

$$\frac{b}{s.e.(b)}.$$

This ratio is commonly referred to as a "t-statistic." It is the "truth" that most applied statistical analysts are concerned with, and it can be confounded by influences that shift the numerator (b) in unforeseen ways. The denominator, the standard error ($s.e.(b)$), also is susceptible to numerous forces that can make it artificially large or small. In either case, avoiding false rejection of the null hypothesis (Type I error) or false acceptance of the null hypothesis (Type II error) is imperative. While the concern with Type I and Type II errors should be of prime importance, that unfortunately is not usually the case. Instead, the focus is on the size of the t-statistic and whether one can get "significant" results. (page 316)

One practice is data mining:

The first tendency in trying to achieve "significant" results is the practice of data mining. Some political scientists put data into a statistical program with minimal theory and run regression after regression until they get either statistically significant coefficients or coefficients that they like. This search is not random and can wither away the strength of causal claims. (page 316)

In a related point, Pfleiderer (2014) argues that since theoretical modeling is often undertaken to understand the implications of a given set of assumptions it is often possible for researchers to "cherry pick" assumptions to produce a desired result. It is reasonable to ask whether a theoretical model is based on assumptions that are generally consistent with what we know about the world and are capturing the most important factors.

The EITM Framework

A related practice is creating overparameterization – by design:

A second practice is that many studies degenerate into garbage-can regression or garbage-can likelihood renditions. By a garbage-can regression or likelihood we mean a practice whereby a researcher includes, in a haphazard fashion, a plethora of independent variables into a statistical package and gets significant results somewhere. But a link with a formal model could help in distinguishing the variables and relations that matter most from those that are ancillary and, probably, statistical artifacts. More often than not there is little or no attention paid to the numerous potential confounding factors that could corrupt statistical inferences. (page 316)

A third empirical modeling practice can be characterized as having the mindset that "we are never wrong, but sometimes we are a little weak on being right":

The first and second practices lead to the third – statistical patching (i.e., the use of weighting procedures to adjust the standard errors $(s.e.(b))$ in the t-statistic ratio above). (page 316)

Statistical patches are seductive because they:

have the potential to deflate the standard error and inflate the t-statistic, which, of course, increases the chance for statistical significance…There are elaborate ways of using error-weighting techniques to "correct" model misspecifications or to use other statistical patches that substitute for a new specification. For example, in almost any intermediate econometrics textbook one finds a section that has the Greek symbol Omega (Ω). This symbol is representative of the procedure whereby a researcher weights the data that are arrayed (in matrix form) so that the statistical errors, and ultimately the standard error noted above, are sometimes reduced in size and the t-statistic then may become significant. (pages 316–317)

Despite these factors, Clarke and Primo further assert:

[In the 2002 EITM Report]…essays written by the [EITM Workshop] participants are hugely ironic as they make clear that the split between theory and empirical analysis is far from problematic…In the executive summary, however, this ambivalence gives way to statements such as "Significant scientific progress can be made by a synthesis of formal and empirical modeling". (page 49)

Clarke and Primo's statement misses various workshop concerns on this matter. One issue was how widespread the divide was. The 2002 EITM Report states that workshop participants, based on their professional experiences and background, believed the divide was broad:

In their deliberations, EITM Workshop participants were in general agreement that the separation was somewhat natural and is not confined to political science. The divide exists in other social sciences, including economics, where individuals specialize in either formal or empirical analysis due to their level of mathematical background and the type and years of training the substantive area or field requires. The divide also exists in the other sciences. It was noted, for example, that epidemiology is much more comfortable with empirical modeling. The primary epidemiology journal, The *American Journal of Public Health (AJPH)*, does not usually publish articles that have substantial formal modeling. The major funding organization for epidemiological research, NIH, tends to support very few formal modeling projects. (page 5)

The 2002 EITM Report also states this natural occurrence had a negative scientific effect:

In sum, EITM Workshop participants were in agreement that compartmentalization was not neutral in its effect. The effect is negative. It was proposed that one way to reduce the effects of compartmentalization was to separate political science into the study of domestic and international politics. Theory, data, and method would cover more general circumstances and lead to deeper understanding.[23] For the purposes of reducing the formal and empirical modeling divide, the effect of reduced compartmentalization by substantive field would encourage integration between formal and empirical analysis. (EITM Report 2002, 7)

Clarke and Primo also express skepticism about the need for EITM in the following passage:

Putting aside the issue of whether empirical models are good at testing theoretical models, these justifications are vague regarding their very premises: how previous practices harm the discipline, and how better theory testing improves the discipline. There is no evidence that continuing our current practices might "delay, or worse, derail the momentum generated over the past 40 years". (Granato and Scioli 2004, 313) (Clarke and Primo 2012, 139)

Again, and contrary to Clarke and Primo's assertions, the 2002 EITM Report provides discussion of current methodological practices. It is a key discussion point in the 2002 NSF EITM Workshop. When it came to sources of the problem workshop participants focused on:

Differences between formal and empirical approaches occur in intellectual outlook, skills, training, and research focus. In terms of outlook, formal modelers typically emphasize, in minute detail, linkages between concepts, whereas empirical modelers do not want to spend their research time parsing through minute details that may not add to their understanding. Formal modeling also requires analytical, logical, and mathematical modeling skills, while empirical modeling is inductive and, therefore, places emphasis on descriptive and statistical skills. Workshop participants noted that the intellectual investment needed for formal modeling is greater; it requires more mathematical knowledge than does empirical modeling to analyze a problem of interest. Training priorities differ as well. Empirical modelers devote their energies to data collection, measurement, and statistical matters, while formal modelers center on mathematical rigor. (EITM Report 2002, 5)

---

[23] Workshop participants noted:

An abbreviated list of research questions that are not studied adequately because of compartmentalization are: political corruption, size of government, levels and types of taxation, economic growth and development, public debt, inflation, failed democracy, democratic stability, regime transitions, the rule of law, property and political rights, ethnic conflict, coups and revolutions, and terrorism (EITM Report 2002, 10–11).

The EITM Framework

As stated previously, the effects were not considered neutral. Creating better ways for testing was not the issue. Instead, current practices were due to self-reinforcing resistance to improvement (EITM Report 2002, 5):

> These differences in outlook, skills, and training are reflected in distinct research practices and outcomes. For empirical modelers, model failures lead to emphasis on more statistical training or more sophisticated uses of statistics – usually to "patch over" – a model failure (see Appendix A). Formal modelers, on the other hand, deal with model controversies by considering alternative mathematical formulations but this is usually done piecemeal. The basic framework, such as expected utility, usually remains in place. The one similarity, however, between these two approaches is that both formal and empirical modelers tend to remain tied to their particular technique despite the warning signals evidenced in model breakdown.

As to evidence of the problems with current practice and their consequences, we can either select past studies or – as an alternative – reference scholars who specialize in particular areas and in different disciplines. We choose the latter option and use Granato and Scioli's (2004) reference to Akerlof (2002) and Achen (2002) in their criticisms of formal modeling and empirical modeling, respectively:

> This conflict between realism and analytical tractability is not new or only a problem in the discipline of political science. Economics is instructive in this regard. In the late 1960s and early 1970s there was a revolution in macroeconomic research, which put great emphasis on the microfoundations of macroeconomic outcomes. Yet, as George Akerlof recently noted:
>
>> [T]he behavioral assumptions were so primitive that the model faced extreme difficulty in accounting for at least six macroeconomic phenomena. In some cases logical consistency with key assumptions of the new classical model led to outright denials of the phenomena in question; in other cases, the explanations offered were merely tortuous. (Granato and Scioli 2004, 315)[24]

As to the scientific problems with specific empirical practices, Granato and Scioli (2004) state:

> If one were to summarize the problem here, one would conclude that the intellectual drift from the virtues of empirical practices means that statistical technique has come to dominate the practices used to help identify causal linkages. But statistical technique alone cannot test generalizations of observed political behavior. Once again, the solution is to find ways to link statistical techniques with formal theory:
>
>> Traditionally we have tried to do both with informal assumptions about the right list of control variables, linearity assumptions, distributional assumptions, and a host of other assumptions, followed by a significance test on a coefficient. But since all the assumptions are somewhat doubtful and largely untested, so are the estimators and the conclusions. The depressing consequence is that at present we have very little useful empirical work with which to guide formal theory. The behavioral work too

---

[24] See Akerlof (2002, 412).

often ignores formal theory. That might not be so bad if it did its job well. But it produces few reliable empirical generalizations because its tests are rarely sharp or persuasive. Thus, empirical findings accumulate but do not cumulate. (page 317)[25]

3.3.2 EITM and the Hypothetico-Deductive (H-D) Method

Clarke and Primo attempt to establish a link between EITM and the H-D method. They describe H-D as follows:

The H-D approach comprises the following:

- a hypothesis H set up for testing or examination;
- an observation sentence O implied by H along with theoretical background statements, mixed statements, boundary conditions, etc.; and
- an experiment or examination of the world where we observe either O or $\neg O$.[26]

If we observe $\neg O$, then we have refuted H. If we observe O, then we have confirmed H or, at the very least, failed to refute H. Less formally, "Theory implies prediction (basic sentence, or observation sentence); if prediction is false, theory is falsified; if sufficiently many predictions are true, theory is confirmed." (Clarke and Primo 2007, 744)

Clarke and Primo "trace the evolution of the initiative" and argue they can "demonstrate" EITM bridges the gap between formal and empirical analysis "using H-D" (page 48). They argue a connection for this assertion can be found in Granato and Scioli (2004, 315):

Granato and Scioli (2004) are quite specific on the role that H-D should play in political science and they elaborate their ideal world:

In an ideal world, where there is unification in approach, political science research should have the following components: 1) theory (informed by field work, or a "puzzle"); 2) a model identifying causal linkages; 3) deductions and hypotheses; 4) measurement and research design; and 5) data collection and analysis.

What Clarke and Primo fail to mention is this quote builds on a more general point about research design competence and overall proposal competitiveness for NSF proposals. Specifically, these same points were discussed in the 2001 EITM Workshop. The 2002 EITM Report summarizes the issues of basic research design construction:

In an ideal world, political scientists should be educated to do research that incorporates five major components: 1) theory (informed by field work or some "puzzle"); 2) a mathematical model identifying causal linkages; 3) deductions and hypotheses; 4) measurement and research design; and 5) data collection and statistics. However, one or more of these components often is absent in political science research and as argued by the EITM Workshop participants, the quality of formal and empirical modeling in political science is substandard. (page 7)

---

[25] This latter quote is from Achen (2002, 445).
[26] Clarke and Primo reference Kyburg (1988, 65) for this definition.

The EITM Framework

The question we have is this. Are students not to be exposed to these elements in a research design (e.g., scope and methods) course? The idea that students should not be trained to know the basics of deductive reasoning, hypothesis formation, data collection, and statistics (analysis) strikes us as impairing student development with harmful future consequences for any scientific discipline. We do not think Clarke and Primo believe this either. But, because they failed to consider the relevant documents – and also never discuss the EITM framework – they have no basis for evaluation of how EITM is implemented and defined at NSF. The appropriate "test" for their assertions is to evaluate the EITM framework.

Clarke and Primo's (2007) solution to their description of the H-D matter is to "abandon the practices of the hypothetico-deductivism" (Clarke and Primo 2007, 748). They suggest the following rules to integrate models and data. We state Clarke and Primo's rules in the following passage and relate them to the EITM framework.

Clarke and Primo's rules are as follows (Clarke and Primo 2007, 748–749):

1. Be clear about the purpose(s) your model is intended to serve.

2. Abandon the goal of "model testing" as currently practiced. "Model testing" implies using statistical analysis to determine the truth or falsity (or any of the synonyms that political scientists use, such as "supported," "confirmed," "verified," or "validated") of a model, but as discussed earlier, the truth or falsity of a model is not the question. Rather, the point is demonstrating that the model is useful in a particular way… [a reason one can forego] data analysis in … [a] structural model is that the field possesses … a number of strong empirical generalizations. In a research area with fewer such generalizations, data analysis would be required to make a compelling case.

3. Include a data analysis only when the purpose(s) of your model is served by it. Not all models require an accompanying data analysis … A researcher should be clear about how the data analysis supports the purpose of the model, and if it does not support the purpose of the model, leave it out.

4. Treat data analysis as more than an endpoint. On those occasions where models and data are integrated, too often the model is carefully developed over the first nine-tenths of the paper while an inconsequential data analysis is tacked on as the final one-tenth of the paper, no doubt to appease reviewers. Seeing data analysis simply as an endpoint is an unfortunate consequence of a focus on model testing … True integration of models and data is not easy. Showing that a model is similar to the world in a particular way for a particular purpose often has description, as opposed to inference, as its goal, and to some political scientists, description is a dirty word evoking atheoretical accounts devoid of conceptual bite. When guided by theory, however, description becomes a powerful tool both for assessing the usefulness of a model and for opening new avenues for theoretical exploration.

Now, recall the EITM framework is as follows:

- Step 1. Relate and Unify Theoretical Concepts and Applied Statistical Concepts

- Step 2. Develop Behavioral (Formal) and Applied Statistical Analogues
- Step 3. Unify and Evaluate the Analogues.

Can one decipher H-D from the EITM framework? How one "tests" a model is of crucial importance and the EITM framework does not preclude any type of testing so long as there is an explicit tie between the formal and empirical analogues.

Clarke and Primo do emphasize that "theoretical models can be used to explain findings or generalizations produced by empirical models. Empirical models, on the other hand, cannot provide explanations" (Clarke and Primo 2012, 137). But, this is consistent with the EITM framework. As Wesley Salmon (1988, 6) notes, a theory is a collection of models or "a set of models." The EITM framework demonstrates the term "models" should include not only theoretical models but also empirical models since both possess concepts and analogues for the concepts.

In Clarke and Primo's view theoretical models are not tested with data; they are tested with models of data, which are far from secure. We do not view testing theoretical models with models of data as problematic because the models of data can represent phenomena of interest. This is precisely the point for using analogues. Therefore, the EITM framework – and analogue development – provides a link between theoretical and statistical concepts. Once the conceptual link is built, we have the opportunity to determine what kind of empirical and formal model analogues best represent the given theoretical and empirical concepts. An important measure of scientific progress is the improvement in analogue development for our concepts of interest.

The H-D method, by way of contrast, begins with a theory about how things work and derives testable hypotheses from it, and its focus is to use empirics to test the hypotheses that then support or discredit a theory. In short, the H-D method concentrates on the relation between hypotheses and empirical tests, but is not necessarily about unification – a transparent and direct link between theory and test.

The EITM framework does allow for the logical "truth-preserving nature" of deduction used by theoretical models (e.g., Arrow 1951), but a logically true conclusion does not mean it fits the facts or serves as an "explanation." Robert Lucas (1988) argues "the role of theory is not to catalogue the obvious, but to help us to sort out effects that are crucial quantitatively, from those that can be set aside (page 13)." But, the matter of ascertaining "crucial quantitative importance" requires the theory fits the facts in addition to achieving substantive significance. Anthony Downs' (1957) classic model of voting is an example of seeking consistency between logic and empirical truths. Downs' model of voting predicts a unique low turnout; however, we find a reasonable number of people go to the polls in the real world. Therefore, the "logical truths" of theoretical models do not guarantee they are empirical

The EITM Framework

truths. Empirical analysis – model testing – assist in developing and revising the explanation.

However, the use of the EITM framework does not mean the disconfirmation of a theoretical model signifies the failure of a theory. The reason is that various theoretical models can be developed from the same theory. In other words, a theoretical model simply reflects a specific dimension of a theory. Clarke and Primo (2012, 50) are correct to criticize Granato and Scioli (2004, 314) for being "ruthless" in their assertion that we can discard a theory based on a limited sample of predictive failure. The issue in model rejection is more complicated: The dialogue requires a far broader testing regimen (e.g., alternative methods, data, and the like) as well as specificity in just what is discarded.

A case in point is rational choice theory. The supposed failure of a rational choice model to account for turnout does not mean the failure of rational choice theory. Other theoretical models derived from rational choice theory might help explain and predict other aspects of human behavior (e.g., Ostrom 2010).[27] Furthermore, even though scholars use the same theoretical model to explain the same behavior, they might have different definitions – or perspectives – concerning the components of a theoretical model. Again, note the dialogue with an empirical component improves the explanation.

Under rational choice theory the turnout decision can be characterized by a decision calculus balancing four factors (i.e., P, B, C, and D).[28] A citizen's turnout decision can be expressed as $R = (BP) - C + D$, where R represents the expected utility of voting. Accordingly, if $R > 0$, the citizen goes to the polls. On the other hand, if $R \leq 0$, a citizen abstains from voting.

The turnout paradox – and the failure of this particular model to fit the facts – led scholars to devise different arguments about these four factors. In terms of the cost of voting, some argue that the opportunity and transportation costs of voting are overblown (Niemi 1976; Hinich 1981; Palfrey and Rosenthal 1985; Aldrich 1993), whereas others contend voting costs are significant (Converse 1964, 1970; Brians and Grofman 1999; Highton 2004). There is also debate on the probability that one's vote influences the outcome P. Some assume P is a fixed quantity, whereas others assume P is a parameter arising endogenously from the strategic interaction of citizens.

---

[27] For example, political scientists developed a number of theoretical models (based on rational choice theory) to explain turnout (e.g., Downs 1957; Morton 1991; Riker and Ordeshook 1968), collective action (e.g., Olson 1965; Oberschall 1980; Hardin 1982; Turner 1987), legislative behavior (e.g., Riker 1958, 1986; Blydenburgh 1971), and electoral competition (e.g., Stokes 1963; McKelvey and Ordeshook 1976; Cox 1984).

[28] P refers to the probability that one's vote influences the outcome; B refers to the benefits a voter receives from seeing her preferred candidate win; C refers to the cost of voting; finally, D refers to the utility one receives as a direct consequence of casting a ballot.

The point here is the same theoretical model, with different assumptions about the components, generates different theoretical explanations and predictions even though they all satisfy the truth-preserving nature of deduction and are logically true. However, when rival explanations are in play, how can we judge which one is better? Accordingly, it is reasonable to argue the theoretical hypotheses derived from a theoretical model should be tested.[29]

Is it inappropriate then to use words such as "test," "support," or similar phrases to describe the evaluation process of the theoretical models? We think wording here is less a concern than the actual activity. Again, the idea of EITM is to develop better "connections" between theory and empirics to improve understanding about the relation between X and Y. In the EITM framework it is accepted that theory can provide clarity to data, but we think the reverse is also possible. We argue the feedback from empirical testing – pursuant to a dialogue – can help revise and further develop theoretical models – even establish new connections between theory and empirical findings. Put differently, better theory can be motivated by previous theoretical assumptions with the assistance of empirical results. For social science questions this dialogue between theory and empirics (tests) (deductive and inductive reasoning) sustains a deeper or a broader exploration.

From Clarke and Primo's rules it is also unclear how they would sort out the usefulness of what they see as useful models. Would not data and testing enter into this process? Even when undertaking logical exercises modelers at some point would need to know how much their arguments for a factor or factors matter. Moreover, a problem with Clarke and Primo's rules is the failure to consider how empirical models cannot be divorced from empirical practice. Destructive empirical practices have been outlined earlier and this is something Clarke and Primo are silent about.

As a final point we are struck by Clarke and Primo's focus on the past and how they try to fit the EITM initiative into a box. Their criticisms about "testing" conjure up old debates, including John Maynard Keynes (1939) critique of econometric methods and their usefulness. Then, as now, formal and empirical tools continue their forward progress but it is a mistake to think this progress in tool development will not foster tighter linkages between theories and tests. Unlike Clarke and Primo's rules, the EITM framework is explicit about creating a dialogue between theory and test. This enhanced dialogue

---

[29] A case in point is that when there exists conflicting results in empirical studies, theoretical models provide guidance explaining how one result differs from another. Would the data collected for one study satisfy one set of assumptions while the data for another study satisfy another set of assumptions? For example, in the literature of foreign direct investment (FDI), the empirical results estimated based on the data from developing countries can be very different from the results based on the data in developed countries (Blonigen and Wang 2005). This circumstance suggests that researchers should carefully impose the assumptions or characteristics of a theoretical model when they are studying different groups of countries.

allows us to improve upon our current assumptions that are often short-cuts for the current state of data and formal and empirical tools.

3.3.3 EITM Limitations

The EITM framework possesses limitations. These shortcomings center on observational equivalence and analogue development. To begin, observational equivalence is related to identification.[30] Also, recall reduced form estimates fail to provide structural parameters and this requires use of model or parameter restrictions so identification is achieved. Observational equivalence occurs when two or more rival models provide statistically indistinguishable reduced form results. Moreover, observational equivalence can occur even if the respective models are identified. An important paper on this issue was written by Thomas Sargent (1976). In his review of this issue, Patrick Minford (1992) summarizes Sargent's (1976) results as follows:

> ... models may be fully identified; that is, the parameters of each may be individually retrieved by estimation of the full model (i.e., subject to all its restrictions). However, there is a useful potential connection with the concept of identification. If two models can be "nested" in a more general model (usually a linear combination of the two), then, provided the coefficients of each model can be identified in this general model, it is possible to test for their significance and accordingly that of each model. In this situation, if (and only if) the coefficients cannot be identified, the models will be "observationally equivalent." (page 425)

The good news is this challenge in distinguishing between rival models can be narrow – occurring in one dependent variable, but not in other dependent variables – but the bad news is its existence is still a problem. Potential solutions do exist but none are generalizable. They are for a specific case. These solutions include either imposing theoretically justified exclusion restrictions or identifying regime shifts that can yield theoretically distinct predictions. A combination of both is also possible, but this would depend on the specific set of models and data.

With regard to analogue development, two technical challenges emerge. One technical challenge is in developing analogues. Unlike the natural sciences, social sciences study human subjects possessing expectations affecting their current behavior. This "dynamic" creates moving targets for many social science questions. How to improve upon current analogues for distinctly human behavioral traits (e.g., norms, reputation, expectations, learning) is a key future hurdle to achieving scientific cumulation.

---

[30] Recall the EITM framework builds on the Cowles Commission's contributions. However, methodological unification is broader than standard econometric tools. We fully expect innovations beyond what we know today to be consistent with the EITM framework and its aim to create a dialogue between theory and test.

A second technical challenge relates to the framework's emphasis on parameters as a building block for ex post and ex ante prediction (see Bamber and van Santen 1985, 2000). It is almost impossible to capture all parameters in complex political, social, and economic systems. However, the EITM framework is useful since it helps researchers open the "black box" relating different theoretical parameters to the estimated coefficients in an empirical model. A more general point concerns the fact that the EITM framework's focus on parameters separates variables that aid in fundamental prediction from other variables considered "causal" but are of minor predictive importance (see Lucas 1988).

3.4 SUMMARY

While it is important to do pure theory and pure empirical work, we have argued a motivation for EITM is that current practices (in some cases) have now reached a point of diminishing returns if not outright harm to the scientific process. Moreover, we think rules proffered by Clarke and Primo, because they fail to engage harmful empirical practices discussed earlier, perpetuate harmful aspects of the methodological status quo. This includes detrimental testing practices, but we think they are more likely to occur when researchers engage in data mining, overparameterization, and statistical patching.

Clarke and Primo's arguments diminishing the use of empirics and testing forgo useful feedback and dialogue from empirical observations in refining theory that can foster cumulation of knowledge. The dilemmas where theory is ahead of data or data are ahead of theory can be dealt with more effectively by employing a form of methodological unification including the EITM framework.

An important issue in the dialogue is whether the tests involved predictions or fitting facts. The distinction between the two is difficult and often blurred. Often they work in concert and their difference distracts from creating a linkage with feedback to create a dialogue between model and test:

> Moreover, this linkage and evaluation provides a clearer (i.e., falsifiable) interpretation of the results because the model's mechanisms are explicit. The specified linkage shows potential sources of inaccuracies and model failure. Further, an inductive and deductive dialogue is created between the data and the technique(s) where new theoretical mechanisms and/or new analogues can be used. (Granato 2005, 12)

Again, this EITM framework should not be interpreted as a substitute for pure formal or pure empirical approaches. The criticisms leveled in Chapter 2 stand, but these approaches are valid out of necessity, particularly when theory or data are underdeveloped, nonexistent, or both. The simple fact is there are numerous examples in many sciences where theory is ahead of data or data are ahead of theory, sometimes for decades (see Rigden 2005). Nor should the quantitative nature of this framework suggest it precludes the use of qualitative procedures

The EITM Framework

(Brady and Collier 2004). Such exclusion would be throwing out information that could otherwise aid in finding underlying mechanisms.

We demonstrate the various linkages in the second part of this book.

3.5 APPENDIX: THE DERIVATION OF THE CONDITIONAL CONVERGENCE HYPOTHESIS

In this appendix we discuss how Eq. (3.22) is derived. We first linearize Eq. (3.8) around its steady state k^* using a first-order Taylor approximation:

$$k_{t+1} - k^* = F'(k^*)(k_t - k^*),$$

where $F'(k^*) \in (0,1)$. We can then rewrite the equation as:

$$\frac{k_{t+1} - k^*}{k^*} = F'(k^*)\left(\frac{k_t - k^*}{k^*}\right),$$

which is approximately:

$$\ln k_{t+1} - \ln k^* = F'(k^*)(\ln k_t - \ln k^*),$$

where $(k_t - k^*)/k^* \approx \ln k_t - \ln k^*$. Since $y_t = k_t^\alpha$ and $y^* = (k^*)^\alpha$, we have $\ln y_t - \ln y^* = \alpha(\ln k_t - \ln k^*)$. We can derive the following approximation for the derivation of $\ln y_{t+1}$ around its steady state:

$$\ln y_{t+1} - \ln y^* = F'(k^*)(\ln y_t - \ln y^*).$$

Subtracting $\ln y_t$ and adding $\ln y^*$ on both sides of the above equation, we have:

$$\ln y_{t+1} - \ln y^* - \ln y_t + \ln y^* = F'(k^*)(\ln y_t - \ln y^*) - \ln y_t + \ln y^*$$
$$\Rightarrow \ln y_{t+1} - \ln y_t - (1 - F'(k^*))(\ln y^* - \ln y_t). \quad (3.24)$$

Now we rewrite Eq. (3.24) as follows:

$$\ln y_{t+1} = [1 - F'(k^*)]\ln y^* + F'(k^*)\ln y_t. \quad (3.25)$$

Then take Eq. (3.25) one period prior:

$$\ln y_t = [1 - F'(k^*)]\ln y^* + F'(k^*)\ln y_{t-1}. \quad (3.26)$$

Similarly, we take Eq. (3.26) one and two prior periods again:

$$\ln y_{t-1} = [1 - F'(k^*)]\ln y^* + F'(k^*)\ln y_{t-2}, \quad (3.27)$$

and:

$$\ln y_{t-2} = [1 - F'(k^*)]\ln y^* + F'(k^*)\ln y_{t-3}. \quad (3.28)$$

Insert Eqs. (3.27) and (3.28) into Eq. (3.26) and simplify the equation and we have:
$$\ln y_t = \left[1 - F'(k^*)^3\right] \ln y^* + F'(k^*)^3 \ln y_{t-3}. \tag{3.29}$$

By inserting the backward (in time) equations into Eq. (3.26) for $s - 1$ times, we have the following equation:
$$\ln y_t = \left[1 - F'(k^*)^s\right] \ln y^* + F'(k^*)^s \ln y_{t-s}.$$

Assuming that $s = t$, we have:
$$\ln y_t = \left[1 - F'(k^*)^t\right] \ln y^* + F'(k^*)^t \ln y_0, \tag{3.30}$$

where $\ln y_{t-t} = \ln y_0$ represents the initial value of output (per effective worker). Equation (3.30) indicates that current level of output $\ln y_t$ at time t depends on the steady state output level $\ln y^*$ and the initial output level $\ln y_0$ in an economy. Since $y_t = Y_t/(A_t L_t)$, we have:
$$\ln y_t = \ln\left(\frac{Y_t}{L_t}\right) - \ln A_t. \tag{3.31}$$

Now insert Eq. (3.31) into Eq. (3.30):
$$\ln\left(\frac{Y_t}{L_t}\right) = \ln A_t + \left[1 - F'(k^*)^t\right] \ln y^* + F'(k^*)^t \left[\ln\left(\frac{Y_0}{L_0}\right) - \ln A_0\right].$$

We then subtract $\ln(Y_0/L_0)$ on both sides of the equation:
$$\ln\left(\frac{Y_t}{L_t}\right) - \ln\left(\frac{Y_0}{L_0}\right) = \ln A_t + \left[1 - F'(k^*)^t\right] \ln y^*$$
$$+ F'(k^*)^t \left[\ln\left(\frac{Y_0}{L_0}\right) - \ln A_0\right] - \ln\left(\frac{Y_0}{L_0}\right).$$

Adding and subtracting $\ln A_0$ on the right-hand side of the equation:
$$\ln\left(\frac{Y_t}{L_t}\right) - \ln\left(\frac{Y_0}{L_0}\right) = \ln A_t + \left[1 - F'(k^*)^t\right] \ln y^*$$
$$+ F'(k^*)^t \left[\ln\left(\frac{Y_0}{L_0}\right) - \ln A_0\right]$$
$$- \ln\left(\frac{Y_0}{L_0}\right) + \ln A_0 - \ln A_0$$
$$\Rightarrow \ln\left(\frac{Y_t}{L_t}\right) - \ln\left(\frac{Y_0}{L_0}\right) = (\ln A_t - \ln A_0)$$
$$+ \left[1 - F'(k^*)^t\right]\left[\ln A_0 + \ln y^* - \ln\left(\frac{Y_0}{L_0}\right)\right].$$

The EITM Framework

Dividing the above equation by t:

$$\frac{\ln(Y_t/L_t) - \ln(Y_0/L_0)}{t} = \frac{\ln A_t - \ln A_0}{t}$$
$$+ \frac{1 - F'(k^*)^t}{t}\left[\ln A_0 + \ln y^* - \ln\left(\frac{Y_0}{L_0}\right)\right]. \tag{3.32}$$

According to Eq. (3.10):

$$y^* = \left(\frac{s}{\delta + \lambda + \tau + \lambda\tau}\right)^{\alpha/(1-\alpha)}$$
$$\Rightarrow \ln y^* = \frac{\alpha}{1-\alpha}Z, \tag{3.33}$$

where $Z = [\ln s - \ln(\delta + \lambda + \tau + \lambda\tau)]$. Finally, if we insert Eq. (3.33) into Eq. (3.32) and set $t = T$, we can derive Eq. (3.22):

$$g_y = g_A + \frac{1 - F'(k^*)^T}{T}\left[\ln A_0 + \frac{\alpha}{1-\alpha}Z - \ln\left(\frac{Y_0}{L_0}\right)\right],$$

where $g_y = [\ln(Y_T/L_T) - \ln(Y_0/L_0)]/T$, $g_A = (\ln A_T - \ln A_0)/T$, and $Z = \ln s - \ln(\delta + \lambda + \tau + \lambda\tau)$.

PART II

EITM IN PRACTICE

4

Economic Voting

4.1 BACKGROUND

Economic voting comprises a substantial literature. It is also one of the most readily accessible and methodologically integrated literatures suitable for a relatively straightforward EITM framework application. The various studies we review refine earlier work and present models of voter sophistication and new applied statistical tests. In the former case, voters possess the capability to deal with uncertainty in assigning blame or credit to incumbents for good or bad economic conditions. For the latter, applied statistical tests include some of the more advanced tools in time series analysis.

Past studies of economic voting normally assume voters hold government responsible for changes in their personal financial situation. Under this assumption, theoretical specifications for the cross-sectional estimates are similar to the time-series estimates in macro-level studies. This similarity in specification led researchers to expect the individual-level studies would produce findings consistent with the aggregate-level ones. At the aggregate level, studies find significant effects of economic performance on election outcomes. Yet, many of the micro-level research findings reveal parameter instability as well as variation in economic vote magnitude. These cross-sectional studies fail to uncover an individual-level basis for the macro-level relation between economic circumstances and vote choice.

Some studies resort to purely statistical fixes in the hope these empirical "tools" solve the conundrum. Among them are studies using instrumental variables to estimate the (reciprocal) links between presidential approval and party competence (Kinder and Kiewiet 1979), logit (Fiorina 1978), and a combination of OLS, probit, and two-stage least squares (Kinder and Kiewiet 1981).

A theoretical explanation for the conflicting empirical results has been offered by Kramer (1983). He argues economic voting has both a governmental-induced component and an exogenous component – the latter determined by the life-cycle and other factors that are beyond government control. Voters respond not to changes in their real income as a whole, but instead only to the portion of the change that is attributable to government policy. This explains, to a large extent, why pure empirical approaches to estimating the effect of personal financial conditions on vote choice fail to produce satisfactory findings.

Kramer's assumption contains important formal and empirical implications. The behavioral relation estimated involves only the government-induced component, but since both the government and non-government components are unobservable to the voter, we have to deal with the "noisy" version of the variable that poses complicated estimation challenges (i.e., a signal extraction problem). More importantly, Kramer's example illustrates the importance of the linkage between theory and empirical analysis in social science research. A number of studies extend Kramer's theoretical innovation to improve understanding of economic voting. Important and noted work can be found in Alesina and Rosenthal (1995). Their economic voting model establishes an important foundation for further theoretical and empirical analyses (e.g., Duch and Stevenson 2010; Alcañiz and Hellwig 2011; Achen 2012; Weschle 2014; Campello and Zucco 2015; Aytaç 2018; Campello 2018).

There is another important EITM-related feature in this work. Some of these authors relate a measurement error problem to the voter capability noted earlier. The theory – the formal model – implies an applied statistical model with measurement error. Consequently, one can examine the joint effects by employing a unified approach.[1] With this all in mind, the Alesina and Rosenthal (1995) EITM approach is this chapter's example. Their work has a strong interdisciplinary flavor as well as a transparent linkage between the theoretical and empirical parameters.[2] Among the issues to consider are the dynamic formulation of expectations, the separation of policy and nonpolicy effects, and ideas about public sophistication and political accountability (see Kiewiet and Rivers 1984). The connection between these issues and the EITM framework

---

[1] Recall that applied statistical tools lack power in disentangling conceptually distinct effects on a dependent variable. This is noteworthy since the traditional applied statistical view of measurement error is that it creates parameter bias, with the typical remedy requiring the use of various estimation techniques (see the Appendix, Section 4.6.1) and Johnston and DiNardo (1997, 153–159)).

[2] Friedman (1957a,b) contributes to the study of the "signal extraction" problems by linking specific empirical coefficients to his behavioral model instead of treating his research question as a pure measurement error problem requiring only applied statistical solutions. Specifically, he merges "error in variables" regression with formal models of expectations and uncertainty concerning permanent and temporary changes in income.

is revealed in the use of concepts and analogues pertaining to expectations, uncertainty, and measurement error.

4.2 STEP 1: RELATING EXPECTATIONS, UNCERTAINTY, AND MEASUREMENT ERROR

Earlier contributors have dealt with "signal extraction" problems (see the Appendix, Section 4.6.3). Friedman's (1957a,b) and Lucas's (1973) substantive findings would not have been achieved had they treated their research question as a pure measurement error problem requiring only an applied statistical analysis (and "fix" for the measurement error). Indeed, both Friedman (1957a,b) and Lucas (1973) linked specific empirical coefficients from their respective formal (behavioral) models: Among their contributions was to merge "error in variables" regression with formal models of expectations and uncertainty. For Friedman (1957a,b), the expectations and uncertainty involve permanent–temporary confusion, while general–relative confusion is the behavioral mechanism in the Lucas model.

4.3 STEP 2: ANALOGUES FOR EXPECTATIONS, UNCERTAINTY, AND MEASUREMENT ERROR

This chapter focuses on Alesina and Rosenthal's (1995) contribution. Their formal model representing the behavioral concepts – expectations and uncertainty – is presented (pages 191–195). To start, the economic growth model is based on an expectations-augmented aggregate supply curve:

$$\hat{y}_t = \hat{y}^n + \gamma \left(\pi_t - \pi_t^e \right) + \varepsilon_t, \tag{4.1}$$

where $\hat{y}_t$ represents the rate of economic growth (GDP growth) in period t, $\hat{y}^n$ is the natural economic growth rate, π_t is the inflation rate at time t, and π_t^e is the expected inflation rate at time t formed at time $t - 1$.

Having established voter inflation expectations, the concept of uncertainty is next. Assume voters want to determine whether to attribute credit or blame for economic growth y_t outcomes to the incumbent administration. Yet, voters are faced with uncertainty in determining which part of the economic outcomes is due to incumbent "competence" (i.e., policy acumen) or simply good luck.

If the uncertainty is based, in part, from Eq. (4.1), then Eq. (4.2) presents the analogue. It is commonly referred to as a "signal extraction" or measurement error problem (see the Appendix, Section 4.6.2):

$$\varepsilon_t = \eta_t + \xi_t. \tag{4.2}$$

The variable ε_t represents a "shock" comprising the two unobservable characteristics noted earlier – competence and good luck. The first, represented by η_t, reflects "competence" attributed to the incumbent administration. The second, symbolized as ξ_t, is shocks to growth beyond administrative control (and competence). Both η_t and ξ_t have zero mean with variance(s) σ_η^2 and σ_ξ^2 respectively. In less technical language, Alesina and Rosenthal describe competence as follows:

> The term ξ_t represents economic shocks beyond the governments control, such as oil shocks and technological innovations. The term η_t captures the idea of government competence, that is the government's ability to increase the rate of growth without inflationary surprises. In fact, even if $\pi_t = \pi_t^e$, the higher is η_t the higher is growth, for a given ξ_t. We can think of this competence as the government's ability to avoid large scale inefficiencies, to promote productivity growth, to avoid waste in the budget process, so that lower distortionary taxes are needed to finance a given amount of government spending, etc. (page 192)

Note also that competence can persist and support reelection. This feature is characterized as a first-order moving average (MA(1)) process:

$$\eta_t = \mu_t + \rho \mu_{t-1}, \tag{4.3}$$

where $0 < \rho \leq 1$ and μ_t is $iid\left(0, \sigma_\mu^2\right)$. The parameter ρ represents the strength of the persistence. The lag allows for retrospective voter judgments.

If we reference Eq. (4.1) again, let us assume voters' judgments include a general sense of the average rate of growth $\hat{y}^n$ and the ability to observe actual growth $\hat{y}_t$. Voters can evaluate their difference $(\hat{y}_t - \hat{y}^n)$. Equation (4.1) also suggests that when voters predict inflation with no systematic error (i.e., $\pi_t^e = \pi_t$), the result is noninflationary growth with no adverse real wage effect.

Next, economic growth performance is tied to voter uncertainty. Alesina and Rosenthal formalize how economic growth rate deviations from the average can be attributed to administration competence or fortuitous events:

$$\hat{y}_t - \hat{y}^n = \varepsilon_t = \eta_t + \xi_t. \tag{4.4}$$

Equation (4.4) shows when the actual economic growth rate is greater than its average or "natural rate" (i.e., $\hat{y}_t > \hat{y}^n$), then $\varepsilon_t = \eta_t + \xi_t > 0$. Again, the voters are faced with uncertainty in distinguishing the incumbent's competence η_t from the stochastic economic shock ξ_t. However, because competence can persist, voters use this property for making forecasts and giving greater or lesser weight to competence over time.

This behavioral effect is demonstrated by substituting Eq. (4.3) in Eq. (4.4):

$$\mu_t + \xi_t = \hat{y}_t - \hat{y}^n - \rho \mu_{t-1}. \tag{4.5}$$

Equation (4.5) suggests voters can observe the composite shock $\mu_t + \xi_t$ based on the observable variables $\hat{y}_t$, $\hat{y}^n$ and μ_{t-1}, which are available at time t and $t-1$. Determining the optimal estimate of competence η_{t+1} when the voters observe $\hat{y}_t$, Alesina and Rosenthal demonstrate this result making a one-period forecast of Eq. (4.3) and solving for its expected value (conditional expectation) at time t (see the Appendix, Section 4.6.3):

Economic Voting 61

$$E_t(\eta_{t+1}) = E_t(\mu_{t+1}) + \rho E(\mu_t|\hat{y}_t) = \rho E(\mu_t|\hat{y}_t), \tag{4.6}$$

where $E_t(\mu_{t+1}) = 0$. Alesina and Rosenthal (1995) argue further that rational voters would not use $\hat{y}_t$ as the only variable to forecast η_{t+1}. Instead, they use all available information, including $\hat{y}^n$ and μ_{t-1}. As a result, a revised Eq. (4.6) is:

$$E_t(\eta_{t+1}) = E_t(\mu_{t+1}) + \rho E(\mu_t|\hat{y}_t - \hat{y}^n - \rho\mu_{t-1}) \tag{4.7}$$
$$= \rho E(\mu_t|\mu_t + \xi_t). \tag{4.8}$$

Using this analogue for expectations in Eq. (4.7), competence η_{t+1} can be forecast by predicting μ_{t+1} and μ_t. Since there is no information available for forecasting μ_{t+1}, rational voters can only forecast μ_t based on observable $\hat{y}_t - \hat{y}^n - \rho\mu_{t-1}$ (at time t and $t-1$) from Eqs. (4.7) and (4.8).

4.4 STEP 3: UNIFYING AND EVALUATING THE ANALOGUES

The method of recursive projections and Eq. (4.5) illustrate how the behavioral analogue for expectations is linked to the empirical analogue for measurement error (an "error-in-variables equation"):

$$E_t(\eta_{t+1}) = \rho E(\mu_t|\hat{y}_t) = \rho \frac{\sigma_\mu^2}{\sigma_\mu^2 + \sigma_\xi^2}(\hat{y}_t - \hat{y}^n - \rho\mu_{t-1}), \tag{4.9}$$

where $0 < \rho\sigma_\mu^2/(\sigma_\mu^2 + \sigma_\xi^2) < 1$. Equation (4.9) shows voters can forecast competence using the difference between $\hat{y}_t - \hat{y}^n$ but also the "weighted" lag of μ_t (i.e., $\rho\mu_{t-1}$). In Eq. (4.9), the expected value of competence is positively correlated with economic growth rate deviations. Voter assessment is filtered by the coefficient $\sigma_\mu^2/(\sigma_\mu^2 + \sigma_\xi^2)$ representing a proportion of competence voters are able to interpret and observe.

The behavioral implications are straightforward. If voters interpret that the variability of economic shocks come solely from the incumbent's competence (i.e., $\sigma_\xi^2 \to 0$), then $\sigma_\mu^2/(\sigma_\mu^2 + \sigma_\xi^2) \to 1$. On the other hand, the increase in the variability of uncontrolled shocks σ_ξ^2 confounds the observability of incumbent competence since the signal-noise coefficient $\sigma_\mu^2/(\sigma_\mu^2 + \sigma_\xi^2)$ decreases. Voters assign less weight to economic performance in assessing the incumbent's competence.

Alesina and Rosenthal test the empirical implications of their theoretical model with United States data on economic outcomes and political parties for the period 1915 to 1988. They first use the growth equation (4.1) to collect the estimated exogenous shocks ε_t in the economy. With these estimated exogenous shocks, they then construct their variance–covariance structure.

Since competence η_t in Eq. (4.3) follows an MA(1) process, they hypothesize that a test for incumbent competence, as it pertains to economic growth, can be performed using the covariances between the current and preceding year.

The specific test centers on whether the changes in covariances with the presidential party in office are statistically larger than the covariances associated with a change in presidential parties. They report null findings (e.g., equal covariances) and conclude that there is little evidence to support that voters are retrospective and use incumbent competence as a basis for support.

Alesina and Rosenthal provide an EITM connection between Eqs. (4.1), (4.3) and their empirical tests. They link the behavioral concepts – expectations and uncertainty – with their respective analogues (conditional expectations and measurement error) and devise a signal extraction relation. While the empirical model resembles an error-in-variables specification, testable by dynamic methods such as rolling regression (Lin 1999), they instead estimate the variance–covariance structure of the residuals.

4.5 SUMMARY

Various scholarship has followed the work of Alesina and Rosenthal (and by extension Kramer). These examples highlight the potential link between theory and test and not only deepen the level of understanding through behavioral representations but also broaden a researcher's ability in modeling voter behavior in different environmental and information contexts. Corresponding with these changes is a focus on alternative measures, theoretical assumptions, and new formal and empirical analogues.

Since not all macroeconomic policies induce politically relevant permanent changes in output, it is reasonable to assume that voters may reward incumbents for permanent growth, but punish them for less desirable cyclical growth. Uncertainty can be tested differently by examining the competence analogue of η_t with alternative measures.

Because the analogue is defined as part of the aggregate supply (AS) shock $\varepsilon_t = \eta_t + \xi_t$, competence η_t can be defined as the incumbent's ability to promote economic growth via the AS function. We can further assume voters reward capacity building on AS policy for generating long-term economic growth, but otherwise punish policy that causes a short-term shift in aggregate demand (AD) with undesirable inflationary effects.

Suzuki and Chappell (1996) make use of similar arguments on permanent and temporary changes in economic growth to evaluate the competence of Eq. (4.9) by *using different measures for uncertainty*. Specifically, the authors replace the restrictive MA(1) process in the original model with flexible empirical specifications, and apply advanced time series techniques to decompose real GNP into permanent and cyclical income components. The authors then jointly estimate a three-equation system for shares of the two-party vote for presidential, Senate, and House elections. Their results shed new light on voting behavior by showing that voters are more sensitive to permanent than cyclical economic growth (in the United States). The policy implication is that voters' preference for permanent growth would encourage politicians to adopt policies that generate long-term rather than short-term growth.

Duch and Stevenson (2008) take a different tack regarding the issue of political responsibility attribution. The authors assume voters distinguish between "electorally dependent decision makers" (mainly political office holders) and those who are "non-electorally dependent," such as bureaucrats, business firms, interest groups, foreign leaders, the WTO, and the like. In the same way as Alesina and Rosenthal, their model uses "signal extraction," which is based on government competence and an exogenous shock to economic growth. But, their model differs in that they assign competency shocks to the governmental decision makers and exogenous shocks to the nongovernmental actors. The specification is useful in examining how electoral outcomes are influenced by the arrangement of domestic political institutions, the ambiguity of policy responsibility, and the influence of the global economy.

In a follow-up study, Duch and Stevenson (2010) apply the competence model of Alesina and Rosenthal but now have voter decisions based on both global and domestic economic outcomes. Using the signal-noise ratio $\sigma_\mu^2/(\sigma_\mu^2+\sigma_\xi^2)$, the expectations-uncertainty-measurement error analogue in Eq. (4.9), the authors provide a "competence signal" explanation for the cross-national and dynamic variations in the magnitude of economic vote. The authors test their proposition with micro-level data from a six-nation survey. Their findings show voters not only have a sense of the total variation in economic shocks (i.e., σ_μ^2 and σ_ξ^2) but they also distinguish between the relative contributions of the different components – domestic and global – of the total variation. When σ_μ^2 is high (low) relative to σ_ξ^2, it suggests a high (low) competency signal. The micro-level results are further confirmed by aggregate-level data of macro-economic time-series of 19 countries. The study further demonstrates open economies, which experience large exogenous economic shocks relative to government-induced ones (i.e., $\sigma_\mu^2 < \sigma_\xi^2$), exhibit a smaller economic vote than countries that are less dependent on global trade.

Building on both Alesina and Rosenthal and Duch and Stevenson, Alcañiz and Hellwig's (2011) work on Latin America treats government competency as the basis for developing expectations about political responsibility. Alcañiz and Hellwig assign responsibility to economic policy decision makers who are electorally dependent from those who are not. The findings from 17 Latin American countries indicate that, instead of punishing political office holders for poor economic outcomes, voters assign blame to international and private-sector actors. Based on survey data, where respondents are allowed to select from a large set of response options with regard to responsibility attribution, Alcañiz and Hellwig demonstrate how signaling models can be used to better understand the attribution of responsibility. They show voters in developing economies seek to reduce uncertainty with regard to attribution based on their knowledge about their countries' position in the global economy (Alcañiz and

Hellwig 2011, 390). On the other hand, the authors point out that political elites are more likely to avoid blame in order to hold on to power (Alcañiz and Hellwig 2011, 408).

By way of contrast, Campello and Zucco (2015) provide an alternative hypothesis. They argue retrospective judgments require a tremendous amount of information (Aidt 2000). Voters who are less attentive to media and political events do not vote based on global or domestic economic conditions. Instead, they are more likely to vote based on exogenous economic conditions, which are not influenced by governments' competency or policy. The authors test this hypothesis based on a dataset that covers 121 presidential elections in 18 Latin American countries in the period 1980–2012. They find that, in the countries which have low savings and rely on commodity exports, voters are more likely to reward incumbents who are in office when the international interest rates are low and commodity prices are higher. The reverse also holds. These exogenous factors are independent of the incumbent's competence and policymaking decisions.

Achen (2012) takes a different tack and uses an alternative formalization of voter retrospection dynamics. Following Alesina and Rosenthal (1995), Achen models growth as a measurement error problem with the voter having uncertainty about how much of the economic performance is due to incumbent competence. However, instead of modeling incumbent competence as a moving average of an MA(1) process, Achen extends voter evaluation of incumbent competence to encompass the full term of an administration. He assumes the more volatile the economy, the more persistent voter memory is with respect to evaluating competence.

The choice of dependent variable is also different in Achen's model: Voters relate competence with growth rates, not income levels (Achen 2012, 9). This change can be found in Eq. (4.10):

$$g_t^* = g_{t-1}^* + \delta_t + \rho \delta_{t-1}, \tag{4.10}$$

where $0 < \rho < 1$. The variable g_t^* denotes the unobserved true growth rate in period t, and g_{t-1}^* denotes the observed true growth rate in period $t-1$. The competence parameters, δ_t and δ_{t-1}, are similar to the parameters, μ_t and μ_{t-1}, in Eq. (4.3). The voter is assumed to know ρ but not δ_t – they have the ability to observe a "noisy" version of the true growth rate g_t^* in period t containing measurement error:

$$g_t = g_t^* + e_t. \tag{4.11}$$

In Eq. (4.11), g_t, is the observed growth rate in period t; e_t is the error in the voter's perception of growth in period t, with mean zero and variance σ_e^2. The term e_t is uncorrelated with e_{t-1} and all of its other past values. Substituting $(g_{t-1} - e_{t-1})$ for g_{t-1}^* in Eq. (4.10) and then rewriting Eq. (4.11) gives:

$$g_t = g_{t-1} + \delta_t + \rho \delta_{t-1} + e_t - e_{t-1}. \tag{4.12}$$

Economic Voting

Equation (4.12) can be simplified to:

$$g_t = g_{t-1} + w_t, \tag{4.13}$$

where $w_t = \delta_t + \rho\delta_{t-1} + e_t - e_{t-1}$. Since w_t is the sum of two MA(1) processes, it can be rewritten as an MA(1) process itself:

$$w_t = \epsilon_t - \epsilon_{t-1}, \tag{4.14}$$

where ϵ_t has zero mean and variance σ_ϵ^2. Equation (4.14) can be expressed as:

$$\epsilon_t - \gamma\epsilon_{t-1} = \delta_t + \rho\delta_{t-1} + e_t - e_{t-1}. \tag{4.15}$$

Achen (2012, 6–7) then solves for γ, the geometric weight parameter, in Eq. (4.15) and relates it to the voter's forecast:

$$g_t - g_{t-1} = \epsilon_t - \gamma\epsilon_{t-1}. \tag{4.16}$$

Using lag operators there exists a white noise process. Equation (4.16) can be written as:

$$g_t - g_{t-1} = (1 - \gamma L)\epsilon_t. \tag{4.17}$$

It follows that:

$$\epsilon_t = \frac{g_t}{(1 - \gamma L)} - \frac{g_{t-1}}{(1 - \gamma L)}. \tag{4.18}$$

Multiplying out gives:

$$\epsilon_t = \left(g_t + \gamma g_{t-1} + \gamma^2 g_{t-2} + \cdots\right) - \left(g_{t-1} + \gamma g_{t-2} + \gamma^2 g_{t-3} + \cdots\right). \tag{4.19}$$

Arranging terms, taking expectations, and truncating lags greater than 4 gives the best forecast for economic growth as follows:

$$\hat{g} = (1 - \gamma) \sum_{k=1}^{4} \gamma^{k-1} g_{t-k}, \tag{4.20}$$

where $\hat{g}_t$ is the expected GDP growth from $t-1$ to t, formed at the end of $t-1$, and γ is the geometric weight parameter.

The growth model in Eq. (4.20) differs from Alesina and Rosenthal. Voters in Achen's model determine incumbent competence by placing weights γ on past economic conditions. Achen conducts a preliminary test of his model using data from the highly volatile economic circumstances of Montana wheat-growing counties in the 1930s. The results show voter memory in evaluating President Hoover's competence persists. Achen contends this contributed (at least partly) to Hoover's defeat in 1932 even though the economy improved during the latter part of his presidency.

Achen's model provides for more accurate estimates through the choices of the lag parameter in the specifications (i.e., pure myopia, persistence, or something in between). The study also points to future directions in the cumulation process. For example, if competence is modeled as an AR(1) process, the model will result in an ARMA(1,2) (autoregressive-moving-average) lag structure. Other ARMA structures can also be used for empirical testing by allowing the four lag coefficients to take on different values (Achen 2012, 17).

Yet another refinement on voter behavior can be found in the work of Mebane (2000). He provides a more sophisticated theory of policy moderation by voters than the basic framework of Alesina and Rosenthal. His model is a useful way in generalizing the approach used by Alesina and Rosenthal (Mebane 2000, 40), by depicting the important difference in the information that voters hold. In Alesina and Rosenthal's model, voters possess common knowledge about the elections and behave strategically to achieve policy moderation but they do not have any private information about election outcomes (Mebane 2000, 38). The individual voters in Mebane's model, on the other hand, possess both common knowledge and private information about the elections – such as individual policy preferences and perceptions of the candidates. It follows that the larger the discrepancy between the voter's policy ideal point and the expected policy given the election outcome, the bigger the expected loss for the voter.

While the basic framework of Alesina and Rosenthal treats the expected policies and expected election outcomes by all voters as identical, the new model explains much more about the information that voters have, by allowing the expected policies and the expected election outcomes to vary across voters (Mebane 2000, 39–40). Based on his model, Mebane further posits that policy moderation is achieved through coordination in the form of a noncooperative rational expectations equilibrium among voters. Empirical evidence obtained from the model's analysis sheds new light by showing there is a small but significant proportion of voters who vote a split ticket in order to improve the chances of policy moderation.

More recently, the focus has again turned to international considerations. Aytaç (2018) argues that the competence model suggested by Alesina and Rosenthal (1995) simply assumes voters are only concerned with domestic economic conditions. The author revisits the competence model where a voter forms the expectations about the incumbent's competence not only based on the growth condition at the domestic level but also at the international level ("relative international performance"). Using data in 475 elections in 62 countries over 40 years, he finds voters are more likely to vote for (or reward) an incumbent when they see the domestic economic performance in the current period as not only better than in the previous period but also better relative to other countries.

4.6 APPENDIX

The tools in this chapter are used to establish a transparent and testable relation between expectations (uncertainty) and forecast measurement error. The applied statistical tools provide a basic understanding of:

- Measurement error in a linear regression context – error-in-variables regression.

The formal tools include a presentation of:

- A linkage to linear regression.
- Linear projections.
- Recursive projections.

These tools, when unified, produce the following EITM relations consistent with research questions termed *signal extraction*. The last section of this appendix demonstrates signal extraction problems that are directly related to Alesina and Rosenthal's model and test.

4.6.1 Empirical Analogues

Measurement Error and Error in Variables Regression

In a regression model it is well known that endogeneity problems (e.g., a relation between the error term and a regressor) can be due to measurement error in the data. A regression model with mis-measured right-hand side variables gives least squares estimates with bias. The extent of the bias depends on the ratio of the variance of the signal (true variable) to the sum of the variance of the signal and the variance of the noise (measurement error). The bias increases when the variance of the noise becomes larger in relation to the variance of the signal. Hausman (2001, 58) refers to the estimation problem with measurement error as the "Iron Law of Econometrics" because the magnitude of the estimate is usually smaller than expected.

To demonstrate the downward bias, consider the classical linear regression model with one independent variable:

$$Y_t = \beta_0 + \beta_1 x_t + \varepsilon_t, \tag{4.21}$$

for $t = 1, \ldots, n$, where ε_t are independent $N(0, \sigma_\varepsilon^2)$ random variables. The unbiased least squares estimator for regression model (4.21) is:

$$\hat{\beta}_1 = \left[\sum_{t=1}^n (x_t - \bar{x})^2 \right]^{-1} \sum_{t=1}^n (x_t - \bar{x})(Y_t - \bar{Y}). \tag{4.22}$$

Now instead of observing x_t directly, observe its value with an error:

$$X_t = x_t + e_t, \tag{4.23}$$

where e_t is an $iid(0, \sigma_e^2)$ random variable. The simple linear error-in-variables model can be written as:

$$Y_t = \beta_0 + \beta_1 X_t + \varepsilon_t, \tag{4.24}$$
$$X_t = x_t + e_t, \text{ for } t = 1, \ldots, n.$$

In model (4.24), an estimate of a regression of Y_t on X_t with an error term mixing the effects of the true error ε_t and the measurement error e_t is presented.[3] It follows that the vector (Y_t, X_t) is distributed as a bi-variate normal vector with mean vector and covariance matrix defined as Eqs. (4.25) and (4.26), respectively:

$$E[(Y, X)] = (\mu_Y, \mu_X) = (\beta_0 + \beta_1 \mu_x, \mu_x), \tag{4.25}$$

and:

$$\begin{bmatrix} \sigma_Y^2 & \sigma_{XY} \\ \sigma_{XY} & \sigma_X^2 \end{bmatrix} = \begin{bmatrix} \beta_1^2 \sigma_x^2 + \sigma_\varepsilon^2 & \beta_1 \sigma_x^2 \\ \beta_1 \sigma_x^2 & \sigma_x^2 + \sigma_e^2 \end{bmatrix}. \tag{4.26}$$

The estimator for the slope coefficient when Y_t is regressed on X_t is:

$$E(\hat{\beta}_1) = E\left\{ \left[\sum_{t=1}^{n}(X_t - \bar{X})^2\right]^{-1} \sum_{t=1}^{n}(X_t - \bar{X})(Y_t - \bar{Y}) \right\} \tag{4.27}$$

$$= (\sigma_X^2)^{-1} \sigma_{XY}$$

$$= \beta_1 \left(\frac{\sigma_x^2}{\sigma_x^2 + \sigma_e^2} \right).$$

The resulting estimate is smaller in magnitude than the true value of β_1. The ratio of $\lambda = \sigma_x^2/\sigma_X^2 = \sigma_x^2/(\sigma_x^2 + \sigma_e^2)$ defines the degree of attenuation. In applied statistics, this ratio λ is termed the *reliability ratio*. A traditional applied statistical remedy is to use a "known" reliability ratio and weight the statistical model accordingly.[4] As presented in Eq. (4.27) the expected value of the least squares estimator of β_1 is the true β_1 multiplied by the reliability ratio, so it is possible to construct an unbiased estimator of β_1 if the ratio of λ is known.

---

[3] To demonstrate this result, we derive $Y_t = \beta_0 + \beta_1 X_t + (\varepsilon_t - \beta_1 e_t)$ from Eq. (4.24). Assuming the $x_t's$ are random variables with $\sigma_x^2 > 0$ and $(x_t, \varepsilon_t, e_t)'$ are iid $N[(e_x, 0, 0)', diag(\sigma_x^2, \sigma_\varepsilon^2, \sigma_e^2)]$, where $diag(\sigma_x^2, \sigma_\varepsilon^2, \sigma_e^2)$ is a diagonal matrix with the given elements on the diagonal.

[4] See Fuller (1987) for other remedies based on the assumption some of the parameters of the model are known or can be estimated (from outside sources). Alternatively, there are remedies that do not assume any prior knowledge for some of the parameters in the model (see Pal 1980).

4.6.2 Formal Analogues

Least Squares Regression

Normally, we think of least squares regression as an empirical tool, but in this case it serves as a bridge between the formal and empirical analogues ultimately creating a behavioral rationale for the ratio in Eqs. (4.6) and (4.9).[5] This section is a review following Sargent (1979, 223–229). Assume there is a set of random variables, $y, x_1, x_2, \ldots, x_n$. Consider that we estimate the random variable y, which is expressed as a linear function of x_i:

$$\hat{y} = b_0 + b_1 x_1 + \cdots + b_n x_n, \tag{4.28}$$

where b_0 is the intercept of the linear function, and b_i presents the partial slope parameters on x_i, for $i = 1, 2, \ldots, n$. As a result, by choosing the b_i, $\hat{y}$ is the "best" linear estimate that minimizes the "distance" between y and $\hat{y}$:

$$\min_{b_i} E(y - \hat{y})^2$$
$$\Rightarrow \min_{b_i} E\left[y - (b_0 + b_1 x_1 + \cdots + b_n x_n)\right]^2, \tag{4.29}$$

for all i. To minimize Eq. (4.29), a necessary and sufficient condition is (in the normal equation(s)):

$$E\left\{[y - (b_0 + b_1 x_1 + \cdots + b_n x_n)] x_i\right\} = 0 \tag{4.30}$$
$$E\left[(y - \hat{y}) x_i\right] = 0, \tag{4.31}$$

where $x_0 = 1$.

The condition expressed in Eq. (4.31) is known as the *orthogonality principle*. It implies that the difference between observed y and the estimated y according to the linear function $\hat{y}$ is not linearly dependent with x_i, for $i = 1, 2, \ldots, n$.

Linear Projections

A least squares projection begins with:

$$y = \sum_{i=0}^{n} b_i x_i + \varepsilon, \tag{4.32}$$

where ε is the forecast error, $E(\varepsilon \sum b_i x_i) = 0$ and $E(\varepsilon x_i) = 0$, for $i = 0, 1, \ldots, n$. Note that the random variable $\hat{y} = \sum_{i=0}^{n} b_i x_i$, is based on b_i's chosen to satisfy the least squares orthogonality condition. This is known as the projection of y on $x_0, x_1, \ldots, x_n$.

---

[5] The following sections are based on Whittle (1963, 1983), Sargent (1979), and Wooldridge (2015).

Mathematically, it is written:

$$\sum b_i x_i \equiv P(y|1, x_1, x_2, \ldots, x_n), \quad (4.33)$$

where $x_0 = 1$. Assuming orthogonality, Eq. (4.30) can be rewritten as a set of normal equations:

$$\begin{bmatrix} Ey \\ Eyx_1 \\ Eyx_2 \\ \vdots \\ Eyx_n \end{bmatrix} = \begin{bmatrix} 1 & Ex_1 & Ex_2 & \cdots & Ex_n \\ Ex_1 & Ex_1^2 & Ex_1x_2 & \cdots & \\ Ex_2 & Ex_1x_2 & \ddots & & \\ \vdots & \vdots & & \ddots & \\ Ex_n & & & & Ex_n^2 \end{bmatrix} \begin{bmatrix} b_0 \\ b_1 \\ b_2 \\ \vdots \\ b_n \end{bmatrix}. \quad (4.34)$$

Given that the matrix of $Ex_i x_j$ in Eq. (4.34) is invertible for $i, j \in \{1, 2, \ldots, n\}$, and solving for each coefficient b_i:

$$\begin{bmatrix} b_0 \\ b_1 \\ \vdots \\ b_n \end{bmatrix} = [Ex_i x_j]^{-1} [Eyx_k]. \quad (4.35)$$

Applying this technique to a simple example:

$$y = b_0 + b_1 x_1 + \varepsilon,$$

and:

$$\begin{bmatrix} Ey \\ Eyx_1 \end{bmatrix} = \begin{bmatrix} 1 & Ex_1 \\ Ex_1 & Ex_1^2 \end{bmatrix} \begin{bmatrix} b_0 \\ b_1 \end{bmatrix}. \quad (4.36)$$

Using normal equation(s), the following estimates are derived for the intercept and slope:

$$b_0 = Ey - b_1 Ex_1,$$

and:

$$b_1 = \frac{E(y - Ey)(x_1 - Ex_1)}{E(x_1 - Ex_1)^2}$$

$$= \frac{\sigma_{x_1 y}}{\sigma_{x_1}^2},$$

Economic Voting

where σ_{x_1y} is the covariance between x_1 and y, and $\sigma^2_{x_1}$ is the variance of x_1.[6]

Recursive Projections

The linear least squares identities can be used in formulating how agents update their forecasts (*expectations*). Recursive projections are a key element of deriving the optimal forecasts, such as the one shown in Eq. (4.9). These forecasts are updated, consistent with the linear least squares rule described previously. The simple univariate projection can be used (recursively) to assemble projections on many variables, such as $P(y|1, x_1, x_2, \ldots, x_n)$.

For example, when there are two independent variables, Eq. (4.33) can be rewritten for $n = 2$ as:

$$y = P(y|1, x_1, x_2) + \varepsilon, \tag{4.37}$$

implying:

$$y = b_0 + b_1 x_1 + b_2 x_2 + \varepsilon, \tag{4.38}$$

where $E\varepsilon = 0$. Assume that Eqs. (4.37) and (4.38) satisfy the orthogonality conditions: $E\varepsilon x_1 = 0$ and $E\varepsilon x_2 = 0$. If we omit the information from x_2 to

---

[6] From Eq. (4.36), we derive a similar equation expressed in Eq. (4.35):

$$\begin{bmatrix} b_0 \\ b_1 \end{bmatrix} = \begin{bmatrix} 1 & Ex_1 \\ Ex_1 & Ex_1^2 \end{bmatrix}^{-1} \begin{bmatrix} Ey \\ Eyx_1 \end{bmatrix}$$

$$= \begin{bmatrix} Ex_1^2 & -Ex_1\left(Ex_1^2 - (Ex_1)^2\right)^{-1} \\ -Ex_1\left(Ex_1^2 - (Ex_1)^2\right)^{-1} & \left(Ex_1^2 - (Ex_1)^2\right)^{-1} \end{bmatrix} \begin{bmatrix} Ey \\ Eyx_1 \end{bmatrix}.$$

The coefficient b_1 can be expressed as:

$$b_1 = -\frac{Ex_1}{Ex_1^2 - (Ex_1)^2} Ey + \frac{Eyx_1}{Ex_1^2 - (Ex_1)^2}$$

$$= \frac{-Ex_1 Ey + Eyx_1}{Ex_1^2 - (Ex_1)^2}.$$

For simplicity, we assume $Ex_1 = 0$ and $Ey = 0$. Consequently:

$$b_1 = \frac{-Ex_1 Ey + Eyx_1}{Ex_1^2 - (Ex_1)^2}$$

$$= \frac{Eyx_1}{Ex_1^2}$$

$$= \frac{\sigma_{x_1y}}{\sigma^2_{x_1}}.$$

project y, then the projection of y can only be formed based on the random variable x_1:

$$P(y|1,x_1) = b_0 + b_1 x_1 + b_2 P(x_2|1,x_1), \quad (4.39)$$

where $P(b_0|1,x_1) = b_0$, $P(x_1|1,x_1) = x_1$, and $P(\varepsilon|1,x_1) = 0$.[7] In Eq. (4.39), $P(x_2|1,x_1)$ is a component where x_2 is projected using 1 and x_1 to forecast y. An alternative expression is to rewrite the forecast error of y given x_1 as simply the "forecast" error of x_2 given x_1 and a stochastic error term ε. Mathematically, Eq. (4.38) is subtracted from Eq. (4.39):

$$y - P(y|1,x_1) = b_2 [x_2 - P(x_2|1,x_1)] + \varepsilon, \quad (4.40)$$

which can be simplified to:

$$z = b_2 w + \varepsilon,$$

where $z = y - P(y|1,x_1)$, and $w = [x_2 - P(x_2|1,x_1)]$. Note that $x_2 - P(x_2|1,x_1)$ is also orthogonal to ε, such that $E\{\varepsilon[x_2 - P(x_2|1,x_1)]\} = 0$ or $E(\varepsilon w) = 0$.

Now writing the following expression as a projection of the forecast error of y that depends on the forecast error of x_2 given x_1:

$$P\{[y - P(y|1,x_1)] | [x_2 - P(x_2|1,x_1)]\} = b_2 [x_2 - P(x_2|1,x_1)], \quad (4.41)$$

---

[7] Formally, Eq. (4.39) can be separated into four projections:

$$P(y|1,x_1) = P(b_0|1,x_1) + b_1 P(x_1|1,x_1) + b_2 P(x_2|1,x_1) + P(\varepsilon|1,x_1). \quad (4.42)$$

To derive Eq. (4.39), we interpret the first two projections, $P(b_0|1,x_1) = b_0$ and $P(x_1|1,x_1) = x_1$, in Eq. (4.39) as follows. First, predicting a constant term b_0 with 1 and x_1 is simply a constant term b_0. Therefore, we have: $P(b_0|1,x_1) = b_0$. Second, when we predict x_1 using 1 and x_1, we simply have x_1, that is $P(x_1|1,x_1) = x_1$.

To show the results mathematically, we rewrite the first projection as the following linear function: $P(b_0|1,x_1) = t_0 + t_1 x_1$, where t_0 and t_1 are estimated parameters. Using normal equations, we can derive t_0 and t_1: $t_0 = Eb_0 - t_1 Ex_1$, and $t_1 = E[(b_0 - Eb_0)(x_1 - Ex_1)]/E(x_1 - Ex_1)^2$. Since $Eb_0 = b_0$, then: $t_1 = t_1 = E[(b_0 - Eb_0)(x_1 - Ex_1)]/E(x_1 - Ex_1)^2 = 0$, and $t_0 = Eb_0 = b_0$. Therefore, $P(b_0|1,x_1) = t_0 + t_1 x_1 = b_0$.

For the last projection of $P(x_1|1,x_1) = x_1$, we perform the similar mathematical operation: $P(x_1|1,x_1) = t_0 + t_1 x_1$. Now $t_0 = Ex_1 - t_1 Ex_1$, and $t_1 = E[(x_1 - Ex_1)(x_1 - Ex_1)]/E(x_1 - Ex_1)^2 = E(x_1 - Ex_1)^2/E(x_1 - Ex_1)^2 = 1$. Therefore $t_0 = Ex_1 - Ex_1 = 0$, and $P(x_1|1,x_1) = t_0 + t_1 x_1 = 0 + x_1 = x_1$. As a result, $P(x_1|1,x_1) = x_1$.

For the projection of $P(\varepsilon|1,x_1) = 0$, we rely on the orthogonality condition for the last expression: $E(\varepsilon) = E(\varepsilon x_1) = 0$. This gives us $P(\varepsilon|1,x_1) = t_0 + t_1 x_1$. Now $t_0 = E\varepsilon - t_1 Ex_1$ and $t_1 = E[(\varepsilon - E\varepsilon)(x_1 - Ex_1)]/E(x_1 - Ex_1)^2 = E(\varepsilon x_1 - \varepsilon Ex_1 - E\varepsilon x_1 + E\varepsilon x_1)/E(x_1 - Ex_1)^2 = 0$. Since $t_1 = 0$, we find $t_0 = E\varepsilon - t_1 Ex_1 = E\varepsilon = 0$. Therefore, $P(\varepsilon|1,x_1) = 0$.

Economic Voting

or in simplified form:

$P(z|w) = b_2 w.$

By combining Eqs. (4.40) and (4.41), the result is:

$$y = P(y|1, x_1) + P\{[y - P(y|1, x_1)] \,|[x_2 - P(x_2|1, x_1)]\} + \varepsilon. \quad (4.43)$$

Consequently, Eq. (4.43) can also be written as:

$$P(y|1, x_1, x_2) = P(y|1, x_1) + P[y - p(y|1, x_1) \,|x_2 - P(x_2|1, x_1)], \quad (4.44)$$

where $P(y|1, x_1, x_2)$ is known as a bivariate projection. The univariate projections are given by: $P(y|1, x_1)$, $P(x_2|1, x_1)$, and $P[y - P(y|1, x_1) \,|x_2 - P(x_2|1, x_1)]$.

In this case, the bivariate projection equals three univariate projections. More importantly, Eq. (4.44) is useful for purposes of describing optimal updating (learning) by the least squares rule:

$$y = P(y|1, x_1) + P[y - P(y|1, x_1) \,|x_2 - P(x_2|1, x_1)] + \varepsilon,$$

where $y - P(y|1, x_1)$ is interpreted as the prediction error of y given x_1, and $x_2 - P(x_2|1, x_1)$ is interpreted as the prediction error of x_2 given x_1.

If we have data only on a random variable x_1 initially, the linear least squares estimates of y and x_2 are $P(y|1, x_1)$ and $P(x_2|1, x_1)$, respectively:

$$P(y|1, x_1) = b_0 + b_1 x_1 + b_2 P(x_2|1, x_1). \quad (4.45)$$

Intuitively, we forecast y based on two components: (i) $b_1 x_1$ alone, and (ii) $P(x_2|1, x_1)$, that is, the forecast of x_2 given x_1. When an observation x_2 becomes available, according to Eq. (4.44), the estimate of y can be improved by adding to $P(y|1, x_1)$, and the projection of unobserved "forecast error" $y - P(y|1, x_1)$ on the observed forecast error $x_2 - P(x_2|1, x_1)$.

On the right-hand side of Eq. (4.44), $P(y|1, x_1)$ is interpreted as the original forecast, $y - P(y|1, x_1)$ is the forecast error of y, given x_1, and $x_2 - P(x_2|1, x_1)$ is the forecast error of x_2 to forecast the forecast error of y given x_1. This concept can be summarized in a general expression:

$$P(y|\Omega, x) = P(y|\Omega) + P\{[y - P(y|\Omega)] \,|[x - P(x|\Omega)]\},$$

where Ω is the original information, x is the new information, and $P(y|\Omega)$ is the prediction of y using the original information. The projection $P\{[y - P(y|\Omega)] \,|[x - P(x|\Omega)]\}$ indicates new information has become available to update the forecast. It is no longer necessary to use the original information to make predictions. In other words, one can obtain $x - P(x|\Omega)$, the difference between the new information and the "forecasted" new information, to predict the forecast error of y (i.e., $y - P(y|\Omega)$).

4.6.3 Signal-Extraction Problems

Based on these tools it can now be demonstrated how conditional expectations with recursive projections have a mutually reinforcing relation with measurement error and error-in-variables regression. There are many examples of this "EITM-like" linkage and they generally fall under the umbrella of signal extraction problems. Consider the following examples.[8]

APPLICATION 1: MEASUREMENT ERROR Suppose a random variable x^* is an independent variable. However, measurement error e exists so that the variable x is only observable:

$$x = x^* + e, \qquad (4.46)$$

where x^* and e have zero mean, finite variance, and $Ex^*e = 0$. Therefore, the projection of x^* given an observable x is:

$$P(x^* \mid 1, x) = b_0 + b_1 x.$$

Based on the least squares and the orthogonality conditions, we have:

$$b_1 = \frac{E(xx^*)}{Ex^2} = \frac{E[(x^* + e)x^*]}{E(x^* + e)^2} = \frac{E(x^*)^2}{E(x^*)^2 + Ee^2}, \qquad (4.47)$$

and:

$$b_0 = 0. \qquad (4.48)$$

The projection of x^* given x can be written as:

$$P(x^* \mid 1, x) = \frac{E(x^*)^2}{E(x^*)^2 + Ee^2} x, \qquad (4.49)$$

where $b_1 = E(x^*)^2 / [E(x^*)^2 + Ee^2]$ is between zero and one. The "measurement error" attenuation is now transparent. As $E(x^*)^2 / Ee^2$ increases, $b_1 \to 1$: the greater $E(x^*)^2 / Ee^2$ is, the larger the fraction of variance in x is due to variations in the actual value (i.e., $E(x^*)^2$).

APPLICATION 2: THE LUCAS (1973) MODEL (RELATIVE-GENERAL UNCERTAINTY) An additional application is the case where there is general-relative confusion. Here, using Lucas's (1973) supply curve, producers observe the prices of their own goods p_i but not the aggregate price level p. The relative price of good i is r_i is defined as:

$$r_i = p_i - p. \qquad (4.50)$$

---

[8] The first example can be found in Sargent (1979, 229).

Economic Voting

The observable price p_i is a sum of the aggregate price level and its relative price:

$$p_i = p + (p_i - p) = p + r_i. \tag{4.51}$$

Assume each producer wants to estimate the real relative price r_i to determine their output level. However, they do not observe the general price level. As a result, the producer forms the following projection of r_i given p_i:

$$P(r_i | p_i) = b_0 + b_1 p_i. \tag{4.52}$$

According to Eq. (4.52), the values of b_0 and b_1 are:

$$b_0 = E(r_i) - b_1 E(p_i) = E(p_i - p) - b_1 E(p_i) = -b_1 E(p_i), \tag{4.53}$$

and:

$$\begin{aligned} b_1 &= \frac{E[r_i - E(r_i)][p_i - E(p_i)]}{E[p_i - E(p_i)]^2} \\ &= \frac{E[r_i - E(r_i)][(p + r_i) - E(p + r_i)]}{E[(p + r_i) - E(p + r_i)]^2} \\ &= \frac{E r_i^2}{E r_i^2 + E p^2} \tag{4.54} \\ &= \frac{\sigma_r^2}{\sigma_r^2 + \sigma_p^2}, \tag{4.55} \end{aligned}$$

where $\sigma_r^2 = E r_i^2$ is the variance of the real relative price, and $\sigma_p^2 = E p^2$ is the variance of the general price level. Inserting the values of $b_0 = -b_1 E(p)$ and b_1 into the projection (4.52), we have:

$$P(r_i | p_i) = b_1 [p_i - E(p)] = \frac{\sigma_r^2}{\sigma_r^2 + \sigma_p^2} [p_i - E(p)]. \tag{4.56}$$

Next, factoring in an output component – the labor supply – and showing it is increasing with the projected relative price we have:

$$l_i = \beta E(r_i | p_i), \tag{4.57}$$

and:

$$l_i = \frac{\beta \sigma_r^2}{\sigma_r^2 + \sigma_p^2} [p_i - E(p)]. \tag{4.58}$$

If aggregated over all producers and workers, the average aggregate production is:

$$y = b[p - E(p)], \qquad (4.59)$$

where $b = \beta\sigma_r^2/\left(\sigma_r^2 + \sigma_p^2\right)$. Equation (4.59) is commonly known as the Lucas Supply Curve.

Lucas's (1973) empirical tests are directed at output-inflation trade-offs in a variety of countries.[9] Equation (4.59) represents the mechanism of the general-relative price confusion:

$$y = \beta \frac{\sigma_r^2}{\sigma_r^2 + \sigma_p^2} [p - E(p)], \qquad (4.60)$$

where σ_p^2 is the variance of the nominal demand shock, and $p - E(p)$ is the nominal demand shock.

APPLICATION 3: ALESINA AND ROSENTHAL'S OPTIMAL FORECAST OF POLITICAL INCUMBENT COMPETENCE This application uses the techniques of recursive projections and signal extraction to derive the optimal forecast of political incumbent competence in Eq. (4.9). In Section 4.3, the public's conditional expectations of an incumbent's competence at time $t+1$ (as expressed in Eqs. (4.7) and (4.8)) is:

$$E_t(\eta_{t+1}) = E_t(\mu_{t+1}) + \rho E(\mu_t | \hat{y}_t - \hat{y}^n - \rho\mu_{t-1})$$

$$E_t(\eta_{t+1}) = \rho E(\mu_t | \mu_t + \xi_t), \qquad (4.61)$$

where $E_t(\mu_{t+1}) = 0$.

Using recursive projections, voters forecast μ_t using $\mu_t + \xi_t$ and obtain the forecasting coefficients a_0 and a_1:

$$P(\mu_t | \mu_t + \xi_t) = a_0 + a_1(\mu_t + \xi_t), \qquad (4.62)$$

with:

$$\begin{aligned}
a_1 &= \frac{cov(\mu_t, \mu_t + \xi_t)}{var(\mu_t + \xi_t)} \\
&= \frac{E(\mu_t(\mu_t + \xi_t))}{E[(\mu_t + \xi_t)(\mu_t + \xi_t)]} \\
&= \frac{\sigma_\mu^2}{\sigma_\mu^2 + \sigma_\xi^2},
\end{aligned}$$

---

[9] The empirical tests are described in Romer (2019, 293–303).

and:

$$a_0 = E(\mu_t) - a_1 E(\mu_t + \xi_t) = 0,$$

where $E(\mu_t) = E(\mu_t + \xi_t) = 0$. The projection for μ_t is written as:

$$E_t(\mu_t|\mu_t + \xi_t) = P(\mu_t|\mu_t + \xi_t) = a_0 + a_1(\mu_t + \xi_t)$$

$$= \frac{\sigma_\mu^2}{\sigma_\mu^2 + \sigma_\xi^2}(\mu_t + \xi_t). \tag{4.63}$$

Placing Eq. (4.5) into Eq. (4.63):

$$E_t(\mu_t|\mu_t + \xi_t) = \frac{\sigma_\mu^2}{\sigma_\mu^2 + \sigma_\xi^2}(\hat{y}_t - \hat{y}^n - \rho\mu_{t-1}). \tag{4.64}$$

The final step is inserting Eq. (4.64) in Eq. (4.61) and obtaining the optimal forecast of competence at $t+1$:

$$E_t(\eta_{t+1}) = \rho E(\mu_t|\mu_t + \xi_t)$$

$$= \rho \frac{\sigma_\mu^2}{\sigma_\mu^2 + \sigma_\xi^2}(\hat{y}_t - \hat{y}^n - \rho\mu_{t-1}).$$

This is the expression in Eq. (4.9).

5

Strategists and Macropartisanship

5.1 BACKGROUND

A vast literature exists on the topic of party identification and the durability of a voter's affiliation. In 1957, Downs published *An Economic Theory of Democracy*, in which he argued voters compare the utilities of competing parties in order to make their voting decisions. However, their loyalties might shift when they are provided with more information. Consequently, party identification in his model is malleable. In contrast, Campbell et al. (1960), in *The American Voter*, provide a model of stable party identification: the funnel model (as it is known) assumes party identification is inherited from parents and learned through socialization and it has staying power – it persists.

One reason Downs places less emphasis on party identification durability is the presence of information uncertainty. The presence of uncertainty makes information gathering even more costly. He argues a rational voter avoids voting since the cost of a vote is greater than the return received. Riker and Ordeshook (1968) amend this argument and explain why people would vote in elections in spite of the associated costs. They suggest new factors such as civic duty, the satisfaction from voting, and the desire to reaffirm their partisanship. Fiorina (1981) then extends Downs' theory by applying Key's (1966) idea of retrospective voting. In Downs' model, there is no independent role of partisanship, whereas in retrospective voting, party identification plays a role.

Building on Downs' and Fiorina's theories, Franklin and Jackson (1983) introduce a new theory of party identification. They show a person's party identification is not fixed as predicted by Campbell et al. (1960). They argue party identification is influenced by "a person's accumulated evaluations from previous elections and are dependent upon the events and the actions of political leaders during these elections and during subsequent terms in office" (Franklin and Jackson 1983, 968).[1]

Behavioral dynamics has also been a focus. An important debate in political science centers on the persistence of party identification, termed macropartisanship (see Erikson et al. 2002, 109–151). There is controversy about the nature of partisanship. On the one hand, the classic American voter model (Campbell et al. 1960) considers party identification highly stable except for rare realignments. On the other hand, scholars such as Fiorina (1981) contend partisanship serves as a standing choice determined by continuous process of reevaluation.

In contrast, Erikson et al. (2002) put forward the idea that (macro) partisanship is a combination of the long-term memory of partisanship and short-term events. Their reasoning is as follows: Citizens respond to economic and political news. When they react to the news their party affiliation can *temporarily* deviate from its long-term path, akin to an error correction.[2]

Based on this brief sketch, the EITM framework used by Clarke and Granato (2004) develops a behavioral model of party identification that merges macropartisanship dynamics with information uncertainty. The model and test incorporate the findings noted earlier that party identification persistence can be influenced by the strategic use of political information. Clarke and Granato's (2004) model assumes political campaign advertisements influence voter party identification.[3] In particular, party identification persistence can be influenced by a political party strategist's use of campaign advertisements. Consequently, shocks to macropartisanship can either be amplified or die out quickly depending on the political strategist's actions.[4]

The EITM linkage in this example is the relation between the behavioral concept of expectations and the empirical concept of persistence. Empirical tools for this example require a basic understanding of autoregressive processes. Formal tools include an extended discussion of conditional expectations modeling, difference equations (various orders), their solution procedures, and relevant stability conditions.

---

[1] Yet another reason leading to partisanship change is the incumbent's less favorable party performance (as in retrospective voting). Following Downs' logic this information gathering is costly, but Lupia and McCubbins (1998) demonstrate people do not need full information in order to make a reasoned choice. People can make reasoned choices by relying on the advice provided by others who are more informed. Along the same lines – utilizing information shortcuts – Cox (1997) introduces the idea of strategic voting whereby the voters might vote for a party other than their favorite one in order to keep a particular party out of office.

[2] Alternatively, Brandt and Freeman (2009) study macro-political dynamics with a structural vector autoregressive (B-SVAR) Bayesian time series model.

[3] See the Appendix for a discussion of policy "treatments."

[4] Note, the issue of managing incumbent popularity has also been a focus of study (see Freeman and Houser 1998 and Houser and Freeman 2001 in chapter 11).

5.2 STEP 1: RELATING EXPECTATIONS AND PERSISTENCE

Clarke and Granato (2004) relate agent expectations to the persistence of agent behavior. It is demonstrated how a political strategist can use campaign advertisements to influence aggregate persistence in party identification.

The model is based on three equations. Each citizen i is subject to an event j at time t. Clarke and Granato then aggregate across individuals and events so the notation will only have the subscript t:

$$M_t = a_1 M_{t-1} + a_2 E_{t-1} M_t + a_3 F_t + u_{1t}, \tag{5.1}$$

$$F_t = b_1 F_{t-1} + b_2 A_t + u_{2t}, \tag{5.2}$$

and:

$$A_t = c_1 A_{t-1} + c_2 \left(M_t - M^*\right) + c_3 F_{t-1}. \tag{5.3}$$

Equation (5.1) specifies what influences aggregate party identification M_t. The variable M_{t-1} accounts for the empirical concept of persistence. The behavioral concept in the model is citizen expectations. It is assumed that citizens have an expectation of what portion of the population identifies with a particular political party $E_{t-1}M_t$. In forming their expectations, citizens use all available and relevant information (up to time $t-1$) as specified in this model (i.e., rational expectations).[5] Further party identification depends on how favorably a citizen views the national party F_t. Finally, party identification can be subject to unanticipated stochastic shocks (realignments) u_{1t}, where $u_{1t} \sim N(0, \sigma_{u_1}^2)$. These relations are assumed to be positive – $a_1, a_2, a_3 > 0$.

Equation (5.2) represents citizens' impression and sense of favorability about a political party F_t. In this equation, favorability is a linear function of the lag of favorability F_{t-1} and an advertising resource variable A_t. u_{2t} is a stochastic shock representing unanticipated events (uncertainty), where $u_{2t} \sim N(0, \sigma_{u_2}^2)$. The parameters b_1 and b_2 are assumed to be positives ($b_1, b_2 > 0$).

Equation (5.3) presents the contingency plan or rule political strategists use. Clarke and Granato posit political strategists track their previous period's advertising resource expenditures A_{t-1}, and react to that period's favorability rating for the national party F_{t-1}. Strategists also base their current expenditure of advertisement resources on the degree to which macropartisanship M_t approximates a prespecified and desired target M^*. The assumption is strategists want to use their campaign resources as efficiently as possible. The parameters c_1 and c_3 are positive.

The parameter c_2 is particularly important for this model's dynamics. It is assumed to be countercyclical ($-1 \leq c_2 < 0$). This countercyclical assumption reflects strategist willingness to increase or conserve their advertising resources

---

[5] Rational expectations (RE) is only one type of expectation modeling. It has particular implications for how fast citizens adjust to new information, which in this case is political advertisements. See the Appendix, Section 5.6.4 for a discussion on the speed of adjustment.

Strategists and Macropartisanship

depending on whether macropartisanship is above or below the target. When macropartisanship M_t is at the desired target level $M_t = M^*$, political strategists spend the campaign resources A_t based its previous level A_{t-1} as well as the favorability level F_{t-1} at time $t-1$. However, if there is a negative shock in the aggregate party identification Eq. (5.1), the macropartisanship level M_t is driven below its target level M^* (i.e., $M_t - M^* < 0$). Given $c_2 < 0$, political strategists attempt to restore (or raise) the macropartisanship level by injecting a larger amount of advertising resources A_t into the campaign. On the other hand, if there is a positive shock that elevates the macropartisanship level M_t above its target level (i.e., $M_t - M^* > 0$), then political strategists lower the advertising expenditures A_t in order to free up some resources.

Note also, the magnitude (in absolute value) of parameter c_2 in Eq. (5.3) signifies how aggressive – responsive – strategists are in correcting deviations from their targeted level. If political strategists set c_2 closer to -1, it implies, given a certain positive (negative) discrepancy between the current level of macropartisanship M_t and the target, they raise (reduce) the advertising expenditure with a larger share of resources. On the other hand, if c_2 is closer to zero, political strategists are less responsive to the macropartisanship deviations and are less willing to change the advertising expenditure level.

5.3 STEP 2: ANALOGUES FOR EXPECTATIONS AND PERSISTENCE

The reduced form for macropartisanship is determined by substituting Eq. (5.3) into Eq. (5.2). Note that there is an autoregressive component $(\Theta_1 M_{t-1})$ in the reduced form for macropartisanship:

$$M_t = \Theta_0 + \Theta_1 M_{t-1} + \Theta_2 E_{t-1} M_t + \Theta_3 A_{t-1} + \Theta_4 F_{t-1} + \varepsilon_t^*, \qquad (5.4)$$

where:

$$\Theta_0 = -\frac{a_3 b_2 c_2}{1 - a_3 b_2 c_2} M^*,$$

$$\Theta_1 = \frac{a_1}{1 - a_3 b_2 c_2},$$

$$\Theta_2 = \frac{a_2}{1 - a_3 b_2 c_2},$$

$$\Theta_3 = \frac{a_3 b_2 c_1}{1 - a_3 b_2 c_2},$$

$$\Theta_4 = \frac{a_3 (b_1 + b_2 c_3)}{1 - a_3 b_2 c_2}, \text{ and}$$

$$\varepsilon_t^* = \frac{a_3 u_{2t} + u_{1t}}{1 - a_3 b_2 c_2}.$$

The system is simplified to a model of macropartisanship that depends on a lagged macropartisanship M_{t-1}, a conditional expectation at time $t-1$ of current macropartisanship $E_{t-1}M_t$, and prior values of advertising A_{t-1}, and favorability F_{t-1}.

This lagged dependent variable is the analogue for persistence (see the Appendix, Section 5.6.3). Because Eq. (5.4) possesses a conditional expectations operator, we "close the model" and solve for the rational expectations equilibrium (REE) by taking the conditional expectation at time $t-1$ of Eq. (5.4) and then substitute the result back into Eq. (5.4) (see the Appendix, Section 5.6.4):

$$M_t = \Pi_1 + \Pi_2 M_{t-1} + \Pi_3 A_{t-2} + \Pi_4 F_{t-2} + \xi'_t, \tag{5.5}$$

where:

$$\Pi_1 = \left(\Theta_0 - \Theta_3 c_2 M^* - \Theta_4 b_2 c_2 M^*\right)(1 - \Theta_2)^{-1},$$

$$\Pi_2 = \left(\Theta_1 + \Theta_3 c_2 + \Theta_4 b_2 c_2\right)(1 - \Theta_2)^{-1},$$

$$\Pi_3 = \left(\Theta_3 c_2 + \Theta_4 b_2 c_1\right)(1 - \Theta_2)^{-1},$$

$$\Pi_4 = \left[\Theta_3 c_3 + \Theta_4 \left(b_1 + b_2 c_3\right)\right](1 - \Theta_2)^{-1}, \text{ and}$$

$$\xi'_t = \Theta_4 (1 - \Theta_2)^{-1} u_{2t-1} + \Theta_4 \epsilon^*_t.$$

Equation (5.5) is the minimum state variable (MSV) solution (McCallum 1983) for macropartisanship. Macropartisanship M_t depends also on its past history, the autoregressive component M_{t-1} (see Appendix for the complete derivation of the MSV solution).

5.4 STEP 3: UNIFYING AND EVALUATING THE ANALOGUES

The persistence of macropartisanship Π_2 is now shown as dependent on the persistence and willingness of political strategists to maintain a macropartisanship target c_2. In other words, the EITM linkage is the MSV with the AR(1) component in Eq. (5.5).

The linkage in this case is the reduced form AR(1) coefficient expression Π_2:

$$\Pi_2 = \frac{\Theta_1 + \Theta_3 c_2 + \Theta_4 b_2 c_2}{1 - \Theta_2}$$

$$= \frac{a_1 + a_3 b_2 c_2 \left(c_1 + b_1 + b_2 c_3\right)}{1 - a_3 b_2 c_2 - a_2}.$$

Strategists and Macropartisanship

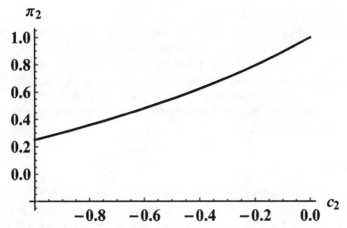

FIGURE 5.1. Macropartisanship persistence (Π_2) and willingness to maintain a macropartisanship target (c_2)

Now, taking the derivative of Π_2 with respect to c_2 we have:

$$\frac{\partial \Pi_2}{\partial c_2} = \frac{a_3 b_2 [a_1 + (1 - a_2) A]}{(1 - a_2 - a_3 b_2 c_2)^2}, \tag{5.6}$$

where $A = b_1 + c_1 + b_2 c_3 > 0$. Given the assumptions about the signs of the coefficients in the model, the numerator is positive when $a_2 < 1$. Therefore, under these conditions, the relation is positive ($\partial \Pi_2 / \partial c_2 > 0$).[6]

The relation between c_2 and Π_2 is demonstrated in Figure 5.1. We find persistence (autocorrelation) in macropartisanship Π_2 is about 0.8 when $c_2 = -0.2$, holding other factors constant.[7] The simulation supports the internal validity of the model: Macropartisanship persistence increases ($\Pi_2 \to 1$)

---

[6] For $\partial \Pi_2 / \partial c_2 > 0$, we note that:

$$\frac{a_3 b_2 [a_1 + (1 - a_2) A]}{(1 - a_2 - a_3 b_2 c_2)^2} > 0$$
$$\Rightarrow a_3 b_2 [a_1 + (1 - a_2) A] > 0$$
$$a_1 + (1 - a_2) A > 0$$
$$a_1 + A > a_2 A$$
$$\frac{a_1 + A}{A} > a_2$$

is the *necessary condition*, and $a_2 < 1$ is the *sufficient condition*, assuming that $a_1 > 0$ and $A = b_1 + c_1 + b_2 c_3 > 0$.

[7] For Figure 5.1, we use the following values: $a_1 = a_2 = a_3 = b_1 = b_2 = c_1 = c_3 = 0.5$. Parameter c_2 ranges from -1.0 to 0.0.

when political strategists fail to react ($c_2 \to 0$) to deviations from their pre-specified target. In other words, when a negative shock drives macropartisanship to a lower level, it will persist for a longer period of time (i.e., a higher value of Π_2) if the political strategists are unable or unwilling to respond to this situation (i.e., a_2 is closer to zero). On the other hand, macropartisanship level can reach (all else equal) the target quicker (i.e., a lower value of Π_2) if political strategists respond to the situation in a more aggressive way (i.e., a larger negative value of c_2).

5.5 SUMMARY

This EITM example is less mature than most. It possesses testable implications but actual data based tests are lacking. In the meantime there are ways to extend the model. One route is to model citizen expectations differently. In this model the use of rational expectations (RE) can limit the complexities of expectation formation. Alternatives could include the use of expectations formation where the public updates at a far slower pace and uses information sets that are far more limited. In this regard, and again with the focus on campaign advertisements, Granato and Wong (2004) modify Clarke and Granato's (2004) model and assume voters initially misspecify their forecasts about a particular candidate's attributes and campaign strategy, but they are able to update their forecasts over time when they receive more information related to the campaign. They show voters can reach a rational expectations equilibrium and eventually discount political advertising ("crystallization"). Their findings are supported by simulations showing that political advertising has little effect in the long run.

In the end, this is an example where the theory is ahead of data. Currently, and as we allude to this issue in this chapter, it is difficult to measure and link specific advertisements to response in real time. One way to deal with this particular design concern is to use experiments and ascertain the treatment and response effects with lags of far shorter duration.

5.6 APPENDIX

5.6.1 The Clarke and Granato (2004) MSV Solution

This section of the appendix illustrates the complete procedure of solving the rational expectations equilibrium for the Clarke and Granato (2004) model. We first present the aggregate party identification equation M_t, the favorability equation F_t, and the advertising equation A_t, respectively, as follows:

$$M_t = a_1 M_{t-1} + a_2 E_{t-1} M_t + a_3 F_t + u_{1t}, \tag{5.7}$$

$$F_t = b_1 F_{t-1} + b_2 A_t + u_{2t}, \text{ and} \tag{5.8}$$

$$A_t = c_1 A_{t-1} + c_2 \left(M_t - M^* \right) + c_3 F_{t-1}. \tag{5.9}$$

Strategists and Macropartisanship

We first insert Eq. (5.9) into Eq. (5.8):

$$F_t = (b_1 + b_2 c_3) F_{t-1} + b_2 c_1 A_{t-1} + b_2 c_2 M_t - b_2 c_2 M^* + u_{2t}, \quad (5.10)$$

Now we substitute Eq. (5.10) into Eq. (5.7):

$$M_t = \Theta_0 + \Theta_1 M_{t-1} + \Theta_2 E_{t-1} M_t + \Theta_3 A_{t-1} + \Theta_4 F_{t-1} + \epsilon_t^*, \quad (5.11)$$

where:

$$\Theta_0 = -a_3 b_2 c_2 \left(1 - a_3 b_2 c_2\right)^{-1} M^*$$

$$\Theta_1 = a_1 \left(1 - a_3 b_2 c_2\right)^{-1}$$

$$\Theta_2 = a_2 \left(1 - a_3 b_2 c_2\right)^{-1}$$

$$\Theta_3 = a_3 b_2 c_1 \left(1 - a_3 b_2 c_2\right)^{-1}$$

$$\Theta_4 = a_3 \left(b_1 + b_2 c_3\right) \left(1 - a_3 b_2 c_2\right)^{-1}, \text{ and}$$

$$\epsilon_t^* = (a_3 u_{2t} + u_{1t}) \left(1 - a_3 b_2 c_2\right)^{-1}.$$

Recall from Eq. (5.10) that:

$$F_t = (b_1 + b_2 c_3) F_{t-1} + b_2 c_1 A_{t-1} + b_2 c_2 M_t - b_2 c_2 M^* + u_{2t}. \quad (5.12)$$

We first set the favorability Eq. (5.12) one period backward:

$$F_{t-1} = (b_1 + b_2 c_3) F_{t-2} + b_2 c_1 A_{t-2} + b_2 c_2 M_{t-1} - b_2 c_2 M^* + u_{2t-1}. \quad (5.13)$$

Similarly, we also set Eq. (5.9) one period backward:

$$A_{t-1} = c_1 A_{t-2} + c_2 (M_{t-1} - M^*) + c_3 F_{t-2}. \quad (5.14)$$

Now we plug Eqs. (5.13) and (5.14) into Eq. (5.11), and we have:

$$M_t = [\Theta_0 - \Theta_3 c_2 M^* - \Theta_4 b_2 c_2 M^*] + [\Theta_1 + \Theta_3 c_2 + \Theta_4 b_2 c_2] M_{t-1}$$
$$+ \Theta_2 E_{t-1} M_t + [\Theta_3 c_2 + \Theta_4 b_2 c_1] A_{t-2}$$
$$+ [\Theta_3 c_3 + \Theta_4 (b_1 + b_2 c_3)] F_{t-2} + \Theta_4 u_{2t-1} + \Theta_4 \epsilon_t^*. \quad (5.15)$$

Finally, to solve the REE, we take expectations E_{t-1} both sides of Eq. (5.15):

$$E_{t-1}M_t = [\Theta_0 - \Theta_3 c_2 M^* - \Theta_4 b_2 c_2 M^*] + [\Theta_1 + \Theta_3 c_2 + \Theta_4 b_2 c_2] M_{t-1}$$
$$+ \Theta_2 E_{t-1} M_t + [\Theta_3 c_2 + \Theta_4 b_2 c_1] A_{t-2}$$
$$+ [\Theta_3 c_3 + \Theta_4 (b_1 + b_2 c_3)] F_{t-2} + \Theta_4 u_{2t-1}$$

$$\Rightarrow E_{t-1} M_t = \frac{\Theta_0 - \Theta_3 c_2 M^* - \Theta_4 b_2 c_2 M^*}{1 - \Theta_2} + \frac{\Theta_1 + \Theta_3 c_2 + \Theta_4 b_2 c_2}{1 - \Theta_2} M_{t-1}$$
$$+ \frac{\Theta_3 c_2 + \Theta_4 b_2 c_1}{1 - \Theta_2} A_{t-2} + \frac{\Theta_3 c_3 + \Theta_4 (b_1 + b_2 c_3)}{1 - \Theta_2} F_{t-2}$$
$$+ \frac{\Theta_4}{1 - \Theta_2} u_{2t-1}.$$

The REE can be obtained as:

$$M_t = \Pi_1 + \Pi_2 M_{t-1} + \Pi_3 A_{t-2} + \Pi_4 F_{t-2} + \xi'_t,$$

where:

$$\Pi_1 = (\Theta_0 - \Theta_3 c_2 M^* - \Theta_4 b_2 c_2 M^*)(1 - \Theta_2)^{-1}$$
$$\Pi_2 = (\Theta_1 + \Theta_3 c_2 + \Theta_4 b_2 c_2)(1 - \Theta_2)^{-1}$$
$$\Pi_3 = (\Theta_3 c_2 + \Theta_4 b_2 c_1)(1 - \Theta_2)^{-1}$$
$$\Pi_4 = [\Theta_3 c_3 + \Theta_4 (b_1 + b_2 c_3)](1 - \Theta_2)^{-1}, \text{ and}$$
$$\xi'_t = \Theta_4 [1 - \Theta_2]^{-1} u_{2t-1} + \Theta_4 \epsilon^*_t.$$

5.6.2 The Concept of Persistence: An EITM Perspective

To assess the degree of persistence in a variable, autoregressive estimation is the most frequently used technique in empirical research. However, in EITM, persistence is behaviorally based. Persistence can be due to many things including brand loyalty and party loyalty. It might also arise because of habit formation, meaning choosing an option in the present period directly increases the probability of choosing it again in future periods.[8]

While the example in this chapter is about party identification – and an appropriate province of political science – the foundations for developing the tools to model expectations are drawn from economics. Since Muth (1961), a great deal of theoretical research uses RE. RE is a particular equilibrium concept representing the optimal choice of the decision rule used by agents depending on the choices of others. "An RE equilibrium (REE) imposes a consistency condition that each agent's choice is a best response to the choices of others" (Evans and Honkapohja 2001, 11). Muth (1961) defined expectations to be rational if they were formed according to the model describing the behavior.

---

[8] See Shachar (2003) for the role of habit formation in voting decisions.

It is also possible to relate RE to autoregressive processes. Let there be a time series generated by a first-order autoregression:

$$z_t = \lambda_0 + \lambda_1 z_{t-1} + v_t, \qquad (5.16)$$

for $z_{t-1} \in I_{t-1}$, where v_t are independent $N(0, \sigma_v^2)$ random variables, $|\lambda_1| < 1$, and I_{t-1} represents all possible information at period $t-1$. Equation (5.16) is treated as the data generating process (DGP). If the agent acts rationally, the mathematical expression of RE corresponding to Eq. (5.16) can be presented as follows:

$$E[z_t | z_{t-1}] = z_t^e = \lambda_0 + \lambda_1 z_{t-1}. \qquad (5.17)$$

With this simple linkage in mind, the tools in this chapter are used to establish a transparent and testable relation between expectations and persistence:

- The applied statistical tools provide a basic understanding of:
  - Autoregressive processes.
- The formal tools include a presentation of:
  - Conditional expectations (naive, adaptive, and rational);
  - Difference equations;
  - Method of undetermined coefficients (minimum state variable procedure).

These tools are used in various applications for models where RE is assumed just as in this chapter.

5.6.3 Empirical Analogues

Autoregressive Processes

An autoregressive process for the time series of Y_t is one in which the current value of Y_t depends upon past values of Y_t and a stochastic disturbance term.[9]

A convenient notation for an autoregressive process is AR(p), where p denotes the maximum lag of Y_t, upon which Y_t depends. Note that in an AR(p)

---

[9] Time series data are discretely ordered by some period. They differ from cross-sectional data in that unlike their cross-sectional cousin, time series are a sequence of data points of the same entity over a period of time. For political science, examples include presidential approval and macropartisanship, while in economics, many macroeconomic data, such as gross domestic product and unemployment rates, are time series. A key property of time series data is stationarity. The consequences of having stationary processes are not trivial. In fact, it is a crucial requirement in that, among other things, most probability moments – the mean, the variance – and all the constituent statistics that derive from these moments are based on the assumption of a stationary time series. No valid inference is achievable absent some assurance that the data and model are stationary. The reason is that nonstationary data affect the moments (mean, variance, for example) of the series and these moments are used in all sorts of inferential statistics such as the t- and F-test.

process, lags are assumed to be present from 1 through to p. For simplicity, we now use AR(1) for illustration. An AR(1) process represents a first-order autoregressive process where Y_t depends upon Y_{t-1} and a disturbance term ε_t:

$$Y_t = \phi Y_{t-1} + \varepsilon_t, \tag{5.18}$$

where ε_t is a white noise that has zero mean, constant variance, and zero autocorrelation. The autoregressive parameter ϕ in Eq. (5.18) can take on values with distinct empirical implications bearing on the persistence of a process. In particular, if $\phi > 1$, the process is explosive, meaning Y_t will grow without limit over time.

Random Walk Processes and the Persistence of Random Shocks
A special case arises when $\phi = 1$. In this case, Eq. (5.18) can be written as:

$$Y_t = Y_{t-1} + \varepsilon_t. \tag{5.19}$$

Equation (5.19) is termed a "pure random walk" process, which indicates that a best guess of Y_{t+1}, given information at period t, is Y_t. The relation between a random walk process and the "persistence" of random shocks is also of importance.

To see this relation, consider the pure random walk process of Eq. (5.19) starts at $t = 1$. The value of Y_t at time $t = 1$ is $Y_1 = Y_0 + \varepsilon_1$. In the next period, $t = 2$, the process is $Y_2 = Y_1 + \varepsilon_2 = (Y_0 + \varepsilon_1) + \varepsilon_2$. Hence, we can generalize the value of Y at time t as:

$$Y_t = Y_0 + \sum_{i=1}^{t} \varepsilon_t. \tag{5.20}$$

Equation (5.20) shows the impact of a particular shock persists and never dies out. The equation also shows that the mean value of Y_t wanders over time. Figure 5.2 illustrates an example of a random walk process over 30 periods based on Eq. (5.20) where the initial value of Y is zero, i.e., ($Y_0 = 0$) and $\epsilon_t \sim N(0, 1)$.

Now, using Eq. (5.18), trace how persistence evolves if we have a stationary process, $0 < \phi < 1$. The result is the shock does die out over time. The process is also mean reverting. To illustrate this, consider an AR(1) process with $\phi = 0.5$:

$$Y_t = 0.5 Y_{t-1} + \varepsilon_t. \tag{5.21}$$

Strategists and Macropartisanship

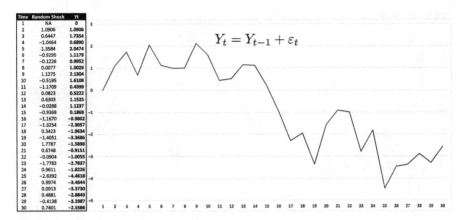

FIGURE 5.2. A random walk process

If we start at $t = 1$, the process is: $Y_1 = 0.5Y_0 + \varepsilon_1$. In successive periods we have:

$$Y_2 = 0.5Y_1 + \varepsilon_2$$
$$= 0.5(0.5Y_0 + \varepsilon_1) + \varepsilon_2$$
$$= 0.5^2 Y_0 + 0.5\varepsilon_1 + \varepsilon_2,$$

and:

$$Y_3 = 0.5Y_2 + \varepsilon_3$$
$$= 0.5\left(0.5^2 Y_0 + 0.5\varepsilon_1 + \varepsilon_2\right) + \varepsilon_3$$
$$= 0.5^3 Y_0 + 0.5^2 \varepsilon_1 + 0.5\varepsilon_2 + \varepsilon_3.$$

In general:

$$Y_t = 0.5^t Y_0 + \sum_{i=1}^{t} 0.5^{t-i} \varepsilon_i. \tag{5.22}$$

Equation (5.22) indicates the effect of a particular shock, say at time $t = 1$, on all the subsequent periods does die out when $t \to \infty$ (i.e, the shock is not persistent).[10] Figure 5.3 presents an AR(1) process of Eq. (5.21) with the identical series of random shocks used in Figure 5.2.

---

[10] Autoregressive processes can be estimated using ordinary least squares (OLS). See Box and Jenkins (1970) for an extensive discussion on the estimation of autoregressive processes. A comprehensive discussion of time series methods can be found in Hamilton (1994). Also, Johnston and DiNardo (1997) provide a basic framework in time series methods, within the broader context of econometric methods.

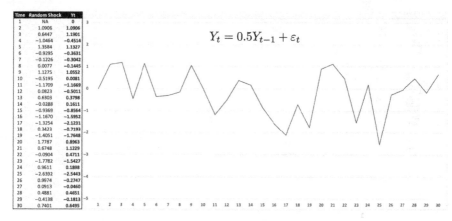

FIGURE 5.3. An autoregressive process

5.6.4 Formal Analogues

Conditional Expectations

The use of expectations in economic models has a long history. While RE is featured in this particular chapter, there are many ways to model expectations and each method has distinct behavioral implications. Here background is provided on three approaches:

1. Naive or static expectations;
2. Adaptive expectations;
3. Rational expectations.

The solution procedures for RE are then presented. Because the development of expectations modeling was largely the creation of economics, the variables and examples are economic in nature. We stay true to those original examples and the variables used. However, as this chapter demonstrates, the application of these tools can be used for any social science questions where expectations are a behavioral and theoretical component.

Static Expectations: The Cobweb Model[11]

Static expectations (also known as naive expectations) assume agents form their expectations of a variable based on their previous period $(t-1)$ observation of the variable. An example illustrating the use of static expectations is the traditional cobweb model, which is one of the most widely used models illustrating dynamic behavior. Kaldor (1934) introduced the cobweb model to explain fluctuations in the agricultural sector when the production process is affected by a time lag. Due to its unique dynamic features, social scientists have applied the cobweb model in different fields, such as agricultural policies

---

[11] See Enders (2014) for background material on the following sections.

(Boussard 1971; Femenia and Gohin 2011; Mitra and Boussard 2012), firm competition (Arifovic 1994; Colucci and Valori 2011), macro-policymaking (Lucas 1973; Branch and Evans 2006), and political campaign dynamics and voting behavior (Granato and Wong 2004).

The cobweb model consists of demand and supply curves, respectively:

$$q_t^d = \alpha - \beta p_t + \epsilon_t^d, \qquad (5.23)$$

and:

$$q_t^s = \gamma + \lambda p_t^e + \epsilon_t^s, \qquad (5.24)$$

where $\beta > 0$, $\lambda > 0$, $\alpha > \gamma > 0$. $\epsilon_t^d \sim iid(0, \sigma_{\epsilon^d}^2)$ and $\epsilon_t^s \sim iid(0, \sigma_{\epsilon^s}^2)$ are stochastic demand and supply shocks with zero mean and constant variance, respectively.

Equation (5.23) is a demand schedule where consumers decide the level of quantity demanded q_t^d given the current price level p_t in the market and other stochastic factors ϵ_t^d at time t. In Eq. (5.24), we assume producers make decisions on the production level q_t^s based on the expected price level at time t, p_t^e. Since the actual market price p_t is not revealed to producers until goods have been produced in the market, producers make a decision on the level of production by forecasting the market price.

The market equilibrium, where $q_t^d = q_t^s$, gives us the dynamic process of the price level:

$$p_t = \frac{\alpha - \gamma}{\beta} - \left(\frac{\lambda}{\beta}\right) p_t^e + \frac{\epsilon_t^d - \epsilon_t^s}{\beta}. \qquad (5.25)$$

Equation (5.25) is known as the cobweb model: The current price level p_t depends on the expected price level p_t^e and a composition of stochastic shocks $(\epsilon_t^d - \epsilon_t^s)/\beta$. Producers form static expectations where they choose the level of production q_t^s at time t by observing the previous price level at time $t-1$ (i.e., $p_t^e = p_{t-1}$). Substituting $p_t^e = p_{t-1}$ into Eq. (5.25):

$$p_t = \frac{\alpha - \gamma}{\beta} - \left(\frac{\lambda}{\beta}\right) p_{t-1} + \frac{\epsilon_t^d - \epsilon_t^s}{\beta}. \qquad (5.26)$$

Equation (5.26) shows the current price level is determined by the past price level and stochastic shocks. Since the initial price level p_t is not in a stationary equilibrium, the price approaches the equilibrium p^* in the long run when certain conditions exist. In this model, $\lambda/\beta < 1$: The model is stable such that the price level will converge in the long run (i.e., $\lim_{t \to \infty} p_t = p^*$). The converging process is shown in Figure 5.4. On the other hand, if $\lambda/\beta > 1$, then the model is unstable and the price will diverge in the long run. This result is known as the Cobweb Theorem.

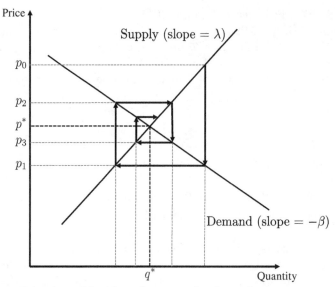

FIGURE 5.4. Cobweb model with static expectation formation

The Use of Difference Equations
The result in Figure 5.4 can be demonstrated using stochastic difference equations. Equation (5.26) is also known as a stochastic first-order difference equation with a constant. Equation (5.26) can be presented in a simpler form:

$$p_t = a + bp_{t-1} + e_t, \tag{5.27}$$

where $a = (\alpha - \gamma)/\beta$, $b = -\lambda/\beta$, and $e_t = (\epsilon_t^d - \epsilon_t^s)/\beta$. To see the sequence of the price level we solve by the method of iterations. Assuming the initial price level is p_0, the price level at time $t = 1$ is:

$$p_1 = a + bp_0 + e_1.$$

Using the previous equation, we solve for p_2:

$$\begin{aligned} p_2 &= a + bp_1 + e_2 \\ &= a + b\left(a + bp_0 + e_1\right) + e_2 \\ &= a + ab + b^2 p_0 + be_1 + e_2. \end{aligned}$$

With a similar substitution, p_3 is:

$$\begin{aligned} p_3 &= a + bp_2 + e_3 \\ &= a + b(a + ab + b^2 p_0 + be_1 + e_2) + e_3 \\ &= a + ab + ab^2 + b^3 p_0 + b^2 e_1 + be_2 + e_3. \end{aligned} \tag{5.28}$$

Strategists and Macropartisanship

If we iterate the equation n times, we have:

$$p_n = a \sum_{i=0}^{n-1} b^i + b^n p_0 + \sum_{i=0}^{n-1} b^i e_{n-i}, \tag{5.29}$$

for $n \geq 1$. Using Eq. (5.29), the current price level p_t depends on the initial level p_0 and the sequence of stochastic shocks $\{e_i\}_{i=1}^t$. Assuming $|b| < 1$, then $\lim_{n \to \infty} b^n = 0$, and $\lim_{n \to \infty} \left(b^0 + b^1 + \cdots + b^n \right) = \lim_{n \to \infty} \sum_{i=0}^n b^i = 1/(1-b)$. Therefore, in the long run, the price level equals:

$$p_{n \to \infty} = \frac{a}{1-b} + \sum_{i=0}^{\infty} b^i e_{n-i}. \tag{5.30}$$

Equations (5.29) and (5.30) show transitory and stationary levels of price, respectively. To illustrate this concept, we assume the following parameter values in the cobweb model: $\alpha = 20$, $\gamma = 10$, $\beta = 1$, $\lambda = 0.8$, and $\lambda/\beta = 0.8 < 1$. Therefore, the stationary price p^* can be derived from Eq. (5.27):

$$p^* = a + bp^*$$
$$= \frac{a}{1-b}$$
$$= \frac{10}{1-(-0.8)} = 5.56.$$

The transitory levels of price can be obtained from Eq. (5.29). Consider there is a one-time temporary shock ($e_1 = 4.44$) in the market such that the price level increases from $p* = 5.56$ to $p_1 = 10$, and $e_i = 0$ for $i > 1$. As a result, the price level for any time period $t = n$ can be presented as follows:

$$p_n = 10 \sum_{i=0}^{n-1} (-0.8)^i + (-0.8)^n p_0 + \sum_{i=0}^{n-1} (-0.8)^i e_{n-i}$$
$$= 10 \sum_{i=0}^{n-1} (-0.8)^i + (-0.8)^n (5.56) + (-0.8)^{n-1} (4.44),$$

for $n \geq 1$. As $t = n \to \infty$, the price level will converge to the stationary level:

$$p_{n \to \infty} = p^* = 10 \sum_{i=0}^{\infty} (-0.8)^i$$
$$= \frac{10}{1-(-0.8)}$$
$$= 5.56,$$

where:

$$\lim_{n\to\infty} (-0.8)^n = 0,$$

and:

$$\lim_{n\to\infty} \left[(-0.8)^0 + (-0.8)^1 + \cdots + (-0.8)^n \right] = \lim_{n\to\infty} \sum_{i=0}^{n} (-0.8)^i$$
$$= \frac{1}{1-(-0.8)}.$$

EXPECTATIONAL ERRORS: SPEED OF ADJUSTMENT An important issue in expectations modeling is the speed of adjustment. Naive or static expectation models contain agents who are relatively slow to adjust and update their forecasts. Using the parameters used previously, we plot the dynamics of price level over time in Figure 5.5. We see that the price level fluctuates and approaches the equilibrium $p^* = 5.56$ in the long run. Intuitively, if there is a one-time shock that shifts the demand or supply curve (or both) producers are assumed to passively determine the current level of production by observing the previous price level. A surplus, or shortage, would exist while the market price deviated from the equilibrium until $t \to \infty$.

The behavioral implication when agents "naively" form expectations based on the past period's observation are as follows: Agents systematically forecast above or below the actual value for an extensive time period. McCallum (1989) terms this sluggishness in error correction systematic expectational errors.

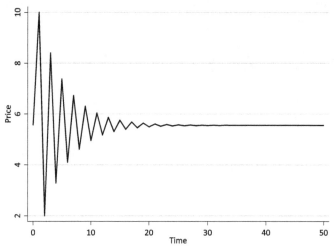

FIGURE 5.5. Price movements in the cobweb model

Adaptive Expectations

Of course, agents can actively revise their expectations when they realize their forecasting mistakes. This alternative formation of expectations is known as adaptive expectations. The revision of current expectations is a function of the expectational error, which is the difference between the actual observation and the past expectation:

$$\text{Expectational Revision} = F(\text{Actual Observation} - \text{Past Expectation})$$
$$= F(\text{Expectational Error}).$$

If agents make forecast errors in the previous period, then they revise their current expectations. Mathematically, adaptive expectations can be written as:

$$p_t^e - p_{t-1}^e = (1-\theta)\left(p_{t-1} - p_{t-1}^e\right), \tag{5.31}$$

where $0 < \theta < 1$ represents the degree (or speed) of expectational revision. When $\theta = 0$, $p_{t-1}^e = p_{t-1}$, agents do not revise their expectations: They have static expectations. On the other hand, if $\theta = 1$, $p_t^e = p_{t-1}^e$, then agents form their current expectations p_t^e based on the past expectations p_{t-1}^e only. By arranging Eq. (5.31), we have:

$$p_t^e = \theta p_{t-1}^e + (1-\theta) p_{t-1}. \tag{5.32}$$

Equation (5.32) also shows that the expectation of the current price p_t^e is the weighted average of past expectation p_{t-1}^e and the past observation p_{t-1}. To recover the expected price level at time t, the method of iterations is applied. The expectations at time $t-1$ and $t-2$ can be presented as follows:

$$p_{t-1}^e = \theta p_{t-2}^e + (1-\theta) p_{t-2}, \tag{5.33}$$

and:

$$p_{t-2}^e = \theta p_{t-3}^e + (1-\theta) p_{t-3}, \tag{5.34}$$

respectively. Substituting Eq. (5.34) into Eq. (5.33) and then inserting it back to Eq. (5.32), we have:

$$p_t^e = \theta^3 p_{t-3}^e + \theta^2 (1-\theta) p_{t-3} + \theta(1-\theta) p_{t-2} + (1-\theta) p_{t-1}. \tag{5.35}$$

Iterating the previous process n times, the expectation of price at time t can be written as:

$$p_t^e = \theta^n p_{t-n}^e + (1-\theta) \sum_{i=1}^{n-1} \theta^{i-1} p_{t-i}.$$

If $n \to \infty$, then:

$$p_t^e = (1 - \theta) \sum_{i=1}^{\infty} \theta^{i-1} p_{t-i}, \tag{5.36}$$

for $|\theta| < 1$, and $\lim_{n \to \infty} \theta^n = 0$.

Equation (5.32) shows the current expectation is the weighted average of the last period expectation and observations. An alternative interpretation based on Eq. (5.36) is that the expected price level for the current period is a weighted average of all price levels observed in the past (with geometrically declining weights).

Under adaptive expectations, agents make their forecast of a variable by weighting its past behavior (Cagan 1956; Friedman 1957a; Nerlove 1958). However, just as with the assumption of static expectations, systematic expectational errors can still be generated. Unexpected stochastic shocks have permanent effects on future expectations formation.

This result is inconsistent with central tenets in economic theory. If agents know that such errors are systematically generated, they have incentives to avoid them. For example, agents have the incentive to collect more (or even all available) information for improving the forecast of the observed variable. Theoretically, one way to avoid the problem of having agents make systematic errors is to assume they have RE (Muth 1961; Lucas 1972, 1973).

Rational Expectations

Under RE, agents are assumed to take conditional (mathematical) expectations of all relevant variables. Agents form their expectations according to all of the information available at time t. The behavioral implications are very different from static or adaptive expectations when it comes to the speed of correcting forecast errors. RE also has very different implications for persistence.

Mathematically, RE can be written as the projection:

$$p_{t+j}^e = E\left(p_{t+j} | I_t\right), \tag{5.37}$$

where p_{t+j}^e is the subjective expectations of p_{t+j} formed in time t, and $E\left(p_{t+j} | I_t\right)$ is a mathematical expectation of p_{t+j} given the information I_t available at time t. Statistically, $E\left(p_{t+j} | I_t\right)$ is interpreted as the mean of the conditional probability distribution of p_{t+j} based on available information I_t at time t. Equation (5.37) implies agents use all information available at time t to forecast the variable of interest for time $t + j$.

More importantly, agents' ability to form a conditional probability distribution of p_{t+j} also implies that agents "know" the structure of the model. For example, agents are able to form a conditional distribution of p_t given the parameters of α, β, γ, and λ as known in Eq. (5.25). It is difficult to

Strategists and Macropartisanship

imagine agents can know the "true" model in the first place and then construct a probability distribution based on the model.[12]

As mentioned earlier, systematic expectational errors are generated when agents form their adaptive expectations given the related information available. These systematic expectational errors can be eliminated under RE. Defining the expectational error as the difference between actual observation at time $t+1$ and the expectation for time $t+1$:

$$p_{t+1} - p^e_{t+1}.$$

If agents systematically over-predict or under-predict the variable of interest, then the "average" of the expectational errors is either larger than or less than zero. Under RE there is no systematic forecast error.

To demonstrate this result under RE we calculate the expected value of the expectational errors as:

$$\begin{aligned} E\left(p_{t+1} - p^e_{t+1}\right) &= E\left[p_{t+1} - E\left(p_{t+1} | I_t\right)\right] \\ &= E\left(p_{t+1}\right) - E\left[E\left(p_{t+1} | I_t\right)\right] \\ &= E\left(p_{t+1}\right) - E\left(p_{t+1}\right) = 0, \end{aligned} \quad (5.38)$$

where $E\left[E\left(p_{t+1} | I_t\right)\right] = E\left(p_{t+1}\right)$ is the unconditional expectation of the conditional expectations of p_{t+1}, given the information set I_t. This is simply the unconditional expectation of p_{t+1}.[13] This result can also be explained by

---

[12] An alternative assumption is agents "learn" the structure of the model over time by least squares to form optimal conditional expectations (Bray 1982; Evans 1985; Bray and Savin 1986; Marcet and Sargent 1989a,b; Evans and Honkapohja 2001). This is known as the adaptive learning approach and is discussed in Chapters 6 and 7.

[13] To show $E\left[E\left(p_{t+1} | I_t\right)\right] = E\left(p_{t+1}\right)$, it is necessary to review some important statistical properties. Let us generalize the statements below and use a variable X. Assume X is a random variable where its numerical values are randomly determined. For the discrete case, the variable X has a set of J random numeral values, $x_1, x_2, \ldots, x_J$. The probability of any numerical value, x_j, for $j = 1, 2, \ldots, J$, can be represented by a probability density function $f(x_j) = Prob\{X = x_j\} \geq 0$. Note that the sum of the probability for all possible numerical values is $\sum_{j=1}^{J} f(x_j) = 1$, and $f(x_k) = 0$, for any $x_k \notin \{x_1, \ldots x_J\}$. Based on the density function, we define the (unconditional) expected value of the random variable X as:

$$E(X) = \sum_{j=1}^{J} x_j f(x_j). \quad (5.39)$$

If $g(x_j)$ is defined as a function for any random value x_j for all $j = 1, 2, \ldots, J$, then the expected value of $g(X)$ is:

$$E[g(X)] = \sum_{j=1}^{J} g(x_j) f(x_j). \quad (5.40)$$

Assuming there is another random variable Y, which has a set of M random values, $y_1, y_2, \ldots, y_M$. Assuming further that X and Y are jointly distributed random variables such that the joint probability density function is $f(x_j, y_m) = Prob\{X = x_j \text{ and } Y = y_m\} \geq 0$, for $j = 1, 2, \ldots J$, and $m = 1, 2, \ldots, M$. Again, note $\sum_{j=1}^{J} \sum_{m=1}^{M} f(x_j, y_m) = 1$, and $f(x_k, y_h) = 0$, for any $x_k \notin \{x_1, \ldots x_J\}$ or $y_h \notin \{y_1, \ldots y_M\}$. Based on the joint density function $f(x_j, y_m)$, the single density function can be calculated for the random variable X by summing up all joint probability of $f(x_j, y_m)$ for any given x_j:

$$f(x_j) = \sum_{m=1}^{M} f(x_j, y_m). \tag{5.41}$$

Similarly, the single density function can be derived for the random variable Y:

$$f(y_m) = \sum_{j=1}^{J} f(x_j, y_m). \tag{5.42}$$

In addition, if there is a multivariate function $g(x_j, y_m)$, then the expected value of $g(X, Y)$ is:

$$E[g(X, Y)] = \sum_{j=1}^{J} \sum_{m=1}^{M} g(x_j, y_m) f(x_j, y_m). \tag{5.43}$$

The last statistical property introduced is the conditional probability density function. This is defined as the conditional probability density function of y given x (subscripts are dropped for convenience) as:

$$f(y|x) = \frac{f(x,y)}{\sum_y f(x,y)} = \frac{f(x,y)}{f(x)}, \tag{5.44}$$

for $f(x) > 0$. As before, the conditional probability density function is the same form but now it is of x given y:

$$f(x|y) = \frac{f(x,y)}{\sum_x f(x,y)} = \frac{f(x,y)}{f(y)}, \tag{5.45}$$

for $f(y) > 0$. Equation (5.44) shows the probability of any numerical value y_m given a specific value of a random variable X. Therefore, we define the conditional expected value of Y given X as:

$$E(Y|X) = \sum_y y f(y|x). \tag{5.46}$$

Based on these statistical properties, we are able to show that $E[E(Y|X)] = E(Y)$ by using the fact that $E[g(X, Y)] = \sum_x \sum_y g(x, y) f(x, y)$ in Eq. (5.43). Assuming that $E(Y|X) = \sum_y y f(y|x) = g(x, y)$ in Eq. (5.46), we have:

$$E[E(Y|X)] = E[g(x,y)] = E\left[\sum_y y f(y|x)\right] = \sum_x \sum_y \left[\sum_y y f(y|x)\right] f(x,y)$$

$$= \sum_x \left\{\left[\sum_y y f(y|x)\right] \sum_y f(x,y)\right\} = \sum_x \left\{\left[\sum_y y f(y|x)\right] f(x)\right\}$$

a statistical property known as the law of iterated expectations.[14] The law of iterated expectations suggests that, given an information set Ω and a subset of information $\omega \subset \Omega$, for a variable of interest x, the conditional expectations of the conditional expectations of x, given a larger information set is just the conditional expectations of x given a subset of information.[15] Mathematically:

$$E[E(x|\Omega)|\omega] = E(x|\omega). \qquad (5.47)$$

If the conditional expectation of x is formed over time according to the available information, then Eq. (5.47) is rewritten as:

$$E\left[E\left(x_{t+1}|I_t\right)|I_{t-1}\right] = E\left(x_{t+1}|I_{t-1}\right),$$

where $I_{t-1} \subset I_t$ for all t.

The second implication of RE is that the expectational errors are uncorrelated with any information available at time t: Any information available to agents to form expectations at time t does not systematically generate forecast errors. To demonstrate this result under RE, consider any information w_t, where $w_t \in I_t$:

$$\begin{aligned}
E\left[\left(p_{t+1} - p_{t+1}^e\right)w_t\right] &= E\left[\left(p_{t+1} - E\left(p_{t+1}|I_t\right)\right)w_t\right] \\
&= E\left(p_{t+1}w_t\right) - E\left[E\left(p_{t+1}|I_t\right)w_t\right] \\
&= E\left(p_{t+1}w_t\right) - E\left(p_{t+1}w_t\right) = 0,
\end{aligned}$$

where $E\left[E\left(p_{t+1}|I_t\right)w_t\right] = E\left[E\left(p_{t+1}w_t|I_t\right)\right] = E\left(p_{t+1}w_t\right)$ and can be shown using the law of iterated expectations.

Solving Rational Expectations Models
The solution procedures for RE models require a different approach. RE models are based on conditional expectations, which is a mathematical expectation with a modified probability distribution ("information set"). Solution procedures involve "closing the model" where unknown variables (i.e., expectations) are expressed in terms of other "known" variables. The method of undetermined coefficients is a particular solution process that closes a model, and the

$$\begin{aligned}
&= \sum_x \sum_y y \frac{f(x,y)}{f(x)} f(x) \quad \text{(from Eq. (5.44))} \\
&= \sum_x \sum_y y f(x,y) = \sum_y y \sum_x f(x,y) = \sum_y y f(y) = E(Y).
\end{aligned}$$

This result validates $E\left[E\left(p_{t+1}|I_t\right)\right] = E\left(p_{t+1}\right)$ in Eq. (5.38).

[14] Note that the expectation operator, $E(\cdot)$, is in linear form. The ideas of recursive expectations and the law of iterated expectations are demonstrated in the discussion of recursive projections in Chapter 4, Appendix, Section 4.6.2.

[15] See Wooldridge (2015), Appendix B for an introductory discussion of conditional expectations.

minimum state variable (MSV) solution is the simplest solution when using the method of undetermined coefficients.

APPLICATION 1: A SIMPLE COBWEB MODEL   The solution(s) for RE models include an REE. Recall that the REE imposes a consistency condition that an agent's choice is a best response to the choices made by others (Evans and Honkapohja 2001, 11). A simple way to demonstrate an REE is to use the cobweb model presented in Eq. (5.25). This particular equation shows that the movements of the price level at time t (i.e., p_t) depend on the RE of the price level form at $t-1$ (i.e., $p_t^e = E\left(p_t|I_{t-1}\right)$), and a composite stochastic error term e_t:

$$p_t = a + bE\left(p_t|I_{t-1}\right) + e_t, \tag{5.48}$$

where $a = (\alpha - \gamma)/\beta$, $b = -\lambda/\beta < 0$, and $e_t = \left(\epsilon_t^d - \epsilon_t^s\right)/\beta$. Agents "know" the model when they form their conditional expectations, so their expectations can be written as:

$$\begin{aligned} E\left(p_t|I_{t-1}\right) &= E\left\{\left[a + bE\left(p_t|I_{t-1}\right) + e_t\right]|I_{t-1}\right\} \\ &= E\left(a|I_{t-1}\right) + E\left\{\left[bE\left(p_t|I_{t-1}\right)\right]|I_{t-1}\right\} + E\left(e_t|I_{t-1}\right) \\ &= a + bE\left[E\left(p_t|I_{t-1}\right)|I_{t-1}\right] \\ &= a + bE\left(p_t|I_{t-1}\right), \end{aligned} \tag{5.49}$$

where $E\left(a|I_{t-1}\right) = a$, $E\left[E\left(p_t|I_{t-1}\right)|I_{t-1}\right] = E\left(p_t|I_{t-1}\right)$, and $E\left(e_t|I_{t-1}\right) = 0$.[16]

Following Eq. (5.49), the right-hand-side expression of $E\left(p_t|I_{t-1}\right)$ is moved to the left-hand side of the equation:

$$(1-b)E\left(p_t|I_{t-1}\right) = a,$$

and $E\left(p_t|I_{t-1}\right)$ is equal to:

$$E\left(p_t|I_{t-1}\right) = \frac{a}{1-b}. \tag{5.50}$$

Equation (5.50) shows that agents form their conditional expectations of p_t using the structural parameters a and b. Inserting Eq. (5.50) into Eq. (5.48) yields the following REE:

---

[16] These identities are based on the following. Since agents know the structure of the model, that is, the parameters a and b, the existing information set would not affect the parameter values. Therefore, $E\left(a|I_{t-1}\right) = a$. We can show, using the law of iterated expectations, that $E\left[E\left(p_t|I_{t-1}\right)|I_{t-1}\right] = E\left(p_t|I_{t-1}\right)$. Intuitively, if an agent forms an expectation of a conditional expectation (based on the same information set), the conditional expectation does not change since there is no added information. Lastly, the conditional expectational of a stochastic error term is zero (i.e., $E\left(e_t|I_{t-1}\right) = 0$) since an agent is unable to "forecast" white noise e_t given past information I_{t-1}.

$$p_t = a + bE\left(p_t|I_{t-1}\right) + e_t$$

$$= a + b\left(\frac{a}{1-b}\right) + e_t$$

$$= \frac{a(1-b) + ab}{1-b} + e_t$$

$$\Rightarrow p_t^{REE} = \frac{a}{1-b} + e_t. \tag{5.51}$$

Furthermore, Eqs. (5.50) and (5.51) also suggest agents have made an optimal forecast in the model since the expectational error is simply stochastic noise:

$$p_t - E\left(p_t|I_{t-1}\right) = \left(\frac{a}{1-b} + e_t\right) - \frac{a}{1-b} = e_t. \tag{5.52}$$

The expected value of the expectational errors is zero:

$$E\left[p_t - E\left(p_t|I_{t-1}\right)\right] = E\left(e_t\right) = 0.$$

APPLICATION 2: A COBWEB MODEL WITH OBSERVABLE VARIABLES In the previous section, it was demonstrated that the variable of interest – the price level at time t – depends on its conditional expectations and a composite stochastic error term in Eq. (5.48). Assuming there are other observable variable(s), w_{t-1}, influencing the quantity supplied in Eq. (5.24):

$$q_t^s = \gamma + \lambda p_t^e + \delta w_{t-1} + \epsilon_t^s. \tag{5.53}$$

For convenience, E_{t-1} is used as an expectation operator to represent the conditional expectations given information available at time $t-1$. The conditional expectation of price level at time t given the information available at time $t-1$ is written as:

$$E_{t-1}p_t = E\left(p_t|I_{t-1}\right). \tag{5.54}$$

In general, the conditional expectation of p_t given the information available at $t - j$ can be written as:

$$E_{t-j}p_t = E\left(p_t|I_{t-j}\right),$$

for all $j \geq 1$.

To solve for the reduced form of the price level, both Eqs. (5.53) and (5.23) are set equal to each other:

$$p_t = \frac{\alpha - \gamma}{\beta} - \frac{\lambda}{\beta}p_t^e - \frac{\delta}{\beta}w_{t-1} + \frac{\epsilon_t^d - \epsilon_t^s}{\beta},$$

or:

$$p_t = a + bp_t^e + dw_{t-1} + e_t',$$

where $a = (\alpha - \gamma)/\beta$, $b = -\lambda/\beta$, $d = -\delta/\beta$, and $e'_t = (\epsilon^d_t - \epsilon^s_t)/\beta$. The RE price at time t is written as:

$$p^e_t = E(p_t|I_{t-1}) = E_{t-1}p_t.$$

Therefore, the revised model of the price level is:

$$p_t = a + bE_{t-1}p_t + dw_{t-1} + e'_t. \tag{5.55}$$

Equation (5.55) is very similar to Eq. (5.48). But, Eq. (5.55) shows the price level p_t now depends on an extra observable variable w_{t-1}. To solve for the REE, conditional expectations of both sides in Eq. (5.55) are taken:

$$\begin{aligned} E_{t-1}p_t &= E_{t-1}\left(a + bE_{t-1}p_t + dw_{t-1} + e'_t\right) \\ &= E_{t-1}a + E_{t-1}\left(bE_{t-1}p_t\right) + E_{t-1}\left(dw_{t-1}\right) + E_{t-1}e'_t \\ &= E_{t-1}a + bE_{t-1}\left(E_{t-1}p_t\right) + dE_{t-1}w_{t-1} + E_{t-1}e'_t. \end{aligned} \tag{5.56}$$

Note $E_{t-1}a = a$, $E_{t-1}\left(E_{t-1}p_t\right) = E_{t-1}p_t$, $E_{t-1}w_{t-1} = w_{t-1}$, and $E_{t-1}e'_t = 0$, thus we have:

$$E_{t-1}p_t = a + bE_{t-1}p_t + dw_{t-1}$$

$$\Rightarrow E_{t-1}p_t = \frac{a}{1-b} + \frac{d}{1-b}w_{t-1}. \tag{5.57}$$

Now substituting Eq. (5.57) into Eq. (5.55) and solving for the REE:

$$p^{REE} = a + b\left(\frac{a}{1-b} + \frac{d}{1-b}w_{t-1}\right) + dw_{t-1} + e'_t$$

$$\Rightarrow p^{REE}_t = \frac{a}{1-b} + \frac{d}{1-b}w_{t-1} + e'_t. \tag{5.58}$$

Equation (5.58) is the REE where the price level depends on a constant term, an observable variable w_{t-1}, and a composite stochastic error term e'_t.

APPLICATION 3: THE CAGAN HYPERINFLATION MODEL   A well-known model, with implications for RE, is the Cagan Hyperinflation model (Cagan 1956) that describes the fundamental relation between the aggregate price level and the money supply. To begin, assume the quantity of real money demanded $(m_t - p_t)^d$ depends on the expected change in the price level:

$$(m_t - p_t)^d = \alpha - \beta\left(E_tp_{t+1} - p_t\right) + \epsilon_t,$$

where $\alpha, \beta > 0$, m_t and p_t are the log levels of money stock and price, respectively, E_tp_{t+1} is the conditional expectations of p_{t+1} formed at t, and ϵ_t is a stochastic money demand shock. Assume also the quantity of real money supplied $(m_t - p_t)^s$ is determined by policymakers:

$$(m_t - p_t)^s = m_t - p_t.$$

Strategists and Macropartisanship

The quantity of money demanded is set with the quantity of money supplied to determine price level dynamics. The reduced form is:

$$p_t = a + bE_t p_{t+1} + dm_t + e_t, \tag{5.59}$$

where $a = -\alpha/(1+\beta)$, $b = \beta/(1+\beta)$, $d = 1/(1+\beta)$, and $e_t = -\epsilon_t/(1+\beta)$.

THE CAGAN MODEL WITH A CONSTANT POLICY OR TREATMENT To make the model as simple as possible the "treatment" is assumed to be constant. In the Cagan model, the "treatment" or "policy" are monetary policy rules. For example, assume the treatment or policy, in this case assume the money stock m_t, does not change over time (i.e., $m_t = \bar{m}$). This implies policymakers decide to fix the money stock level in the economy. Equation (5.59) is rewritten as:

$$p_t = a' + bE_t p_{t+1} + e_t, \tag{5.60}$$

where $a' = a + d\bar{m}$, and $e_t = -\epsilon_t/(1+\beta)$.

The method of undetermined coefficients is used to solve for Eq. (5.60). From Eq. (5.60), the price level depends only on a constant term, its expectations, and a stochastic error term. We conjecture the RE solution is in the following form:

$$p_t = \Pi + e_t, \tag{5.61}$$

where Π is an unknown coefficient. Equation (5.61) is extended one period forward and conditional expectations for time t are taken:

$$\begin{aligned} E_t p_{t+1} &= E_t \left(\Pi + e_{t+1} \right) \\ &= E_t \Pi + E_t e_{t+1} \\ &= \Pi, \end{aligned} \tag{5.62}$$

where $E_t e'_{t+1} = 0$. Substituting Eq. (5.62) into Eq. (5.60):

$$\begin{aligned} p_t &= a' + bE_t p_{t+1} + e_t \\ &= a' + b\Pi + e_t. \end{aligned} \tag{5.63}$$

In Eq. (5.63), we see the actual law of motion (ALM) of p_t depends only on a constant term $a' + b\Pi$, and a stochastic term e_t, when RE is formed. By setting Eqs. (5.61) and (5.63) equal to each other, we have:

$$\Pi = a' + b\Pi. \tag{5.64}$$

It is straightforward to solve the unknown parameter Π from Eq. (5.64):

$$\Pi = \frac{a'}{1-b}. \tag{5.65}$$

Equation (5.65) is put back in Eq. (5.62):

$$E_t p_{t+1} = \frac{a'}{1-b}. \tag{5.66}$$

Equation (5.66) is the RE agents form. Inserting Eq. (5.66) into Eq. (5.60), we get the dynamics of the price level:

$$p_t = a' + b E_t p_{t+1} + e_t$$
$$= a' + b \left[\frac{a'}{1-b} \right] + e_t$$
$$p_t^{REE} = \frac{a'}{1-b} + e_t. \tag{5.67}$$

THE CAGAN MODEL WITH AN AUTOREGRESSIVE POLICY OR TREATMENT We can also have alternative treatment regimes. Assume the movement of the money supply follows a first-order autoregressive (AR(1)) policy rule:

$$m_t = \lambda + \gamma m_{t-1} + \xi_t, \tag{5.68}$$

where ξ_t is a stochastic factor. Substituting Eq. (5.68) into Eq. (5.59) to get the reduced form for the price level:

$$p_t = a'' + b E_t p_{t+1} + h m_{t-1} + u_t + e_t, \tag{5.69}$$

where $a'' = (\lambda - \alpha)/(1+\beta)$, $b = \beta/(1+\beta)$, $h = \gamma/(1+\beta)$, $u_t = \xi_t/(1+\beta)$, and $e_t = -\epsilon_t/(1+\beta)$.

Applying the method of undetermined coefficients, based on Eq. (5.69), our conjecture for the RE solution is:

$$p_t = \Pi_0 + \Pi_1 m_{t-1} + \Pi_2 u_t + \Pi_3 e_t. \tag{5.70}$$

Using Eq. (5.70), the equation is moved one period forward and then expectations for t are taken:

$$E_t p_{t+1} = E_t \left(\Pi_0 + \Pi_1 m_t + \Pi_2 u_{t+1} + \Pi_3 e_{t+1} \right)$$
$$= \Pi_0 + \Pi_1 m_t, \tag{5.71}$$

where $E_t m_t = m_t$ and $E_t u_{t+1} = E_t e_{t+1} = 0$. Substituting Eq. (5.68) into Eq. (5.71):

$$E_t p_{t+1} = \Pi_0 + \Pi_1 \lambda + \Pi_1 \gamma m_{t-1} + \Pi_1 \xi_t. \tag{5.72}$$

Inserting Eq. (5.72) into Eq. (5.69):

$$p_t = a'' + b \left(\Pi_0 + \Pi_1 \lambda + \Pi_1 \gamma m_{t-1} + \Pi_1 \xi_t \right) + h m_{t-1} + u_t + e_t$$
$$= \left(a'' + b \Pi_0 + b \lambda \Pi_1 \right) + \left(b \gamma \Pi_1 + h \right) m_{t-1} + \left[b(1+\beta) \Pi_1 + 1 \right] u_t + e_t, \tag{5.73}$$

Strategists and Macropartisanship   105

where $\xi_t = (1 + \beta) u_t$. According to Eqs. (5.70) and (5.73), these two equations are identical when:

$$\Pi_0 = a'' + b\Pi_0 + b\lambda\Pi_1, \tag{5.74}$$

$$\Pi_1 = b\gamma\Pi_1 + h, \tag{5.75}$$

$$\Pi_2 = b(1 + \beta)\Pi_1 + 1, \text{ and} \tag{5.76}$$

$$\Pi_3 = 1. \tag{5.77}$$

From conditions (5.75)–(5.77), the unknown coefficients can be solved:

$$\Pi_0 = \frac{a'' + b\lambda\Pi_1}{1 - b} = \frac{a''(1 - b\gamma) + bh\lambda}{(1 - b\gamma)(1 - b)}, \tag{5.78}$$

$$\Pi_1 = \frac{h}{1 - b\gamma}, \tag{5.79}$$

$$\Pi_2 = b(1 + \beta)\Pi_1 + 1 = \frac{bh(1 + \beta)}{1 - b\gamma} + 1, \text{ and} \tag{5.80}$$

$$\Pi_3 = 1. \tag{5.81}$$

Substituting Eqs. (5.78)–(5.81) into Eq. (5.70), the RE solution is obtained:

$$p_t^{REE} = \frac{a''(1 - b\gamma) + bh\lambda}{(1 - b\gamma)(1 - b)} + \frac{h}{1 - b\gamma}m_{t-1} + \left[\frac{bh(1 + \beta)}{1 - b\gamma} + 1\right]u_t + e_t. \tag{5.82}$$

APPLICATION 4: MODELS WITH MULTIPLE EXPECTATIONS In this application a RE model is introduced with two rational expectations formulations. An example is Sargent and Wallace's (1975) "ad hoc" model consisting of an aggregate supply equation, an IS equation, and a LM equation. A general reduced-form model is:

$$y_t = a + bE_{t-1}y_t + dE_{t-1}y_{t+1} + e_t. \tag{5.83}$$

Equation (5.83) implies agents' expectations of y_t and y_{t+1} are formed at time $t - 1$. Using the simplest REE:

$$y_t = \Pi_0 + \Pi_1 e_t. \tag{5.84}$$

The expression of Eq. (5.84) one period forward is:

$$y_{t+1} = \Pi_0 + \Pi_1 e_{t+1}. \tag{5.85}$$

Taking expectations of Eqs. (5.84) and (5.85) at time $t - 1$, respectively:

$$E_{t-1}y_t = \Pi_0, \tag{5.86}$$

and:

$$E_{t-1}y_{t+1} = \Pi_0. \tag{5.87}$$

Substituting Eqs. (5.86) and (5.87) into Eq. (5.83):

$$y_t = a + b\Pi_0 + d\Pi_0 + e_t. \tag{5.88}$$

Solving for Π_0:

$$\Pi_0 = \frac{a}{1-b-d}.$$

From Eq. (5.88), we see that:

$$\Pi_1 = 1.$$

Therefore, the REE is:

$$y_t^{REE} = \frac{a}{1-b-d} + e_t. \tag{5.89}$$

Equation (5.89) is also known as the minimum state variable (MSV) solution or "fundamental" solution (McCallum 1983). This is a linear solution that depends on a minimal set of variables. In this example, the REE of y_t depends only on an intercept, $\Pi_0 = a/(1-b-d)$, and a stochastic error term e_t. Note, a variation of this procedure is applied in this chapter.

Another possible solution for Eq. (5.83) is an AR(1) solution. We conjecture the AR(1) solution:

$$y_t = \Pi_0 + \Pi_1 y_{t-1} + \Pi_2 e_t. \tag{5.90}$$

The expectations of y_t and y_{t+1} formed at $t-1$ are, respectively:

$$E_{t-1} y_t = \Pi_0 + \Pi_1 y_{t-1}, \tag{5.91}$$

and:

$$\begin{aligned} E_{t-1} y_{t+1} &= \Pi_0 + \Pi_1 E_{t-1} y_t \\ &= \Pi_0 + \Pi_0 \Pi_1 + \Pi_1^2 y_{t-1}. \end{aligned} \tag{5.92}$$

Substituting Eqs. (5.91) and (5.92) into Eq. (5.83):

$$y_t = \left(a + b\Pi_0 + d\Pi_0 + d\Pi_0 \Pi_1\right) + \left(b\Pi_1 + d\Pi_1^2\right) y_{t-1} + e_t. \tag{5.93}$$

Using Eqs. (5.90) and (5.93), Π_0, Π_1, and Π_2 can be solved:

$$\Pi_0 = -\frac{a}{d},$$

$$\Pi_1 = \frac{1-b}{d},$$

and:

$$\Pi_2 = 1.$$

Therefore, the AR(1) REE is:

$$y_t^{REE} = -\frac{a}{d} + \frac{1-b}{d}y_{t-1} + e_t. \tag{5.94}$$

McCallum (1983) also terms this AR(1) REE a "bubble" solution since it involves the concept of a "self-fulfilling prophecy."[17] The reason is Eq. (5.89) can fundamentally determine the dynamic behavior of y_t, but if agents "believe" and use y_{t-1} to form expectations, then the RE solution becomes Eq. (5.94) and a self-fulfilling prophecy. McCallum (1983) argues the MSV solution – not necessarily the AR(1) REE – should be the solution of interest unless an alternative assumption is made to focus on the bubble solution in the model.[18]

---

[17] A more general REE for this model can be derived. The general solution is:

$$y_t^{REE} = -\frac{a}{d} + \frac{1-b}{d}y_{t-1} + e_t + he_{t-1} + ku_{t-1}, \tag{5.95}$$

where h, k are arbitrary values of coefficients, and u_t is an extra stochastic term (i.e., a sunspot variable), where $E_{t-1}u_t = 0$. This general solution in Eq. (5.95) is also known as the ARMA(1,1) sunspot solution for Eq. (5.83).

[18] Empirical analysis can serve as an alternative way to identify which REE solution is a more valid solution in the theoretical model. For example, if we estimate the AR(1) REE solution (5.90) and find out the estimated coefficient on the lagged dependent variable y_{t-1} is not significantly different from zero, then we would conclude the MSV solution (5.89) would be more reasonable both theoretically and empirically. We thank the reviewer for the comment.

6

Macro Policy

6.1 BACKGROUND

Post–World War II economies experienced macroeconomic policy regime shifts with varying degrees of macroeconomic stabilization success (see Taylor 1999; Bernanke et al. 2001). Subsequent research has argued policy can be used as a coordination device to aid the public's ability to make more accurate forecasts of various macroeconomic outcomes (i.e., RE forecasts). This newer view of macro policy – when properly implemented – creates a stable path for public expectations and learning policy targets. The expected result of this relation between policy and the public is greater stability in important macroeconomic outcomes (e.g., inflation and output). But, how to characterize policy? One particular line of research has focused on the use of interest rate rules in New Keynesian models (see Clarida et al. 2000).

The literature on how policy influences public expectations and learning can be traced back to, for example, Evans and Honkapohja (2001). Evans and Honkapohja (2003a) follow with a review of work on the monetary policy design pertaining to the performance of interest rate rules and how they influence the public's ability to learn a policy target. The monetary authority's policy rule is important in determining convergence or nonconvergence of the learning process. They argue "expectations-based optimal rules" do encourage learning and, by extension, greater macroeconomic stability.[1]

Evans and Honkapohja (2003a) explain two potential difficulties in existing studies on monetary policy design: (1) the proposed interest rate rules may not perform well when the expectations of the agents are initially out of equilibrium

---

[1] Expectations-based optimal rules are defined as "the interest rate rules with appropriate private expectations and economic fundamentals, which satisfy the structure of the economy and optimize the policymaker's objective function" (see Eq. (17) in Evans and Honkapohja 2003b, 813–814).

Macro Policy

(the public makes temporary forecast errors as a result of structural economic shifts) and (2) monetary policy rules can lead to indeterminacy of equilibria. The key to the stability results is the feedback from public expectations to interest rate rules, so that expectation deviations from RE forecasts are offset by policy in such a way that the public is guided to learn and form expectations consistent with the optimal REE.[2] They also argue that when computing the optimal expectations-based rule, it is important for the monetary authority to use the correct structural model of the IS and price-setting relationships, which in turn depend on the specific form of rational individual behavior.

Preston (2005) argues care must be taken in specifying an individual agent's knowledge. His study focuses on the manner in which agents update their decision rules, and whether additional data lead them to adopt perceived laws of motion that are closer to the actual laws of motion of the economy. He considers an important source of model misspecification in the design of policy rules affecting how expectations are formed: (1) a policy should be robust to small deviations from rationality even if rational expectations provide a reasonably accurate description of economic agents' behavior and (2) some desirable policies will have disastrous consequences in practice by allowing self-fulfilling expectations to propagate (Preston 2005, 82). There are two main results in Preston's (2005) study: (1) interest-rate rules that are specified as depending only on the history of exogenous disturbances do not facilitate learning and updating forecasts and (2) for the Taylor rule (1993), expectational stability hinges critically on satisfaction of the Taylor principle.[3]

With this background in mind, the focus of this chapter is one aspect of Granato and Wong (2006). They use a model with New Keynesian properties for determining the relation between inflation-stabilizing policy (as defined by the Taylor Rule and the Taylor Principle) and inflation persistence. The EITM linkage is the relation between the behavioral concepts – expectations and learning – and the applied statistical concept – persistence. Substantively speaking, the model and test show that implementation (and shifts) in the aggressiveness of maintaining an inflation target affects inflation persistence. The empirical tools for this example require a basic understanding of autoregressive processes. These tools have been presented earlier (Chapter 5). The formal tools include an extended presentation of tools from Chapters 4 and 5 (i.e., RE and linear difference equations) in addition to the components of adaptive learning. These adaptive learning components include RE modeling, an understanding of recursive stochastic algorithms, and relevant stability conditions.

---

[2] See Chapter 5 for a discussion of REE.
[3] The Taylor principle applies to changes in the Taylor Rule. Specifically, nominal interest rates are to respond on a one-to-one basis with deviations from inflation targets.

6.2 STEP 1: RELATING EXPECTATIONS, LEARNING, AND PERSISTENCE

The model's intuition is as follows: Monetary policy influences inflation expectations by encouraging the public to substitute an inflation target for past inflation. The testable prediction is a negative relation between periods of aggressive inflation-stabilizing policy and inflation persistence.[4] The model is a small structural model of macroeconomic outcomes and policy in the Cowles Commission tradition, but it also includes behavioral analogues for expectations and learning (Evans and Honkapohja 2001). Under the REE, aggressive implementation of an inflation target guides agents to the unique and stable equilibrium, and thereby reduces inflation persistence.[5]

However, in this chapter, Granato and Wong do not impose RE. Rather they leave the possibility open that an REE can be reached via adaptive learning. Under adaptive learning, expectations are formed by extrapolating from the historical data. One of the key differences between the assumption of RE and that of adaptive learning concerns whether the agent uses full information for forecasting.

Unlike RE – which assumes agents exhaust all possible information for forecasting – adaptive learning assumes agents choose only to use cost-effective information in a presumably known econometric model for forecasting.[6] Over time, by updating the data and running the same econometric model repeatedly, the agent is expected to learn and obtain the REE. The ability to reach the REE is formalized via stability conditions. These conditions are important because they have direct implications for how, and if, agents learn from policymakers. Adaptive learning models make use of what are known as E-stability conditions (see the Appendix, Section 6.6.1).

6.3 STEP 2: ANALOGUES FOR EXPECTATIONS, LEARNING, AND PERSISTENCE

The model is based on a two-period contract. For simplicity, prices reflect a unitary markup over wages. The price p_t at time t is expressed as the average of the current x_t and the lagged x_{t-1} contract wage:[7]

---

[4] Aggressive inflation-stabilizing policy is defined as one that includes a willingness to respond forcefully to deviations from a prespecified implicit or explicit inflation target.
[5] Adaptive learning has gained popularity in inflation persistence research (see Milani 2007 as a representative study).
[6] Or, in more technical terms, adaptive learning is used so that agents update parameters of a forecasting rule (a perceived law of motion (PLM)) – associated with the stochastic process of the variable in question – to learn an REE. This process requires a condition establishing convergence to the REE – the E-stability condition. The E-stability condition determines the stability of the equilibrium in which the perceived law of motion (PLM) parameters adjust to the implied actual law of motion (ALM) parameters. See Evans and Honkapohja (2001) for details.
[7] See Wang and Wong (2005) for the details of the general theoretical framework.

Macro Policy

$$p_t = \frac{1}{2}(x_t + x_{t-1}), \tag{6.1}$$

where p_t is the logarithm of the price level, and x_t is the logarithm of the wage level at period t.

Additionally, agents are concerned with their real wages over the lifetime of the contract:

$$x_t - p_t = \frac{1}{2}\left[x_{t-1} - p_{t-1} + E_t(x_{t+1} - p_{t+1})\right] + \theta z_t, \tag{6.2}$$

where $x_t - p_t$ represents the real wage rate at time t, $E_t(x_{t+1} - p_{t+1})$ is the expectation of the future real wage level at time $t+1$ formed at time t, and $z_t = y_t - y_t^n$ is the excess demand for labor at time t.

Next, the inflation rate π_t is defined as the difference between the current and lagged price level $(p_t - p_{t-1})$. With this definition, substituting Eq. (6.2) into Eq. (6.1) obtains:

$$\pi_t = \frac{1}{2}(\pi_{t-1} + E_t \pi_{t+1}) + \theta z_t + u_{1t}, \tag{6.3}$$

where $E_t \pi_{t+1}$ is the expected inflation rate over the next period and u_{1t} is $iid(0, \sigma_{u_1}^2)$. Equation (6.3) captures the main characteristic of inflation persistence. Since agents make plans about their real wages over both past and future periods, the lagged price level p_{t-1} is taken into consideration as they adjust (negotiate) their real wage at time t. This model feature allows the inflation rate to depend on the expected inflation rate as well as past inflation.

Let Eq. (6.4) represent a standard IS curve: The quantity demanded on output relative to natural output z_t is negatively associated with the changes in real interest rates:

$$z_t = -\varphi(i_t - E_t \pi_{t+1} - r^*) + u_{2t}, \tag{6.4}$$

where $\varphi > 0$, i_t is nominal interest rate, r^* is the target real interest rate, and u_{2t} is $iid(0, \sigma_{u_2}^2)$.

Assume policymakers use an interest rate rule in linking policy and outcomes – the Taylor rule (Taylor 1993) – when conducting monetary policy:

$$i_t = \pi_t + \alpha_y z_t + \alpha_\pi (\pi_t - \pi^*) + r^*. \tag{6.5}$$

Positive values of α_π and α_y indicate a willingness to raise (lower) nominal interest rates in response to the positive (negative) deviations from the target inflation rate $(\pi_t - \pi^*)$, the output gap z_t, or both. An aggressive inflation-stabilizing policy is consistent with $\alpha_\pi > 0$.

The equilibrium inflation rate can be found by solving for the reduced form of the system. We first substitute Eq. (6.5) into Eq. (6.4) to solve for z_t and then put that result into Eq. (6.3). If we solve this expression for π_t, the result is:

$$\pi_t = \Gamma_0 + \Gamma_1 \pi_{t-1} + \Gamma_2 E_t \pi_{t+1} + \xi_t, \tag{6.6}$$

where:

$$\Gamma_0 = (\theta\varphi\alpha_\pi\pi^*)\Phi^{-1},$$
$$\Gamma_1 = (1+\varphi\alpha_y)(2\Phi)^{-1},$$
$$\Gamma_2 = (1+\varphi\alpha_y+2\theta\varphi)(2\Phi)^{-1},$$
$$\xi_t = [\theta u_{2t} + (1+\varphi\alpha_y)u_{1t}]\Phi^{-1}, \text{ and}$$
$$\Phi = 1+\varphi\alpha_y+\theta\varphi(1+\alpha_\pi).$$

Equation (6.6) shows that current inflation depends on the first-order lag of inflation and also expected inflation. When Eq. (6.6) is "closed," the MSV solution can be expressed as an AR(1) process. Thus, the AR(1) process is the empirical analogue for persistence.[8]

6.4 STEP 3: UNIFYING AND EVALUATING THE ANALOGUES

Solving for the REE ensures methodological unification since this solution involves merging the behavioral analogue of expectations with the empirical analogue for persistence. By taking the conditional expectations at time $t+1$ of Eq. (6.6) and substituting this result into Eq. (6.7):

$$\pi_t = A + B\pi_{t-1} + \tilde{\xi}_t, \tag{6.7}$$

where:

$$A = \Gamma_0(1-\Gamma_2 B - \Gamma_2)^{-1},$$
$$B = \left(1 \pm \sqrt{1-4\Gamma_1\Gamma_2}\right)(2\Gamma_2)^{-1}, \text{ and}$$
$$\tilde{\xi}_t = \xi_t(1-\Gamma_2 B)^{-1}.$$

Equation (6.7) is the MSV solution of inflation – which depends solely on the lagged inflation rate.[9]

This solution also highlights an important formal modeling and analogue attribute.[10] Using an adaptive learning analogue, one potential confounding factor that we are alerted to, with important empirical implications, is the

---

[8] Wang and Wong (2005) and Granato and Wong (2006) demonstrate the public can learn the AR(1) equilibrium if the policymaker conducts a more aggressive monetary policy (a larger value of α_π).
[9] The MSV is solved for in Section 6.6.1.
[10] To reinforce this point, see Section 2.3 for an illustration when the inner workings of a system are improperly developed.

nature of the coefficient for lagged inflation, B. This parameter is a quadratic where the two values are defined as:

$$B^+ = \frac{1 + \sqrt{1 - 4\Gamma_1\Gamma_2}}{2\Gamma_2}, \text{ and}$$

$$B^- = \frac{1 - \sqrt{1 - 4\Gamma_1\Gamma_2}}{2\Gamma_2}.$$

Behaviorally, when policymakers adopt an aggressive inflation-stabilizing policy, a stationary AR(1) solution can be obtained (i.e., B^-), while an explosive AR(1) solution (i.e., B^+) would also be possible. Here adaptive learning serves as an important selection criteria (i.e., determining stable solutions) where only the stationary solution (i.e., B^-) is attainable and the explosive solution (i.e., B^+) is not possible (see the Appendix, Section 6.6.1, and McCallum 2003).

In other words, if agents learn the equilibrium in an adaptive manner and they form expectations as new data becomes available over time, B^- is the only learnable (E-stable) equilibrium when policymakers aggressively stabilize inflation (i.e., $\alpha_\pi > 0$). The intuition with this selection criterion is that the model is internally consistent: People can learn the inflation target and begin to rely less on the past history of inflation in making their forecasts.[11]

To test the relation between the policy parameter(s) and inflation persistence quarterly, the US data are used (for the period 1960:I to 2000:III). According to the model, inflation persistence should fall significantly under an aggressive inflation-stabilizing policy (i.e., $\alpha_\pi > 0$.). From Eq. (6.7) Granato and Wong estimate a first-order autoregressive process (i.e., AR(1)) of the inflation rate in the United States. As a consequence of the more aggressive inflation-stabilizing policy stance during the Volcker–Greenspan period (August 1979 through August 2000), the expectation is that the inflation-persistence parameter (B_t) in the Volcker–Greenspan period should be (statistically) smaller relative to the pre-Volcker period.

Granato and Wong estimate Eq. (6.5) to contrast the parameter movements in α_π and α_y.[12] Figure 6.1 provides point estimates of inflation persistence B_t and policy rule parameters, α_π and α_y, for a 15-year rolling sample starting in the first quarter of 1960 (1960:I). The results show that inflation persistence starts falling after 1980. Figure 6.1 also indicates both α_π and α_y de-emphasize inflation and output stability in approximately 1968. Prior to 1968, policy emphasized output stability ($\alpha_y > 0$). Aggressive inflation stabilizing policy occurs only after 1980, when $\alpha_\pi > 0$.

---

[11] The stability condition(s) show this hypothesis is possible in this model: B^- is a unique stationary solution when $\alpha_\pi \geq 0$. The empirical implications of the model – and ex-ante prediction – as represented in Eq. (6.7) is that an increase in α_π reduces persistence under B^-.
[12] See also Granato and Wong (2006, 198–211).

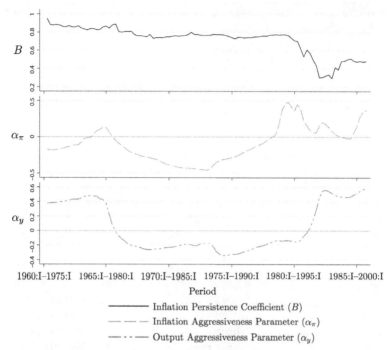

FIGURE 6.1. Taylor rule parameters and inflation persistence

6.5 SUMMARY

This chapter finds that monetary authorities show considerable inertia when adjusting monetary policy in response to changing economic conditions, considering possible imprecision in our knowledge of structural parameters. Bullard and Mitra (2002, 2007) argue it is necessary to understand when agents must form expectations concerning economic events using the actual data produced by the economy. The learning approach admits the possibility that expectations might not initially be fully rational, and that, if economic agents make forecast errors and try to correct them over time, the economy may or may not reach the REE asymptotically. Therefore, it is important to show the potential for agents to learn that equilibrium, beyond showing that a particular policy rule reliably induces a determinate REE.

There are various ways to extend the model – within the EITM framework – in this chapter. One extension of the model is to make both the inflation target variable π^* and the response parameters (α_π, α_y) endogenous to political and social factors, including (but not limited to) partisanship, elections, and social interaction where public information levels are heterogeneous.[13]

---

[13] See Converse (2000) for a literature review on information heterogeneity in the electorate, and Granato et al. (2008) for a model with heterogeneous information levels and adaptive learning.

One could also think of ways to endogenize the policy rule to international economic factors.

In addition, there is little in the way of microfoundations or the strategic interaction between policymakers and the public. Strategic interaction, in particular, points to issues of reputation and credibility, which could, in turn, lead to alternative predictions on public response. Bullard and Mitra's (2007) work on whether a particular policy rule is determinate and learnable is one promising line of inquiry. Lubik and Matthes (2016), for example, have followed up to investigate the equilibrium indeterminacy of the monetary policy during the Great Inflation of the 1970s (see also Pruitt 2012). The authors modify a standard New Keynesian model by imposing more realistic assumptions: (1) the central bank does not know the structure of the economy but updates its beliefs using least-squares learning and (2) it observes the true state of the economy with measurement error. They find agents tend to overestimate the persistence process in the economy. As a result, the central bank is unable to determine if the economy is in equilibrium.

Alternatively, Pfajfar and Žakelj (2016) investigate the formation of inflation expectations in a laboratory experiment. The authors set up a simple New Keynesian model with Taylor-type monetary policy rules, then they estimate how subjects form their expectations in this controlled environment. They find subjects form inflation expectations based on various expectation-formation mechanisms. More importantly, they find policy rules that use actual rather than forecasted inflation produce lower inflation variability, and help to ameliorate inflation cycles (see also Evans and McGough 2018).[14]

6.6 APPENDIX

Using the tools in this chapter, a transparent and testable relation is established among expectations, learning, and persistence. The applied statistical analogue for persistence is located in Section 5.6.3 and will not be repeated. The formal tools include a presentation of adaptive learning building on tools used in Chapters 4 and 5. The formal tools include a presentation of:

- An extended discussion of difference equations (variations on the minimum state variable solution procedure);
- Adaptive learning (recursive stochastic algorithms and relevant stability conditions).

---

[14] Evans and McGough (2018) examine, in a similar New Keynesian model with learning dynamics, how setting an interest rate at a higher level (known as the Neo-Fisherian policy) affects output and inflation volatility. The authors find pegging an interest rate at a higher fixed level can "impart unavoidable instability."

These tools are subsequently used in various applications for models where RE is assumed. The discussion ends by showing how adaptive learning, under certain conditions, translates into showing how an REE can be attained.

6.6.1 Formal Analogues

Equation (6.6) can be solved using an MSV solution and a special case of the method of undetermined coefficients. Referring to Section 5.6.4, the technique is extended to RE models with lagged variables.

Equation (6.6) is of a particular form. A general RE model with persistence is presented as follows:

$$y_t = a + bE_t y_{t+1} + dy_{t-1} + e_t, \tag{6.8}$$

where y_t is a variable of interest (e.g., the inflation rate at time t), $E_t y_{t+1}$ is the rational expectation of y_{t+1} formed at time t, y_{t-1} is the lagged dependent variable, and e_t is a stochastic term.

Solving for the RE in Eq. (6.8), conjecture the solution is:

$$y_t = \Pi_0 + \Pi_1 y_{t-1} + \Pi_2 e_t. \tag{6.9}$$

Moving Eq. (6.9) one period forward and then taking expectations at time t:

$$\begin{aligned} E_t y_{t+1} &= E_t \left(\Pi_0 + \Pi_1 y_t + \Pi_2 e_{t+1} \right) \\ &= \Pi_0 + \Pi_1 y_t. \end{aligned} \tag{6.10}$$

Equation (6.10) indicates that agents form their expectations of y_{t+1} based on the current information y_t. Substituting Eq. (6.10) into Eq. (6.8):

$$y_t = a + b \left(\Pi_0 + \Pi_1 y_t \right) + dy_{t-1} + e_t.$$

After algebraic manipulations:

$$y_t = \frac{a + b\Pi_0}{1 - b\Pi_1} + \frac{d}{1 - b\Pi_1} y_{t-1} + \frac{1}{1 - b\Pi_1} e_t. \tag{6.11}$$

Comparing Eqs. (6.9) and (6.11):

$$\Pi_0 = \frac{a + b\Pi_0}{1 - b\Pi_1}, \tag{6.12}$$

$$\Pi_1 = \frac{d}{1 - b\Pi_1}, \text{ and} \tag{6.13}$$

$$\Pi_2 = \frac{1}{1 - b\Pi_1}. \tag{6.14}$$

Macro Policy 117

Next, use Eq. (6.13):

$$\Pi_1 = \frac{d}{1 - b\Pi_1}$$

to find:

$$b\Pi_1^2 - \Pi_1 + d = 0. \tag{6.15}$$

Equation (6.15) demonstrates there are two possible solutions for the model:

$$\Pi_1 = \frac{1 \pm \sqrt{1 - 4bd}}{2b}. \tag{6.16}$$

From Eq. (6.16), we define $\Pi_1^+ = (1+\sqrt{1-4bd})/(2b)$ and $\Pi_1^- = (1-\sqrt{1-4bd})/(2b)$.

Although there are two possible solutions in the model, we find that one solution is more intuitive and reasonable than the other one. To show this, assuming the lagged dependent variable y_{t-1} has no effect on y_t (i.e., $d = 0$), then y_{t-1} should not be in the solution in Eq. (6.9) ($\Pi_1 = 0$). By substituting $d = 0$ into both possible solutions:

$$\Pi_1^+ = \frac{1 + \sqrt{1 - 4bd}}{2b} = \frac{1 + \sqrt{1 - 4b(0)}}{2b} = \frac{1}{b}, \tag{6.17}$$

and:

$$\Pi_1^- = \frac{1 - \sqrt{1 - 4bd}}{2b} = \frac{1 - \sqrt{1 - 4b(0)}}{2b} = 0. \tag{6.18}$$

From solutions (6.17) and (6.18), the conclusion is that Π_1^- would be a plausible solution consistent with the model.

6.6.2 Adaptive Learning

At this point a brief introduction to adaptive learning and expectational stability is discussed. These two matters were explicated by Evans (1985, 1989) and Evans and Honkapohja (1995, 2001). For purposes of continuity the example in Section 5.6.4 is further developed using the following cobweb model (as defined in Eq. (5.55)):

$$p_t = a + bE_{t-1}p_t + dw_{t-1} + e'_t.$$

Solving for the REE:

$$p_t^{REE} = \frac{a}{1-b} + \frac{d}{1-b}w_{t-1} + e'_t.$$

As mentioned in Chapter 5, the REE shows that agents rationally forecast the price level that depends on a constant term $a/(1-b)$, and the observable w_{t-1} with the coefficient of $d/(1-b)$.

Under the assumption of rational expectations, agents are assumed to be very "smart" and able to make an optimal forecast of p_t using w_{t-1} with a coefficient of $d/(1-b)$ in the forecasting process. Acquiring all available information immediately, agents are able to form conditional (mathematical) expectations, which is a very strong assumption. Sargent (1993) points out that agents with RE are even more sophisticated than the economist who sets up the economic model.

Instead of assuming agents possess rational expectations, we assume agents *learn* in an adaptive manner by forming expectations as new data becomes available. Further, we analyze the conditions of expectational stability (E-stability) under which the parameters in agents' forecasting rules – perceived law of motion (PLM) – are slowly adjusted to (or mapped to) the parameters in the actual law of motion (which can contain the REE).

This E-stability condition determines if agents are able to learn (locally) the correct forecasting rule – the REE. Evans (1989) and Evans and Honkapohja (1992) show that the mapping from the PLM to the ALM is generally consistent with the convergence to REE under least squares learning. This correspondence is known as the E-stability principle. Assuming that agents continuously form the forecast of p_t by estimating the following econometric model as new information of w_t becomes available over time we present:

$$p_t = \alpha_0 + \alpha_1 w_{t-1} + \epsilon_t. \tag{6.19}$$

Equation (6.19) is also known as the PLM. Determining the condition(s) such that the estimated coefficients, α_0 and α_1, can converge to the REE, $a/(1-b)$ and $d/(1-b)$, respectively (when $t \to \infty$) is the goal in this regard.

This principle has additional attributes. If the equilibrium is E-stable, then the RE method may be an appropriate technique for solving long run equilibria. Moreover, E-stability conditions are important selection criteria in determining stable solutions when a model has multiple equilibria.

Employing advanced technical terms, Evans (1989) defines the E-stability condition in terms of the ordinary differential equation (ODE):

$$\frac{d\theta}{d\tau} = T(\theta) - \theta, \tag{6.20}$$

where θ is a finite dimensional parameter specified in the perceived law of motion, $T(\theta)$ is a mapping (so-called T-mapping) from the perceived to the actual law of motion, and τ denotes "notional" or "artificial" time. The REE $\bar{\theta}$ corresponds to fixed points of $T(\theta)$. The stability condition of $\bar{\theta}$ is given under the following definition:

Definition 6.1. $\bar{\theta}$ is expectationally stable (E-stable) if there exists $\varepsilon > 0$ such that $\theta(\tau) \to \bar{\theta}$ as $\tau \to \infty$, for all $\|\theta_0 - \bar{\theta}\| < \varepsilon$, where $\theta(\tau)$ is the trajectory that solves (6.20) subject to the initial condition $\theta(0) = \theta_0$.

Evans and Honkapohja (2001) show that the notional time concept of expectational stability is generally consistent with the stability under real-time least squares learning. Additionally, this correspondence is known as the *E-stability principle*. Evans and Honkapohja (2001) mention that E-stability conditions are often easy to develop, but the convergence condition of adaptive learning involves a more technical analysis.

Least Squares Learning and Stochastic Recursive Algorithms

To understand the general correspondence between E-stability and adaptive learning it is necessary to outline the least squares learning technique and appropriate convergence conditions[15] (see Bray 1982; Bray and Savin 1986; Marcet and Sargent 1989a,b). Assuming that agents use recursive least squares (RLS) for updating their expectations each period up to time $t - 1$:

$$y_t^e = \psi_{t-1}' x_{t-1}, \tag{6.21}$$

where:

$$\psi_t = \psi_{t-1} + t^{-1} R_t x_{t-1} \left(y_t - \psi_{t-1}' x_{t-1} \right) \tag{6.22}$$

$$R_t = R_{t-1} + t^{-1} \left(x_{t-1} x_{t-1}' - R_{t-1} \right), \tag{6.23}$$

and x_t and y_t^e are $m \times 1$ vectors of independent and forecast dependent variables, respectively, ψ_t is a $1 \times m$ coefficient vector updated by the system (6.22) and (6.23), R_t denotes the moment matrix for x_t. Equation (6.21) represents agents' PLM generating a corresponding ALM for y_t:

$$y_t = T(\psi_{t-1})' x_{t-1} + v_t, \tag{6.24}$$

where $v_t \sim iid(0, \sigma_v^2)$. Substituting Eq. (6.24) into Eq. (6.22) gives the stochastic recursive system:

$$\psi_t = \psi_{t-1} + t^{-1} R_t x_{t-1} \left(x_{t-1}' \left(T(\psi_{t-1}) - \psi_{t-1}' \right) + v_t \right), \text{ and} \tag{6.25}$$

$$R_t = R_{t-1} + t^{-1} \left(x_{t-1} x_{t-1}' - R_{t-1} \right). \tag{6.26}$$

The system (6.25) and (6.26) can also be formed as a standard stochastic recursive algorithm (SRA) determining the asymptotic stability for linear regression models:

$$\theta_t = \theta_{t-1} + \gamma_t Q(t, \theta_{t-1}, X_t),$$

---

[15] See Evans and Honkapohja (2001) for further mathematical details.

where $\theta'_t = \left(vec\left(\psi_t\right), vec\left(R_{t+1}\right)\right), X_t = \left(x_t, x_{t-1}, v_t\right)$ and $\gamma_t = t^{-1}$. This SRA relates to the ODE:

$$\frac{d\theta}{d\tau} = h\left(\theta\left(\tau\right)\right), \tag{6.27}$$

where the limit of $h(\theta)$ exists as:

$$h(\theta) = \lim_{t \to \infty} EQ(t, \theta, X_t),$$

and E represents the expectation of $Q(\cdot)$ with the fixed value of θ.

Following the set-up of the SRA, $\bar{\theta}$ is an equilibrium point if $h(\theta) = 0$ in Eq. (6.27). This result provides a standard mathematical definition of asymptotic stability for the differential equation:

> **Definition 6.2.** $\bar{\theta}$ is locally stable if for every $\varepsilon > 0$ there exists $\delta > 0$ such that $|\theta(t) - \bar{\theta}| < \varepsilon \ \forall \ |\theta(0) - \bar{\theta}| < \delta$. $\bar{\theta}$ is said to be locally asymptotically stable if $\bar{\theta}$ is stable, and that $\theta(\tau) \to \bar{\theta} \ \forall \ \theta(0)$ is somewhere in the neighborhood of $\bar{\theta}$ (Evans and Honkapohja 2001, 35).

We now show the local stability condition of $\bar{\theta}$ by computing the Jacobian matrix $Dh(\bar{\theta})$ and using the following lemma. This lemma is generally consistent with the the E-stability condition:

> **Lemma 6.3.** *If all eigenvalues of $Dh(\bar{\theta})$ have negative real parts, then $\bar{\theta}$ is a locally stable equilibrium point of $\frac{d\theta}{d\tau} = h(\theta)$. If some eigenvalues of $Dh(\bar{\theta})$ have a positive real part, then $\bar{\theta}$ is not a locally stable equilibrium point of $\frac{d\theta}{d\tau} = h(\theta)$ (Evans and Honkapohja 2001, 35–36).*

Application: Deriving Expectational Stability (or E-Stability) Conditions
With this background we derive the E-stability condition for the cobweb model in Eq. (5.55):

$$p_t = a + bE_{t-1}p_t + dw_{t-1} + e'_t. \tag{6.28}$$

Assuming that agents do not know the REE while they are able to update their forecasts (the parameters) over time, the PLM is:

$$p_t = \alpha_0 + \alpha_1 w_{t-1} + \epsilon_t. \tag{6.29}$$

Therefore, the forecast of p_t generated by the agents based on the PLM at time $t - 1$ is:

$$E_{t-1}p_t = \alpha_0 + \alpha_1 w_{t-1}.$$

Macro Policy

As a result, the actual price p_t will be affected by agents' forecasts in this case:

$$\begin{aligned}
p_t &= a + bE_{t-1}p_t + dw_{t-1} + e'_t \\
&= a + b(\alpha_0 + \alpha_1 w_{t-1}) + dw_{t-1} + e'_t \\
&= (a + b\alpha_0) + (d + b\alpha_1)w_{t-1} + e'_t.
\end{aligned} \quad (6.30)$$

Equation (6.30) is the implied ALM showing that the parameters in the model are adjusted given the parameters from the PLM. According to Evans (1989) and Evans and Honkapohja (2001), the E-stability condition determines the stability of the equilibrium in which the PLM parameters $\theta = (\alpha_0, \alpha_1)$ adjust to the implied ALM parameters $(a + b\alpha_0, d + b\alpha_1)$. This is written as the following ODE:

$$\frac{d\theta}{d\tau} = T(\theta) - \theta,$$

where τ is a notional time period, and $T(\theta)$ is a mapping (T-mapping) of the PLM parameters θ, that is, $T(\theta) = (a + b\alpha_0, d + b\alpha_1)$. The ODE can also be rewritten as follows:

$$\begin{aligned}
\frac{d}{d\tau}\begin{pmatrix}\alpha_0 \\ \alpha_1\end{pmatrix} &= T\begin{pmatrix}\alpha_0 \\ \alpha_1\end{pmatrix} - \begin{pmatrix}\alpha_0 \\ \alpha_1\end{pmatrix} \\
&= \begin{pmatrix}a + b\alpha_0 \\ d + b\alpha_1\end{pmatrix} - \begin{pmatrix}\alpha_0 \\ \alpha_1\end{pmatrix}.
\end{aligned} \quad (6.31)$$

As a result, the REE corresponds to the fixed points of $T(\theta)$. To determine the E-stability condition, the associated ODE in Eq. (6.31) can be viewed as the dynamic process of the forecasting parameters:

$$\dot{\alpha}_0 = \frac{d\alpha_0}{d\tau} = (a + b\alpha_0) - \alpha_0, \text{ and} \quad (6.32)$$

$$\dot{\alpha}_1 = \frac{d\alpha_1}{d\tau} = (d + b\alpha_1) - \alpha_1. \quad (6.33)$$

According to Eqs. (6.32) and (6.33), the E-stability condition is shown as $b < 1$, implying that agents are able to learn the REE over time only if $b < 1$ is satisfied.

Understanding the result mathematically, the REE is attainable when the dynamic processes for α_0 and α_1 are in steady state, such that $\dot{\alpha}_0 = 0$ and $\dot{\alpha}_1 = 0$. In Eqs. (6.32) and (6.33), we simplify them as follows:

$$\dot{\alpha}_0 = a + (b - 1)\alpha_0, \text{ and} \quad (6.34)$$

$$\dot{\alpha}_1 = d + (b - 1)\alpha_1. \quad (6.35)$$

An explanation of the E-stability condition is illustrated by the values of $\dot{\alpha}_0$ against α_0. This is based on the ODE function (6.32) when $b < 1$ and $b > 1$. If $b < 1$, the slope of Eq. (6.34) is negative and can be presented in the left panel of Figure 6.2. However, the function is positively sloped if $b > 1$ (the right panel).

On the left panel of Figure 6.2, with $b < 1$, any local value of $\alpha_{0,t}$ at time t that is less than its REE (i.e., $\alpha_{0,t} < \alpha_0^{REE}$) gives a positive value of $\dot{\alpha}_0$ (i.e., $\dot{\alpha}_0 = d\alpha_0/d\tau > 0$). Consequently, $\alpha_{0,t}$ increases over time and approaches α_0^{REE} for $t \to \infty$. Similarly, if $\alpha_{0,t}$ is initially larger than α_0^{REE} (locally), the condition, $\dot{\alpha}_0 < 0$, indicates $\alpha_{0,t}$ decreases over time but also approaches α_0^{REE} for $t \to \infty$.

However, considering the case where $b > 1$ (the right panel of Figure 6.2), for any initial value of $\alpha_{0,t}$ less than α_0^{REE}, we have $\dot{\alpha}_0 < 0$. This result implies that $\alpha_{0,t}$ decreases over time and diverges from its REE. Based on the same reasoning, if $\alpha_{0,t} > \alpha_0^{REE}$ for any t, then $\dot{\alpha}_0 > 0$ indicates α_0 increases over time and moves away from its REE.

The same procedure can be applied to show that $\alpha_{1,t}$ converges (in Eq. (6.35)) to α_1^{REE} only if $b < 1$: The PLM parameters converge to the REE only under the condition of $b < 1$. The conclusion therefore is that $b < 1$ satisfies the

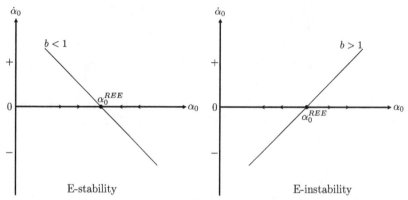

FIGURE 6.2. E-stability versus E-instability

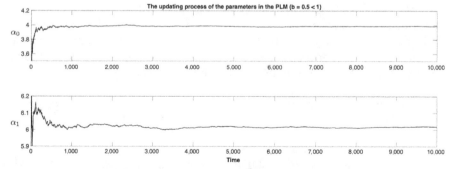

FIGURE 6.3. Simulation with E-stable condition ($b < 1$)

Macro Policy

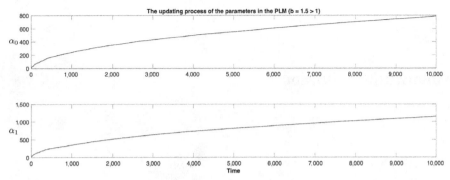

FIGURE 6.4. Simulation with E-unstable condition $(b > 1)$

E-stability condition and $b > 1$ is the E-instability condition. Consequently, this result demonstrates that, if $b < 1$ is satisfied, agents will obtain the REE if they recursively update their forecasts by using the adaptive learning mechanism.

These properties are illustrated further with numeric simulations for the model (6.28)–(6.30). We assign the values $a = 2$, $d = 3$, $\sigma_w = 1$, and $\sigma_{e'} = 1$ in the first simulation. By assigning $b = 0.5$, we can solve for the REE: $\alpha_0^{REE} = 4$ and $\alpha_1^{REE} = 6$. Since $b = 0.5$ is less than 1, the model is E-stable and agents are able to learn the REE in the long run. The result is presented in Figure 6.3. On the other hand, if $b = 1.5$ is assigned, the REE can be solved ($\alpha_0^{REE} = -4$ and $\alpha_1^{REE} = -6$). However, given the condition for $b > 1$ – the REE is not learnable since the parameters diverge in the long run (see Figure 6.4).

7

Information Diffusion

7.1 BACKGROUND

This chapter focuses on information diffusion – the transfer of information from one group to another. It should come as no surprise that information diffusion is an important research area for social scientists. While political scientists have been working on information diffusion processes for many decades (see Lazarsfeld et al. 1944), there is also a very robust tradition in economics (see Chamley 2004).[1] Financial economists, for example, have studied explanations for herding behavior, in which rational investors demonstrate some degree of behavioral convergence (Devenow and Welch 1996). Recent studies in monetary economics investigate how information diffusion influences economic forecasting behavior. Information diffusion, as it pertains to the formation and distribution of expectations, specifically over economic variables, such as inflation, have also been examined. Other studies focus on the relation between information acquisition and forecasting behavior. For example, Pfajfar (2013) introduces information frictions and heterogeneity in the process of expectation formation in a simple dynamic supply–demand model.[2]

By way of background, and a sketch, consider the influence of Lazarsfeld et al. (1944). Their two-step communication model has been applied in various contexts to explain information diffusion processes. Granato and

---

[1] Stigler (1961) introduces an information searching model where an imperfectly informed consumer acquires an optimal level of information based on search costs (Stigler 1962; McCall 1965; Nelson 1970). On the other hand, Aidt (2000) points out voters choose to be less-informed due to the high cost of understanding or consuming information.

[2] Due to limited availability of information, Guse (2014) assumes individuals are unable to determine the best approach when conducting political-economic forecasts. The individuals in his model are required to adopt one of two forecasting models, and they are able to switch to another forecasting model via an evolutionary process. The author shows economic fluctuations exist when individuals are allowed to switch from one forecasting model to another.

Information Diffusion

Krause (2000), for example, examine the connection between information and expectations and test for the diffusion of information among the public. As in the Lazarsfeld et al. two-step communication model, Granato and Krause (2000) assume information transmission is asymmetric, which means predictions of more informed citizens influence the predictions of their less informed counterparts. They use differences in educational attainment as a proxy for information heterogeneity and vector autoregression (VAR) to find out whether communication flows within the electorate are asymmetric between more or less educated citizens. Their VAR results examining monthly surveys of expectations support the asymmetric transmission hypothesis: Educational differences contribute to an asymmetric diffusion of information, and the expectations of the less informed groups within the electorate are shaped by the expectations of more informed groups. *These findings are suggestive but there is no formalization of the dynamic process.*

Communication models in economics have focused on the learning process. Evans and Honkapohja (2001) provide a systematic treatment using adaptive learning. Recall the adaptive learning approach introduces a specific form of bounded rationality where, at each moment in time, agents are assumed to maximize their utility using forecast functions based on available data. But, they also learn in an adaptive manner by revising forecast functions as new data become available.

Learning does occur but what about the issue of heterogeneity? The short answer is it does not make a difference theoretically when adaptive learning is involved. Using a stochastic recursive algorithm, Evans and Honkapohja (1996) find the stability condition for learning (with heterogeneous expectations) is identical to the corresponding condition in the homogeneous case. In more technical language, when different classes of agents have different expectations, global convergence of least squares learning to the unique REE under a simple stability condition exists. In theory, then, learning is feasible given heterogeneous information levels.

Another issue is the effect of social interaction on learning. Granato et al. (2008) introduce a process of information diffusion in a modified cobweb model with a Stackelberg framework, where there are two types of agents – first and second moving firms. The leading firms form initial forecasts and the following firms observe and use the leading firms' forecasts when forming their expectations. They showed the conditions for at least one learnable equilibrium are similar to those under homogeneous expectations. A final issue is how error free the information is when transmitted. Learning occurs but now when information transmission is noisy between leading and following firms, a boomerang effect adversely affects the leading firm's forecast efficiency.[3]

---

[3] In this model we define the boomerang effect as a situation where the inaccurate forecasts of a less-informed group confound a more-informed group's forecasts.

In this chapter, we use an example based on Granato et al. (2008) and Granato et al. (2011). In the spirit of a traditional two-step flow model of communication, less-informed agents learn the expectations of more-informed agents. The tests support the theoretical finding: When there is misinterpretation in the information acquisition process, a boomerang effect exists.[4]

The EITM linkage for this example involves unifying the behavioral concepts of social interaction, expectations, and learning, with the empirical concepts of simultaneity and prediction error. While expectations are again used (as in prior chapters), it is the social interaction that is crucial in this chapter.[5] Specifically, the social interaction involves information diffusion from better informed to less informed agents. The formal tools used – expectations and learning – are found in Chapters 4 and 5. The empirical tools include an analogue for prediction error – defined as the mean square error – contained in the chapter's text. Additionally, the time series tools used in this chapter dealing with simultaneity (endogeneity) and stationarity are contained in the Appendix.

7.2 STEP 1: RELATING SOCIAL INTERACTION, EXPECTATIONS, AND LEARNING TO SIMULTANEITY AND PREDICTION ERROR

Information diffusion is characterized here as a situation where less informed agents can receive information from more informed agents for the purpose of enhancing their – the less informed agents – forecast accuracy. Further, the relation is not simply one group informing another. Instead, the relation between less- and more-informed agents – social interaction – involves expectations and learning.[6] When these behavioral traits are linked with forecast error (forecast accuracy), the result is a set of distinct predictions based on these behavioral concepts and new equilibrium predictions about behavior. The EITM framework allows for an investigation of a boomerang effect.

---

[4] Research suggests that agents do not interpret public information in an identical manner. For example, Kandel and Zilberfarb (1999) examine the assumption that agents interpret information identically. They use a survey of Israeli inflation forecasts from 1980 to 1993 and apply a methodology and test for identical interpretation. Their results, based in differences between the sample variance of forecasts and predicted values, reject the identical interpretation hypothesis. Bernanke and Woodford (1997) study the effectiveness of monetary policy. They argue that some private-sector agents may be "incompetent" at using their information to produce optimal forecasts (page 659).

[5] Note that under EITM, the empirical concept of simultaneity is used as a modeling and testing attribute and not a statistical nuisance. The simultaneity bias is given a behavioral rationale and is explicitly modeled.

[6] Granato et al. (2008) and (2011) investigate the social interaction of inflation forecast behavior in a simple supply and demand model.

7.3 STEP 2: ANALOGUES FOR SOCIAL INTERACTION, EXPECTATIONS, LEARNING, SIMULTANEITY, AND PREDICTION ERROR

In developing a formal model of inflation's behavior, Granato et al. (2011) link a standard Lucas aggregate supply model (Lucas 1973) with an aggregate demand function (Evans and Honkapohja 2001). The aggregate supply and demand functions, respectively, are:

$$y_t = \bar{y} + \theta \left(p_t - E^*_{t-1} p_t\right) + \epsilon_t, \tag{7.1}$$

where $\theta > 0$, and:

$$m_t + v_t = p_t + y_t. \tag{7.2}$$

The variables are as follows: p_t and y_t are the price and output level at time t, respectively, $\bar{y}$ is the natural rate of output level, $E^*_{t-1} p_t$ is the expectation (may not be rational) of the price level at time t, m_t is the money supply, and v_t is a velocity shock. If agents form expectations rationally, it suggests people use all the available information to make the best possible forecasts of the economic variables relevant to them (Lucas 1972). In more technical terms, rational expectations (RE) is an equilibrium condition where the subjective expectations of some variable of interest are equivalent to the objective mathematical expectations conditional on all available information at the time the expectation is formed.[7]

It is assumed velocity depends on some exogenous observables, w_{t-1}:

$$v_t = \kappa + \lambda w_{t-1} + \varepsilon_t, \tag{7.3}$$

where $\lambda > 0$, and the money supply m_t is determined by the monetary policy rule:

$$m_t = \bar{m} + p_{t-1} + \phi w_{t-1} + \xi_t, \tag{7.4}$$

where $\phi > 0$, $\bar{m}$ is a constant money stock, and ϵ_t, ε_t, and ξ_t are iid stochastic shocks.

Using Eqs. (7.1) through (7.4) and defining $\pi_t = p_t - p_{t-1}$ and $E^*_{t-1} \pi_t = E^*_{t-1} p_t - p_{t-1}$, inflation dynamics are presented as follows:

$$\pi_t = \alpha + \beta E^*_{t-1} \pi_t + \gamma w_{t-1} + \eta_t, \tag{7.5}$$

---

[7] See Chapter 5, Section 5.6.4 for the description of rational expectations.

where:

$$\alpha = (1+\theta)^{-1}\left(\kappa + \bar{m} - \bar{y}\right),$$
$$\beta = \theta(1+\theta)^{-1} \in (0,1),$$
$$\gamma = (1+\theta)^{-1}(\phi + \lambda), \text{ and}$$
$$\eta_t = (1+\theta)^{-1}(\epsilon_t + \varepsilon_t + \xi_t).$$

Equation (7.5) is a self-referential model where inflation depends on its expectations $E_{t-1}^*\pi_t$, exogenous variables w_{t-1}, and the stochastic shocks η_t. Since RE is assumed, the unique rational expectations equilibrium (REE) is:

$$\pi = \bar{a}^{REE} + \bar{b}^{REE}w_{t-1} + \eta_t, \tag{7.6}$$

where $\bar{a}^{REE} = \alpha/(1-\beta)$, and $\bar{b}^{REE} = \gamma/(1-\beta)$. From the (7.6), agents can make rational forecasts $E_{t-1}\pi_t$ if they have the full information set w_{t-1} at time $t-1$ such that:

$$E_{t-1}\pi_t = \bar{a}^{REE} + \bar{b}^{REE}w_{t-1}. \tag{7.7}$$

A body of research suggests forecast accuracy is associated with education, a common proxy for information levels (w_{t-1}) (Granato and Krause 2000; Carlson and Valev 2001). Agents possessing more education have more accurate forecasts. An extension of this finding is a second implication relating to information diffusion: More-informed agent forecasts and expectations (e.g., with higher education levels) influence less-informed agent forecasts and expectations (Granato and Krause 2000).

With these findings in mind, take Eq. (7.5) and partition the information set w_{t-1} into two parts: $w_{t-1} = (x_{t-1}, z_{t-1})$, where x_{t-1} is "common" information, and z_{t-1} represents the "advanced" information:

$$\pi_t = \alpha + \beta E_{t-1}^*\pi_t + \gamma_1 x_{t-1} + \gamma_2 z_{t-1} + \eta_t, \tag{7.8}$$

where $\gamma = (\gamma_1, \gamma_2)$. Following Granato et al. (2008) populations are separated into two groups of agents. In the spirit of the classic two-step flow model (Lazarsfeld et al. 1944), the groups are separated by the amount of information and interest they possess. Group L signifies the less-informed group. These agents are assumed to be less current on political and economic events. Members of the second group, Group H, are opinion leaders (e.g., issue publics) who are generally up-to-date on political and economic events. Opinion leaders are key in any information diffusion process since they are recognized by the less-informed group as having more and better information.

It follows that these two groups possess different information sets (x_{t-1}, w_{t-1}). Group H has the complete information set of $w_{t-1} = (x_{t-1}, z_{t-1})$, while Group L only obtains the common information set x_{t-1}. The model also assumes that there is a continuum of agents located on the unit interval $[0, 1]$

Information Diffusion

of which a proportion of $1 - \mu$, where $\mu \in [0, 1)$, are agents in Group H who are more informed when forecasting inflation, and the rest of agents (the proportion of μ) are in Group L.

Agents are interactive. Group L observes Group H's expectations to make its forecasts (but not vice versa). However, Group L agents may interpret (or even misinterpret) Group H's forecasts differently or may not be able to obtain the exact information from the more-informed agents. The next step is to introduce a distribution of observational errors, e_{t-1}, for Group L during the information diffusion process.[8] This gives Group L's forecasting model of inflation:

$$\pi_t = a_L + b_L x_{t-1} + c_L \widehat{\pi}_{t-1} + v_t, \qquad (7.9)$$

and:

$$\widehat{\pi}_{t-1} = E^*_{H,t-1} \pi_t + e_{t-1}, \qquad (7.10)$$

where $e_{t-1} \sim iid\,(0, \sigma_e^2)$ represents the observational errors that are uncorrelated with v_t and w_{t-1}, and $\widehat{\pi}_{t-1}$ is the observed information that Group L obtains from Group H, $E^*_{H,t-1} \pi_t$ (see Eq. (7.12)) with observational error e_{t-1} at time $t - 1$. Since Group L obtains the observed information after Group H forms its expectations, Group L treats the observed information as a predetermined variable.

The forecasting model for Group H is different since this group possesses the full information set to forecast inflation:

$$\pi_t = a_H + b_{1H} x_{t-1} + b_{2H} z_{t-1} + v_t. \qquad (7.11)$$

In this model, Group L and Group H do not directly obtain RE initially. Instead, Group L and Group H recursively forecast following the process of Eqs. (7.9) and (7.11), respectively, and have data on the political-economic system for periods $t_i = T_i, \ldots, t - 1$, where $i \in \{L, H\}$. At time $t - 1$, the information set for the less-informed group, Group L, is $\{\pi_i, x_i, \widehat{\pi}_i\}_{i=T_L}^{t-1}$, but that for Group H is $\{\pi_i, w_i\}_{i=T_H}^{t-1}$.

With analogues for expectations and social interaction established, the analogue for learning is derived (see Evans and Honkapohja 2001; Granato et al. 2008).[9] Based on the adaptive learning method, agents attempt to learn the stochastic process by updating their forecasts (expectations) as new

---

[8] Agents are unable to obtain the exact information from others (Kandel and Zilberfarb 1999). Granato et al. (2011) assume that a distribution of observational errors e_{t-1} is imposed to indicate the degree of misinterpretation of others' actions.

[9] Evans and Honkapohja (2001) argue the assumption of RE is rather strong. They suggest the assumption can be relaxed by allowing agents to "learn" or update their conditional forecasts over time to obtain RE in the long run. This is known as the adaptive learning approach (see Chapter 6, Section 6.6.2).

information becomes available. Both groups use Eq. (7.12) for their perceived law of motion (PLM) when they forecast the variable of interest (inflation rate):

$$E^*_{i,t-1}\pi_t = \varphi'_i q_{i,t-1}, \tag{7.12}$$

where $i \in \{L, H\}$, $q'_{L,t-1} \equiv (1, x_{t-1}, \hat{\pi}_{t-1})$, $q'_{H,t-1} \equiv (1, x_{t-1}, z_{t-1})$, $\varphi'_L \equiv (a_L, b_L, c_L)$ and $\varphi'_H \equiv (a_H, b_{1H}, b_{2H})$. The inflation expectations $E^*_{t-1}\pi_t$ in the society can be calculated as the weighted average of the expectations from both groups:

$$E^*_{t-1}\pi_t = \mu E^*_{L,t-1}\pi_t + (1-\mu) E^*_{H,t-1}\pi_t. \tag{7.13}$$

Using Eqs. (7.8) through (7.11) and (7.13) results in the actual law of motion (ALM):

$$\pi_t = \Omega_\alpha + \Omega_x x_{t-1} + \Omega_z z_{t-1} + \Omega_e e_{t-1} + \eta_t, \tag{7.14}$$

where:

$$\Omega_\alpha = \alpha + \beta\mu a_L + \beta(1-\mu) a_H,$$
$$\Omega_x = \beta\mu b_L + [\beta\mu c_L + \beta(1-\mu)] b_{1H} + \gamma_1,$$
$$\Omega_z = [\beta\mu c_L + \beta(1-\mu)] b_{2H} + \gamma_2, \text{ and}$$
$$\Omega_e = \beta\mu c_L.$$

Equations (7.5), (7.12), and (7.14) represent a system that now incorporates adaptive learning. Both Group H and Group L use their PLM's (i.e., Eq. (7.12)) to update their forecasts of inflation ($E^*_{i,t-1}\pi_t$ in Eq. (7.5)) based on information, $q_{i,t-1}$.

Evans (1989) and Evans and Honkapohja (1992) show that mapping the PLM to the ALM is generally consistent with the convergence to REE under least squares learning. Further, assuming agents have a choice of using one of several forecasting models and that there are equilibrium predictions in these models, Guse (2005, 2010) refers to a resulting stochastic equilibrium as a "mixed expectations equilibrium" (MEE).[10] Computing the linear projections on Eqs. (7.8), (7.12), and (7.13), the MEE coefficients result in the following:[11]

$$\bar{\varphi}_L = \begin{pmatrix} \bar{a}_L \\ \bar{b}_L \\ \bar{c}_L \end{pmatrix} = \begin{pmatrix} \frac{\alpha}{1-\beta}(1-\bar{c}_L) \\ \frac{\gamma_1}{1-\beta}(1-\bar{c}_L) \\ \frac{\bar{b}_{2H}^2 \sigma_z^2}{\bar{b}_{2H}^2 \sigma_z^2 + (1-\beta\mu)\sigma_e^2} \end{pmatrix} \tag{7.15}$$

---

[10] In this model, agents have a choice to be either in Group H or in Group L when they form their forecasting models.
[11] To obtain the MEE, one can solve for the orthogonality condition (OC) using ALM (7.14) and PLM (7.12). For Group H, the OC is $E(\pi_t - E^*_{H,t-1}\pi_t)(1, x_{t-1}, z_{t-1}) = 0$. For Group L, the OC is: $E(\pi_t - E^*_{L,t-1}\pi_t)(1, x_{t-1}, \hat{\pi}_{t-1}) = 0$.

and:

$$\bar{\varphi}_H = \begin{pmatrix} \bar{a}_H \\ \bar{b}_{1H} \\ \bar{b}_{2H} \end{pmatrix} = \begin{pmatrix} \frac{\alpha}{1-\beta} \\ \frac{\gamma_1}{1-\beta} \\ \frac{\gamma_2}{1-\beta+\beta\mu(1-\bar{c}_L)} \end{pmatrix}. \tag{7.16}$$

The MEE (7.15) and (7.16) is the equilibrium of the forecasting models for Group L and Group H, respectively. Recall from (7.6) the REE is $\bar{a}^{REE} = \alpha/(1-\beta)$ and $\bar{b}^{REE} = \gamma/(1-\beta)$. Both groups can obtain the REE if they are able to receive the same complete information. However, because of this particular information diffusion process, Groups L and H fail to obtain the REE.

The observational error e_{t-1} plays a significant role in the model. Whether Group L uses the observed information from Group H depends on how accurately the less-informed group understands information (the expectations) from the more-informed group. The accuracy is represented by the variance of the observational error σ_e^2.

Equation (7.15) implies $0 < \bar{c}_L \leq 1$ for $\beta < 1/\mu$. If Group L can fully understand and make use of Group H's expectations (i.e., $\sigma_e^2 \to 0$), then $\bar{c}_L = 1$ (by solving Eqs. (7.15) and (7.16) with $\sigma_e^2 = 0$). In addition, $\bar{c}_L \to 0$ as $\sigma_e^2 \to \infty$. The values of $\bar{c}_L$ also affect $\bar{a}_L$ and $\bar{b}_L$. If $\bar{c}_L \to 0$, then $\bar{a}_L \to \alpha/(1-\beta)$ and $\bar{b}_L \to \gamma_1/(1-\beta)$. Both $\bar{a}_L, \bar{b}_L \to 0$ if $\bar{c}_L \to 1$.

In the case of Group H, and under the assumption the covariance between x_t and $w_{2,t}$ is zero, $\bar{c}_L$ does not affect $\bar{a}_H$ and $\bar{b}_{1H}$. Both parameters approach the REE,[12] $(\bar{a}_H, \bar{b}_{1H}) \to (\alpha/(1-\beta), \gamma_1/(1-\beta))$. However, Eq. (7.16) shows $\bar{b}_{2H}$ is affected by $\bar{c}_L$, where $|\bar{b}_{2H}| \in (|\gamma_2|/[1-\beta(1-\mu)], |\gamma_2|/(1-\beta))$ for $\beta \in [0, 1)$, and $|\bar{b}_{2H}| \in (|\gamma_2|/(1-\beta), |\gamma_2|/[1-\beta(1-\mu)])$ for $\beta \in (-\infty, 0)$. This latter relation is evidence of the boomerang effect on expectations: The observational error of the less-informed group biases the parameter(s) of the highly informed group's forecasting rule.[13]

The applied statistical analogue for prediction (forecast) error is the mean square error (MSE). For the inflation forecast error in the model, the mean square error is represented by the following formula:

$$MSE_i \equiv E\left(\pi_t - E^*_{i,t-1}\pi_t\right)^2,$$

for $i \in \{L, H\}$.

---

[12] If the $cov(x_t, w_{2,t}) \neq 0$, then $\bar{b}_{1H}$ can also be affected by the less informed group's forecast errors.

[13] See Granato et al. (2008, 358–360) for details.

7.4 STEP 3: UNIFYING AND EVALUATING THE ANALOGUES

The formal model demonstrates that Group L places a weight $\bar{c}_L$ on the observed information from Group H. Group L makes use of Group H's expectations (i.e., a higher $\bar{c}_L$) as long as Group L face smaller variation in observation error when interpreting Group H's information (i.e., lower σ_e^2). Linking the formal and applied statistical analogues shows how expectations and information diffusion create testable dynamics.

To show this, calculate the mean squared error (MSE) for the forecasts of Groups L and H, respectively:[14]

$$MSE_L = \left[\frac{\gamma_2 (1 - \bar{c}_L)}{1 - \beta + \beta (1 - \bar{c}_L) \mu}\right]^2 \sigma_z^2 + (1 - \beta\mu)^2 \bar{c}_L^2 \sigma_e^2 + \sigma_\eta^2, \text{ and} \quad (7.17)$$

$$MSE_H = (\beta\mu\bar{c}_L)^2 \sigma_e^2 + \sigma_\eta^2, \quad (7.18)$$

where $MSE_i \equiv E(\pi_t - E^*_{i,t-1}\pi_t)^2$, for $i \in \{L, H\}$.

Equation (7.17) depicts the accuracy of the less-informed group's predictions. If Group L is able to fully understand the expectations from Group H (i.e., without any observation errors $\sigma_e^2 = 0$), the result is that Group L obtains the minimum MSE (i.e, $MSE_L = \sigma_\eta^2$). Otherwise, the finite σ_e^2 reduces the less-informed agents' predictive accuracy (i.e., $MSE_L > \sigma_\eta^2$).

More importantly, due to the information diffusion, Group H fails to obtain the most accurate forecast. If there is no information diffusion process, then both groups form their forecasts independently, and Group H obtains the minimum forecast error, $MSE_H = \sigma_\eta^2$. However, if the process exists, with a finite σ_e^2, Group H has higher forecast errors: $MSE_H = (\beta\mu\bar{c}_L)^2 \sigma_e^2 + \sigma_\eta^2 > \sigma_\eta^2$ in Eq. (7.18). This result is known as the boomerang effect on the MSE.[15]

The results for Group H indicate only the two limit points of the variance observation errors ($\sigma_e^2 = 0$ or $\sigma_e^2 \to \infty$) produce the most efficient outcome. Stated differently, Group L uses the expectations from the highly informed group (i.e., when $\sigma_e^2 = 0$, $\bar{c}_L = 1$); this implies Group L's expectations become exactly the same as those of Group H, resulting in both groups forecasting efficiently. However, if $\sigma_e^2 \to \infty$, then $\bar{c}_L = 0$. In this case, Group L is unable to interpret Group H's expectations and eventually discards them. Both groups learn independently and the boomerang effect is absent.

Surveyed inflation expectations from the SRC at the University of Michigan are used to test the dynamics embedded in Eq. (7.5). The tests are directed at two things. First, the theoretical model assumes information diffusion

---

[14] For comparison, the MSE's are calculated for situations in which both groups have the same (full) information set and learn independently. Both groups' MSE's are at a minimum when $MSE_L = MSE_H = \sigma_\eta^2$.

[15] See Proposition 4 in Granato et al. (2008, 360–361).

Information Diffusion 133

is asymmetric: The expectations of Group H influence the expectations of Group L. The first test serves as a necessary condition for the second test. The second test examines whether the boomerang effect exists and involves examining whether larger observation errors made by Group L agents σ_e^2 result in greater inaccuracy in inflation predictions by Group H agents MSE_H.[16]

Granger causality tests are used to test for endogeneity. Since there is evidence the data possess unit roots, first differences for all classes of inflation forecasts are employed. The Akaike information criterion (AIC) and Lagrange multiplier (LM) test statistics suggest that the VAR system with lag order of seven is preferable on the basis of a minimum AIC and no serial correlation or heteroskedasticity in the residuals.[17]

Table 7.1 reports the Granger causality test results. The null hypotheses that Group H does not Granger-cause Group L2 is rejected (p-value equals 0.030). However, Group H does not Granger-cause Group L1 (p-value equals 0.122). Note, too, Group L1 Granger-causes Group L2 (p-value equals 0.047). In contrast, Groups L1 and L2 do not Granger-cause Group H. Another finding is Group L2 does not Granger-cause Group L1's forecasts. Overall, the testing results in Table 7.1 clearly indicate asymmetric information diffusion exists: The inflation forecasts of the more-educated affect the less-educated.

---

[16] Inflation expectations surveys are conducted by the SRC at the University of Michigan and the results are published in the Survey of Consumer Attitudes. Since 1978 the center has conducted monthly telephone interviews from a sample of at least 500 households randomly selected to represent all American households, excluding those in Alaska and Hawaii. Each monthly sample is drawn as an independent cross-section sample of households. Respondents selected in the drawing are interviewed once and then re-interviewed six months later. This rotating process creates a total sample made up of 60 percent new respondents and 40 percent prior respondents.

Survey respondents are asked approximately 50 core questions that cover three broad areas of consumer opinions: personal finances, business conditions, and buying conditions. The following questions relate to measuring inflation expectations:

1. During the next 12 months, do you think that prices in general will go up, or go down, or stay where they are now?
2. By about what percent do you expect prices to go (up/down), on the average, during the next 12 months?

If respondents expect that the price level will go up (or down) on question 1, they are asked in the second question to provide the exact percent the price level will increase (or decrease); otherwise the second question is coded as zero percent. Then divide the inflation expectation survey data into different educational categories. To be consistent with the theory, the respondents with college or graduate degrees are put in the highly informed group (Group H) and those without a college degree are categorized as the less-informed group (Group L). Based on the unique characteristics of the data set, it is possible to further separate Group L into two distinct levels: (1) high school diploma or some college (denoted as "L1") and (2) less than high school or no high school diploma (denoted as "L2").

[17] The unit root test results are based on both the augmented Dickey–Fuller test (1979), and the Elliott–Rothenberg–Stock test (1996). The results of the unit root tests and of the lag order selection for the VAR are available from the current authors on request.

TABLE 7.1. *Granger causality test results: Group H, Group L1, and Group L2*

If forecasts of the higher educated group Granger-cause those of the less educated group?	
Null hypothesis	Chi-sq statistics [*p*-value]
a. Group H does not Granger-cause Group $L1$	11.401 [0.122]
b. Group H does not Granger-cause Group $L2$	15.522** [0.030]
c. Group $L1$ does not Granger-cause Group $L2$	14.253** [0.047]

If forecasts of the less educated group Granger-cause those of the higher educated group?	
Null hypothesis	Chi-sq statistics [*p*-value]
d. Group $L1$ does not Granger-cause Group H	3.897 [0.792]
e. Group $L2$ does not Granger-cause Group H	7.583 [0.371]
f. Group $L2$ does not Granger-cause Group $L1$	2.603 [0.919]

** indicates statistical significance at 5 percent.

To test for the existence of the boomerang effect requires a determination of whether a "positive" relation exists between the size of observation errors of less-informed agents and more-informed agents' forecast inaccuracy size. The size of observation error e_t is based on its variance σ_e^2, while the forecast (prediction) accuracy of the more-informed is the size of the mean square error of Group H's forecasts MSE_H.

Using Eqs. (7.9) and (7.10), we present the following regression model:

$$E^*_{Lj,t-1}\pi_t = a_{Lj} + b_{Lj}x_{t-1} + c_{Lj}(E^*_{H,t-1}\pi_t + e_{Lj,t-1}), \qquad (7.19)$$

where $E^*_{Lj,t-1}\pi_t$ and $E^*_{H,t-1}\pi_t$ represent the inflation forecasts of less and more-informed groups, respectively, $j \in \{1, 2\}$, and x_t is the information set for inflation forecasts for Group L, which includes the current and lagged federal funds rate, the current inflation rate, and oil prices.[18] The series $\sigma^2_{e_{Lj}}$ is constructed using a rolling regression technique in which the regression window of (7.19) is set at 12 years and moved forward every quarter.[19]

The observational error generated from Eq. (7.19) for the less-informed groups is:

$$e_{Lj,t-1} = \frac{E^*_{Lj,t-1}\pi_t - a_{Lj} - b_{Lj}x_{t-1} - c_{Lj}E^*_{H,t-1}\pi_t}{c_{Lj}}.$$

---

[18] The data are from the FRED database provided by the Federal Reserve Bank of St. Louis.
[19] 15-year and 10-year rolling regression windows are used in this empirical analysis. However, results from using different choices of regression windows do not show any substantive or statistical difference.

The variances of the observational error $\sigma^2_{e_{Lj},t}$ for the less-informed groups are:

$$\sigma^2_{e_{Lj},t} = \frac{\sum_t^{t+s} e^2_{Lj,t}}{s-1}, \forall t,$$

where s represents the number of quarters (size of the window for the rolling regression).

Applying the same rolling regression technique to estimate the mean square error for Group H:

$$MSE_{H,t} = \frac{\sum_t^{t+s} \left(\pi_t - E^*_{H,t-1}\pi_t\right)^2}{s}, \forall t.$$

A concern is the long-run (inter-)relation between MSE_H and $\sigma^2_{e_{Lj}}$ and also whether a larger value of $\sigma^2_{e_{Lj}}$ causes MSE_H to increase. This result would support the boomerang effect hypothesis. To obtain consistent estimates of the unknown parameters entering the system consisting of MSE_H, $\sigma^2_{e_{L1}}$, and $\sigma^2_{e_{L2}}$, we first characterize the stochastic properties of these underlying variables.

Table 7.2 presents the augmented Dickey–Fuller (1979) and Elliott–Rothenberg–Stock (1996) test results: MSE_H, $\sigma^2_{e_{L1}}$, and $\sigma^2_{e_{L2}}$ all contain a unit root and the cointegration methodology is appropriate for exploring the long-run (inter-)relation among the variables and the existence of a boomerang effect.[20] We now turn to the boomerang effect. Recall, the empirical implication of the model (see Eq. (7.18)) is that when information diffusion exists – with a finite σ^2_e – Group H will have a higher forecast error since $MSE_H = (\beta\mu\bar{c}_L)^2 \sigma^2_e + \sigma^2_\eta > \sigma^2_\eta$.

Panel A in Table 7.3 reports the results of the cointegration tests of the long-run relation between MSE_H and $\sigma^2_{e_{Lj}}$. Columns 1 and 2 in Panel A summarize the results of cointegrating relations for two pairs of variables, $(MSE_H, \sigma^2_{e_{L1}})$ and $(MSE_H, \sigma^2_{e_{L2}})$. Both the maximum eigenvalues and trace statistics indicate that there are long-run equilibrium relations for both. Using the Johansen cointegration procedure, they find the cointegrating vectors of $\left(MSE_H, \sigma^2_{e_{Lj}}\right)$ are $(1, -29.58)$ and $(1, -21.54)$, for $j \in \{1, 2\}$.

These results show a positive long-run equilibrium relation with the existence of the boomerang effect between MSE_H and σ^2_e. It suggests the mean square error on inflation forecasts for the respondents who hold a college degree or above (MSE_H) are positively related with the measurement errors resulting from the nondegree-holding respondents σ^2_e.

The results in column (3), where the cointegrating system consists of all three variables of MSE_H, $\sigma^2_{e_{L1}}$, and $\sigma^2_{e_{L2}}$, provide further evidence to support the

---

[20] Granato et al. (2011) use the Johansen test for this particular task. See the application section of the Appendix.

TABLE 7.2. *Unit root test results for* MSE_H, $\sigma^2_{e,L1}$, *and* $\sigma^2_{e,L2}$

A. Data in levels

	Augmented Dickey–Fuller test			Elliott–Rothenberg-Stock Test		
Variable	$DF_\mu{}^a$	$DF_\tau{}^b$	Optimal lags	$DF - GLS_\mu{}^c$	$DF - GLS_\tau{}^c$	Conclusion
MSE_H	−2.222	−0.661	3	−0.305	−1.690	$I(1)$
$\sigma^2_{e,L1}$	−0.826	−2.797	3	−0.531	−2.638	$I(1)$
$\sigma^2_{e,L2}$	−1.896	−3.327*	6	−0.743	−3.327**	$I(1)$

B. Data in first differences

			Optimal			
Variable	$DF_\mu{}^a$	$DF_\tau{}^b$	lags	$DF - GLS_\mu{}^c$	$DF - GLS_\tau{}^c$	Conclusion
MSE_H	−4.536***	−4.966***	2	−2.041*	−2.371**	$I(0)$
$\sigma^2_{e,L1}$	−7.616***	−7.588***	2	−2.957***	−2.973*	$I(0)$
$\sigma^2_{e,L2}$	−7.002***	−6.926***	7	−3.367***	−3.440**	$I(0)$

***,**, and * indicate statistical significance at 1, 5, and 10 percent, respectively.
[a]Test allows for a constant; one-sided test of the null hypothesis that the variable is nonstationary. Fuller (1976) 1 and 5 percent critical values for a sample size of 41 equal −3.597 and −2.934, respectively.
[b]Test allows for a constant; one-sided test of the null hypothesis that the variable is nonstationary. Fuller (1976) 1 and 5 percent critical values for a sample size of 41 equal −4.196 and −3.522, respectively.
[c]Test allows for a constant; one-sided test of the null hypothesis that the variable is nonstationary. The critical values, not reported here, are calculated from the response surface estimates of table 1, Cheung and Lai (1995).

boomerang effect found in columns (1) and (2). With an estimated cointegrating vector of $(MSE_H, \sigma^2_{e_{L1}}, \sigma^2_{e_{L2}}) = (1, -20.52, -0.79)$, this robustness check shows both $\sigma^2_{e_{L1}}$ and $\sigma^2_{e_{L2}}$ are positively related with MSE_H in the long run; that is, $MSE_H = 20.52\sigma^2_{e_{L1}} + 0.79\sigma^2_{e_{L2}}$. The results in column (4) also show the robust cointegrating vector among the three variables is solely the result of the boomerang effect since the variances of the measurement errors in the two levels of Group L are not cointegrated.

Furthermore, Granato et al. (2011) examine if the boomerang effect is robust when both levels of Group L are combined. They determine this case by averaging the inflation expectations from Groups L1 and L2 to obtain σ^2_e. The cointegration estimation indicates (results available from the authors) the boomerang effect is still robust: σ^2_e is positively related with MSE_H.

Additional support for a boomerang effect occurs if the direction of causality runs from σ^2_e to MSE_H (but not vice versa). Panel B of Table 7.3 gives the results of the Granger-causality tests. The results from systems (1) and (2) indicate rejection of the null hypotheses that $\sigma^2_{e_{Lj}}$ does not Granger-cause MSE_H, for

Information Diffusion

TABLE 7.3. *Johansen cointegration tests and Granger causality tests:* MSE_H, $\sigma^2_{e,L1}$, *and* $\sigma^2_{e,L2}$

A. Rank test and cointegrating relation

	\multicolumn{8}{c}{Variables in the system}
	$MSE_H, \sigma^2_{e,L1}$ [a] (1)		$MSE_H, \sigma^2_{e,L2}$ [b] (2)		$MSE_H, \sigma^2_{e,L1}, \sigma^2_{e,L2}$ [c] (3)		$\sigma^2_{e,L1}, \sigma^2_{e,L2}$ [d] (4)	
Null hypothesis	$\hat{\lambda}_{max}$	Trace	$\hat{\lambda}_{max}$	Trace	$\hat{\lambda}_{max}$	Trace	$\hat{\lambda}_{max}$	Trace
No rank	12.82** [11.44]	15.22** [12.53]	8.00 [11.44]	12.20* [12.53]	48.60*** [22.00]	87.52*** [34.91]	6.52 [11.44]	8.80 [12.53]
At most 1 rank	2.40 [3.84]	2.40 [3.84]	4.20 [3.84]	4.20 [3.84]	32.65*** [15.67]	38.92*** [19.96]	2.28 [3.84]	2.28 [3.84]
At most 2 ranks	-	-	-	-	6.27 [9.24]	6.27 [9.24]	-	-
Conclusion	\multicolumn{2}{c}{1 cointegrating relation}	\multicolumn{2}{c}{1 cointegrating relation}	\multicolumn{2}{c}{2 cointegrating relations}	\multicolumn{2}{c}{None}
Estimated Cointegration Vector	\multicolumn{2}{c}{$(MSE_H, \sigma^2_{e,L1}) =$ $(1, -29.58)$}	\multicolumn{2}{c}{$(MSE_H, \sigma^2_{e,L1}) =$ $(1, -21.54)$}	\multicolumn{2}{c}{$(MSE_H, \sigma^2_{e,L1}, \sigma^2_{e,L2}) =$ $(1, -20.52, -0.79)$}	\multicolumn{2}{c}{None}

B. The direction of causality in VECM

	\multicolumn{4}{c}{Variables in the system}
	$MSE_H, \sigma^2_{e,L1}$ [a] (1)	$MSE_H, \sigma^2_{e,L2}$ [b] (2)	$MSE_H, \sigma^2_{e,L1}, \sigma^2_{e,L2}$ [c] (3)	$\sigma^2_{e,L1}, \sigma^2_{e,L2}$ [d] (4)
Null hypothesis	Chi-sq statistics [*p*-value]	Chi-sq statistics [*p*-value]	Chi-sq statistics [*p*-value]	Chi-sq statistics [*p*-value]
$\sigma^2_{e,L1}$ does not cause MSE_H	14.36*** [0.006]	-	21.04*** [0.007]	-
MSE_H does not cause $\sigma^2_{e,L1}$	3.82 [0.430]	-	5.68 [0.682]	-
$\sigma^2_{e,L2}$ does not cause MSE_H	-	19.43*** [0.000]	30.87*** [0.000]	-
MSE_H does not cause $\sigma^2_{e,L1}$	-	4.72 [0.194]	7.15 [0.512]	-

***, **, and * indicate statistical significance at 1, 5, and 10 percent, respectively. We use the AIC criterion to choose the optimal number lags to be included in each empirical model. 5 percent critical values, from Osterwald-Lenum (1992), for rank tests are in parentheses.
[a] Test allows for a constant but no trend in the data space and 4 lags are included in the system.
[b] Test allows for a constant but no trend in the data space and 3 lags are included in the system.
[c] Test allows for a constant but no trend in the cointegration space and 4 lags are included in the system and 8 lags are included in the system.
[d] Test allows for a constant but no trend in the data space and 4 lags are included in the system.

$j \in \{1, 2\}$. The respective test statistics are equal to 14.36 and 19.43 and are significant at the 0.05 level. On the other hand, the null hypothesis (for reverse causation) is not rejected. Column (3) in Panel B reports associated results are consistent with findings in columns (1) and (2).

To sum up, the tests indicate a boomerang effect exists: The long run "cointegrated" relation between the variance of observational errors from the less educated group influence the mean square error of the more educated group's expectations.

7.5 SUMMARY

In this chapter, we demonstrate how Granato et al. (2011) test information diffusion and the boomerang effect. This model and test may be extended in various ways. First, the model itself assumes the less informed agents are passive recipients of the information. There is a point in this model where the variance of the information transmission leads the less informed agents to discard the information. However, this process is not modeled and there is no estimation of how long it would take for the less informed agents to discard the information.

A second point of examination is adding more information on the characteristics of various groups and their willingness to cooperate and use information. Jasso (2008), for example, has shown how various group characteristics can lead to situations where there is enhanced or reduced cooperation.

A third way of extending the model and test is to use experiments and vary not only the size of the information set but also the proportions of more-informed and less-informed agents (Granato et al. 2008). These population proportions, along with alternative types of information (not related to inflation expectations), and repeated play would add to the robustness and the circumstances when various information diffusion scenarios contribute to a boomerang effect.

7.6 APPENDIX

The tools in this chapter are used to create a transparent and testable linkage using social interaction, expectations, learning, and combining these behavioral concepts with empirical concepts – simultaneity and prediction error. The formal analogues for social interaction is mathematical substitution and the analogues for expectations and learning have been presented in Chapters 4 through 6 and will not be repeated. The applied statistical tools used in this chapter require further background in the use of advanced time series methods. We then demonstrate the use of these tools in the empirical application for this chapter.

The Granger Causality Test

The applied statistical tools used in this chapter assist in sorting out issues of simultaneity (endogeneity) and causality. One basic tool to determine what variables are exogenous or endogenous is the Granger causality test (1969). Implementing single equation Granger causality tests is straightforward. In the case of single equation estimation, Freeman (1983) gives a clear exposition and we follow it here. The test requires estimating two equations in a manner similar to F-tests for the relevance of a regressor. One unrestricted regression (including both variables) and one restricted regression (including only one variable) are estimated separately and the residuals are compared to see if there is a significant "difference" going from the unrestricted model to the restricted model. To test whether X_t Granger causes Y_t, we estimate the unrestricted model as:

$$Y_t = \sum_{i=1}^{T} \alpha_{1i} Y_{t-i} + \sum_{i=1}^{T} \beta_{1i} X_{t-i} + v_{1t}, \qquad (7.20)$$

and the restricted model as:

$$Y_t = \sum_{i=1}^{T} \delta_{1i} Y_{t-i} + v_{2t}. \qquad (7.21)$$

Then, we construct the following null and alternative hypotheses:

$$H_0 : \sum_{i=1}^{T} \beta_{1i} X_{t-i} = 0 \rightarrow \text{"}x_t \text{ does not Granger-cause } y_t\text{"}$$

$$H_A : \sum_{i=1}^{T} \beta_{1i} X_{t-i} \neq 0 \rightarrow \text{"}x_t \text{ Granger-causes } y_t\text{"}.$$

By obtaining the residual sum of squares from both models, we compute the following F-statistic:

$$\frac{\frac{RSS_R - RSS_U}{K_R}}{\frac{RSS_U}{(T-K)}} \sim F(K_R, T-K), \qquad (7.22)$$

where T represents sample size, RSS_R the residual sum of squares in the restricted model, RSS_U the residual sum of squares in the unrestricted model, K_R the number of restrictions (i.e., the number of X_{t-i}'s removed), and K the number of regressors (including the intercept) in the unrestricted regression.

As might be expected, it is also necessary to reverse the test and see if Y_t Granger-causes X_t. But, Granger causality tests, while important, can be misleading without an accounting of the behavior of time series data.

Unit Root and Cointegration Tests

In the early 1990s, research in applied econometrics went through a major revolution. The revolution was triggered by the fact that a large number of macroeconomic time series are nonstationary: Their means and variances change over time. Standard estimation methods assume that the means and variances of the variables are constant and independent of time.[21] Classical estimation methods with nonstationary variables lead to a spurious regression problem.

One way to avoid spurious regressions is to transform a non-stationary series into a stationary series by differencing. However, the method of differencing also removes long-term relations among a set of non-stationary variables. The challenge then is to account for spurious regressions without removing vital long-term equilibrium relations. Engle and Granger (1987) introduce the concept of cointegration, which addresses the spurious regression problem and captures a long-run linear combination of non-stationary variables. Johansen (1995) emphasizes the importance of cointegration:

> An economic theory is often formulated as a set of behavioural relations or structural equations between the levels of the variables, possibly allowing for lags as well. If the variables are $I(1)$, that is, non-stationary with stationary differences, it is convenient to reformulate them in terms of levels and differences, such that if a structural relation is modeled by a stationary relation then we are led to considering stationary relations between levels, that is, cointegrating relations (page 5).

An essential condition of estimating cointegration relations is that the variables of interest are integrated (or non-stationary) and the linear combination of the integrated variables is stationary. Hence, determining the stationarity of a variable is often the priority of the time series analysis. There are various ways for testing a variable's stationary properties: (1) the Dickey–Fuller test and (2) the Augmented Dickey–Fuller test.

Dickey–Fuller (DF) Test

The Dickey–Fuller (1979) test determines whether a series is stationary in an autoregressive model. To see the motivation for the DF test procedure, we start with a first-order autoregressive model (an AR(1) model) without an intercept:[22]

---

[21] A series of Y_t is considered a stationary time series if it satisfies the following properties:

1. Constant mean: $E(Y_t) = \mu$;
2. Constant variance: $\text{var}(Y_t) = E(Y_t - \mu)^2 = \sigma^2$; and
3. Time-invariant covariance: $\gamma_k = E[(Y_t - \mu)(Y_{t+k} - \mu)]$, where γ_k is the covariance between the values of Y_t and Y_{t+k}.

   If $k = 0$, then we have $\gamma_0 = E[(Y_t - \mu)(Y_t - \mu)] = \sigma^2$.

[22] See Chapter 5 Section 5.6.3 for the detailed discussion on the autoregressive process.

Information Diffusion

$$Y_t = \phi Y_{t-1} + \varepsilon_t, \tag{7.23}$$

where ε_t has a zero mean and is independently and identically distributed, i.e., $\varepsilon_t \sim iid(0, \sigma^2)$ (see Eq. (5.18)). The parameter ϕ determines the stationarity of the series. If $|\phi| < 1$, then Y_t is stationary. Therefore, the estimate of ϕ is efficient and the usual t-statistics can be used to test if ϕ is statistically different from zero. However, if $\phi = 1$, the series of Y_t becomes non-stationary.[23] Furthermore, we describe this non-stationary series of Y_t as integrated of order one, that is, Y_t is $I(1)$, since the first difference of Y_t (i.e., $\Delta Y_t = \varepsilon_t$) is stationary.[24] The Y_t is $I(1)$, implying future changes do not depend on the current level. As a result, the DF test simply determines whether ϕ is significantly less than one. If ϕ is significantly less than one, the series of Y_t is stationary (no unit root). However, if ϕ is not significantly less than one, we conclude that the series of Y_t is a unit root process.

To perform the DF test, we first rewrite the AR(1) model by subtracting Y_{t-1} from both sides of Eq. (7.23):

$$\Delta Y_t = \gamma Y_{t-1} + \varepsilon_t, \tag{7.24}$$

where $\gamma = \phi - 1$. We estimate Eq. (7.24) and form the following null hypothesis $H_0 : \gamma = 0$ implying $Y_t = Y_{t-1} + \varepsilon_t$ (i.e., the existence of a unit root process),

---

[23] The series of Y_t presented in Eq. (7.23) is not stationary since the variance of Y_t is not time invariant if $\phi = 1$. To show this, we first calculate the expected value of Y_t:

$$E(Y_t) = E\left(Y_0 + \sum_{i=1}^{t} \varepsilon_i\right) = E(Y_0) + E\left(\sum \varepsilon_i\right) = Y_0,$$

where $E(\varepsilon_i) = 0$ (see Eq. (5.20)). Now, we compute the variance of Y_t as follows:

$$E\left[(Y_t - E(Y_t))^2\right] = E\left[(Y_t - Y_0)^2\right]$$

$$= E\left[\left(Y_0 + \sum_{i=1}^{t} \varepsilon_i - Y_0\right)^2\right] = E\left[\left(\sum \varepsilon_i\right)^2\right]$$

$$= E\left[(\varepsilon_1 + \varepsilon_2 + \cdots + \varepsilon_3)(\varepsilon_1 + \varepsilon_2 + \cdots + \varepsilon_3)\right]$$

$$= E\left(\varepsilon_1^2\right) + E\left(\varepsilon_2^2\right) + \cdots + E\left(\varepsilon_t^2\right)$$

$$= t\sigma^2,$$

where $E\left(\varepsilon_i^2\right) = \sigma^2$ and $E\left(\varepsilon_i \varepsilon_j\right) = 0$, for $i, j = 1, 2, \ldots, t$, and $i \neq j$. As t increases, the variance $E\left[(Y_t - E(Y_t))^2\right] = t\sigma^2$ increases.

[24] If Y_t is required to be differenced d times to become a stationary series, then Y_t is integrated of order d (i.e., $I(d)$).

and alternative hypothesis $H_a : \gamma < 0$ (i.e., Y_t is a stationary process).[25] The test statistic is referred to as $\hat{\tau}$, and the corresponding critical values depend on the sample size. The critical values can be found in Fuller (1976) or MacKinnon (1991).

The Dickey–Fuller test can also be used to test for the existence of a unit root with the following extended specifications:

$$Y_t = \mu + \phi Y_{t-1} + \varepsilon_t, \tag{7.25}$$

and:

$$Y_t = \mu + \beta t + \phi_1 Y_{t-1} + \varepsilon_t. \tag{7.26}$$

Compared with Eq. (7.23), Eq. (7.25) has an additional deterministic term μ, which is known as a drift, whereas Eq. (7.26) has both a drift and a deterministic trend βt. To test for the presence of a unit root, we apply the similar procedure on Eqs. (7.25) and (7.26) by subtracting Y_{t-1} from both sides, respectively:

$$\Delta Y_t = \mu + \gamma Y_{t-1} + \varepsilon_t, \tag{7.27}$$

and:

$$\Delta Y_t = \mu + \beta t + \gamma Y_{t-1} + \varepsilon_t. \tag{7.28}$$

Given the null hypothesis is $H_0 : \gamma = 0$ against the alternative hypothesis $H_a : \gamma < 0$, the test statistic $\hat{\tau}_\mu$ can be obtained for Eq. (7.27), and $\hat{\tau}_\beta$ for Eq. (7.28).

Augmented Dickey–Fuller (ADF) Test
The Augmented Dickey–Fuller test is an extended version of the DF test. This test allows for the possibility of persistence in the difference process. Consider a general series that follows an AR(p) process:

$$Y_t = \mu + \phi_1 Y_{t-1} + \phi_2 Y_{t-2} + \cdots + \phi_p Y_{t-p} + \varepsilon_t. \tag{7.29}$$

If we do not determine (or even ignore) the higher order of autoregressive process (i.e., $\phi_2 Y_{t-2} + \cdots + \phi_p Y_{t-p}$) but we simply estimate Y_t with a simplest specification of the first-order of AR process ($\phi_1 Y_{t-1}$) only, then the implicit regression model looks as follows:

$$Y_t = \mu + \phi_1 Y_{t-1} + \upsilon_t, \tag{7.30}$$

where the residual term υ_t consists of a linear combination of the higher order autoregressive process $(\phi_2 Y_{t-2} + \cdots + \phi_p Y_{t-p})$ and a stochastic error term ε_t:

$$\upsilon_t = \phi_2 Y_{t-2} + \phi_3 Y_{t-3} + \cdots + \phi_p Y_{t-p} + \varepsilon_t. \tag{7.31}$$

---
[25] We note that $\gamma > 0$ is not assumed in the alternative hypothesis because it corresponds to $\phi > 1$. Under this condition, the process generates an unstable (explosive) series of Y_t, which is not commonly observed in the real world.

Information Diffusion

According to this empirical model, the estimated residual v_t possesses serial correlation, where the lagged values of Y_t are present in v_t and v_{t-k}, for $k \geq 1$. To address the issue of serial correlation, a common strategy is to increase the orders of the AR process in Eq. (7.30) until the residual becomes a white noise.

Practically speaking, this searching strategy begins by selecting a maximum lag length (or the maximum order of AR process), say p^*, that likely generates (7.30) with white noise residuals. For example, if Y_t is monthly data, a researcher can choose the maximum lag length p^* at 12. Then, the researcher successively estimates the model by reducing the order of AR process, such as AR($p^* - 1$), AR($p^* - 2$), and so on, and ceases the process when the residual is no longer a white noise. Alternatively, the researcher can choose the optimal level of p according to various information criteria, such as Akaike Information Criterion (AIC) and Schwarz Information Criterion (SIC).

Assuming that the variable of interest has a higher-order of AR process (i.e, $p > 1$), the original DF test cannot be applied to determine the present of the unit root process due to the problem of serial correlation. Fuller (1976) suggests an alternative unit root test by rewriting the AR(p) process as follows:

$$\Delta Y_t = \mu + \gamma Y_{t-1} + \sum_{j=1}^{p-1} \alpha_j \Delta Y_{t-j} + \varepsilon_t. \tag{7.32}$$

Under the null hypothesis of $\gamma = 0$, Y_t is a unit root process and is not stationary. On the other hand, under the alternative hypothesis of $\gamma < 0$, Y_t is stationary. The associated test statistic is referred as $\hat{\tau}_\mu$. This unit root test under the AR(p) specification is known as the augmented Dickey–Fuller (ADF) test.

To understand the concept of the ADF test, we use an AR(2) process as an example (i.e., $p = 2$). Equation (7.29) is simplified as the following AR(2) process:

$$Y_t = \mu + \phi_1 Y_{t-1} + \phi_2 Y_{t-2} + \varepsilon_t. \tag{7.33}$$

By adding and subtracting $\phi_2 Y_{t-1}$ on the right hand of Eq. (7.33), we have:

$$Y_t = \mu + (\phi_1 + \phi_2) Y_{t-1} - \phi_2 (Y_{t-1} - Y_{t-2}) + \varepsilon_t. \tag{7.34}$$

Now we subtract Y_{t-1} from both sides of Eq. (7.34):

$$\Delta Y_t = \mu + \gamma Y_{t-1} + \alpha_1 \Delta Y_{t-1} + \varepsilon_t, \tag{7.35}$$

where $\gamma = \phi_1 + \phi_2 - 1$ and $\alpha_1 = -\phi_2$. Equation (7.35) is known as the first-order Augmented Dickey–Fuller (ADF(1)) model.

Similarly, the ADF test can be extended to Eq. (7.29) with a deterministic trend. The ADF(p) model can be written as:

$$\Delta Y_t = \mu + \beta t + \gamma Y_{t-1} + \sum_{j=1}^{p-1} \alpha_j \Delta Y_{t-j} + \varepsilon_t. \quad (7.36)$$

In this case, the unit-root test statistic for $H_0 : \gamma = 0$ is referred as $\hat{\tau}_\beta$.

Testing for Cointegration: The Engle-Granger (EG) Procedure

The difference between a cointegrating regression and a spurious regression is whether a linear combination of $I(1)$ variables is stationary. Suppose the variables X_t and Y_t are random walk processes, their linear combination can be written as:

$$Y_t = \varphi_1 + \varphi_2 X_t + \xi_t, \quad (7.37)$$

where ξ_t is the error term. If the error term is stationary (i.e., $\xi_t \sim I(0)$), then Eq. (7.37) is known as a cointegrating regression. On the other hand, if $\xi_t \sim I(1)$, then Eq. (7.37) is known as a spurious regression or a misspecified regression involving some omitted relevant $I(1)$ variables.

To systematically determining cointegration relations, Engle and Granger (1987) suggest a two-step procedure. The first step of the test is to use either the DF or ADF tests to assess the order of integration for each time series in the regression. For simplicity, consider the bivariate case involving X_t and Y_t.

- **Step 1:** Use the DF or ADF procedures to determine if both X_t and Y_t are $I(1)$. If both X_t and Y_t are $I(1)$, regress Y_t on X_t and extract the residual ξ_t from the estimated regression model:

$$Y_t = \varphi_1 + \varphi_2 X_t + \xi_t.$$

- **Step 2:** Perform an ADF test for $\hat{\xi}_t$:

$$\Delta \hat{\xi}_t = \gamma \hat{\xi}_{t-1} + \sum_{i=1}^{p-1} \alpha_i \Delta \hat{\xi}_{t-i} + v_t,$$

where the hypotheses are:

$H_0 : \gamma = 0 \Rightarrow \xi_t \sim I(1)$ "X_t and Y_t are not cointegrated."

$H_A : \gamma < 0 \Rightarrow \xi_t \sim I(0)$ "X_t and Y_t are cointegrated."

The second step is to assess whether the residuals ξ_t are consistent with $I(1)$ process. If it is $I(1)$, Eq. (7.37) is not a cointegrating regression. On the other hand, if it is $I(0)$, then Eq. (7.37) is a cointegrating regression.

Note that the Engle–Granger procedure requires that one of the jointly endogenous variables is treated as the dependent variable in the regression.

Choosing different variables as the dependent variable might lead to different conclusions about the cointegrating relation.

The Johansen Procedure

Johansen (1988, 1992) introduces an alternative multivariate – system-based – approach. This approach has an advantage over the Engle–Granger procedure since all variables are treated as endogenous. Within a system of equations, testing for cointegration relations is based on the rank of a matrix.

The Johansen procedure can be illustrated by considering a kth-order vector autoregressive model (VAR(k)) with N variables:

$$X_t = \Pi_1 X_{t-1} + \Pi_2 X_{t-2} + \cdots + \Pi_k X_{t-k} + \Phi D_t + \epsilon_t, \text{ for } t = 1, \ldots, T, \quad (7.38)$$

where X_t is a $N \times 1$ vector, D_t is a $d \times 1$ vector of deterministic terms which can contain a constant, a trend, and (seasonal or event) dummy variables. Equation (7.38) can be re-parameterized as:

$$\Delta X_t = \Pi_1 X_{t-1} + \Gamma_1 \Delta X_{t-1}$$
$$+ \Gamma_2 \Delta X_{t-2} + \cdots + \Gamma_{k-1} \Delta X_{t-(k-1)} + \Phi D_t + \epsilon_t \quad (7.39)$$
$$= \Pi_1 X_{t-1} + \sum_{i=1}^{k-1} \Gamma_i \Delta X_{t-i} + \Phi D_t + \epsilon_t, \text{ for } t = 1, \ldots, T,$$

where Π_1 is a coefficient matrix on the lagged level X_{t-1}, and k is a lag length that can be chosen based on various information criteria (e.g., AIC and SIC) or a test for the absence of serial correlation in the residuals.

In Eq. (7.39), Johansen (1995) decomposes Π_1 into two matrices α and β and the effect of the levels is isolated in the matrix $\Pi_1 = \alpha \beta'$. The row of β' (i.e., the column of β) gives cointegrating vectors, and the associated hypothesis test is whether any column of β is statistically different from zero. Furthermore, the matrix α is a weight matrix determining how each cointegrating vector is involved in the N-equation VAR model.

To determine the number of cointegrating vectors in the system, it is required to compute the cointegration rank of $\Pi_1 = \alpha \beta'$.[26] To do so, we simplify the notations of Eq. (7.39) as follows:

$$Z_{0t} = \alpha \beta' Z_{1t} + \Psi Z_{2t} + \epsilon_t, \quad (7.40)$$

where $Z_{0t} = \Delta X_t$ is an $N \times 1$ vector, $Z_{1t} = X_{t-1}$ is an $N \times 1$ vector, $Z_{2t} = (\Delta X_{t-1}, \Delta X_{t-2}, \ldots, \Delta X_{t-(k-1)}, D_t)'$ is an $[N(k-1) + d] \times 1$ vector, and $\Psi = (\Gamma_1, \Gamma_2, \ldots, \Gamma_{k-1}, \Phi)$ is an $N \times [N(k-1) + d]$ matrix. The model is then estimated by maximizing the log likelihood function $\log L(\Psi, \alpha, \beta, \Omega)$.

---

[26] See Johansen (1995) for the complete mathematical derivation.

The corresponding first-order conditions can be presented as:

$$\sum_{t=1}^{T}(Z_{0t} - \alpha\beta' Z_{1t} - \widehat{\Psi} Z_{2t})Z_{2t}' = 0. \tag{7.41}$$

Using a product moment matrix, we rewrite Eq. (7.41) as:

$$M_{02} = \alpha\beta' M_{12} + \widehat{\Psi} M_{22}, \tag{7.42}$$

where the product matrix is:

$$M_{ij} = T^{-1}\sum_{t=1}^{T} Z_{it} Z_{jt}', \tag{7.43}$$

for $i, j = 0, 1, 2$. Multiplying Eq. (7.43) by M_{22}^{-1} and solving for $\widehat{\Psi}$ gives:

$$\Psi(\alpha, \beta) = M_{02} M_{22}^{-1} - \alpha\beta' M_{12} M_{22}^{-1}. \tag{7.44}$$

The residuals are therefore:

$$R_{0t} = Z_{0t} - M_{02} M_{22}^{-1} Z_{2t}, \tag{7.45}$$
$$R_{1t} = Z_{1t} - M_{12} M_{22}^{-1} Z_{2t}.$$

Note that R_{0t} (R_{1t}) gives residuals obtained by regressing ΔX_t (X_{t-1}) on ΔX_{t-1}, $\Delta X_{t-2},...,\Delta X_{t-(k+1)}$, and D_t. By substituting Ψ from Eq. (7.44) into Eq. (7.40), we solve for the residuals of $\widehat{\epsilon}_t$:

$$\begin{aligned}\widehat{\epsilon}_t &= Z_{0t} - \alpha\beta' Z_{1t} - \Psi Z_{2t} \\ &= Z_{0t} - \alpha\beta' Z_{1t} - (M_{02} M_{22}^{-1} - \alpha\beta' M_{12} M_{22}^{-1}) Z_{2t} \\ &= Z_{0t} - M_{02} M_{22}^{-1} Z_{2t} - \alpha\beta'(Z_{1t} - M_{12} M_{22}^{-1} Z_{2t}) \\ &= R_{0t} - \alpha\beta' R_{1t}. \end{aligned} \tag{7.46}$$

Now we rewrite Eq. (7.46) as a regression equation, where R_{0t} is regressed on R_{1t}:

$$R_{0t} = \alpha\beta' R_{1t} + \widehat{\epsilon}_t. \tag{7.47}$$

Information Diffusion

For any fixed β, we estimate α and Ω by regressing R_{0t} on $\beta' R_{1t}$:

$$\hat{\alpha}(\beta) = S_{01}\beta(\beta' S_{11}\beta)^{-1}, \tag{7.48}$$

and:

$$\hat{\Omega}(\beta) = S_{00} - \hat{\alpha}(\beta)(\beta' S_{11}\beta)\hat{\alpha}(\beta') \quad \text{(by substituting for } \hat{\alpha}\text{)} \tag{7.49}$$
$$= S_{00} - S_{01}\beta(\beta' S_{11}\beta)^{-1}\beta' S_{10},$$

where $S_{ij} = T^{-1}\sum_{t=1}^{T} R_{it}R_{jt}' = M_{ij} - M_{i2}M_{22}^{-1}M_{2j}$, for $i,j = 0,1$. Apart from the constant, which disappears when forming ratios, the likelihood function to be maximized is now presented as:

$$L(\beta) = |\hat{\Omega}(\beta)| = |S_{00} - S_{01}\beta(\beta' S_{11}\beta)^{-1}\beta' S_{10}|. \tag{7.50}$$

Johansen (1995) shows that the maximum of $L(\beta)$ can be obtained by deriving the corresponding eigenvalues λ and solving the following equation:

$$|\lambda S_{11} - (S_{11} - S_{10}S_{00}^{-1}S_{01})| = 0. \tag{7.51}$$

For N solutions, there are n eigenvalues $\lambda_1, \lambda_2,..., \lambda_N$ with corresponding eigenvectors $v_1, v_2,..., v_N$, where each λ_i is a scalar and each v_i is a $N \times 1$ vector. Then the eigenvalues are arranged in descending order such that $\lambda_1 > \lambda_2 > \cdots > \lambda_N$. The space spanned by the eigenvectors corresponding to the r largest eigenvalues is the r-dimensional "cointegrating space." The estimated $\hat{\beta}$ with a dimension $N \times r$ corresponds to the first r eigenvectors ($r = 0 \sim N$). For example, if $r = 2$, then $\hat{\beta}$ is $N \times 2$. Therefore, the first column is the eigenvector corresponding to the largest eigenvalue, and the second column is the eigenvector corresponding to the second largest eigenvalue. On the other hand, if $r = 0$, then $\Pi_1 = 0$ and all the eigenvalues are zero, denoting the eigenvalues and eigenvectors as $\hat{\lambda}_i$ and $\hat{\beta}$, respectively. Given the choice of $\hat{\beta}$, the resulting value of $L(\beta)$ in Eq. (7.50) becomes:

$$L(\beta) = L(H(r))$$
$$= |S_{00}|\frac{|\hat{\beta}'(S_{11} - S_{10}S_{00}^{-1}S_{01})\hat{\beta}|}{|\hat{\beta}' S_{11}\hat{\beta}|} \tag{7.52}$$
$$= |S_{00}|\prod_{i=1}^{r}(1 - \hat{\lambda}_i),$$

where $H(r)$ denotes the hypothesis that the rank of Π_1 is r. The likelihood ratio test statistic for $H(r)$ against $H(N)$ is:

$$LR(r|N) = L(H(r))/L(H(N))$$
$$= \frac{|S_{00}|\prod_{i=1}^{r}(1-\hat{\lambda}_i)}{|S_{00}|\prod_{i=1}^{N}(1-\hat{\lambda}_i)}. \tag{7.53}$$

After cancelling $|S_{00}|$ in Eq. (7.53), we obtain the Johansen's trace test statistic:

$$Trace(r|N) = -2ln[LR(r|N)] \tag{7.54}$$
$$= -T \sum_{i=r+1}^{N} ln(1-\hat{\lambda}_i),$$

and the nonrejection hypothesis of $H(r)$ means the cointegration rank $\leq r$.

To determine the "exact" cointegration rank for the estimation system, Johansen suggests a sequence of tests. The test sequence starts with a test setting $r = 0$, and the associated test statistic is $Trace(0|N) = -T\sum_{i=1}^{N} ln(1-\hat{\lambda}_i)$. If $Trace(0|N)$ is larger than the critical value (which can be found in Johansen and Juselius 1990), then reject $H(0)$ and test $H(1)$. Otherwise, if $Trace(0|N)$ is smaller than the critical value, then we conclude that there is no cointegrating relation in the system.

For the second test statistic, we set $r = 1$ and the test statistic is $Trace(1|N) = -T\sum_{i=2}^{N} ln(1-\hat{\lambda}_i)$. Similarly, if $Trace(1|N)$ is larger than the critical value, then $H(1)$ is rejected and the next test of $H(2)$ is estimated. The sequence of tests continues until $Trace(N-1|N) = -ln(1-\hat{\lambda}_N)$ in the test of $H(N-1)$. If $Trace(N-1|N)$ exceeds the critical value, then $H(N-1)$ is rejected. Hence, the evidence is in favor of $H(N)$.

A test statistic alternative to the trace test is the maximum eigenvalue test, known as λ_{max}. The λ_{max} test is used to test a cointegrating rank of r against a cointegrating rank of $r + 1$:

$$\lambda_{max} = -2ln[LR(r|r+1)]$$
$$= -Tln(1-\hat{\lambda}_{r+1}). \tag{7.55}$$

The λ_{max} test also involves a sequence of tests. The test sequence starts with $H(0|1)$. If $H(0)$ is not rejected, then the sequence stops. Otherwise, $H(1|2)$ is then tested. This process continues until $H(N-1|N)$ is not rejected. In general, the Johansen procedure can be summarized:

1. Choose an autoregressive order k for estimating a system of variables.
2. Regress ΔX_t on $(\Delta X_{t-1}, \Delta X_{t-2}, \ldots, \Delta X_{t-(k+1)}, D_t)'$ and obtain the residual γ_t^1.

3. Regress X_{t-1} on $(\Delta X_{t-1}, \Delta X_{t-2}, \ldots, \Delta X_{t-(k+1)}, D_t)'$ and obtain the residual γ_t^2.
4. Compute the squares of the canonical correlations between γ_t^1 and γ_t^2, calling these $\varrho_1^2 > \varrho_2^2 > \cdots > \varrho_n^2$.
5. Let T denote the number of time periods available in the sample, and compute the trace test statistic $-T \sum_{i=k+1}^{N} \ln(1 - \varrho_i^2)$. The null hypothesis indicates that there are no more than k cointegrating vectors in the system. Alternatively, one can use the maximum eigenvalue test, which gives the statistic $-T \ln(1 - \varrho_{r+1}^2)$. The null hypothesis in this case is that there are r cointegrating vectors and the alternative hypothesis is that there are $r + 1$ cointegrating vectors.
6. Finally, compare the test statistic to the appropriate table in Johansen and Juselius (1990).

8

Political Parties and Representation

8.1 BACKGROUND

The study of political parties and representation contains various works involving the use or potential linkage of formal and empirical analysis. One well researched area focuses on when and why voters choose one party over the others. This choice is based on the relative political positions of parties on key policies. Spatial theory has played a large role in this literature. The proximity model is a particular type of spatial model of vote choice that assumes voters care about the distance between the policy position of the political parties and candidates compared to their own ideal points: A voter chooses the party who has the policy position closest to their preferred policy position. Under the assumption of vote-maximizing parties and utility maximizing voters, the proximity model predicts policy convergence between political parties (Downs 1957; Black 1958).[1]

Another vote choice model is the discounting model. In the discounting model, voters not only care about the policy proximity to the candidates but also take into account the candidates' ability to deliver on these policies. The ability of candidates to deliver promised policies is influenced by the rules of political institutions. Using a modified discounting model, Calvo and Hellwig (2011) investigated the impact of electoral rules on the policy positions implemented in electoral equilibrium. Voters in this model not only care about

---

[1] Proximity theory implications create an empirical anomaly. Political parties do choose divergent and sometimes extreme policy positions, contrary to the proximity model's predictions. Consequently, the EITM framework provides a fertile platform to explain this empirical anomaly with necessary modification of the theory. For example, the assumption that voters only care about policy proximity is insufficient to explain the empirical reality of policy divergence among political parties. Moreover, among the candidates on their side, voters choose the candidate who is more intense about their issue positioning.

proximity to the party policy but they also take into consideration the electoral rule effect on the seat premium of a party. Seat premium is the difference between the share of seats and the share of votes for a party, and parties that are favored by the electoral rules in terms of seat premium are more likely to take policy positions closer to the center. The small parties that are adversely affected by nonproportional electoral rules take more extreme policy positions.

Kedar's (2005) work on the discounting model is the focus of this chapter. Her EITM linkage centers on the behavioral concept of decision making and the applied statistical concept of nominal choice. Empirical tools in this chapter involve discrete choice estimation methods. Formal tools include the application of basic decision theory, including an understanding of random utility models.

8.2 STEP 1: RELATING DECISION MAKING AND NOMINAL CHOICE

Voting provides a useful window into methodological unification. Hotelling (1929) and Downs (1957) argue that voters choose one party over the others based on the relative political positions of parties – proximity voting theory. Voters are more likely to vote for a political party if the position of the party is closer to a voters' ideal position. As the party's position further deviates from a voter's ideal position, the voter receives less utility and is less likely to vote for it.[2] While the voting literature finds some empirical support for the proximity model, Kedar (2005) believes that this effect would be reduced if the institutional environment involves power-sharing.

Specifically, Kedar (2005) uses the discounting voting model to show that voters may choose candidates with extreme policy positions compared to their ideal points when the institutional environment is characterized by a high degree of coalitional bargaining in multi-party democracy setting – termed compensational voting. In the coalitional set-up the policy is determined by the coalition bargaining process. The presence of more extreme parties may bring the negotiated policy platform of the coalition closer to the voters.

8.3 STEP 2: ANALOGUES FOR DECISION MAKING AND NOMINAL CHOICE

Kedar (2005) asserts that, along with the proximity of parties' positions, voters are also concerned about each party's contribution to the aggregate policy outcome. Beginning with the proximity model:

---

[2] Applications of this particular utility function abound. Erikson et al. (2002), for example, assume that voters' utility is an inverse function of the squared distance of party political position and the voters' ideal position.

$$U_{ij} = -\beta_1 (v_i - p_j)^2, \qquad (8.1)$$

where U_{ij} is the utility of voter i for party j, v_i is the ideal point of voter i, p_j is the position of party j, and β_1 is a scalar representing the importance of party-position deviations. In Kedar's analogue for decision making, Eq. (8.1), voter i perceives disutility for party j when the position of party j deviates from voter i's ideal point. On the other hand, if the position of party j is equivalent to his ideal point (i.e., $v_i = p_j$), no disutility is perceived to result from party j.

Assuming that party positions can affect policy outcomes, Kedar (2005) specifies the policy outcome as a weighted average of policy positions of the respective parties:

$$P = \sum_{k=1}^{m} s_k p_k, \qquad (8.2)$$

where there are m parties in the legislature, $0 < s_k < 1$ is the relative share of party k, and $\sum_{k=1}^{m} s_k = 1$, for all k.

If voters are policy-outcome oriented and concerned the policy outcome may deviate from their ideal point if party j is not elected, then the utility of voter i pertaining to party j becomes:

$$U_{ij} = -\beta_2 \left[(v_i - P)^2 - (v_i - P_{-p_j})^2 \right], \qquad (8.3)$$

where:

$$P_{-p_j} = \left(\frac{1}{\sum_{k \neq j} s_k} \right) \sum_{k \neq j} s_k p_k. \qquad (8.4)$$

Equation (8.4) represents the policy outcome if party j is not in the legislature, and β_2 is a scalar weighting the deviations of the policy outcome when party j is excluded.

Equation (8.3) provides an important insight into how voters view the contribution of party j to the policy outcome affecting their utility. If party j takes part in policy formulation and makes the policy closer to voter i's ideal point v_i, that is, $(v_i - P_{-p_j})^2 > (v_i - P)^2$, then voter i will gain positive utility when party j is involved in the policy formation process (i.e., $U_{ij} > 0$). However, if the inclusion of party j makes the policy outcome increase in distance from voter i's idea point such that $(v_i - P_{-p_j})^2 < (v_i - P)^2$, then the utility of voter i for party j is negative.

Now, consider the expectations analogue. Assume voter i has expectations (an expected value) concerning party j based on the weighted average of both

Political Parties and Representation

the party's relative position and its contribution to policy outcomes. This analogue, in the context of voter i's utility for party j, can be written as:[3]

$$U_{ij} = \theta \left\{ -\gamma (v_i - p_j)^2 - (1-\gamma) \left[(v_i - P)^2 - (v_i - P_{-p_j})^2 \right] \right\} + \delta_j z_i, \tag{8.5}$$

where θ is a scalar, δ_j is a vector of coefficients on voter i's observable variables z_i for party j, and $\gamma \equiv \beta_1/(\beta_1 + \beta_2)$. When $\gamma \to 1$, the implication is that voters are solely concerned with a party's positions. This situation is known as representational voting behavior. On the other hand, if $\gamma \to 0$ then voters vote for a party such that the policy outcome can be placed at the voter's desired position(s). This outcome is known as compensational voting behavior.

From Eq. (8.5), we obtain voter i's optimal or "desired" position for party j by solving the first-order condition of U_{ij} with respect to p_j:

$$p_j^* = v_i \left[\frac{\gamma(1-s_j) + s_j}{\gamma(1-s_j^2) + s_j^2} \right] - \frac{(1-\gamma)\left(s_j \sum_{k=1,k\neq j}^{m} s_k p_k\right)}{\gamma(1-s_j^2) + s_j^2}. \tag{8.6}$$

When $\gamma \to 1$ (representational voting), we have:

$$p_j^* = v_i. \tag{8.7}$$

But, when $\gamma \to 0$ (compensational voting), we have:

$$p_j^* = \frac{v_i - \sum_{k=1,k\neq j}^{m} s_k p_k}{s_j}, \tag{8.8}$$

and the policy outcome would be:

$$\begin{aligned} P\Big|_{\gamma\to 0, p_j = p_j^*} &= \sum_{k=1}^{m} s_k p_k = s_j p_j + \sum_{k=1,k\neq j}^{m} s_k p_k \\ &= s_j p_j^* + \sum_{k=1,k\neq j}^{m} s_k p_k \\ &= s_j \frac{v_i - \sum_{k\neq j}^{m} s_k p_k}{s_j} + \sum_{k=1,k\neq j}^{m} s_k p_k \\ &= v_i. \end{aligned} \tag{8.9}$$

---

[3] Note the analogue here for expectations is not to be confused with conditional expectation analogues discussed in earlier chapters.

8.4 STEP 3: UNIFYING AND EVALUATING THE ANALOGUES

In Eqs. (8.7) through (8.9), voters make an optimal voting decision based on representational (proximity) and compensational voting considerations. These two considerations reflect the levels of political bargaining in different institutional systems. For majoritarian systems, where the winning party is able to implement its ideal policy with less need for compromise, voters place greater value on γ and vote for the party positioned closest to their ideal position. However, in the case where institutional power sharing (γ is small) exists, voters select a party whose position is further from their ideal positions to draw the collective outcome closer to the voter's ideal point.

Kedar tests these empirical implications using survey data from Britain, Canada, Netherlands, and Norway:

> **Hypothesis 1:** *Voters' behavior in the countries with a majoritarian system follows the proximity model more closely (larger γ) than those in the countries with a consensual system (smaller γ).*
> **Hypothesis 2:** *The pure proximity model ($\gamma = 1$) does not sufficiently represent voting behavior.*

For Hypothesis 1, Kedar (2005) first identifies the institutional features of Britain, Canada, Norway, and the Netherlands. Using the indicators of majoritarianism and power-sharing in Lijphart (1984), she concludes Britain and Canada are more unitary, whereas the Netherlands and Norway are more consensual.

Methodological unification occurs when Kedar estimates issue voting in four political systems by deriving the following empirical analogue for nominal choice – the multinomial logit model based on Eq. (8.5):

$$\text{Prob}\left(vote_i = j\right) = \frac{e^{U_{ij}}}{\sum_{k=1}^{m} e^{U_{ik}}},$$

where:

$$U_{ij} = \theta \left[-\gamma \cdot \text{representational}_{ij} - (1 - \gamma) \cdot \text{compensational}_{ij} \right] + \delta_j z_i. \tag{8.10}$$

According to Eq. (8.10), representational$_{ij}$ represents voter i's perceived position of party j, and compensational$_{ij}$ represents the voter perception of party impact measured by: (i) seat shares in the parliament; (ii) vote shares; and (iii) the average of seat share and portfolio allocation in the government.

Figure 8.1 presents the estimated coefficient on the representational voting strategy γ in four institutional systems. The empirical results support the first theoretical hypothesis: Voting behavior in majoritarian systems (i.e., Britain and Canada) is more consistent with the proximity model relative to consensual systems (i.e., the Netherlands and Norway). Hypothesis 2 is tested using a

Political Parties and Representation

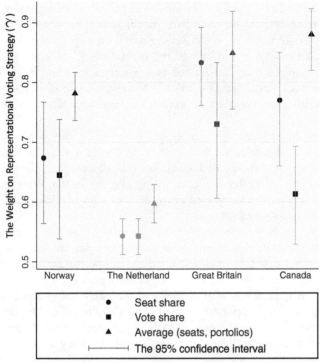

FIGURE 8.1. Estimated results of the compensational-voting model

likelihood ratio (LR) test. Kedar shows the hypothesis of $\gamma = 1$ is rejected. In other words, the LR tests show that, in all four political systems, compensational voting behavior exists while the pure proximity model is an insufficient explanation.[4]

8.5 SUMMARY

In this chapter we focus on Kedar's study, which represents a clear EITM framework. This research provides a close link between formal and empirical analysis from different theoretical perspectives. As shown in this chapter, in forming the behavioral mechanism for decision making, Kedar chooses utility maximization as an analogue: Voters select their ideal party position and/or policy outcome by maximizing their utility. The author links the theoretical findings of the optimal choice model to multinomial estimation – the empirical analogue.

---

[4] See Section 8.6.3 for the discussion on the empirical estimation in detail.

One way to build on the formal model is to relax the behavioral assumption that voters' expectations are error free since it is well-known that equilibrium predictions change when expectations are based on imperfect or limited information. The extension would amend the formal model of voter expectations to incorporate modern refinements on how voters adjust and learn from their expectation errors. Leveraging Kedar's EITM design allows drawing (empirical) implications on how voter expectations and learning affect ex-ante model predictions.

On the empirical side, recall she tested the implications of this theoretical models with four democracies. She found that voting in the consensual/power sharing democracies are guided more by this discounting theory, whereas the proximity model better explains voting choices in majoritarian systems. However, extending the sample to more democracies in different eras would also be a useful robustness check.

Some alternative theories have been introduced in the literature. They assume party candidates not only have policy motivations but also have the desire to maximize votes. In other words, while a candidate desires to get elected, she also wants to implement her desired policies. Adams and Merrill (2006) used this framework to model a three-party competition to predict policy divergence among parties in an electoral equilibrium. The basic proposition of the work is that the presence of a small centrist third party compels major parties to propose divergent policy positions. They have compared the model predictions with the estimated policy positions of the candidates in post-war Britain, but their work would be a useful extension to Kedar's model and test.

Yet, another example is Bargsted and Kedar (2009). They extend Kedar's (2005) model and study the effect of coalition expectations on voter choice. They argue a policy-outcome oriented voter not only chooses a candidate whose political ideal position is closer to hers, but she also considers how likely the favorite candidate affects the coalition of the government. If the voter perceives her favorite candidate is likely to participate in the governing coalition, she may consider selecting an alternative candidate instead. Bargsted and Kedar (2009) termed this voting decision as "strategic coalition voting." The authors find the theoretical argument is supported using coalition expectations data from the 2006 Israeli elections. The authors conclude that "[w]hen voters perceive membership in the coalition to be out of reach for their preferred party, they often desert it and instead support the lesser of evils among those parties they perceive as potential coalition members" (page 321). One final example is Wagner (2012). He argues political parties have an incentive to strategically differentiate themselves from others by taking a more extreme position. The author finds that a party that has a smaller vote share or is more distinctive from other parties tends to emphasize a more extreme position.

8.6 APPENDIX

In contrast to standard regression models which have continuous dependent variables, discrete choice models focus on a choice made by individuals among a finite set of discrete alternatives. They can be classified according to the number of available alternatives. A discrete model for explaining the outcome as a choice between two alternatives is referred to as a binomial model (i.e., binary choice model). Discrete choice problems involving choices between more than two alternatives are termed multinomial models. Examples of the application of multinomial models include the decision regarding which job/occupation to take, which shopping area to go to, which car to buy, which candidate to vote for, and which mode of transportation to use for travel.

Discrete choice models estimate the probability that a person chooses a particular alternative. These models statistically link the choice made by each individual to a set of relevant factors. The factors typically include the characteristics of the individual (such as education level, gender, income level, and marital status) and the attributes of the alternatives (such as travel time, and costs in a study of which mode of transportation to take).

A general framework for such probability models can be written as:

$$Prob(\text{Individual } i \text{ chooses alternative choice } j) \equiv P_{ij}$$
$$= F(X_{ij} : \beta), \tag{8.11}$$

where $X_{ij} = [Z_i, x_{ij}, x_{ik}]$, $\forall j \neq k$, Z_i is a vector of characteristics of individual i, x_{ij} (x_{ik}) is a vector of attributes of alternative j (other alternatives k) for individual i, and β is a set of parameters that are estimated by the probability model. In the binary choices setting, these models are binary probit and binary logit models. For multinomial choice settings, these models include multinomial logit and conditional logit models. Here we briefly discuss these statistical choice models in the following sections.

8.6.1 Empirical Analogues

Binary Choice Models

THE PROBIT MODEL In the binary choice models, researchers estimate the probability that a person makes a selecting decision when faced with two possibilities. For instance, suppose we are interested in understanding why some individuals choose to take on an activity ($Y = 1$) and others do not ($Y = 0$). We can formulate an index function model as follows:

$$Y^* = \beta'X + \epsilon, \tag{8.12}$$

$$Y = \begin{cases} 1, & \text{if } Y^* > 0 \\ 0, & \text{otherwise,} \end{cases} \tag{8.13}$$

where Y^* represents a latent variable indicating the net benefit of taking on the activity, and $\epsilon \sim$ standard normal. Condition (8.13) suggests an individual takes on an activity ($Y = 1$) if her associated utility is positive (i.e., $Y^* > 0$). With the assumption that error terms ϵ follow a standard normal distribution, the probability of choosing an activity can be presented by the following probit model:[5]

$$Prob(Y = 1) = \int_{-\infty}^{\beta'X} \phi(t)dt = \Phi(\beta'X), \qquad (8.14)$$

where $\Phi(\cdot)$ denotes the function of a cumulative standard normal distribution.

Instead of deciding whether to take an action or not, the binary choice model can be extended to study the decision of choosing between two alternative activities: activity 1 ($Y_{i1} = 1$) or activity 2 ($Y_{i1} = 0$). The specification of the model is written as follows:

$$U_{i1} = \beta'X_{i1} + \epsilon_{i1} \qquad (8.15)$$
$$U_{i2} = \beta'X_{i2} + \epsilon_{i2}, \qquad (8.16)$$

and:

$$Y_{i1} = \begin{cases} 1, & \text{if } U_{i1} > U_{i2} \\ 0, & \text{otherwise,} \end{cases} \qquad (8.17)$$

where U_{i1} and U_{i2} are utility values that individual i obtains from choosing activities 1 and 2, respectively, and $\epsilon_{i1}, \epsilon_{i2}$ are iid and distributed as standard normal. Based on the system of Eqs. (8.15)–(8.17), the probability of choosing activity 1 over activity 2 is presented by the following probit model:

$$\begin{aligned} Prob(Y_{i1} = 1) &= Prob(U_{i1} > U_{i2}) \\ &= Prob(\beta'X_{i1} + \epsilon_{i1} > \beta'X_{i2} + \epsilon_{i2}) \\ &= Prob(\epsilon_{i2} - \epsilon_{i1} < \beta'X_{i1} - \beta'X_{i2}) \\ &= \Phi(\beta'(X_{i1} - X_{i2})/\sqrt{2}). \end{aligned} \qquad (8.18)$$

THE LOGIT MODEL The specification of the logit model is identical to the model expressed in Eqs. (8.12)–(8.13), except the error terms are assumed to have a logistic distribution (i.e., $\epsilon \sim logistic$). The probability of choosing an activity is written as:

$$Prob(Y = 1) = \frac{e^{\beta'X}}{1 + e^{\beta'X}}. \qquad (8.19)$$

---

[5] In this appendix we assume the error term ϵ is distributed standard normal (i.e., $\epsilon \sim N(0, 1)$). We can also consider a case where ϵ has a general normal distribution, $\epsilon \sim N(0, \sigma^2)$. In this case the probit model can be written as: $Prob(Y = 1) = \Phi(\beta'X/\sigma)$.

Political Parties and Representation

Similarly, for the system of Eqs. (8.15)–(8.17), when both error terms are iid extreme values, their difference is distributed logistically. We therefore present the probability of choosing activity 1 by the following logit model:

$$Prob(Y_{i1} = 1) = \frac{e^{\beta' X_{i1}}}{e^{\beta' X_{i1}} + e^{\beta' X_{i2}}}. \tag{8.20}$$

Multinomial Choice Models

The probit and logit models discussed in the previous section focus on binary choice estimation. However, when decisions involve more than two available alternatives, it is more difficult to perform probit estimations due to the intensive computation of multiple integrals of the normal distributions. As a result, researchers commonly estimate multinomial choice models with the logistic distribution. These models are known as the multinomial logit model and conditional logit model.

MULTINOMIAL LOGIT MODEL The multinomial logit (MNL) model is estimated when data consist of individual-specific characteristics. A general form of the MNL model can be written as:

$$U_{ij} = \beta'_j Z_i + \epsilon_{ij}, \tag{8.21}$$

where U_{ij} is individual i's utility of choosing the jth alternative, Z_i gives a vector of an individual's characteristics, and ϵ_{ij} is iid extreme value. The model estimates a set of regression coefficients on each alternative β_j. The utility for all alternatives depends on the characteristics of the individual, but the coefficients vary across alternatives.

The multinomial logit model is fundamentally similar to the random utility model (RUM). The model assumes individual i maximizes her utility by selecting option j from a list of m alternatives. Since only differences in utility matter when choosing an alternative with the highest utility, it is more convenient to normalize a coefficient on one of the alternatives to zero, for example, $\beta_1 = 0$. Then, the resulting choice probabilities are:

$$Prob(Y = j) = Prob(U_{ij} > U_{ik}), \forall j \neq k$$

$$= \frac{e^{\beta'_j Z_i}}{1 + \sum_{k=2}^{m} e^{\beta'_k Z_i}}, \tag{8.22}$$

for $j = 1, 2, 3, \ldots, m$, and $\beta_1 = 0$.

CONDITIONAL LOGIT MODEL When data consist of choice-specific attributes, the conditional logit (CL) model proposed by McFadden (1974) is more appropriate (see Manski 2001). The general form of the CL model is:

$$U_{ij} = \beta' X_{ij} + \epsilon_{ij}, \tag{8.23}$$

where $X_{ij} = [x_{ij}, Z_i]$, x_{ij} gives a vector of alternative-specific attributes, Z_i gives a vector of individual-specific characteristics, and ϵ_{ij} is iid extreme value. For an individual choosing an alternative j among m alternatives, it implies that she obtains the highest level of utility from option j in the choice set. The resulting probability of selecting j is as follows:

$$Prob(Y = j) = Prob(U_{ij} > U_{ik}), \forall j \neq k$$

$$= \frac{e^{\beta' X_{ij}}}{\sum_{j=1}^{m} e^{\beta' X_{ij}}}, \tag{8.24}$$

where $j = 1, 2, 3, \ldots, m$. Compared to the MNL model, McFadden's CL model expands an additional dimension of choice-specific x_{ij} in individual i's utility function:

$$U_{ij} = f(x_{ij}, Z_i) + \epsilon_{ij}, \tag{8.25}$$

where U_{ij} represents the level of utility for individual i choosing alternative j based on both choice-specific attributes x_{ij} and individual-specific attributes Z_i. More importantly, the attribute X_{ij} varies across choices and possibly across individuals as well. Under this setting, the utility of alternative j for individual i can be determined as long as attributes x_{ij} and Z_i can be observed and the functional form of utility can also be partially observed such that ϵ_{ij} captures the unexplanatory factors in the utility function. The individual's choice behavior can therefore be tested.

Estimation and Hypothesis Tests

ESTIMATION The discrete choice models are commonly estimated by the maximum likelihood method (ML). For binary choice models, each observation is treated as a single draw from a Bernoulli distribution. The corresponding likelihood function (or the joint probability) for a sample of n observations can be written as:

$$L = \prod_{i=1}^{n} \pi_{i1}^{Y_{i1}} \pi_{i2}^{Y_{i2}}. \tag{8.26}$$

By taking the logarithm in Eq. (8.26), we have:

$$\ln L = \sum_{i=1}^{n} \left(Y_{i1} \ln \pi_{i1} + Y_{i2} \ln \pi_{i2} \right), \tag{8.27}$$

where $Y_{ij} = 1$ if individual i chooses alternative j, and $Y_{ij} = 0$ otherwise, and π_{ij} is the probability of individual i choosing alternative j, for $i = 1, 2, \ldots, n$, and $j \in \{1, 2\}$.

Political Parties and Representation

The estimation of multinomial models is an extension of binary choice models. The likelihood function of a multinomial choice model can be presented by the following form:

$$L = \prod_{i=1}^{n} \prod_{j=1}^{m} \pi_{ij}^{Y_{ij}}. \tag{8.28}$$

As with Eq. (8.27), we take the logarithm in Eq. (8.28):

$$\ln L = \sum_{i=1}^{n} \sum_{j=1}^{m} Y_{ij} \ln \pi_{ij}, \tag{8.29}$$

where π_{ij} is the probability of individual i choosing alternative j, for $i = 1, 2, \ldots, n$, and $j = 1, 2, \ldots, m$, and $Y_{ij} = 1$ if alternative j is chosen by individual i, and 0 otherwise, for m possible outcomes.

HYPOTHESIS TESTS   A relevant hypothesis test mentioned in Chapter 8 (and used in Kedar (2005)) is a likelihood ratio test. The likelihood ratio statistics based on the log likelihood function (8.29) can be computed as:

$$LR = -2(\ln \hat{L}_r - \ln \hat{L}), \tag{8.30}$$

where $\hat{L}_r$ and $\hat{L}$ are estimates in restricted and unrestricted models, respectively. Kedar (2005) proposes a hypothesis test whether $\gamma = 1$ in Eq. (8.10). The coefficient γ captures the individuals' voting behavior. A larger value of γ indicates that a voter's voting behavior is more proximity-driven (representational) and less compensational.

8.6.2 Formal Analogues

In the contemporary choice theory literature, researchers generally suggest two types of decision rules determining how an individual reaches a decision when faced with a set of choices: (1) the marginal decision rule and (2) the utility-maximization rule.

The Marginal Decision Rule

The marginal decision rule states that an individual takes on an additional activity ($Y = 1$) or not ($Y = 0$) based on whether she receives a positive net benefit Y^* by doing the activity. However, the net benefit is subjective and not observable because an individual's utility function is not revealed. Although the net benefit of taking the action cannot be measured, the choice outcome can be observed directly. Consequently, an individual's decision can be formulated using an index function model:

$$Y^* = \beta'X + \epsilon, \tag{8.31}$$

and:

$$Y = \begin{cases} 1, & \text{if } Y^* > 0 \\ 0, & \text{otherwise.} \end{cases}$$

The choice probability can be presented as:

$$\begin{aligned} Prob(Y = 1) &= Prob(Y^* > 0) \\ &= Prob(\beta'X + \epsilon > 0) \\ &= Prob(\epsilon > -\beta'X). \end{aligned} \quad (8.32)$$

Greene (2011) notes that discrete dependent variable models are often cast in the form of an index function model (see also Nakosteen and Zimmer 1980).

Utility-Maximization Rule: Random Utility Models

McFadden's pioneering work (1973, 1974) introduced random utility models (RUM) to modern econometric analysis of discrete choices. RUM assumes an individual faces a finite choice set and makes a choice decision by maximizing her utility.

Let U_{ij} and U_{ik} be utility levels that individual i obtains from choosing alternatives j and k, respectively. According to the method of utility-maximization, individual i chooses the alternative j, which gives the individual the highest level of utility. Since an individual's utility is not observable, researchers assume that some observable and unobservable factors, X and ϵ_j, respectively, can influence the utility level of choosing option j. Mathematically, we have:

$$U_{ij} = \beta_j' X + \epsilon_j, \quad (8.33)$$

where $X = (x_{ij}, Z_i)$, x_{ij} is a vector of choice-specific attributes, and Z_i is a vector of individual-specific characteristics for individual i.

Although individual i's utility levels of both alternatives j and k are not observable, the choice outcome implies that the chosen alternative gives a higher level of utility than others. Hence we designate an indicator variable of the choice outcome Y_{ij} with a dummy variable. The individual choices can be modeled based on the following RUM:

$$U_{ij} = \beta_j' X + \epsilon_j$$
$$U_{ik} = \beta_k' X + \epsilon_k,$$

and:

$$Y_{ij} = \begin{cases} 1, & \text{if } U_{ij} > U_{ik}, \forall j \neq k \\ 0, & \text{otherwise.} \end{cases} \quad (8.34)$$

Political Parties and Representation

The probability of option j being chosen is written as:

$$\begin{aligned} Prob(Y_{ij} = 1) &= Prob(U_{ij} > U_{ik}) \\ &= Prob(\beta_j' X + \epsilon_j > \beta_k' X + \epsilon_k) \\ &= Prob(\epsilon_k - \epsilon_j < \beta_j' X - \beta_k' X) \\ &= Prob(\epsilon < -\beta' X). \end{aligned} \quad (8.35)$$

In the RUM, the utility levels are conceptualized as random variables. McFadden interprets the "randomness" in the RUM is based on cross-sectional variations in utility functions across individuals in the population. In other words, an individual can perceive different levels of utility under identical conditions. This assumption of heterogeneity is reflected in the random variations of utility assessment and measurement errors.

8.6.3 Details on the Kedar (2005) Application

Kedar (2005) sets up a framework of utility-maximization multinomial response models to empirically test the validity of the representational-compensational voting model. As discussed in Section 8.3, the key Eq. (8.5) gives voter i's utility for party j:

$$U_{ij} = \theta \left\{ -\gamma (v_i - p_j)^2 - (1 - \gamma) \left[(v_i - P)^2 - (v_i - P_{-p_j})^2 \right] \right\} + \delta_j z_i. \quad (8.36)$$

The first component $(v_i - p_j)^2$ indicates the representational voting behavior, and the second component, $\left[(v_i - P)^2 - (v_i - P_{-p_j})^2 \right]$, the compensational voting behavior. We therefore rewrite Eq. (8.36) as:

$$U_{ij} = \theta \left[-\gamma \cdot \text{representational}_{ij} - (1 - \gamma) \cdot \text{compensational}_{ij} \right] + \delta_j z_i. \quad (8.37)$$

Since Eq. (8.37) involves data that consist of choice-specific attributes (i.e., representational$_{ij}$ and compensational$_{ij}$) in addition to individual-specific characteristics z_i, Kedar's (2005) model is equivalent to the CL model. The resulting choice probability function can be written as:

$$Prob(Voter_i = j) \equiv \pi_{ij} = \frac{f(U_{ij})}{\sum_{k=1}^{m} f(U_{ik})}, \quad (8.38)$$

where π_{ij} denotes the probability of voter i ($i = 1, 2, 3, \ldots, n$) voting for party j ($j = 1, 2, 3, \ldots, m$). The maximum likelihood function is presented as follows:

$$\ln L = \sum_{i=1}^{n} \sum_{j=1}^{m} Y_{ij} \ln \pi_{ij}, \quad (8.39)$$

where $Y_{ij} = 1$ if voter i's votes for party j, and $Y_{ij} = 0$ otherwise.

9

Voter Turnout

9.1 BACKGROUND

Voter turnout studies have a rich history (e.g., Merriam and Gosnell 1924; Milbrath 1965; Blais 2000). The influence of Downs (1957) also looms large: Prospective voters are assumed to weigh the benefits and the costs of voting. When the difference between the benefits and the costs of voting for the incumbent is positive, the voter should select the incumbent. If this difference is negative, the voter should choose a challenger. However, if this difference is zero, and voters do not perceive advantages in voting over staying at home, the rational behavior should be to abstain from casting a ballot. Under this framework, a perfectly rational citizen should abstain most of the time, because the probability that one vote will change the outcome of the election is close to zero.

Recall from Chapter 5, Riker and Ordeshook (1968) offered an alternative to Downs. They argued voters give credence concerning the value of democracy. They determine the rewards of voting as $R = (P \times B) + D - C$, with P as the probability of influencing the outcome by casting the decisive vote, B as the benefits of your candidate winning, D as duty and other unobservables, and C as the costs. P varies if the electorate size varies, and by extension if the election is of less importance.

Turnout can also be based on voter judgment of past performance. Fiorina (1981) adds the element of the public's ability to judge the incumbent based on current term performance. The public punishes or rewards an incumbent based on their satisfaction with past job performance. This retrospective voting framework assumes a process of observation from voters and serves as an accountability measure for the incumbent. Of course, some argue prospective considerations also influence turnout. Powell (2000) argues potential voters evaluate candidates based on their promises and their plans for the future, and voters gamble on the future instead of relying solely on a retrospective evaluation.

In this chapter we present Achen's (2006) voter turnout model. As outlined in the opening brief sketch, there are elements of prospective, retrospective, and Downsian elements to the voter turnout question. Achen ties all of these factors together. In addition, his EITM linkage is between the behavioral concepts – rational decision making and learning – and the applied statistical concept of nominal choice. What is also important about Achen's approach is the ability to link formalization with known distribution functions. For prior examples the EITM link was accomplished in ways not involving distribution functions.[1]

The empirical tools in this chapter include discrete choice estimation methods. The background for these empirical tools was presented earlier in Chapter 8. The formal tools involve the use of Bayesian updating and a basic understanding of distribution functions is also required.[2]

9.2 STEP 1: RELATING DECISION MAKING, LEARNING, AND DISCRETE CHOICE

In prior studies of turnout, researchers used discrete choice models to estimate the probability of voting. The explanatory variables in these empirical models include ad-hoc transformations. For example, age, the square of age, education level, and the square of education level are used. However, there is weak theoretical justification for the squared terms. The variables are included typically for the sake of a better statistical fit within sample. Yet, Achen (2006) argues this:

... lack of theoretical structure leaves researchers free to specify their statistical models arbitrarily, so that even closely related research teams make different choices...These modeling choices have substantial implications if we really mean them: If age measures learning, for example, it makes a difference whether over a lifetime, political learning accelerates, decelerates, or is constant. Alas, the theory that would provide the interpretation and structure our specifications is missing. (pages 2–3)

With this criticism in mind, Achen (2006) provides an estimated model with a theoretical interpretation (i.e., no "squared" variables). The intuition behind his behavioral model, the way he conceptualizes the decision to vote, is that it

---

[1] Some studies develop alternative empirical tests. For example, Meredith (2009) studies the persistence in voter turnout with a regression discontinuity design. One of the major findings is that voters who just turned 18 and were eligible to vote in the previous presidential election are more likely to vote in the subsequent election. The author argues these findings are consistent with those presented in Achen (2006) (see also Niemi and Hammer 2010).

[2] Note in this chapter Achen demonstrates an alternative learning analogue. In previous chapters adaptive learning tools were used as a learning analogue.

is an "expressive act"[3] *where potential voters learn* about the candidates via party label or contact from a trusted source. He further asserts that:

> written down formally, these simple ideas generate mathematical implications that map directly onto the behavioral literature and connect closely to what the voters are actually doing... Moreover, the model implies new functional forms for the statistical modeling of voter turnout. The resulting predictions go through the data points, while those from the most widely used statistical specifications in the behavioral literature do not. (pages 4–5)

Turning now to the analogues for decision making, learning and discrete choice, we discuss how they can be linked.

9.3 STEP 2: ANALOGUES FOR DECISION MAKING, LEARNING, AND DISCRETE CHOICE

Achen's theoretical model assumes a voter receives positive utility by voting if she expects the true value of the difference between two parties in the next period u_{n+1} to be different from zero, where n is the number of prior elections that the voter experiences. Achen assumes, too, the voter does not have perfect foresight on the true value of the party differences. Instead the voter "learns" the expected value based on her information set (updated by a Bayesian mechanism).

The subjective (expected) distribution of u_{n+1} can be written as:

$$f\left(u_{n+1} | I\right), \tag{9.1}$$

where $f(\cdot)$ is the probability density distribution based on the voter's information set I given the period of n. The corresponding cumulative distribution function (CDF) from Eq. (9.1) is:

$$F\left(u_{n+1} | I\right), \tag{9.2}$$

where $F(\cdot)$ is the cdf with the mean $\hat{u}_{n+1}$ and variance σ^2_{n+1}.

For theoretical convenience, Achen (2006) assumes $\hat{u}_{n+1}$ is nonnegative: the voter only votes for the party valued higher than another. The probability of the voter making a correct decision when $u_{n+1} \geq 0$ is therefore:

$$Prob\,(\text{correct}) = 1 - F\left(0 | I\right), \tag{9.3}$$

whereas the probability of an incorrect decision is:

$$Prob\,(\text{incorrect}) = F\left(0 | I\right). \tag{9.4}$$

---

[3] Achen defines an expressive act as "a decision to do one's duty or take pleasure in a collective enterprise or cheer for one's team without imagining that one might personally determine the outcome of the game (Milbrath 1965, 12–13)" (page 5).

If we assume a voter will vote only if the probability of making a correct decision exceeds that of making an incorrect decision, then we can present the expected benefit of voting $E(D_{n+1})$ in the next period as the difference between the two probabilities:

$$\begin{aligned} E(D_{n+1}) &= \alpha \left[Prob \text{ (correct)} - Prob \text{ (incorrect)} \right] \\ &= \alpha \left[1 - F(0|I) - F(0|I) \right] \\ &= \alpha \left[1 - 2F(0|I) \right], \end{aligned}$$

where $\alpha > 0$ represents the weight (importance) of voting.

Following Downs (1957), Achen (2006) suggests the utility of voting in period $n+1$ is the difference between the expected benefit of voting $E(D_{n+1})$ and the cost of voting:

$$\begin{aligned} U &= E(D_{n+1}) - c \\ &= \alpha \left[1 - 2F(0|I) \right] - c, \end{aligned} \quad (9.5)$$

where c is the cost of voting. Assuming u_{n+1} is normally distributed, we transform Eq. (9.5) to:

$$U = \alpha \left[1 - 2\Phi\left(-\hat{u}_{n+1}/\sigma_{n+1}\right) \right] - c, \quad (9.6)$$

where $\Phi(\cdot)$ is a standard normal CDF. Since $\Phi(-z) = 1 - \Phi(z)$, we rewrite Eq. (9.6) as:

$$U = \alpha \left[2\Phi\left(\hat{u}_{n+1}/\sigma_{n+1}\right) - 1 \right] - c. \quad (9.7)$$

Achen argues voters use a Bayesian updating procedure (assuming a normal distribution of u_{n+1}) and voters "learn" the true u_{n+1} based on: (1) the difference(s) in party identification (PID) from the last period u_n; (2) the campaign information c_{n+1}; and (3) a trusted information source q_{n+1} received from a political party.[4]

The learning process can now be characterized. The posterior mean as it pertains to party identification is:

$$u_t = \delta + v_t, \quad (9.8)$$

where $u_t \sim N(\delta, w^2)$. The voter first updates the posterior mean of his PID up to time n using the standard Bayesian formulation:

$$\hat{\delta}_n = \frac{h_1 \bar{u}_n}{h_0 + h_1}, \quad (9.9)$$

where $\bar{u}_n = \Sigma u_t / n$ is the mean of PID based on past voting experience, $h_1 = \left(w^2/n\right)^{-1}$ is the inverse of the sample variance, and $h_0 = \left(\sigma_0^2\right)^{-1}$

---

[4] Achen (2006) also suggests that trusted information can also come from the voter's spouse or some interest groups.

represents the inverse of the prior variance σ_0^2. In the next period, the voter also receives new information from the party campaign:

$$c_{n+1} = u_{n+1} + \theta_{n+1} + \epsilon_{n+1}, \tag{9.10}$$

where $\theta \sim N(0, \varphi^2)$ and $\epsilon \sim N(0, \tau^2/m)$.

Based on the posterior mean of PID at time n (i.e., $\hat{\delta}_n$ in Eq. (9.9)), the campaign information c_{n+1} in Eq. (9.10), and the trusted information source q_{n+1} at time $n+1$, we use the same Bayesian updating procedure to update the posterior mean of the PID difference $\hat{u}_{n+1}$:

$$\hat{u}_{n+1} = \frac{h_c \hat{\delta}_n + h_\tau c_{n+1} + h_q q_{n+1}}{h_c + h_\tau + h_q}, \tag{9.11}$$

where $h_c \equiv \left[(h_0 + h_1)^{-1} + w^2\right]^{-1}$, $h_\tau \equiv (\varphi^2 + \tau^2/m)^{-1}$, and h_q is the inverse of known variance of the trusted information source. The posterior variance of $\hat{u}_{n+1}$ is presented as:

$$\sigma_{n+1}^2 = \frac{1}{h_c + h_\tau + h_q}. \tag{9.12}$$

To derive the utility function of voting with the feature of Bayesian learning, we substitute Eqs. (9.11) and (9.12) into Eq. (9.7):

$$U = \alpha \left[2\Phi \left(\left(\frac{h_c \hat{\delta}_n + h_\tau c_{n+1} + h_q q_{n+1}}{h_c + h_\tau + h_q} \right) \Big/ \left(\frac{1}{(h_c + h_\tau + h_q)^{1/2}} \right) \right) - 1 \right] - c$$

$$= \alpha \left[2\Phi \left(\frac{h_c \hat{\delta}_n + h_\tau c_{n+1} + h_q q_{n+1}}{(h_c + h_\tau + h_q)^{1/2}} \right) - 1 \right] - c. \tag{9.13}$$

9.4 STEP 3: UNIFYING AND EVALUATING THE ANALOGUES

To estimate the determinants of voter turnout, Achen presents the probit model that follows from Eq. (9.13). Let there be a critical level of utility, call it U^*, such that if $U > U^*$, the voter will vote; otherwise the voter will not. Given the normality assumption for the utility distribution, we construct the probability that U^* is less than or equal to U based on the normal CDF:

$$\text{Prob}\left(vote = 1 \,\middle|\, \text{PID, Campaign Information, and Trusted Source}\right)$$
$$= \text{Prob}\left(U^* \leq U\right)$$
$$= \Phi \left(\alpha \left[2\Phi \left(\frac{h_c \hat{\delta}_n + h_\tau c_{n+1} + h_q q_{n+1}}{(h_c + h_\tau + h_q)^{1/2}} \right) - 1 \right] - c \right). \tag{9.14}$$

In Eq. (9.14), we see the inner normal CDF represents the Bayesian learning process and the outer normal CDF is used for the purpose of discrete choice estimation. At this point unification is achieved.

Using maximum likelihood estimation, Achen (2006) estimates simultaneously two normally distributed CDF's in Eq. (9.14): a double-probit. To interpret the coefficients, we first focus on the inner normal CDF. If the voter does not have accurate information about the party, then $\Phi\left(\frac{h_c\hat{\delta}_n + h_\tau c_{n+1} + h_q q_{n+1}}{(h_c + h_\tau + h_q)^{1/2}}\right) = \Phi(0) = 1/2$. In this case Eq. (9.14) is equivalent to:

$$\begin{aligned}\Pr(vote = 1 | I) &= \Phi\left(\alpha\left[2\Phi\left(\frac{h_c\hat{\delta}_n + h_\tau c_{n+1} + h_q q_{n+1}}{(h_c + h_\tau + h_q)^{1/2}}\right) - 1\right] - c\right) \\ &= \Phi(\alpha[2\Phi(0) - 1] - c) \\ &= \Phi(-c).\end{aligned} \quad (9.15)$$

Achen (2006) assumes c is the z-value, which ranges between 2 and 3. Therefore, $-c$ will range between -2 and -3, implying the probability of voting will be very low.[5]

On the other hand, if the voter is fully informed and the posterior precision of information is quite large, then $\Phi\left(\frac{h_c\hat{\delta}_n + h_\tau c_{n+1} + h_q q_{n+1}}{(h_c + h_\tau + h_q)^{1/2}}\right) = \Phi(\infty) \to 1$. Therefore, we have:

$$\begin{aligned}\Pr(vote = 1 | I) &= \Phi(\alpha[2(1) - 1] - c) \\ &= \Phi(\alpha - c).\end{aligned} \quad (9.16)$$

Note that α is assumed to be in a range between 4 and 5. Therefore, $\alpha - c$ will range between 1 and 3. This relation shows that the probability of voting will be high and close to 1.[6]

To estimate Eq. (9.14), Achen uses the variables, systemtime and education, as the proxies for PID, $\hat{\delta}_n$, and campaign information c_{n+1}, respectively. Systemtime is defined as the voter's age subtracted from 18 years. Education is measured as the voter's education level – classified in six categories: (1) No High-School, (2) Some High-School, (3) High-School Degree, (4) Some College, (5) College Degree, and (6) Postgraduate Level.

---

[5] Achen (2006, 18) expects $-c$ "to equal -2 or -3; that is, only a percent or two of the population would vote in the completely uninformed condition."

[6] Achen (2006) points out that α is assumed to be 4 or 5, which makes $\alpha - c$ to be "approximately 2, meaning that in the fully informed condition, all but 2-3% of the population would vote. (At any given time, approximately that many are unexpectedly out of town, sick, having a baby, attending a family funeral, and so on, as many surveys have shown)" (page 19).

Achen argues the age of voters (systemtime) shows the strength of PID, while voters' education level are attributes in understanding campaign information.[7] Based on the availability of data, the theoretical model (9.14) is used to estimate the following double-probit model:

$$\Pr(vote = 1) = \Phi\left(\lambda_0 + \lambda_1\left[2\Phi\left(\beta_1 systemtime + \beta_2 education\right) - 1\right]\right), \quad (9.17)$$

where the empirical component, $\Phi\left(\beta_1 systemtime + \beta_2 education\right)$, is theoretically equivalent to the Bayesian learning procedure $\Phi\left(\frac{h_c\hat{\delta}_n + h_\tau c_{n+1} + h_q q_{n+1}}{(h_c + h_\tau + h_q)^{1/2}}\right)$, and λ_0 and λ_1 are equivalent to $-c$ and α in Eq. (9.14), respectively.

To test the EITM relation, Achen (2006) uses voter turnout data from the 1998 and 2000 Current Population Surveys (CPS) and the Annenberg 2000 presidential election study. Contrasting the EITM-based model with traditional applied statistical models in the existing literature, he finds that his models have a better fit. Equally important, when the focus turns to the parameters in Achen's model he finds the empirical estimates are consistent with the theoretical predictions of the model (see Eq. (9.14)). For example, he finds that the estimated values of c and α range between 1.212 and 2.424 and between 3.112 and 4.865, respectively. These values are statistically indistinguishable from the values predicted in the model.

9.5 SUMMARY

Achen uses the behavioral concepts of rational decision making and learning. His behavioral analogues are basic utility maximization and Bayesian learning, respectively. He links these behavioral analogues with the applied statistical analogue for discrete choice – probit. To accomplish this EITM linkage he assumes the voting decision and Bayesian learning are normally distributed events. With that assumption in place the formal model is tested using two probit regressions simultaneously.

Achen's EITM model can be leveraged in a number of ways. One of the more important extensions is to take advantage of the dynamic properties in his theory and model. Retrospective evaluations are assumed in the model but there is no specification or test on how long these evaluations persist or how long a voter's memory lasts. We know, for example, that in matters of policy, retrospective judgments by the public can have a profound influence on policy effectiveness. Equally importantly, there are analogues for persistence that can be linked to a formal extension of the model.

As a final thought, institutional arguments should be considered as possible modifications for the formalization. Blais (2006), for example, expands the rationale for voters to include the variation in institutional designs across

---

[7] Note, there is no proxy measure used for trusted source. Therefore q_{n+1} is dropped from Eq. (9.14).

Voter Turnout

democracies to explain the variation in voter turnout. This means – in addition to candidate-related variables analyzed in previous readings – variables such as the electoral system, the party system, the ballot structure, and the voting system could all have significant effects on voter turnout.

9.6 APPENDIX

The applied statistical analogue for discrete choice is presented in Chapter 8. In this appendix we provide some background on distribution functions since they aid in prediction. For the formal tools we include a brief presentation of Bayesian updating methods to estimate the mean and variance.

9.6.1 Empirical Analogues

Probability distributions are typically defined in terms of the probability density function (PDF). In probability theory, a PDF of a random variable describes the relative frequencies (or likelihood) of different values for that variable. If the random variable X is discrete, the PDF provides the probability associated with each outcome:

$$f(x) = Prob(X = x).$$

If the random variable X is continuous, the probability associated with any single point is zero. In this case, the PDF is expressed in terms of an integral between two points:

$$Prob(a \leq X \leq b) = \int_a^b f(x)dx.$$

The PDF of a continuous variable is a continuous function of $f(x)$, and the area under $f(x)$ provides the probability for a range of outcomes. Note that probabilities are always positive or zero and they should total 1 (i.e., $\sum_X f(x) = 1$, if X is discrete, and $\int_{-\infty}^{+\infty} f(x) = 1$, if X is continuous).

The cumulative distribution function (CDF) gives the probability that a random variable (X) takes a value of less than or equal to x:

$$F(x) = Prob(X \leq x).$$

Conceptually, the CDF accumulates the probabilities (PDF) of single events x_j, such that $x_j \leq x$. For a discrete distribution, the CDF is:

$$\begin{aligned} F(x) &= Prob(X \leq x) \\ &= Prob(X = x_1) + Prob(X = x_2) + \cdots + Prob(X = x_j) \\ &= f(x_1) + f(x_2) + \cdots + f(x_j) \\ &= \sum_{x_j \leq x} f(x_j). \end{aligned}$$

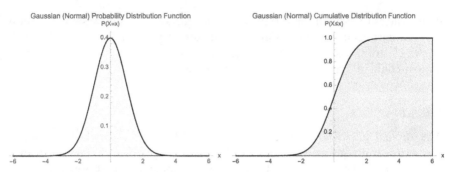

FIGURE 9.1. Normal PDF and CDF

For a continuous distribution, the CDF is:

$$F(x) = Prob(X \leq x)$$
$$= \int_{-\infty}^{x} f(t)dt,$$

and:

$$f(x) = \frac{dF(x)}{dx}.$$

Note that $F(x)$ has the following properties: (1) $0 \leq F(x) \leq 1$, (2) if $x_2 > x_1$, then $F(x_2) \geq F(x_1)$, and (3) $F(-\infty) = 0$ and $F(+\infty) = 1$.

THE NORMAL PDF AND CDF   In Figure 9.1, we plot the normal PDF and CDF. The CDF of the standard normal distribution is denoted with the capital Greek letter Φ. For a generic normal random variable with mean of u and variance of σ^2, its CDF is denoted as $\Phi((x-u)/\sigma) = F(x; u; \sigma^2)$. An important property of the standard normal CDF is that it is two-fold rotationally symmetric at point $(0, 1/2)$, such that $\Phi(-x) = 1 - \Phi(x)$.

DETAILS ON THE ACHEN (2006) APPLICATION   Achen uses the statistical concept of CDF from a normal distribution to derive the utility function for voting as expressed in Eq. (9.7). Specifically, using the notation discussed previously, $F(u_{n+1} = 0|I)$ gives the CDF that the voter decided to vote when the PID takes a value of less than or equal to zero. Since Achen argues the voter only votes for the party valued higher than another (i.e., $u_{n+1} > 0$), the CDF of $F(0|I)$ in Eq. (9.4) gives the probability that the voter is making an incorrect decision. Adding the assumption that u_{n+1} is normally distributed, he then derived the utility of voting as in Eq. (9.7).

9.6.2 Formal Analogues

Bayesian statistics is a system for describing uncertainty using the language of probability. Bayesian methods start with existing "prior" beliefs and update these beliefs using new sample information to generate "posterior" beliefs.

Voter Turnout

To derive the utility function for voting with the feature of Bayesian learning shown in Eq. (9.13), Achen applies Bayesian updating methods to the utility function of Eq. (9.7). Moreover, Achen uses Bayesian methods to update voter's prior belief that the PID u_{n+1} is a normal distribution. This prior belief (distribution) expresses the uncertainty about the mean value of the process. The mean of this prior is the mean of the process, while the variance is the process variance divided by the sample size. Voters update the prior belief (distribution) to generate the posterior distribution based on the sample of new information when it becomes available. The updated distribution can be characterized in terms of its mean and variance (which are referred to as posterior mean, and posterior variance, respectively). The required formulations to obtain the posterior mean μ'' and posterior variance σ''^2 from the Bayesian updating scheme with a prior normal distribution can be expressed as:

$$\mu'' = \frac{\frac{1}{\sigma'^2}\mu' + \frac{1}{\sigma^2/n}\bar{x}}{\frac{1}{\sigma'^2} + \frac{1}{\sigma^2/n}}, \qquad (9.18)$$

and:

$$\sigma''^2 = \frac{1}{\frac{1}{\sigma'^2} + \frac{1}{\sigma^2/n}}, \qquad (9.19)$$

where $\bar{x}$ is the sample mean, $s^2 = \sigma^2$ for a sample variance with a sufficiently large sample; μ' is the prior mean; and σ'^2 is the prior variance. Equation (9.18) is the basis for Eq. (9.11), while Eq. (9.19) is the same for Eq. (9.12).

10

International Political Economy

10.1 BACKGROUND

This chapter explicates the EITM linkage between the behavioral concepts of decision making, bargaining, and strategic interaction with the empirical concept of discrete/nominal choice.[1] This linkage – captured by the use of quantal response equilibrium (QRE) – was developed in a series of papers by McKelvey and Palfrey (1995, 1996, 1998).[2] An early and important application of QRE is Signorino's (1999) work on international conflict and cooperation. Signorino used QRE and contrasts it with stand-alone discrete choice estimation. In particular, Signorino demonstrates that discrete choice estimation such as logit and probit or Heckman selection models possess shortcomings. The reason is they do not incorporate a situation where the observed outcome, followed by an agent's choice, depends on decisions strategically made by another. By ignoring the possibility of strategic decision making, these nonstrategic choice models can lead to incorrect inferences (Signorino 2002; Signorino and Yilmaz 2003).[3]

---

[1] Note, in Chapter 7 social interaction was nonstrategic – one group accepted information from another group. The form of social interaction in this chapter is strategic: Taking other decision-makers choice of action as given, a decision-maker chooses the best action (among all the actions available) in accordance with her preferences. This form of social interaction requires the use of game theory.

[2] The approach has also been used in studies of political choice (Carson 2003), international conflict (Signorino and Tarar 2006), and other areas (e.g., Carter 2010; Helmke 2010; McLean and Whang 2010). Carson (2003), for example, examines the likelihood Congress members choose to seek reelection or retire based on the decisions of potential challengers. Signorino and Tarar (2006) study the determinants of extended immediate deterrence in the context of strategic interaction between attackers and defenders.

[3] Along the same lines, Bas et al. (2008, 22) argue "the 'indirect' statistical tests of formal models generally fail to properly characterize the hypothesized relationships in statistical testing."

International Political Economy

The example we use in this chapter is from the field of international political economy. Leblang's (2003) study of speculative currency attacks employs QRE. Traditional studies on speculative exchange rate attacks examine the role of economic and political conditions that lead a country to be more or less likely to experience a currency attack by international financial markets (Krugman 1979; Obstfeld 1994; Eichengreen et al. 1996; Drazen 2000b; Grier and Lin 2010).

Leblang refines these arguments and suggests currency crises may not merely depend on domestic economic conditions. Instead, the observed outcome of currency attack can also be the result of strategic interaction between speculators and the domestic government. Speculators are likely to attack a currency if the policymakers are unwilling and unable to defend the currency peg. Yet, if speculators expect the government is willing and able to defend its currency peg, they are less likely to attack the currency in the first place since the expected cost of initiating the attack is too high. The exchange rate status quo prevails. As noted earlier, and in the language of EITM, the relations and reactions Leblang discusses involve the behavioral concepts – decision making, bargaining, strategic social interaction – and the empirical concept of nominal choice. The QRE links these concepts and provides the basis for unification.

10.2 STEP 1: RELATING DECISION MAKING, BARGAINING, STRATEGIC INTERACTION, AND NOMINAL CHOICE

The concepts decision making, bargaining, strategic social interaction, and nominal choice are related in the following way. Leblang (2003) assumes there are two players in an economy: international financial markets (*markets*) and policymakers in government (*governments*). The model is summarized in Figure 10.1. The financial markets have two choices: (1) they can initiate a speculative attack against a currency peg or (2) they can choose not to attack.

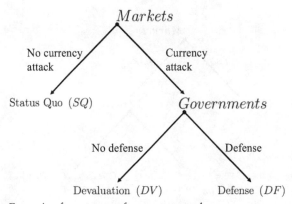

FIGURE 10.1. Extensive-form game of currency attacks

If *markets* choose not to attack, then the exchange rate situation will remain the status quo (*SQ*) and the game is over. On the other hand, if *markets* choose to attack, then *governments* must choose either devaluing the currency (*DV*) or defending the currency peg (*DF*).

10.3 STEP 2: ANALOGUES FOR DECISION MAKING, BARGAINING, STRATEGIC INTERACTION, AND NOMINAL CHOICE

The model assumes players are concerned about the utility over each outcome (see Figure 10.2). Let *markets'* utility for *SQ*, *DV*, and *DF* be defined as $U_M(SQ)$, $U_M(DV)$, and $U_M(DF)$, respectively, where $U_M(\cdot)$ represents the utility function of each observed outcome for *markets*. We also define $U_G(DV)$ and $U_G(DF)$ as the utility of devaluation and currency defense for *governments*, respectively.

Leblang (2003) assumes the true utility U_i^* for an outcome for each player i can be represented as an observable component $U_i(m)$ and an unobservable (or private) component ω_m^i:

$$U_i^*(m) = U_i(m) + \omega_m^i,$$

where $i \in \{markets, governments\}$ and $m \in \{SQ, DV, DF\}$. ω_m^i is defined as a random variable that has a normal distribution with mean 0 and variance σ^2 (i.e., $\omega_m^i \sim N(0, \sigma^2)$). For instance, we interpret ω_{DV}^M as private information for devaluation for *markets*, but it is unobservable to *governments* and to the analysts: *Governments* and analysts only know a statistical distribution of ω_{DV}^M.

Following Signorino (2003), Leblang derives equilibrium choice probabilities for each of the actions in the model. Let p_{AK} denote the probability *markets* attack the currency, and p_{DF} represents the probability *governments* defend the currency peg. *Governments'* decision calculus is as follows: It defends the currency peg only if the utility of defending the currency is larger than the utility of devaluation.

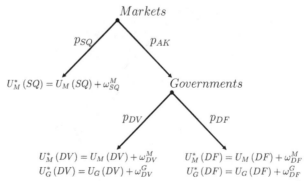

FIGURE 10.2. Extensive-form game with true utility

We can derive the corresponding probability of defending the currency as:

$$p_{DF} = \Phi\left(\frac{U_G(DF) - U_G(DV)}{\sigma\sqrt{2}}\right), \tag{10.1}$$

and the corresponding probability of devaluation as $p_{DV} = 1 - p_{DF}$, where $\Phi(\cdot)$ is the standard normal cumulative distribution function (CDF).[4]

Similarly, *markets* attack the currency only if the utility of attacking the currency is greater than the status quo utility. The corresponding probability of attacking the currency peg is:

$$p_{AK} = \Phi\left(\frac{p_{DV}U_M(DV) + p_{DF}U_M(DF) - U_M(SQ)}{\sigma\sqrt{1 + p_{DV}^2 + p_{DF}^2}}\right), \tag{10.2}$$

and the corresponding probability of the economic status quo is $p_{SQ} = 1 - p_{AK}$.

10.4 STEP 3: UNIFYING AND EVALUATING THE ANALOGUES

Given the derivation of Eqs. (10.1) and (10.2), we construct a likelihood equation based on these probabilities to obtain maximum likelihood estimates. For each observation n, let $y_{AK,n} = 1$ if the variable *markets* attacks the currency peg in observation n, and zero if the currency crisis remains in a status quo outcome. Let $y_{DF,n} = 1$ if the variable *governments* defends the currency peg, and zero otherwise. The log-likelihood function to be maximized is:

$$\ln L = \sum_{n=1}^{N} \left[(1 - y_{AK,n})\ln p_{SQ} + y_{AK,n}(1 - y_{DF,n})(\ln p_{AK} + \ln p_{DV})\right.$$
$$\left. + y_{AK,n}y_{DF,n}(\ln p_{AK} + \ln p_{DF})\right], \tag{10.3}$$

where N is the total number of observations.

With a sample of 90 developing countries over the period 1985–1998, Leblang defines a set of factors determining *markets'* utility and *governments'* utility. For *markets'* utility, Leblang considers the following factors affecting the probability of speculative attacks: expansionary monetary policy, overvaluation, large external imbalances, banking sector conditions, and the capital account conditions. For *governments'* utility, Leblang groups the factors into two areas: (1) the factors that influence the willingness to defend the currency peg and (2) the factors that reflect the ability to defend.

The factors influencing the willingness to defend are: electoral timing, constituent interests, and partisanship. The factors reflecting the ability to defend are: foreign exchange reserves, interest rates, capital controls, and policy

---

[4] See the Appendix for the theoretical background and estimation procedure.

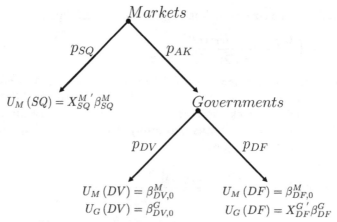

FIGURE 10.3. Leblang (2003) Model with regressors and parameters

decisiveness. Figure 10.3 shows the general specification of the expected utility functions employed in the data analysis. We also summarize the estimation system, known as a *strategic probit model*, as follows:

$$U_M(SQ) = \sum_{k=1}^{K} \beta_{SQ,k}^{M} x_{SQ,k}^{M} \tag{10.4}$$

$$U_M(DV) = \beta_{DV,0}^{M} \tag{10.5}$$

$$U_M(DF) = \beta_{DF,0}^{M} \tag{10.6}$$

$$U_G(DV) = \beta_{DV,0}^{G} \tag{10.7}$$

$$U_G(DF) = \sum_{h=1}^{H} \beta_{DF,h}^{G} x_{DF,h}^{G}, \tag{10.8}$$

where $\beta_{DV,0}^{M}$, $\beta_{DF,0}^{M}$, and $\beta_{DV,0}^{G}$ are constant terms, the vectors of control variables are as follows:[5]

- X_{SQ}^{M} = [Capital controls$_{t-1}$, Log(reserve/base money)$_{t-1}$, Real exchange rate overvaluation, Domestic credit growth$_{t-1}$, US domestic interest rate$_{t-1}$, External debt service$_{t-1}$, Contagion, Number of prior speculative attacks],
- X_{DF}^{G} = [Unified government, Log(exports/GDP)$_{t-1}$, Campaign and election period, Post-election period, Right government, Real interest rate$_{t-1}$, Capital controls$_{t-1}$, Log(reserves/base money)$_{t-1}$],

---

[5] See Leblang (2003) for the definitions of the variables.

and β_{SQ}^M and β_{DF}^G are the corresponding vector of coefficients on X_{SQ}^M and X_{DF}^G, respectively. For the specification of the dependent variable, there are several ways the dependent variable can be specified in the dataset. These include:

- $y = 1$ if there is no currency attack (SQ),
- $y = 2$ if the government devalues the currency in response to an attack (DV),
- $y = 3$ if the government defends the currency in response to an attack (DF).

The EITM linkage can be seen in Figures 10.1, 10.2, and 10.3. Starting with a two-player game theoretic model illustrated in Figure 10.1, *markets* are the first mover. They decide on a currency attack. The follower, *governments*, respond to the market action. Leblang converts the model so players' decisions are associated with specific utility functions presented in Figure 10.2. As a result, the utility function for each outcome in the model can be estimated based on the system of Eqs. (10.4)–(10.6) in Figure 10.3.

We estimate the model using the **games** package in the **R** program.[6] The estimated result of the strategic probit model is provided in Table 10.1, and is directly linked with Eqs. (10.4)–(10.8). The first three columns of Table 10.1 correspond to Eqs. (10.4)–(10.6) in the model. The estimated results shows some economic fundamentals, such as capital control policy, lack of foreign reserves, real exchange rate overvaluation, domestic credit growth, international economic instability and number of past speculative attacks, can significantly raise the likelihood of speculative attacks in the market. The last column in Table 10.1 is associated with Eqs. (10.7) and (10.8). The results here show real interest rates, foreign reserves, campaign and election period, post-election period, and right of center governments are significantly associated with the likelihood of defending the currency peg in the country.

10.5 SUMMARY

Leblang (2003) applies a unified framework to test the model of speculative currency attacks. He uses the behavioral concepts of rational decision making and strategic interaction. His behavioral analogues are expected utility maximization and game theory. These behavioral analogues are linked with an applied statistical analogue for discrete choice: the probit model with random utility – QRE.

Subsequent international political economy research has extended QRE applications. Whang et al. (2013), for example, develop a game theoretic model to study the informational and coercive effects of sanction threats. The authors estimate – using QRE – the model using the Threat and Imposition of Sanctions (TIES) database, which covers all sanctions cases from 1971 to 2000. They

---

[6] The **games** package is written by Brenton Kenkel and Curtis S. Signorino (see Kenkel and Signorino 2014).

TABLE 10.1. *Leblang's (2003) results*

	Markets Equations (10.4)–(10.6)			Governments Equations (10.7) and (10.8)
	U_M (SQ)	U_M (DV)	U_M (DF)	U_G (DF)
Intercept		−3.6648*** (0.3855)	−3.1385*** (0.4057)	0.4269 (1.7442)
Capital control$_{t-1}$	−0.4525** (0.3352)			0.0656 (1.7098)
Log(reserve/base money)$_{t-1}$	0.2292*** (0.0629)			0.3099* (0.2046)
Real exchange rate overvaluation	−0.4413*** (0.1400)			
Domestic credit growth$_{t-1}$	−0.0648** (0.0380)			
US domestic interest rate$_{t-1}$	−0.0505 (0.0507)			
External debt service$_{t-1}$	−0.0288 (0.0401)			
Contagion	−0.1159** (0.0435)			
Number of prior speculative attacks	−0.1218** (0.0457)			
Unified government				−0.3568 (0.3862)
Log(exports/GDP)$_{t-1}$				−0.1997 (0.1891)
Campaign and election period				1.6632** (1.9215)
Post-election period				1.0623* (0.9031)
Right government				−0.9358** (0.5176)
Real interest rate$_{t-1}$				1.7955*** (1.0693)
Log-likelihood	−482.0155			
Number of observations	7240			

Notes: Standard errors in brackets. *** significant at 1%, ** significant at 5%, * significant at 10%.

International Political Economy

find sanction threats are an instrument of coercion. Bapat and Kwon (2015) investigate the optimal strategy of sanction threats when the sender's share of the target's market is considered. Again using the TIES database, they find the sender's share of a target's market significantly affects the likelihood of sanction success and imposition. In a different research context, Carter and Stone (2015) develop a strategic voting model to understand how other nations make decisions of voting with or against the United States in the UN General Assembly. The authors find poor democracies vote with the United States because of the linkage of foreign aid with the United States, but not the shared democratic values.

Leblang's EITM model can be leveraged in other ways as well. One of the extensions is to include monetary factors (e.g., policy rules) in the model since exchange rate policy largely depends on the monetary policy stance. Moreover, because the current model is based on a bilateral strategic interaction between speculators and the government a revised model could incorporate self-fulfilling expectations to allow for the possibility of currency crisis contagion (Keister 2009).

10.6 APPENDIX

The tools in this chapter are used to establish a transparent and testable relation between strategic social interaction and discrete choice. The formal tools include a presentation of basic game theory. The applied statistical tools are slightly different in that the estimation method already incorporates fusing game theory with discrete choice estimation – quantal response equilibrium (QRE). The last section of this appendix provides the code and data in applying QRE to Leblang (2003).

10.6.1 Formal Analogues

A Simple Game Theoretic Model

This appendix describes a basic idea of strategic choice analysis using a simple strategic model with two players and three observable outcomes. The model, as depicted in Figure 10.4, has two players, a and b. These players make one of the following two choices: left or right. Assume player a is a first-mover (or leader) and player b is a second-mover (or follower). If player a chooses L, the game is over and player b does not choose: The final outcome is L. On the other hand, if player a chooses R, then player b chooses either left l or right r. There are two possible outcomes in this case: Rl or Rr, respectively.

Assuming players are rational and well-informed, we determine via backward induction the equilibrium of a finite extensive game – the subgame perfect Nash equilibrium (SPE). We solve the optimal decision players a and b choose by starting at the end of the game (the end decision nodes) and working backward.

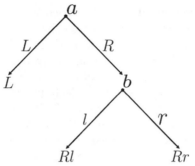

FIGURE 10.4. Two-player, three-outcome game

Figure 10.5 illustrates the three possible outcomes of the two-player, three-outcome game described in Figure 10.4. Given the three possible outcomes, suppose player a's preferences are $Rl \succ L \succ Rr$, and player b's are $Rl \succ Rr$.[7] We start with the decision made by player b since she makes the final decision in the game. If player a chooses R, player b will choose l over r as player b prefers the outcome of Rl to Rr. When player a is well-informed about player b's decision, player a will evaluate the outcome between L and Rl and make a decision of choosing R at the beginning. Therefore, the subgame perfect Nash equilibrium is Rl, where a chooses R and b chooses l as their optimal decision and they will not deviate from their optimal decision. We illustrate this result in Figure 10.5(a). We also present other possible SPE when we alter the preferences for players a and b in Figures 10.5(b) and 10.5(c).

To simplify the preference description, we use a utility function $U(\cdot)$ to assign a number to every possible outcome such that the more-preferred outcomes get assigned larger values than less-preferred outcomes. According to our previous example, player b prefers Rl to Rr if and only if the utility of Rl is larger than the utility of Rr. In symbols, $Rl \succ Rr$ if and only if $U_b(Rl) > U_b(Rr)$, where $U_i(\cdot)$ represents the utility function for player i. Similarly, we describe player a's preferences in terms of utility as follows: $U_a(Rl) > U_a(L) > U_a(Rr)$. We revise the extensive game in Figure 10.6.

Quantal Response Equilibrium (QRE)

The assumptions of rationality and perfect information provide greater ease in computation. The (Nash) equilibrium can be derived with certainty. However, Signorino (1999, 281) argues that, "[t]raditional equilibrium concepts prove

---

[7] We denote the symbol $\succ$ to mean that one option (or bundle) is strictly preferred to another. For example, $x \succ y$ implies that x is preferred to y. Furthermore, $x \succ y \succ z$ implies that $x \succ y$ and $y \succ z$, and $x \succ z$ according to the property of transitivity.

International Political Economy

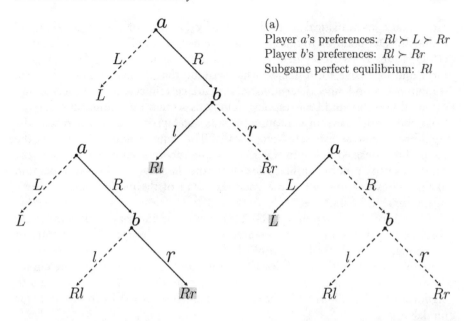

(a)
Player a's preferences: $Rl \succ L \succ Rr$
Player b's preferences: $Rl \succ Rr$
Subgame perfect equilibrium: Rl

(b)
Player a's preferences: $Rr \succ L \succ Rl$
Player b's preferences: $Rr \succ Rl$
Subgame perfect equilibrium: Rr

(c)
Player a's preferences: $L \succ Rl \succ Rr$
Player b's preferences: $Rl \succ Rr$
Subgame perfect equilibrium: L

⎯⎯⎯→ An option that player i chooses
- - - - -→ An option that player i does not choose

FIGURE 10.5. Subgame perfect equilibrium in a two-player, three-outcome game

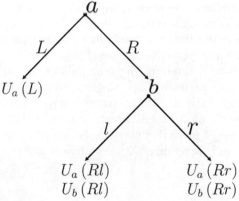

FIGURE 10.6. A two-player, three-outcome game with utility functions

problematic in statistical analysis primarily because of the zero-likelihood problem." One solution to this challenge can be found in McKelvey and Palfrey (1995, 1996, 1998). They develop a random utility model (RUM) for normal form and extensive form games. They assume that agents' utilities and best responses are no longer deterministic. Instead, certain stochastic processes are assumed in utility and best response functions so that the equilibrium derived from the model can have meaningful statistical properties. As a result, the equilibrium can be estimated empirically. This equilibrium is known as the quantal response equilibrium (QRE) – a game-theoretic equilibrium under the assumption of random utility. McKelvey and Palfrey (1995) use maximum likelihood estimation to test the goodness of fit of the model using a variety of experimental data.

Signorino (1999) applies QRE to a study of international conflict. In contrast to prior work in this research area, he incorporates the structure of the strategic interdependence into a broader empirical estimation procedure. Here, we introduce the idea (described above) of the strategic discrete choice estimation based on a two-player, three-outcome model. We refer readers to Signorino (1999, 2003) and Kenkel and Signorino (2014) for other strategic models.

We noted earlier that rationality and perfect information assumptions result in "zero-likelihood" for statistical analysis. Signorino (1999, 2003) relaxes these assumptions and assumes one of two forms of uncertainty: (1) agent error and (2) private information. The uncertainty assumptions impose a certain structure for the stochastic process, a process which is crucial for the estimation of utility parameters in the game-theoretic model. In the case of agent error, each player's utility over outcomes is fixed and observable for other players. However, player i might not be able to choose the utility-maximizing option correctly. There exists an unobservable stochastic stock ϵ^i, which can lead player i to pick an alternative option, where the stochastic shock is assumed to be either normally or logistically distributed.

Figure 10.7 illustrates the basic structure of a strategic choice model with agent error. We assume player a chooses L and R with the probability of p_L and p_R, respectively. Similarly, the probabilities for player b to choose l and r are p_l and p_r, respectively. Each player's utility depends on the strategic outcome in the game. To demonstrate how both players a and b determine their decisions, we solve the model by backward induction. Assume that player b's true utility of choosing l, given that player a chooses R, is the sum of observable utility $U_a(Rl)$ – a linear function of X^i_{Rl} explanatory variables, and a stochastic shock ϵ^b_{Rl}:

International Political Economy

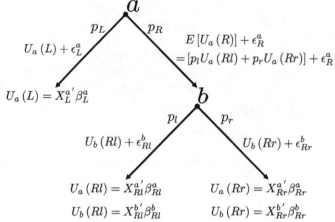

FIGURE 10.7. The case of agent error

$$U_b^*(Rl) = U_b(Rl) + \epsilon_{Rl}^b$$
$$= X_{Rl}^{b'}\beta_{Rl}^b + \epsilon_{Rl}^b, \quad (10.9)$$

where $U_b(Rl) = X_{Rl}^{b'}\beta_{Rl}^b$ and $\epsilon_{Rl}^b \sim N(0, \sigma^2)$ is a stochastic shock (perceptual error) to player b's true utility function of choosing l. Similarly, the true utility for player b to choose r is:

$$U_b^*(Rr) = U_b(Rr) + \epsilon_{Rr}^b$$
$$= X_{Rr}^{b'}\beta_{Rr}^b + \epsilon_{Rr}^b, \quad (10.10)$$

when player a's action is R, where $U_b(Rr) = X_{Rr}^{b'}\beta_{Rr}^b$ and $\epsilon_{Rr}^b \sim N(0, \sigma^2)$ is a stochastic shock to the true utility function of choosing r. Using Eqs. (10.9) and (10.10), player b's decision of choosing r over l is based on the following ex ante probability:

$$p_r = Prob\left[U_b^*(Rr) \geq U_b^*(Rl)\right]$$
$$= Prob\left(X_{Rr}^{b'}\beta_{Rr}^b + \epsilon_{Rr}^b \geq X_{Rl}^{b'}\beta_{Rl}^b + \epsilon_{Rl}^b\right)$$
$$= Prob\left(\epsilon_{Rl}^b - \epsilon_{Rr}^b \leq X_{Rr}^{b'}\beta_{Rr}^b - X_{Rl}^{b'}\beta_{Rl}^b\right)$$
$$= \Phi\left(\frac{X_{Rr}^{b'}\beta_{Rr}^b - X_{Rl}^{b'}\beta_{Rl}^b}{\sigma\sqrt{2}}\right), \quad (10.11)$$

where $\Phi(\cdot)$ is the standard normal cumulative distribution function (CDF).[8] The probability for player b to choose l is $p_l = 1 - p_r$.

Next we apply a similar procedure to determine player a's propensities for action. Since player a's utility of choosing R depends on the action chosen by player b, we first express player a's expected utility of choosing R as the a weighted average of observable utilities from two player b's actions, that is:

$$E[U_a(R)] = p_l U_a(Rl) + p_r U_a(Rr)$$
$$= p_l X_{Rl}^{a'} \beta_{Rl}^a + p_r X_{Rr}^{a'} \beta_{Rr}^a.$$

As a result, player a's true utility of choosing R can be written as follows:

$$U_a^*(R) = E[U_a(R)] + \epsilon_R^a$$
$$= [p_l U_a(Rl) + p_r U_a(Rr)] + \epsilon_R^a$$
$$= p_l X_{Rl}^{a'} \beta_{Rl}^a + p_r X_{Rr}^{a'} \beta_{Rr}^a + \epsilon_R^a,$$

where $\epsilon_R^a \sim N(0, \sigma^2)$ is the stochastic shock to player a's utility when choosing R. Similarly, the true utility of choosing L for player a is:

$$U_a^*(L) = U_a(L) + \epsilon_L^a$$
$$= X_L^{a'} \beta_L^a + \epsilon_L^a,$$

where $\epsilon_L^a \sim N(0, \sigma^2)$ is the perceptual error in the utility function for choosing L. Finally, we can apply a similar method for computing the probabilities of player a's actions. The ex ante probability for player a to choose R over L is:

$$p_R = Prob[U_a^*(R) \geq U_a^*(L)]$$
$$= Prob\left[\left(p_l X_{Rl}^{a'} \beta_{Rl}^a + p_r X_{Rr}^{a'} \beta_{Rr}^a\right) + \epsilon_R^a \geq X_L^{a'} \beta_L^a + \epsilon_L^a\right]$$

---

[8] The CDF of a random variable X is the probability that takes a value less than or equal to x_0, where x_0 is some specified numerical value of X, that is, $\Phi(X = x_0) = Prob(X \leq x_0)$. For a variable X, which follows the normal distribution with mean μ and variance σ^2, its probability density function (PDF) is:

$$\phi(X) = \frac{1}{\sqrt{2\sigma^2 \pi}} \exp\left(-(X-\mu)^2 / 2\sigma^2\right),$$

and its CDF is:

$$\Phi(X) = \int_{-\infty}^{X_0} \frac{1}{\sqrt{2\sigma^2 \pi}} \exp\left(-(X-\mu)^2 / 2\sigma^2\right).$$

See the Appendix in Chapter 8 for a detailed discussion of probit and logit models and the Appendix in Chapter 9 for a discussion of CDF's and PDF's.

$$= \text{Prob}\left(\epsilon_L^a - \epsilon_R^a \leq p_l X_{Rl}^{a'}\beta_{Rl}^a + p_r X_{Rr}^{a'}\beta_{Rr}^a - X_L^{a'}\beta_L^a\right)$$

$$= \Phi\left(\frac{p_l X_{Rl}^{a'}\beta_{Rl}^a + p_r X_{Rr}^{a'}\beta_{Rr}^a - X_L^{a'}\beta_L^a}{\sigma\sqrt{2}}\right). \tag{10.12}$$

It follows that the probability of taking option L is $p_L = 1 - p_R$.

Next, instead of relaxing the assumption of perfect rationality in the case of agent error model, Signorino (2002) suggests an alternative approach to include an unobservable private (information) component or shock (denoted as ω_m^i), where $\omega_m^i \sim N(0, \sigma^2)$, for $i \in \{a, b\}$ and $m \in \{L, Rl, Rr\}$. The unobservable private shock limits the analyst or the player to evaluate the other player's preferences over outcomes. Figure 10.8 summarizes the basic concept of private information. We now calculate the probabilities of actions for both players according to their true utilities. For player b, the ex ante probability of choosing r is:

$$p_r = \text{Prob}\left(U_b^*(Rr) \geq U_b^*(Rl)\right)$$

$$= \text{Prob}\left(U_b(Rr) + \omega_{Rr}^b \geq U_b(Rl) + \omega_{Rl}^b\right)$$

$$= \text{Prob}\left(\omega_{Rl}^b - \omega_{Rr}^b \leq U_b(Rr) - U_b(Rl)\right)$$

$$= \text{Prob}\left(\omega_{Rl}^b - \omega_{Rr}^b \leq X_{Rr}^{b'}\beta_{Rr}^b - X_{Rl}^{b'}\beta_{Rl}^b\right)$$

$$= \Phi\left(\frac{X_{Rr}^{b'}\beta_{Rr}^b - X_{Rl}^{b'}\beta_{Rl}^b}{\sigma\sqrt{2}}\right). \tag{10.13}$$

For choosing l, the probability is $p_l = 1 - p_r$. On the other hand, when player a chooses R, her expected true utility is:

$$U_a^*(R) = p_l\left(X_{Rl}^{a'}\beta_{Rl}^a + \omega_{Rl}^a\right) + p_r\left(X_{Rr}^{a'}\beta_{Rr}^a + \omega_{Rr}^a\right).$$

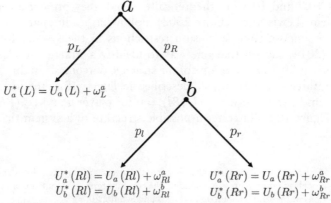

FIGURE 10.8. The case of private information

Therefore, player a's probability for choosing R over L is:

$$p_R = Prob\left(U_a^*(R) \geq U_a^*(L)\right)$$

$$= Prob\left(p_l\left(X_{Rl}^{a'}\beta_{Rl}^a + \omega_{Rl}^a\right) + p_r\left(X_{Rr}^{a'}\beta_{Rr}^a + \omega_{Rr}^a\right) \geq X_L^{a'}\beta_L^a + \omega_L^a\right)$$

$$= Prob\left(\omega_L^a - p_l\omega_{Rl}^a - p_r\omega_{Rr}^a \leq p_l X_{Rl}^{a'}\beta_{Rl}^a + p_r X_{Rr}^{a'}\beta_{Rr}^a - X_L^{a'}\beta_L^a\right)$$

$$= \Phi\left(\frac{p_l X_{Rl}^{a'}\beta_{Rl}^a + p_r X_{Rr}^{a'}\beta_{Rr}^a - X_L^{a'}\beta_L^a}{\sigma\sqrt{1 + p_l^2 + p_r^2}}\right), \tag{10.14}$$

and the probability for L is $p_L = 1 - p_R$.

Assuming there are N repeated plays in the game. In each play n, we define $y_{an} = 1$ if the observable action of player a is R, and $y_{an} = 0$ if the observable action is L. Similarly, we define $y_{bn} = 1$ if the observable action of player b is r, and $y_{bn} = 0$ if the observable action is l. We present the following likelihood function for all N plays:

$$L = \Pi_{n=1}^N p_L^{(1-y_{an})} \left(p_R p_l\right)^{y_{an}(1-y_{bn})} \left(p_R p_r\right)^{y_{an}y_{bn}}. \tag{10.15}$$

We can then estimate the model parameters (either in the agent error model or in the private information model) by maximizing the following log of the likelihood function (10.16):

$$\ln L = \sum_{n=1}^N \left[(1 - y_{an})\ln p_L + y_{an}(1 - y_{bn})(\ln p_R + \ln p_l)\right.$$
$$\left. + y_{an}y_{bn}(\ln p_R + \ln p_r)\right]. \tag{10.16}$$

Since the log-likelihood function is nonlinear, we do not obtain a closed-form solution for β's. However, we can perform numerical maximization since Eq. (10.16) is globally concave. While the strategic systems presented in Figures 10.7 and 10.8 are theoretically sound, they present an identification problem (Lewis and Schultz 2003). Following traditional practice, it is necessary to impose some exclusion restrictions in the system. Kenkel and Signorino (2014) suggest that one way to identify a strategic model is to set each player's utility to zero for one of the strategic outcomes.[9] In this particular two-player, three-outcome model, described in Figure 10.6, the identification condition can be satisfied when $U_a(Rl) = 0$ for player a and $U_b(Rl) = 0$ for player b. Figure 10.9 illustrates a possible structure of a system that satisfies

---

[9] Kenkel and Signorino (2014) indicate that, in general, a necessary condition for identification in a strategic model is that no regressor, including the constant term, is included in all of a player's utility functions of the strategic outcomes (Lewis and Schultz 2003).

International Political Economy

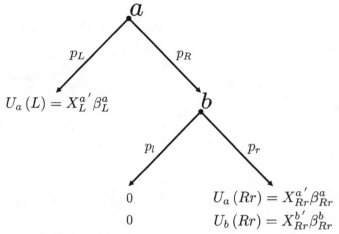

FIGURE 10.9. Identified model with regressors and parameters

the identification condition for estimating the model. We impose the following specification:

$$U_a(L) = \beta^a_{L,0} + \beta^a_{L,1} x_1$$
$$U_a(Rl) = 0$$
$$U_a(Rr) = \beta^a_{Rr,0} + \beta^a_{Rr,1} x_1 + \beta^a_{Rr,2} x_2$$
$$U_b(Rl) = 0$$
$$U_b(Rr) = \beta^b_{Rr,0} + \beta^b_{Rr,2} x_2 + \beta^b_{Rr,3} x_3,$$

and define: $X^a_L = [1, x_1]$, $X^a_{Rr} = [1, x_1, x_2]$, $X^a_{Rr} = [1, x_2, x_3]$, $\beta^a_L = [\beta^a_{L,0}, \beta^a_{L,1}]$, $\beta^a_{Rr} = [\beta^a_{Rr,0}, \beta^a_{Rr,1}, \beta^a_{Rr,2}]$, and $\beta^b_{Rr} = [\beta^b_{Rr,0}, \beta^b_{Rr,2}, \beta^b_{Rr,3}]$.

Details on the Leblang (2003) Application

In 2001, Signorino developed **STRAT**, a program for analyzing statistical strategic models written in Gauss language. Since then, Kenkel and Signorino (2014) further developed the program and implemented a new package, called **games**, in R language. The **games** package provides estimation and analysis for different forms of game-theoretic models. In this appendix, we illustrate the usage of **egame12** in the package for the estimation of the two-player, three-outcome model based on Leblang's (2003) estimation results.

Here we present the estimation procedure for the system of Eqs. (10.4)–(10.8) presented in the chapter.[10] The **games** package also allows other

---

[10] The data set can be downloaded from uh.edu/hobby/eitm/eitmbook/.

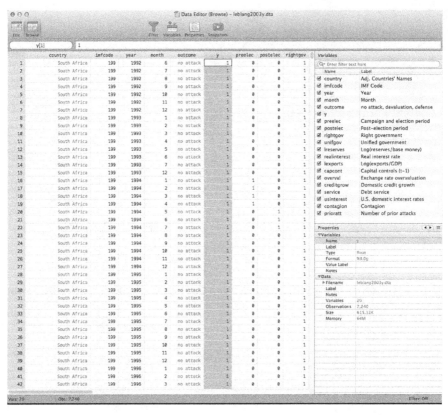

FIGURE 10.10. Leblang (2003) data set in **STATA**

specifications for defining the dependent variable.[11] To estimate the model using **R**, first-time **R** users need to install the **games** package in **R** by typing:

install.packages("games", dependencies=TRUE)

R uses a specific package that can be linked to other packages. If the dependencies=TRUE argument is specified, then **R** uses the full capacity of the specific package by downloading and installing other packages. Then we load the **games** package from the library by typing:

library("games")

Since the data set we use is in **STATA** format (Figure 10.10), we import the **STATA** data file (leblang2003y.dta) into **R** using a package called **foreign**. We first install the **foreign** package by typing:

install.packages("foreign", dependencies=TRUE)

---

[11] We refer interested readers to the tutorial of **games** packages by Kenkel and Signorino (2014).

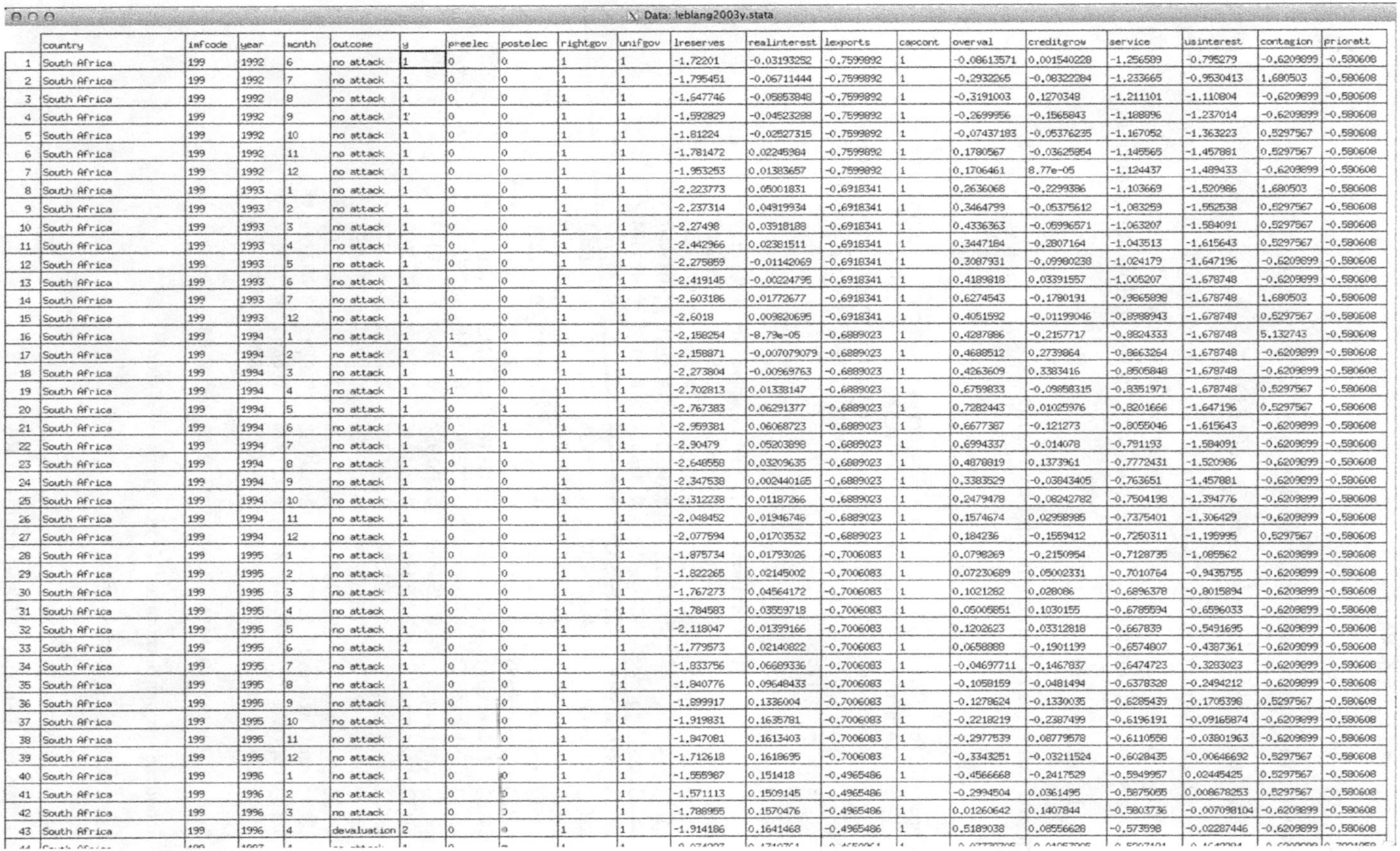

Data: leblang2003y.stata

	country	imfcode	year	month	outcome	y	preelec	postelec	rightgov	unifgov	lreserves	realinterest	lexports	capcont	overval	creditgrow	service	usinterest	contagion	prioratt
1	South Africa	199	1992	6	no attack	1	0	0	1	1	-1.72201	-0.03193252	-0.7599892	1	-0.08613571	0.001540228	-1.256589	-0.795279	-0.6209899	-0.580608
2	South Africa	199	1992	7	no attack	1	0	0	1	1	-1.795451	-0.06711444	-0.7599892	1	-0.2932265	-0.08322284	-1.233665	-0.9530413	1.680503	-0.580608
3	South Africa	199	1992	8	no attack	1	0	0	1	1	-1.647746	-0.05853848	-0.7599892	1	-0.3191003	0.1270348	-1.211101	-1.110804	-0.6209899	-0.580608
4	South Africa	199	1992	9	no attack	1	0	0	1	1	-1.592829	-0.04523288	-0.7599892	1	-0.2699956	-0.1565843	-1.188896	-1.237014	-0.6209899	-0.580608
5	South Africa	199	1992	10	no attack	1	0	0	1	1	-1.81224	-0.02527315	-0.7599892	1	-0.07437183	-0.05376235	-1.167052	-1.363223	0.5297567	-0.580608
6	South Africa	199	1992	11	no attack	1	0	0	1	1	-1.781472	0.02245984	-0.7599892	1	0.1780567	-0.03625854	-1.145565	-1.457881	0.5297567	-0.580608
7	South Africa	199	1992	12	no attack	1	0	0	1	1	-1.953253	0.01383657	-0.7599892	1	0.1706461	8.77e-05	-1.124437	-1.489433	-0.6209899	-0.580608
8	South Africa	199	1993	1	no attack	1	0	0	1	1	-2.223773	0.05001831	-0.6918341	1	0.2636068	-0.2299386	-1.103669	-1.520986	1.680503	-0.580608
9	South Africa	199	1993	2	no attack	1	0	0	1	1	-2.237314	0.04919934	-0.6918341	1	0.3464799	-0.05375612	-1.083259	-1.552538	0.5297567	-0.580608
10	South Africa	199	1993	3	no attack	1	0	0	1	1	-2.27498	0.03918188	-0.6918341	1	0.4336363	-0.05996571	-1.063207	-1.584091	0.5297567	-0.580608
11	South Africa	199	1993	4	no attack	1	0	0	1	1	-2.442966	0.02381511	-0.6918341	1	0.3447184	-0.2807164	-1.043513	-1.615643	0.5297567	-0.580608
12	South Africa	199	1993	5	no attack	1	0	0	1	1	-2.275859	-0.01142069	-0.6918341	1	0.3087931	-0.09980238	-1.024179	-1.647196	-0.6209899	-0.580608
13	South Africa	199	1993	6	no attack	1	0	0	1	1	-2.419145	-0.00224795	-0.6918341	1	0.4189818	0.03391557	-1.005207	-1.678748	-0.6209899	-0.580608
14	South Africa	199	1993	7	no attack	1	0	0	1	1	-2.603186	0.01772677	-0.6918341	1	0.6274543	-0.1780191	-0.9865838	-1.678748	1.680503	-0.580608
15	South Africa	199	1993	12	no attack	1	0	0	1	1	-2.6018	0.009820695	-0.6918341	1	0.4051592	-0.01199046	-0.8988943	-1.678748	0.5297567	-0.580608
16	South Africa	199	1994	1	no attack	1	1	0	1	1	-2.158254	-8.79e-05	-0.6889023	1	0.4287886	-0.2157717	-0.8824333	-1.678748	5.132743	-0.580608
17	South Africa	199	1994	2	no attack	1	1	0	1	1	-2.158871	-0.007079079	-0.6889023	1	0.4688512	0.2739864	-0.8663264	-1.678748	-0.6209899	-0.580608
18	South Africa	199	1994	3	no attack	1	1	0	1	1	-2.273804	-0.00969763	-0.6889023	1	0.4263609	0.3383416	-0.8505848	-1.678748	-0.6209899	-0.580608
19	South Africa	199	1994	4	no attack	1	1	0	1	1	-2.702813	0.01338147	-0.6889023	1	0.6759833	-0.09858315	-0.8351971	-1.678748	0.5297567	-0.580608
20	South Africa	199	1994	5	no attack	1	0	1	1	1	-2.767383	0.06291377	-0.6889023	1	0.7282443	0.01025976	-0.8201666	-1.647196	0.5297567	-0.580608
21	South Africa	199	1994	6	no attack	1	0	1	1	1	-2.959381	0.06068723	-0.6889023	1	0.6677387	-0.121273	-0.8055046	-1.615643	-0.6209899	-0.580608
22	South Africa	199	1994	7	no attack	1	0	1	1	1	-2.90479	0.05203898	-0.6889023	1	0.6994337	-0.014078	-0.791193	-1.584091	-0.6209899	-0.580608
23	South Africa	199	1994	8	no attack	1	0	0	1	1	-2.648558	0.03209635	-0.6889023	1	0.4878819	0.1373961	-0.7772431	-1.520986	-0.6209899	-0.580608
24	South Africa	199	1994	9	no attack	1	0	0	1	1	-2.347538	0.002440165	-0.6889023	1	0.3383529	-0.03843405	-0.763651	-1.457881	-0.6209899	-0.580608
25	South Africa	199	1994	10	no attack	1	0	0	1	1	-2.312238	0.01187266	-0.6889023	1	0.2479478	-0.08242782	-0.7504198	-1.394776	-0.6209899	-0.580608
26	South Africa	199	1994	11	no attack	1	0	0	1	1	-2.048452	0.01946746	-0.6889023	1	0.1574674	0.02958985	-0.7375401	-1.306429	-0.6209899	-0.580608
27	South Africa	199	1994	12	no attack	1	0	0	1	1	-2.077594	0.01703532	-0.6889023	1	0.184236	-0.1559412	-0.7250311	-1.195995	0.5297567	-0.580608
28	South Africa	199	1995	1	no attack	1	0	0	1	1	-1.875734	0.01793026	-0.7006083	1	0.0798269	-0.2150954	-0.7128735	-1.085562	-0.6209899	-0.580608
29	South Africa	199	1995	2	no attack	1	0	0	1	1	-1.822265	0.02145002	-0.7006083	1	0.07230689	0.05002331	-0.7010764	-0.9435755	-0.6209899	-0.580608
30	South Africa	199	1995	3	no attack	1	0	0	1	1	-1.767273	0.04564172	-0.7006083	1	0.1021282	0.028086	-0.6896378	-0.8015894	-0.6209899	-0.580608
31	South Africa	199	1995	4	no attack	1	0	0	1	1	-1.784583	0.03559718	-0.7006083	1	0.05005851	0.1030155	-0.6785594	-0.6596033	-0.6209899	-0.580608
32	South Africa	199	1995	5	no attack	1	0	0	1	1	-2.118047	0.01399166	-0.7006083	1	0.1202623	0.03312818	-0.667839	-0.5491695	-0.6209899	-0.580608
33	South Africa	199	1995	6	no attack	1	0	0	1	1	-1.779573	0.02140822	-0.7006083	1	0.0658888	-0.1901199	-0.6574807	-0.4387361	-0.6209899	-0.580608
34	South Africa	199	1995	7	no attack	1	0	0	1	1	-1.833756	0.06689336	-0.7006083	1	-0.04697711	-0.1467837	-0.6474723	-0.3283023	-0.6209899	-0.580608
35	South Africa	199	1995	8	no attack	1	0	0	1	1	-1.840776	0.09648433	-0.7006083	1	-0.1058159	-0.0481494	-0.6378328	-0.2494212	-0.6209899	-0.580608
36	South Africa	199	1995	9	no attack	1	0	0	1	1	-1.899917	0.1336004	-0.7006083	1	-0.1278624	-0.1330035	-0.6285439	-0.1705398	0.5297567	-0.580608
37	South Africa	199	1995	10	no attack	1	0	0	1	1	-1.919831	0.1635781	-0.7006083	1	-0.2218219	-0.2387499	-0.6196191	-0.09165874	-0.6209899	-0.580608
38	South Africa	199	1995	11	no attack	1	0	0	1	1	-1.847081	0.1613403	-0.7006083	1	-0.2977539	0.08779578	-0.6110558	-0.03801963	-0.6209899	-0.580608
39	South Africa	199	1995	12	no attack	1	0	0	1	1	-1.712618	0.1618695	-0.7006083	1	-0.3343251	-0.03211524	-0.6028435	-0.00646692	0.5297567	-0.580608
40	South Africa	199	1996	1	no attack	1	0	0	1	1	-1.555987	0.151418	-0.4965486	1	-0.4566668	-0.2417529	-0.5949957	0.02445425	0.5297567	-0.580608
41	South Africa	199	1996	2	no attack	1	0	0	1	1	-1.571113	0.1509145	-0.4965486	1	-0.2994504	0.0361495	-0.5875065	0.008678253	0.5297567	-0.580608
42	South Africa	199	1996	3	no attack	1	0	0	1	1	-1.788955	0.1570476	-0.4965486	1	0.01260642	0.1407844	-0.5803736	-0.007098104	-0.6209899	-0.580608
43	South Africa	199	1996	4	devaluation	2	0	0	1	1	-1.914186	0.1641468	-0.4965486	1	0.5189038	0.08556628	-0.573598	-0.02287446	-0.6209899	-0.580608

FIGURE 10.11. Leblang (2003) data set in **R**

and then load the package:

`library("foreign")`

Now we can import the Leblang's data into **R** by typing:

`leblang2003y.stata <- read.dta("file_path/leblang2003y.dta")`

where `file_path/` is the location where the STATA file is saved. After importing, the data file in **R** is now called leblang2003y.stata. We can view the data set as presented in Figure 10.11 using the following command:

`View(leblang2003y.stata)`

Now we estimate Leblang's model by typing:

```
Call:
egame12(formulas = y ~ capcont + lreserves + overval + creditgrow +
    usinterest + service + contagion + prioratt - 1 | 1 | 1 | 1 |
    unifgov + lexports + preelec + postelec + rightgov + realinterest +
        capcont + lreserves, data = leblang2003y.stata, link = "probit",
    type = "private")

Coefficients:
                     Estimate Std. Error   z value  Pr(>|z|)
u1(1):capcont        -0.452469   0.246015   -1.8392  0.065887 .
u1(1):lreserves       0.229181   0.056868    4.0301 5.576e-05 ***
u1(1):overval        -0.441258   0.085546   -5.1581 2.494e-07 ***
u1(1):creditgrow     -0.064819   0.028834   -2.2480  0.024574 *
u1(1):usinterest     -0.050541   0.055535   -0.9101  0.362787
u1(1):service        -0.028797   0.054734   -0.5261  0.598807
u1(1):contagion      -0.115889   0.047754   -2.4268  0.015233 *
u1(1):prioratt       -0.121824   0.048525   -2.5105  0.012055 *
u1(2):(Intercept)    -3.664825   0.298936  -12.2596 < 2.2e-16 ***
u1(3):(Intercept)    -3.138530   0.286409  -10.9582 < 2.2e-16 ***
u2(3):(Intercept)     0.426935   0.782241    0.5458  0.585214
u2(3):unifgov        -0.356759   0.357950   -0.9967  0.318923
u2(3):lexports       -0.199745   0.174444   -1.1450  0.252193
u2(3):preelec         1.663190   0.746972    2.2266  0.025976 *
u2(3):postelec        1.062284   0.592304    1.7935  0.072896 .
u2(3):rightgov       -0.935812   0.454065   -2.0610  0.039306 *
u2(3):realinterest    1.795540   0.600695    2.9891  0.002798 **
u2(3):capcont         0.065582   0.757930    0.0865  0.931047
u2(3):lreserves       0.309912   0.165696    1.8704  0.061433 .
---
Signif. codes:  0 '***' 0.001 '**' 0.01 '*' 0.05 '.' 0.1 ' ' 1

Standard errors estimated from inverse Hessian

Log-likelihood: -482.0155
AIC: 1002.031
No. observations: 7240
```

FIGURE 10.12. Leblang's (2003) results in **R**

```
m1 <- egame12(y ~ capcont + lreserves + overval +
creditgrow + usinterest + service + contagion + prioratt
- 1 | 1 | 1 | unifgov + lexports + preelec + postelec +
rightgov + realinterest + capcont + lreserves,

data = leblang2003y.stata, link = "probit", type = "private")
```

where the result is saved as m1.

The command **egame12** estimates a two-player, three-outcome extensive-form game. `y` is the dependent variable, which is defined as follows: $y = 1$ if the outcome = SQ, $y = 2$ if the outcome = DV, and $y = 3$ if the outcome = DF. The first expression after ~, that is, `capcont + lreserves + overval + creditgrow + usinterest + service + contagion + prioratt − 1`, represents the linear model for estimating the utility of the markets when the situation is the status quo (i.e., $U_M(SQ)$ in Eq. (10.4)).

The "minus 1" in the expression excludes the model's constant term. The expression "1" followed by the first vertical stroke represents the constant term for markets' utility when governments devalues the currency (i.e., Eq. (10.5). Similarly, the next expression of "1" followed by the second vertical stroke presents the constant term for the markets' utility when the governments defends the currency (i.e., Eq. (10.6)).

Finally, the last expression after the third stroke presents the linear model for estimating the governments' utility in taking action to defend the currency. The command `data` retrieves the data file for the estimation. The command `link` defines the distribution of the stochastic shocks in the game, where "probit" is set as the default for normally distributed stochastic shocks, and "logit" can be imposed for the logistic distribution of the stochastic shocks. The command `type` determines if the stochastic structures fall under the assumption of agent-error ("agent" as default) or private information ("private"). To retrieve the estimation results, we type:

```
summary(m1)
```

Figure 10.12 shows the results in **R** that are equivalent to those in Leblang (2003). Figure 10.13 depicts all codes for the estimation.

FIGURE 10.13. R codes for Leblang's (2003) results

11

Macro Political Economy

11.1 BACKGROUND

In earlier chapters (e.g., Chapters 5 and 6) we provided EITM examples reflecting structural equation modeling and the influence of the Cowles Commission. Recall also the criticisms of the approach (e.g., Chapter 1). One restriction in structural modeling is the dependence on closed form solutions. For this chapter we present a formal and empirical method that is, in part, a response to the criticisms (including reliance on closed forms) of the Cowles Commission "method."[1]

One research technique that addresses criticisms of the Cowles Commission methodology is real business cycle (RBC) modeling. It was developed by Kydland and Prescott (1982).[2] RBC establishes an important EITM linkage between theoretical predictions (using various behavioral equations at the micro and macro level) and actual observations.[3] The RBC methodology

---

[1] In particular, researchers typically solve closed-form solutions (or equilibria), which describe the predictable and measurable relationship among variables from a model of structural equations. Then they compare the predictions against the observable patterns estimated from secondary data sources. However, closed-form solutions are unobtainable for some models: This challenge arises because the model's complexity and nonlinearity are prohibitive. When closed-form solutions are infeasible, researchers consider alternative approaches, such as numerical solution procedures, to solve the equilibrium (equilibria). These solution procedures involve calibration and simulation. Model testing involves comparing the simulated data (model generated) with observed data.

[2] Stadler (1994) provides a detailed discussion and assessment of Real Business Cycle theory.

[3] In their seminal paper published in 1982, Kydland and Prescott set up a representative-agent general equilibrium model that consists of a forward-looking household and a firm. The representative household chooses the optimal levels of consumption, labor, and savings to maximize the present value of expected utility, and the representative firm chooses the optimal levels of labor and capital to maximize its profit based on a production function with productivity shocks. The authors then simulate the model to obtain the business cycle data, and compare the simulated data with the post-WWII macroeconomic data. They find about 70 percent of post-WWII business cycle volatilities can be explained by the stochastic shocks to technology.

evolved in the ensuing years and is now typically referred to as dynamic, stochastic general equilibrium (DSGE) modeling.[4]

This chapter presents the work of Freeman and Houser (1998) who use a DSGE model to study an important issue in macro political economy – the relation between economic performance and presidential approval. In the spirit of Chappell and Keech (1983) they build a structural model but with modifications inspired by criticisms of the Cowles Commission's approach. Specifically, Freeman and Houser argue that economic decisions and political decisions are often studied separately in the literature. They argue there is "a lack of theoretical balance between economic and political theory" (Freeman and Houser 1998, 628).

Freeman and Houser's pioneering work develops a computable general equilibrium model combining the Ramsey-type RBC model – based on Kydland and Prescott (1982, 1990, 1996) – with a policymaker's objective function of approval ratings. An important contribution of their work is that they model standard economic sectors – households and firms – and relate them to government strategists who are trying to manage presidential popularity. Not only do they capitalize on the power of calibration and simulation to mimic data but they also can engage in counterfactual analysis. The authors stress this attribute and state: "[t]he baseline model allows us to gauge the importance of various structural features of the political economy in ways that are not possible with reduced form set-up like VARs and ECMs, for example" (p. 650).

Subsequent studies have followed Freeman and Houser. Grafstein (2002) and Blomberg and Hess (2003) investigate the effects of public policies and political business cycles in the United States. Grafstein (2002) specifically focuses on the impact of social insurance on an individual's reaction to changes in government based on a DSGE model. Blomberg and Hess (2003) merge a real business cycle (RBC) model with a political business cycle (PBC) model. The calibrations show that their model captures some empirical characteristics observed in the United States, where the economy, on average, expands early under a Democratic presidency and contracts early under a Republican presidency. Additionally, incumbent presidents are more likely to be reelected for a second term when the economy grows faster than average in the second half of their first term (Basak et al. 2019).

In the language of EITM, Freeman and Houser link the behavioral concept of decision making with the empirical concept of prediction. The formal analogue is dynamic optimization (utility maximization, volatility minimization), and the empirical analogue relates to model calibration (and attendant descriptive statistics). A review of the analogues is presented in the Appendix.

---

[4] See Kremer et al. (2006) for a detailed discussion.

11.2 STEP 1: RELATING DECISION MAKING TO PREDICTION

The model consists of a representative household and a policymaker. The representative household makes the optimal decisions on consumption, savings, and labor to maximize her lifetime utility function. Similarly, the policymaker also makes the optimal decisions on tax rates and interest rates on public debt in order to minimize her objective function of approval rating volatility (conditional on the decisions made by the household). Freeman and Houser (1998) calibrate the formal (behavioral) model to generate simulated data, and compare the statistical properties of the simulated data with actual data in the United States.

11.3 STEP 2: ANALOGUES FOR DECISION MAKING AND PREDICTION

11.3.1 Household Utility Maximization

Assume that a representative household optimizes the present value of lifetime utility by choosing the levels of consumption c and labor l at time t:

$$\max_{c,l} \sum_{t} \sum_{s^t} \beta^t \mu(s^t) u[c(s^t), l(s^t)], \quad (11.1)$$

subject to the following constraints:

1. production function:

$$y(s^t) = z(s^t)(1+\rho)^t f(l(s^t)), \quad (11.2)$$

2. income identity:

$$c(s^t) + (1+\rho)^t g(s^t) \leq z(s^t)(1+\rho)^t f(l(s^t)), \quad (11.3)$$

3. government budget constraint:

$$b(s^t) + \tau(s^t) w(s^t) l(s^t) = R(s^t) b(s^{t-1}) + (1+\rho)^t g(s^t), \quad (11.4)$$

where $\beta < 1$ is the discount factor, s^t is the state of the economy at time t, $\mu(s^t)$ is the probability that a particular state happens at time t for $s^t \in S^t$, $u(\cdot)$ is the utility function that depends on the consumption level $c(s^t)$ and labor $l(s^t)$ in the state s at time t. We also define the following: $u_c = \partial u/\partial c > 0$, $u_l = \partial u/\partial l > 0$, $u_{cc} = \partial^2 u/\partial c^2 < 0$, and $u_{ll} = \partial^2 u/\partial l^2 < 0$.

Equation (11.2) shows that the output level y depends on the production function $f(l)$, the productivity shock z, and the economic growth rate ρ. The equation also indicates the production process does not depend on the capital stock (for simplicity). Equation (11.3) states the sum of household spending (consumption) and government expenditure g, growing at the rate of

ρ over time, cannot be greater than the total income $y(s^t)$ generated at time t. Equation (11.4) shows the sum of government-issued bonds $b(s^t)$ and taxes collected from the public $\tau(s^t) w(s^t) l(s^t)$ is equal to the sum of government spending and repayment of bonds issued at time $t-1$ with interest, where τ is the tax rate, w is the wage rate, and R is the gross rate of interest on bonds.

By combining Eqs. (11.2)–(11.4), we derive the household budget constraint and present the household utility maximization problem:

$$\max_{c,l} \sum_t \sum_{s^t} \beta^t \mu(s^t) u[c(s^t), l(s^t)],$$

subject to:

$$c(s^1) + b(s^1) = [1 - \tau(s^1)] w(s^1) l(s^1)$$
$$+ R(s^1) b(s^0) + v(s^1) + A, \text{ for } t = 1, \quad (11.5)$$

and:

$$c(s^t) + b(s^t) = [1 - \tau(s^t)] w(s^t) l(s^t)$$
$$+ R(s^t) b(s^{t-1}) + v(s^t), \forall t = 2, 3, \ldots \quad (11.6)$$

where Eqs. (11.5) and (11.6) represent the household budget constraint indicating that the total spending on consumption and bond purchases equals the sum of disposable income $[1 - \tau(s^t)][w(s^t) l(s^t)]$, the principal and interest received from the bonds purchased in the previous period, and the profits $v(s^t)$ for all time $t = 2, 3, \ldots$ where $v(s^t) = y(s^t) - w(s^t) l(s^t)$. We also assume the household obtains her initial endowment A at time $t = 1$.

To derive the optimal result, we solve the system by writing the following Lagrangian equation:

$$\mathcal{L} = \beta^t \mu(s^t) u(c(s^t), l(s^t)) + \beta^{t+1} \mu(s^t) u(c(s^t), l(s^t)) + \cdots$$
$$- p(s^t) \{c(s^t) + b(s^t) - [1 - \tau(s^t)] w(s^t) l(s^t) - R(s^t) b(s^{t-1}) - v(s^t)\}$$
$$- p(s^{t+1}) \{c(s^{t+1}) + b(s^{t+1}) - [1 - \tau(s^{t+1})] w(s^{t+1}) l(s^{t+1})$$
$$- R(s^{t+1}) b(s^t) - v(s^{t+1})\} - \cdots, \quad (11.7)$$

where $p(s^t)$ is the Lagrangian multiplier. The following first-order conditions from the Lagrangian equation (11.7) are:

1. $\partial \mathcal{L}/\partial c(s^t) = 0$:

$$\beta^t \mu(s^t) u_c(s^t) - p(s^t) = 0$$
$$\Rightarrow p(s^t) = \beta^t \mu(s^t) u_c(s^t) \quad (11.8)$$

Macro Political Economy

2. $\partial \mathcal{L}/\partial l(s^t) = 0$:

$$\beta^t \mu(s^t) u_l(s^t) + p(s^t)[1 - \tau(s^t)] w(s^t) = 0$$
$$\Rightarrow \beta^t \mu(s^t) u_l(s^t) = -p(s^t)[1 - \tau(s^t)] w(s^t) \quad (11.9)$$

3. $\partial \mathcal{L}/\partial b(s^t) = 0$:

$$-p(s^t) + p(s^{t+1}|s^t) R(s^{t+1}|s^t) = 0$$
$$\Rightarrow p(s^t) = \sum_{s^{t+1}|s^t} p(s^{t+1}) R(s^{t+1}) \quad (11.10)$$

4. $\partial \mathcal{L}/\partial p(s^t) = 0$:

$$c(s^1) + b(s^1) - [1 - \tau(s^1)] w(s^1) l(s^1)$$
$$+ R(s^1) b(s^0) + v(s^1) + A = 0, \text{ for } t = 1, \quad (11.11)$$
$$c(s^t) + b(s^t) - [1 - \tau(s^t)] w(s^t) l(s^t)$$
$$+ R(s^t) b(s^{t-1}) + v(s^t) = 0, \forall t = 2, 3, \ldots, \quad (11.12)$$

5. Transversality condition:

$$\lim_{s^t \in s^\infty} \sum_{s^t} p(s^t) b(s^t) = 0. \quad (11.13)$$

11.3.2 Firm Profit Maximization

Since we define the profit $v(s^t)$ as the difference between output $y(s^t)$ and the total cost of labor $w(s^t) l(s^t)$, each firm maximizes its profit by choosing the optimal level of labor in each period:

$$\max_l v(s^t) = y(s^t) - w(s^t) l(s^t)$$
$$\Rightarrow \max_l v(s^t) = z(s^t)(1+\rho)^t f(l(s^t)) - w(s^t) l(s^t), \quad (11.14)$$

where $y(s^t) = z(s^t)(1+\rho)^t f(l(s^t))$ and $w(s^t) = \partial y(s^t)/\partial l(s^t) = z(s^t)(1+\rho)^t f_l(l(s^t))$ according to Eq. (11.2).

11.3.3 Governmental Approval Target Deviation Minimization

Freeman and Houser (1998), using a traditional equilibrium model, introduce a public approval motivated government as a sector in this model. The authors investigate whether business cycles are driven, in part, by electoral and other political forces. Building on the model suggested by Chappell and Keech (1983), the authors add a unitary, politically motivated actor – the government – that optimizes a political objective function, but it is also subject to the optimizing behavior of a representative economic agent.

The government is assumed to be a representative agent that optimally chooses tax rate τ and gross interest rate R on public bonds in order to minimize the present value of the expected sum of deviations of approval ratings $APP\left(s^{t}\right)$ from its approval targets APP^{*} (for all time t):

$$\min_{\tau,R} \sum_{t} \sum_{s^{t}} \bar{\beta} u\left(s^{t}\right)\left[APP\left(s^{t}\right) - APP^{*}\right]^{2}, \tag{11.15}$$

subject to the approval rating condition $APP\left(s^{t}\right)$, which depends on consumption and labor:

$$APP\left(s^{t}\right) = \alpha_{0} + \alpha_{1}\frac{c\left(s^{t}\right)}{\left(1+\rho\right)^{t}} + \alpha_{2}l\left(s^{t}\right) + e\left(s^{t}\right). \tag{11.16}$$

The government budget is constrained by the household's consumption, saving, and labor decisions given the policy choices $\eta = \left(\tau\left(s^{t}\right), R\left(s^{t}\right)\right)$:

$$b\left(s^{t}|\eta\right) + \tau\left(s^{t}\right) w\left(s^{t}|\eta\right) l\left(s^{t}|\eta\right) = R\left(s^{t}\right) b\left(s^{t-1}|\eta\right) + \left(1+\rho\right)^{t} g\left(s^{t}\right). \tag{11.17}$$

For Eqs. (11.15) and (11.16), respectively, $\bar{\beta}$ is the discount factor for the government, $c\left(s^{t}\right)/\left(1+\rho\right)^{t}$ represents the "present value" of consumption adjusted for the economic growth rate at time t, and $e\left(s^{t}\right)$ is a shock to the approval rating. Equation (11.16) indicates the approval rating is influenced by the adjusted consumption and labor weighted by α_{1} and α_{2}, respectively, and the stochastic shock at time t. Equation (11.17) is the optimal government budget when the household and firm choose c and l to maximize their utility and profit (described in the system of Eqs. (11.1)–(11.4) and (11.14)), respectively, for every policy $\eta = \eta'$.

With this structure in place, the government chooses optimal policy η to minimize the approval target deviations given the optimal decisions made by the household and the firm. The complete system can be written as follows:

$$\min_{\tau,R} \sum_{t} \sum_{s^{t}} \bar{\beta} u\left(s^{t}\right)\left[APP\left(s^{t}\right) - APP^{*}\right]^{2}, \tag{11.18}$$

such that:

1. income identity:

$$c\left(s^{t}\right) + \left(1+\rho\right)^{t} g\left(s^{t}\right) = z\left(s^{t}\right)\left(1+\rho\right)^{t} f\left(l\left(s^{t}\right)\right); \tag{11.19}$$

Macro Political Economy

2. household optimal behavior:[5]

$$\sum_t \sum_{s^t} \beta^t \mu(s^t) \left[u_c(s^t) c(s^t) + u_l(s^t) l(s^t) \right] = u_c(s^1)[R(s^1)b(s^0) + A];$$

(11.20)

3. firm optimal behavior:[6]

$$v(s^t) = z(s^t)(1+\rho)^t f(l(s^t)) - w(s^t) l(s^t) = 0;$$

(11.21)

4. government approval condition:

$$APP(s^t) = \alpha_0 + \alpha_1 \frac{c(s^t)}{(1+\rho)^t} + \alpha_2 l(s^t) + e(s^t).$$

(11.22)

11.4 STEP 3: UNIFYING AND EVALUATING THE ANALOGUES

Freeman and Houser (1998) simulate the system of Eqs. (11.16)–(11.22). The authors define the functional forms of the household's utility and firm's production functions, respectively:

$$u(c,l) = \left[c^{1-\gamma}(1-l)^\gamma \right]^\phi / \phi,$$

(11.23)

and:

$$y = z(s^t)(1+\rho)^t l^\theta,$$

(11.24)

where ϕ represents the degree of risk aversion, and γ is the relative weight between leisure $(1-l)$ and consumption c. We can derive the marginal utility of consumption as $u_c = (1-\gamma)\left[c^{1-\gamma}(1-l)^\gamma\right]^{\phi-1}(1-l)^\gamma c^{-\gamma}$, the marginal utility of labor as $u_l = \gamma\left[c^{1-\gamma}(1-l)^\gamma\right]^{\phi-1} c^{1-\gamma}(1-l)^{\gamma-1}$ (from Eq. (11.23)), and the marginal product of labor as $y_l = \partial y/\partial l = \theta z(s^t)(1+\rho)^t l^{\theta-1}$ (from Eq. (11.24)). The parameter values for the household utility and firm profit maximization problems come from the previous studies in the literature.

Freeman and Houser estimate the coefficients of the approval function (11.22) using approval data obtained from the American National Election Study. The parameter values are presented in Table 11.1. They also account for supply shocks (the productivity shock z from Eq. (11.24)), demand shocks (the government spending shock g from Eq. (11.19)), and political shocks (the approval shock e from Eq. (11.22)).[7] Table 11.2 describes the values

---

[5] Equation (11.20) determines the household's optimal consumption decisions over time according to Eqs. (11.8)–(11.13). We describe the derivation of the equation in the Appendix.
[6] By assuming a constant return to scale (CRS) production function, the profit level is zero in a competitive market. See FN 13 in the Appendix.
[7] These stochastic shocks are generated by the Markov Chain process.

TABLE 11.1. *Parameter values (Freeman and Houser 1998)*

Parameter	Value	Parameter	Value
ρ	0.006	α_0	−0.025
β	0.99	α_1	2.5
$\bar{\beta}$	0.988	APP^*	0.55
γ	0.66	$b(s^0)$	1
θ	1	$R(s^1)$	1
ϕ	−1	A	2

TABLE 11.2. *Shock values and corresponding transition probabilities (Freeman and Houser 1998)*

A. Shock values

	Productivity shock (z)	Govt. spending shock (g)	Approval shock (e)
Low value	0.99	0.074	−0.014
High value	1.010	0.078	−0.014

B. Corresponding Markov Chain transition probabilities

	To	Low	High	Low	High	Low	High
From	Low	0.95	0.05	0.91	0.09	0.5	0.5
	High	0.05	0.95	0.91	0.09	0.64	3.6

of the shocks and the corresponding transition probabilities of the Markov Chain process.

For each combination of shocks $(z(s^t), g(s^t), e(s^t))$ in the economy, the authors determine the optimal policy $\eta^* = (\tau^*, R^*)$ that minimizes the approval target deviations as described in Eqs. (11.16)–(11.22).

The authors simulate the model 1,000 times. Each simulation has $t = 200$ periods (i.e., quarters). They compare the actual patterns of key variables observed in the United States for the period 1980–1990 with the patterns of the same variables predicted in the model simulations. Based on the total of 1,000 simulations, the authors show that "the model mimics the United States actual data rather well" (Freeman and Houser 1998, 648).[8]

The results are summarized in Figure 11.1. The bar chart on the left in Figure 11.1 compares volatilities of the variables between the actual and simulated data. It shows the standard deviations of Hodrick and Prescott

---

[8] See FN 15 in Chapter 12 for further discussion about the linkage between simulations and empirical tests.

Macro Political Economy

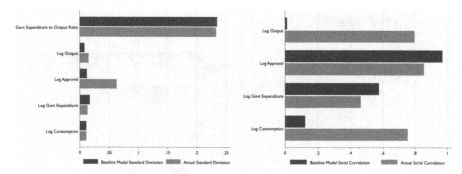

FIGURE 11.1. Baseline model simulated data and actual data (Freeman and Houser 1998)

(HP)-filtered cyclical components of consumption, government expenditure, and output in the simulated model are comparable to those in the United States economy.[9] However, there is a larger discrepancy between the actual and simulated standard deviations of approval (log approval). We also see that the volatilities of the actual government expenditure to output ratio is almost identical to that obtained from the simulated data. The bar chart on the right in Figure 11.1 shows the movement patterns of the variables between the simulated model and the United States economy: It shows the simulated serial correlations of approval ratings and government expenditure are similar to those of the actual data, but output and consumption variables are dissimilar.

Freeman and Houser (1998) also experiment with approval dynamics. For example, they focus on larger approval shocks (LAS) and a higher approval target (HAT) in the model. The authors first allow the magnitude of approval shocks e to increase by 220 percent in absolute value, that is, from $e = \{e_{low}, e_{high}\} = \{-0.014, 0.014\}$ to $e = \{-0.03, 0.03\}$ in the LAS model. Figure 11.2 shows the simulated patterns of key variables are consistent with those from the actual data. Next, the authors raise the approval rate target APP^* from 0.55 to 0.7 in the HAT model. The simulated results remained

---

[9] The Hodrick–Prescott filter (Hodrick and Prescott 1981, 1997) is a high-pass filter (i.e., detrending the data to uncover high-frequency components of a series). Mathematically speaking, let a time-series variable be y_t. The trend component y_t^{trend} can be solved using the following minimization problem:

$$min_{y_t^{trend}} \left\{ \sum_{t=1}^{T} \left(y_t - y_t^{trend} \right)^2 + \lambda \sum_{t=2}^{T-1} \left[\left(y_{t+1}^{trend} - y_t^{trend} \right) - \left(y_t^{trend} - y_{t-1}^{trend} \right) \right]^2 \right\},$$

where the smoothing parameter λ is set to a fixed value. If λ is set to be zero, then the trend component y_t^{trend} is simply the original series y_t. On the other hand, if $\lambda \to \infty$, the trend component becomes the estimated series from a linear regression with a time trend only, where $y_t^{trend} = \alpha_0 + \alpha_1 t$. For estimating the trend component with quarterly time series, the rule of thumb is to set $\lambda = 1600$. For annual time series, Ravn and Uhlig (2002) recommend $\lambda = 6.25$.

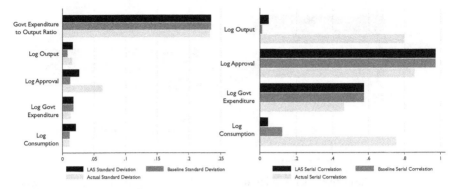

FIGURE 11.2. Simulated data for baseline and LAS models and actual data (Freeman and Houser 1998)

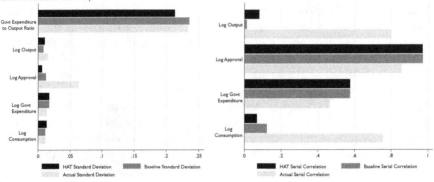

FIGURE 11.3. Simulated data for baseline and HAT models and actual data (Freeman and Houser 1998)

largely unchanged as shown in Figure 11.3. Freeman and Houser find that the dynamics of the simulated model remain robustly consistent with the United States economy.

11.5 SUMMARY

The DSGE model devised by Freeman and Houser (1998) develops an important connection between economic decisions and political decisions in a macroeconomic setting. The policymaker optimally implements policy to minimize the volatility of approval ratings (which is influenced by the household's consumption, labor, and saving decisions). More importantly, the dynamics of the theoretical model mimic the statistical properties of the actual data in the United States.[10]

---

[10] We note calibration is not empirical estimation. Mimic assessments are not statistical tests in the sense frequentists use. Some researchers may see a disconnect to "frequentism" since researchers can do "resampling" many times via simulation, but they have only one realization/history for comparing simulated data moments. We thank John Freeman for this comment.

Macro Political Economy

Houser and Freeman (2001) extend their model to study the relation between political approval management and business cycles. Since the decision of fiscal policy depends on the approval function of the policymaker, Houser and Freeman (2001) argue when governments are less insulated from public approval, they have a stronger incentive to manage their level of popular support by implementing sub-optimal fiscal policy.

To answer this question, the authors study the business cycles and fiscal policy outcomes in the United States and the United Kingdom. They point out that the United States has a presidential system: Governmental executives are elected for a fixed term. The United Kingdom, on the other hand, has a parliamentary system: Executives are not elected for a fixed term and are relatively more vulnerable for removal due to coalition volatility and the prospect of a no confidence vote.[11] As a consequence, Houser and Freeman argue executives in parliamentary systems (in comparison to their presidential system counterparts) are more likely to implement short-term fiscal policies to reduce their removal vulnerability.

Houser and Freeman (2001) test this vulnerability hypothesis in the following ways. They suggest two sets of parameters in the theoretical model that mimic the statistical properties of economic variables and approval ratings (using national economic and survey data for the period of 1977–1995 and the period of 1980–1995) for the United States and the United Kingdom, respectively. The authors then simulate the model with negative approval shocks and compute the difference in output losses for the two countries. They find the simulated costs for the United States and the United Kingdom constitute about 0.20 percent and 0.35 percent of the annual output level, respectively. Houser and Freeman (2001) conclude:

Institutions that hold governments relatively accountable for their actions, e.g., by making it relatively easy for legislatures to change governments, may lead incumbents to be rather more responsive to a wide variety of the citizenry's public policy concerns. However, such institutions also leave governments with an incentive to manage their political approval ratings through relatively active fiscal policy and such behavior might not be optimal with respect to the citizenry's long-run economic welfare. (page 713)

More recent studies have adopted the DSGE approach to investigate other topics in political economy. Basak et al. (2019) develop a DSGE model to describe political business cycles. The authors assume the ruling party has an incentive to gain popularity in the next election by lowering the inflation rate and/or unemployment rate. The model calibrations show that the ruling party gains more popularity by lowering the inflation rate. The authors conclude that "electoral pressures drive the government to engage in cost control rather than productive investment (e.g., boosting employment or output growth), even as better technology becomes available near the end of the term" (page 139).

---

[11] Note that the Fixed-term Parliaments Act was implemented in 2011. The act introduced fixed-term elections in the UK, stating that a general election must be held every five years, and early elections may only be held under specified circumstances.

Yet another example is Andreasen et al. (2018). The authors develop a DSGE model to show how political constraints, such as the resistance of raising tax revenues or income redistribution, can affect the likelihood of sovereign default. Their calibrations indicate the likelihood of sovereign default increases when income inequality and regressive taxes are higher for a given level of debt in an economy.

11.6 APPENDIX

The tools in this chapter are used to link the behavioral concept of decision making with the empirical concept of prediction. The formal tool is dynamic optimization. The applied statistical tool is model calibration. This appendix discusses the following topics: the derivation of the optimal household behavior in Freeman and Houser (1998); general equilibrium modeling; and an extended discussion on dynamic optimization.

11.6.1 The Derivation of Optimal Household Behavior

The first objective in this appendix is to demonstrate the derivation of optimal household behavior presented in Eq. (11.20). We consider the household budget constraint (11.6):

$$c(s^t) + b(s^t) = [1 - \tau(s^t)] w(s^t) l(s^t) + R(s^t) b(s^{t-1}) + v(s^t).$$

Now we multiply $p(s^t)$ on both sides and sum all periods and all possible states of the economy:

$$\sum_{t=1}^{T} \sum_{s^t} p(s^t) [c(s^t) + b(s^t)]$$

$$= \sum_{t=1}^{T} \sum_{s^t} p(s^t) \{[1 - \tau(s^t)] w(s^t) l(s^t) + R(s^t) b(s^{t-1}) + v(s^t)\} + p(s^1) A$$

$$\Rightarrow \sum_{t=1}^{T} \sum_{s^t} p(s^t) c(s^t) + \sum_{t=1}^{T} \sum_{s^t} p(s^t) b(s^t)$$

$$= \sum_{t=1}^{T} \sum_{s^t} p(s^t) [1 - \tau(s^t)] w(s^t) l(s^t) + \sum_{t=1}^{T} \sum_{s^t} p(s^t) R(s^t) b(s^{t-1})$$

$$+ \sum_{t=1}^{T} \sum_{s^t} p(s^t) v(s^t) + p(s^1) A$$

$$\Rightarrow \sum_{s^T} p(s^T) b(s^T) + \sum_{t=1}^{T-1} \sum_{s^t} p(s^t) b(s^t)$$

Macro Political Economy

$$+ \sum_{t=1}^{T} \sum_{s^t} p(s^t) \{c(s^t) - [1 - \tau(s^t)] w(s^t) l(s^t)\}$$

$$= \sum_{t=1}^{T} \sum_{s^t} p(s^t) R(s^t) b(s^{t-1}) + \sum_{t=1}^{T} \sum_{s^t} p(s^t) v(s^t) + p(s^1) A. \quad (11.25)$$

Note that:

$$\sum_{t=1}^{T} \sum_{s^t} p(s^t) R(s^t) b(s^{t-1}) = p(s^1) R(s^1) b(s^0)$$

$$+ \sum_{s^t} p(s^2) R(s^2) b(s^1) + \cdots$$

$$+ \sum_{s^T} p(s^T) R(s^T) b(s^{T-1})$$

$$\sum_{t=1}^{T} \sum_{s^t} p(s^t) R(s^t) b(s^{t-1}) = p(s^1) R(s^1) b(s^0)$$

$$+ \sum_{t=1}^{T-1} \sum_{s^t} p(s^{t+1}) R(s^{t+1}) b(s^t),$$

we can rewrite Eq. (11.25) as:

$$\sum_{s^T} p(s^T) b(s^T) + \sum_{t=1}^{T-1} \sum_{s^t} p(s^t) b(s^t)$$

$$+ \sum_{t=1}^{T} \sum_{s^t} p(s^t) \{c(s^t) - [1 - \tau(s^t)] w(s^t) l(s^t)\}$$

$$= p(s^1) R(s^1) b(s^0) + \sum_{t=1}^{T-1} \sum_{s^t} p(s^{t+1}) R(s^{t+1}) b(s^t)$$

$$+ \sum_{t=1}^{T} \sum_{s^t} p(s^t) v(s^t) + p(s^1) A$$

$$\Rightarrow \sum_{s^T} p(s^T) b(s^T) + \sum_{t=1}^{T-1} \sum_{s^t} \left[p(s^t) b(s^t) - p(s^{t+1}) R(s^{t+1}) b(s^t) \right]$$

$$+ \sum_{t=1}^{T} \sum_{s^t} p(s^t) \{c(s^t) - [1 - \tau(s^t)] w(s^t) l(s^t)\}$$

$$= p(s^1) R(s^1) b(s^0) + \sum_{t=1}^{T} \sum_{s^t} p(s^t) v(s^t) + p(s^1) A. \quad (11.26)$$

According to Eq. (11.10) and the transversality condition (11.13), the first two rows of Eq. (11.26) are zero. Assuming the production function has the property of constant return to scale (CRS), the profit $v(s^t)$ is equal to zero. As a result, Eq. (11.26) can be simplified as follows:

$$\sum_{t=1}^{T}\sum_{s^t} p(s^t)\{c(s^t) - [1-\tau(s^t)]w(s^t)l(s^t)\} = p(s^1)R(s^1)b(s^0) + p(s^1)A. \quad (11.27)$$

Now, using Eqs. (11.8) and (11.9), we are able to obtain Eq. (11.20).

11.6.2 General Equilibrium Modeling

In this section, we first describe a simple general equilibrium model – a real business cycle (RBC) model. Note that an RBC model is a representative-agent general equilibrium model that consists of a forward-looking household and a firm. The representative household chooses the optimal levels of consumption, labor, and savings to maximize the present value of expected utility, and the representative firm chooses the optimal levels of labor and capital to maximize its profit based on a production function with productivity shocks.

Household Behavior – Utility Maximization

Consider a representative agent i maximizing the following present value of expected aggregate utility at time t:

$$\max_{C_{it}, L_{it}, K_{it+1}} E_t \sum_{t=0}^{\infty} \beta^t u(C_{it}, L_{it}), \quad (11.28)$$

subject to the following conditions:

$$Y_{it} = C_{it} + I_{it}, \quad (11.29)$$

$$Y_{it} = F(K_{it}, L_{it}), \quad (11.30)$$

$$K_{it+1} = (1-\delta)K_{it} + I_{it}, \text{ and} \quad (11.31)$$

$$Y_{it} = w_t L_{it} + r_t K_{it}, \quad (11.32)$$

where E_t represents the expectation operator discussed in Chapter 5, $\beta < 1$ is the discount factor, and C_{it} and L_{it} are agent i's consumption and labor at time t, respectively. The utility function u satisfies regular properties where $\partial u/\partial C = u_C > 0$, $\partial^2 u/\partial C^2 = u_{CC} < 0$, $\partial u/\partial L = u_L < 0$, and $\partial^2 u/\partial L^2 = u_{LL} < 0$.

The utility function is maximized subject to four constraints (i.e., Eqs. (11.29)–(11.32)). The first constraint of Eq. (11.29) is known as an income identity, suggesting that agent i's income (Y_{it}) can be allocated between consumption and investment (I_{it}). Equation (11.30) is the production function where income or output is generated by two production factors: labor L and capital K. The third condition (11.31) is known as the capital accumulation function, in which the capital stock in the next period K_{it+1} is the sum of the remaining capital stock in period t after depreciation (with the depreciation rate of δ) and investment at t. Finally, assuming the economy is competitive and operating under constant returns to scale, one can show that the total revenue Y_{it} equals the sum of the labor cost $w_t L_{it}$ and the capital cost $r_t K_{it}$ (as presented in Eq. (11.32)), where w_t is the wage rate, and r_t is the rental rate at time t.[12] As a result, no profit will be generated in the economy.

To determine the optimal solution, we solve the system of (11.28)–(11.32) by setting up a Lagrangian equation:

$$\mathcal{L} = E_t \sum_{t=0}^{\infty} \beta^t \left\{ u\left(C_{it}, L_{it}\right) - \mu_{it} \left[C_{it} + K_{it+1} - (1-\delta) K_{it} - w_t L_{it} - r_t K_{it} \right] \right\}, \tag{11.33}$$

where μ is the Lagrange multiplier. To solve the Lagrangian equation, we rewrite Eq. (11.33) as follows:

$$\begin{aligned}\mathcal{L} = E_t \Big\{ &u\left(C_{it}, L_{it}\right) + \beta u\left(C_{it+1}, L_{it+1}\right) + \beta^2 u\left(C_{it+2}, L_{it+2}\right) + \cdots \\ &- \mu_{it} \left[C_{it} + K_{it+1} - (1-\delta) K_{it} - w_t L_{it} - r_t K_{it} \right] \\ &- \mu_{it+1} \beta \left[C_{it+1} + K_{it+2} - (1-\delta) K_{it+1} - w_{t+1} L_{it+1} - r_{t+1} K_{it+1} \right] \\ &- \mu_{it+2} \beta^2 \left[C_{it+2} + K_{it+3} - (1-\delta) K_{it+2} \right. \\ &\left. - w_{t+2} L_{it+2} - r_{t+2} K_{it+2} \right] - \cdots \Big\}. \end{aligned} \tag{11.34}$$

We can obtain the first-order conditions from the Lagrangian Eq. (11.34):

1. $\frac{\partial \mathcal{L}}{\partial C_{it}} = 0$:

$$u_C\left(C_{it}, L_{it}\right) - \mu_{it} = 0; \tag{11.35}$$

2. $\frac{\partial \mathcal{L}}{\partial L_{it}} = 0$:

$$-L_{it}^{\phi} + \mu_{it} w_t = 0; \tag{11.36}$$

3. $\frac{\partial \mathcal{L}}{\partial K_{it+1}} = 0$:

$$\begin{aligned}-\mu_{it} + E_t \left\{ \mu_{it+1} \beta \left[(1-\delta) - r_{t+1} \right] \right\} &= 0 \\ -\mu_{it} + E_t \mu_{it+1} \beta (1-\delta) - \beta E_t \mu_{it+1} r_{t+1} &= 0; \end{aligned} \tag{11.37}$$

4. $\frac{\partial \mathcal{L}}{\partial \mu_{it}} = 0$:

$$C_{it} + K_{it+1} - (1-\delta) K_{it} - w_t L_{it} - r_t K_{it} = 0. \tag{11.38}$$

---

[12] For simplicity, we normalize the price level $P_t = 1$ for all t such that normal values and real values are equal in the economy. See FN 13 for a discussion.

Now we rewrite Eq. (11.35):

$$u_C(C_{it}, L_{it}) - \mu_{it} = 0$$
$$\Rightarrow \mu_{it} = u_C(C_{it}, L_{it}). \tag{11.39}$$

Then by plugging Eq. (11.39) into Eq. (11.37), we have:

$$-u_C(C_{it}, L_{it}) + \beta(1-\delta)E_t u_C(C_{it+1}, L_{it+1}) + \beta E_t r_{t+1} E_t u_C(C_{it+1}, L_{it+1}) = 0$$
$$-u_C(C_{it}, L_{it}) + \beta[(1-\delta) + E_t r_{t+1}] E_t u_C(C_{it+1}, L_{it+1}) = 0.$$

Finally, we obtain the well-known Euler equation:

$$u_C(C_{it}, L_{it}) = \beta[(1-\delta) + E_t r_{t+1}] E_t u_C(C_{it+1}, L_{it+1}) \tag{11.40}$$

Equation (11.40) determines the household's optimal consumption decisions over time. The optimal decision is achieved when agent i is indifferent between consuming one more unit today (time t) on the one hand and saving that unit and consuming in the next period (time $t+1$) on the other.

To be more specific, consider agent i consumes today (t) with a marginal utility of consumption $u_C(C_{it}, L_{it})$ at time t. However, if the agent decides to save the unit of consumption as investment I_t instead, they would expect to receive $(1-\delta) + E_t r_{t+1}$ units at $t+1$. As a result, agent i would expect to get $[(1-\delta) + E_t r_{t+1}] E_t u_C(C_{it+1}, L_{it+1})$ extra units of utility at $t+1$. This extra amount of utility will be discounted by β at time $t+1$. The agent's consumption behavior is optimal when they do not substitute their present consumption for future consumption.

Furthermore, we can derive the labor supply function by inserting (11.39) into (11.36):

$$-L_{it}^{\phi} + u_C(C_{it}, L_{it}) w_t = 0$$
$$L_{it}^{\phi} = u_C(C_{it}, L_{it}) w_t. \tag{11.41}$$

Equation (11.41) represents the optimal labor supply function. When the real wage w_t increases, agent i is more willing to work, i.e., L_{it} increases, ceteris paribus.

Finally, to study the model numerically, we assume that the utility function is separable in consumption and labor:

$$u(C_{it}, L_{it}) = \frac{C_{it}^{1-\sigma}}{1-\sigma} - \frac{L_{it}^{1+\phi}}{1+\phi}, \tag{11.42}$$

for $\sigma, \phi > 0$, where σ is the degree of risk aversion, and ϕ is the marginal disutility of labor. Next, we substitute Eq. (11.42) into Eq. (11.40) to obtain the following Euler equation:

$$E_t C_{it+1}^{\sigma} = \beta[(1-\delta) + E_t r_{t+1}] C_{it}^{\sigma}, \tag{11.43}$$

Macro Political Economy 211

and the optimal labor supply from Eq. (11.41):

$$L_{it}^{\phi} = C_{it}^{-\sigma} w_t. \tag{11.44}$$

Firm Behavior – Profit Maximization

The production side of the economy is modeled as if production comes from household i who produces output Y_{it}, with labor L_{it}, and capital stock K_{it}, which is saved. A standard production function can be presented as:

$$Y_{it} = F(K_{it}, L_{it}).$$

The production function has the following properties:

1. Constant returns to scale (or homogenous of degree one):
   A production function has constant returns to scale if an increase of an equal percentage in both capital and labor of production causes an increase in output of the same percentage. Mathematically,

   $$F(\lambda K_{it}, \lambda L_{it}) = \lambda F(K_{it}, L_{it}), \text{ for all } \lambda > 0.$$

2. Positive marginal products:
   The marginal product of capital (MPK) is defined as an additional level of output generated by an extra unit of capital. The mathematical representation of MPK is:

   $$\frac{\partial F(K_{it}, L_{it})}{\partial K_{it}} = F_K(\cdot) > 0,$$

   Similarly, the marginal product of labor (MPL) can be written as:

   $$\frac{\partial F(K_{it}, L_{it})}{\partial L_{it}} = F_L(\cdot) > 0,$$

   for all $K_{it} > 0$ and $L_{it} > 0$.

3. Diminishing marginal returns:
   We also assume that, holding another factor constant, the marginal products decrease in the amount of the factor used such that:

   $$\frac{\partial^2 F(K_{it}, L_{it})}{\partial K_{it}^2} = F_{KK}(\cdot) < 0,$$

   and:

   $$\frac{\partial^2 F(K_{it}, L_{it})}{\partial L_{it}^2} = F_{LL}(\cdot) < 0,$$

where F_{KK} is the second derivative of the production function with respect to K_{it}, and F_{LL} is the second derivative of the production function with respect to L_{it}.

4. Positive cross-marginal products:
The marginal product of one factor goes up when the input of the other factor increases:

$$F_{KL}(\cdot) = F_{LK}(\cdot) > 0,$$

where $F_{KL} = \partial^2 F(K_{it}, L_{it}) / \partial K \partial L$, and $F_{LK} = \partial^2 F(K_{it}, L_{it}) / \partial L \partial K$.

Given that firm i faces input prices in factor markets, it chooses K_{it} and L_{it} to maximize the profit function π_{it}:

$$\max_{K_{it}, L_{it}} \pi_{it} = Y_{it} - (r_t K_{it} + w_t L_{it}),$$

subject to the constraint:

$$Y_{it} = F(K_{it}, L_{it}),$$

where r_t and w_t are the rental rate and the wage rate for each unit of capital and labor, respectively (hired in the market). Hence, the firm-level maximization problem can be written as:

$$\max_{K_{it}, L_{it}} \pi_{it} = F(K_{it}, L_{it}) - r_t K_{it} - w_t L_{it}.$$

As a result, the competitive market clears when their factor prices are set at their marginal products:

$$F_K(K_{it}, L_{it}) = r_t, \text{ and} \tag{11.45}$$

$$F_L(K_{it}, L_{it}) = w_t. \tag{11.46}$$

Next, the shares of capital and labor in total income at time t can be expressed as:

$$\frac{r_t K_{it}}{Y_{it}} = \frac{F_K(\cdot) K_{it}}{F(\cdot)}, \tag{11.47}$$

and:

$$\frac{w_t L_{it}}{Y_{it}} = \frac{F_L(\cdot) L_{it}}{F(\cdot)}, \tag{11.48}$$

Macro Political Economy

where $r_t K_{it}$ and $w_t L_{it}$ are total capital and labor incomes, respectively. According to Eqs. (11.47) and (11.48), we can show that:

$$\frac{r_t K_{it}}{Y_{it}} = \frac{F_K K_{it}}{Y_{it}} = \frac{\partial Y_{it}}{\partial K_{it}} \frac{K_{it}}{Y_{it}} = \frac{\partial Y_{it}}{Y_{it}} \Big/ \frac{\partial K_{it}}{K_{it}}, \tag{11.49}$$

and:

$$\frac{w_t L_{it}}{Y_{it}} = \frac{F_L L_{it}}{Y_{it}} = \frac{\partial Y_{it}}{\partial L_{it}} \frac{L_{it}}{Y_{it}} = \frac{\partial Y_{it}}{Y_{it}} \Big/ \frac{\partial L_{it}}{L_{it}}. \tag{11.50}$$

Equations (11.49) and (11.50) suggest the capital income as a share of total output ($r_t K_{it}/Y_{it}$) and the labor income as a share of total output ($w_t L_{it}/Y_{it}$) can be interpreted as output elasticities with respect to capital and labor, respectively. Since the production function exhibits the property of constant returns to scale and the market is competitive, the total profit for the firm is equal to zero.[13] Mathematically, the optimal level of profit is:

$$\pi_{it}^* = Y_{it} - r_t K_{it} - w_t L_{it} = 0 \tag{11.51}$$
$$\Rightarrow Y_{it} = r_t K_{it} + w_t L_{it}. \tag{11.52}$$

Equation (11.52) implies that the sum of the factor incomes equals the total output in the market. When both sides are divided by Y_t, we have:

$$\frac{r_t K_t}{Y_t} + \frac{w_t L_t}{Y_t} = 1. \tag{11.53}$$

Equation (11.53) indicates that the sum of capital share of output and labor share of output equals the entire output produced in the economy.

Assuming the production function is in a Cobb–Douglas form (Cobb and Douglas 1928):

$$Y_{it} = A_t K_{it}^\alpha L_{it}^{1-\alpha}, \tag{11.54}$$

---

[13] To see this, we consider a CRS production function:

$$\lambda Y_{it} = F(\lambda K_{it}, \lambda L_{it}).$$

Now taking the derivative on both sides of the equation with respect to λ:

$$Y_{it} = F_K K_{it} + F_L L_{it}.$$

Since $F_K = r_t$ and $F_L = w_t$, we can show:

$$Y_{it} = r_t K_{it} + w_t L_{it},$$

therefore, profit π_{it} equals zero.

where α and $(1-\alpha)$ are capital and labor shares of output, respectively,[14] and A_t represents the technological productivity, which follows an AR(1) process and is affected by stochastic factors:[15]

$$\ln A_t = \rho \ln A_{t-1} + \epsilon_t. \tag{11.55}$$

In Eq. (11.55) $\epsilon \sim N(0, \sigma_\epsilon)$ is a productivity shock to the economy. Note, the productivity shock is the primary source generating business cycles in the model. Using Eqs. (11.45) and (11.46), we have:

$$\begin{aligned} r_t &= \alpha A_t K_{it}^{\alpha-1} L_{it}^{1-\alpha} \\ r_t &= \frac{\alpha A_t K_{it}^{\alpha} L_{it}^{1-\alpha}}{K_{it}} \\ r_t &= \frac{\alpha Y_{it}}{K_{it}} \\ \Rightarrow K_{it} &= \frac{\alpha Y_{it}}{r_t}, \end{aligned} \tag{11.56}$$

and:

$$\begin{aligned} w_t &= (1-\alpha) A_t K_{it}^{\alpha} L_{it}^{-\alpha} \\ w_t &= \frac{(1-\alpha) A_t K_{it}^{\alpha} L_{it}^{1-\alpha}}{L_{it}} \\ w_t &= \frac{(1-\alpha) Y_{it}}{L_{it}} \\ \Rightarrow L_{it} &= \frac{(1-\alpha) Y_{it}}{w_t}. \end{aligned} \tag{11.57}$$

---

[14] To show that α is the capital share of output in the production process, we first derive the equation where the rental rate (r_t) equals marginal product of capital (MPK) (from the Cobb–Douglas production function):

$$\begin{aligned} r_t &= \alpha A_t K_{it}^{\alpha-1} L_{it}^{1-\alpha} \\ r_t &= \frac{\alpha A_t K_{it}^{\alpha} L_{it}^{1-\alpha}}{K_{it}} \\ r_t &= \frac{\alpha Y_{it}}{K_{it}}. \end{aligned}$$

Now we rewrite this equation as the capital share of output:

$$\frac{r_t K_{it}}{Y_{it}} = \alpha.$$

Therefore, we see α is simply the capital share of output in the Cobb–Douglas production specification. We can repeat a similar computation to show that $1-\alpha$ is the labor share of output.

[15] For simplicity, we assume the productivity growth rate is zero.

Finally, we derive the relation between rental rate r_t and wage rate w_t in order to obtain the equilibrium (steady state) level in the long run. Using Eqs. (11.56) and (11.57), we have the following expressions, respectively:

$$K_{it}^{\alpha} = \left(\frac{\alpha Y_{it}}{r_t}\right)^{\alpha}, \tag{11.58}$$

and:

$$L_{it}^{1-\alpha} = \left[\frac{(1-\alpha) Y_{it}}{w_t}\right]^{1-\alpha}. \tag{11.59}$$

We multiply Eq. (11.58) by Eq. (11.59):

$$K_{it}^{\alpha} L_{it}^{1-\alpha} = \left(\frac{\alpha Y_{it}}{r_t}\right)^{\alpha} \left[\frac{(1-\alpha) Y_{it}}{w_t}\right]^{1-\alpha}$$

$$K_{it}^{\alpha} L_{it}^{1-\alpha} = \left(\frac{\alpha}{r_t}\right)^{\alpha} \left(\frac{1-\alpha}{w_t}\right)^{1-\alpha} Y_{it}$$

$$\Rightarrow \frac{K_{it}^{\alpha} L_{it}^{1-\alpha}}{Y_{it}} = \left(\frac{\alpha}{r_t}\right)^{\alpha} \left(\frac{1-\alpha}{w_t}\right)^{1-\alpha}$$

$$\Rightarrow \frac{K_{it}^{\alpha} L_{it}^{1-\alpha}}{A_t K_{it}^{\alpha} L_{it}^{1-\alpha}} = \left(\frac{\alpha}{r_t}\right)^{\alpha} \left(\frac{1-\alpha}{w_t}\right)^{1-\alpha}$$

$$\Rightarrow 1 = A_t \left(\frac{\alpha}{r_t}\right)^{\alpha} \left(\frac{1-\alpha}{w_t}\right)^{1-\alpha}$$

$$\Rightarrow w_t^{1-\alpha} = A_t \left(\frac{\alpha}{r_t}\right)^{\alpha} (1-\alpha)^{1-\alpha}$$

$$w_t = (1-\alpha) A_t^{\frac{1}{1-\alpha}} \left(\frac{\alpha}{r_t}\right)^{\frac{\alpha}{1-\alpha}}. \tag{11.60}$$

Equation (11.60) represents the optimal relation between wage rate w_t and rental rate r_t.

The Complete Structure of the Model and Its Steady State

The previous subsections show a household maximizes her utility by choosing the optimal levels of consumption, savings, and labor, and a firm maximizes its profits by choosing the optimal levels of labor and capital. We can summarize the complete model in Table 11.3.

The model predicts that the variables of interest converge to particular steady state levels in the long run. The steady state consumption level is given as the

TABLE 11.3. *The complete RBC model*

The demand side of the economy		
Equation (11.43)	Euler Equation	$(E_t C_{it+1}/c_{it})^\sigma = \beta\left[(1-\delta)+E_t r_{t+1}\right]$
Equation (11.44)	Labor Supply Function	$L_{it}^\phi = C_{it}^{-\sigma} w_t$
Equation (11.29)	Income Identity	$Y_{it} = C_{it} + I_{it}$
Equation (11.31)	Capital Accumulation Function	$K_{it+1} = (1-\delta)K_{it} + I_{it}$

The supply side of the economy		
Equation (11.54)	Production Function	$Y_{it} = A_t K_{it}^\alpha L_{it}^{1-\alpha}$
Equation (11.55)	Productivity Function	$\ln A_t = \rho \ln A_{t-1} + \epsilon_t$
Equation (11.57)	Demand for Labor	$L_{it} = (1-\alpha) Y_{it}/w_t$
Equation (11.56)	Demand for Capital	$K_{it} = \alpha Y_{it}/r_t$

unique constant solution, $C_{it+1} = C_{it} = C_i^*$, from Eq. (11.43), and the steady state condition for the Euler equation is:

$$E_t C_{it+1}^\sigma = \beta\left[(1-\delta) + E_t r_{t+1}\right] C_{it}^\sigma$$
$$\Rightarrow E_t C_i^{*\sigma} = \beta\left[(1-\delta) + E_t r^*\right] C_i^{*\sigma}$$
$$C_i^{*\sigma} = \beta\left[(1-\delta) + r^*\right] C_i^{*\sigma} \tag{11.61}$$
$$1 = \beta\left[(1-\delta) + r^*\right], \tag{11.62}$$

where $E_t C_i^* = C_i^*$, and $E_t r^* = r^*$, for r^* represent the steady state level of the rental rate. Hence, we are able to determine the steady state levels for all the endogenous variables, $r^*, w^*, Y^*, K^*, I^*, C^*, L^*$, and A^* in the model:

1. The rental rate in steady state (11.62):

$$r^* = \frac{1}{\beta} - (1-\delta); \tag{11.63}$$

2. The wage rate in steady state (11.60):

$$w^* = (1-\alpha)\left(\frac{\alpha}{r^*}\right)^{\alpha/(1-\alpha)}; \tag{11.64}$$

3. The output level in steady state:[16]

$$Y^* = \left(\frac{r^*}{r^* - \delta\alpha}\right)^{\frac{\sigma}{\sigma+\phi}} \left[\frac{w^{*\frac{1+\phi}{\sigma+\phi}}}{(1-\alpha)^{\frac{\phi}{\sigma+\phi}}}\right]; \tag{11.65}$$

[16] Equation (11.65) is obtained from the income identity (11.29). In the steady state, the income identity equation can be written as:

$$Y^* = C^* + I^*. \tag{11.66}$$

Macro Political Economy

We derive the steady state level of output by solving steady state levels of C^* and I^*. To solve C^*, we note that the steady states for Eqs. (11.57) and (11.44), respectively, are:

$$L^* = \frac{(1-\alpha)Y^*}{w^*}, \tag{11.67}$$

and:

$$L^{*\phi} = C^{*-\sigma} w^*$$
$$\Rightarrow L^* = C^{*\frac{-\sigma}{\phi}} w^{*\frac{1}{\phi}}. \tag{11.68}$$

We set (11.67) equal to (11.68):

$$\frac{(1-\alpha)Y^*}{w^*} = C^{*\frac{-\sigma}{\phi}} w^{*\frac{1}{\phi}}$$

$$\Rightarrow C^{*\frac{\sigma}{\phi}} = \frac{w^*}{(1-\alpha)Y^*} \times w^{*\frac{1}{\phi}}$$

$$\Rightarrow C^* = \left[\frac{w^*}{(1-\alpha)Y^*} \times w^{*\frac{1}{\phi}}\right]^{\frac{\phi}{\sigma}}$$

$$C^* = \left[(1-\alpha)Y^*\right]^{-\frac{\phi}{\sigma}} w^{*\frac{1+\phi}{\sigma}}. \tag{11.69}$$

We then solve for I^* using Eqs. (11.56) and (11.31). The steady states for those equations are:

$$K^* = \alpha Y^*/r^*, \tag{11.70}$$

and:

$$I^* = \delta K^*, \tag{11.71}$$

where $K_{t+1} = K_t = K^*$ in steady state. Inserting Eq. (11.70) into Eq. (11.71), we have:

$$I^* = \delta \alpha Y^*/r^*. \tag{11.72}$$

Finally, we plug Eqs. (11.69) and (11.72) into Eq. (11.66), and we have:

$$Y^* = \left\{\left[(1-\alpha)Y^*\right]^{-\frac{\phi}{\sigma}} w^{*\frac{1+\phi}{\sigma}}\right\} + \left(\delta\alpha Y^*/r^*\right)$$

$$Y^* = Y^{*-\frac{\phi}{\sigma}} \left\{(1-\alpha)^{-\frac{\phi}{\sigma}} w^{*\frac{1+\phi}{\sigma}}\right\} + Y^*\left(\frac{\delta\alpha}{r^*}\right)$$

$$\Rightarrow Y^*\left(1 - \frac{\delta\alpha}{r^*}\right) = Y^{*-\frac{\phi}{\sigma}}\left[(1-\alpha)^{-\frac{\phi}{\sigma}} w^{*\frac{1+\phi}{\sigma}}\right]$$

$$Y^{*1+\frac{\phi}{\sigma}} = \left(1 - \frac{\delta\alpha}{r^*}\right)^{-1}\left[(1-\alpha)^{-\frac{\phi}{\sigma}} w^{*\frac{1+\phi}{\sigma}}\right]$$

$$\Rightarrow Y^{*\frac{\sigma+\phi}{\sigma}} = \left(1 - \frac{\delta\alpha}{r^*}\right)^{-1}\left[(1-\alpha)^{-\frac{\phi}{\sigma}} w^{*\frac{1+\phi}{\sigma}}\right]$$

$$Y^* = \left(1 - \frac{\delta\alpha}{r^*}\right)^{-\frac{\sigma}{\sigma+\phi}}\left[(1-\alpha)^{-\phi} w^{*1+\phi}\right]^{\frac{1}{\sigma+\phi}}$$

$$Y^* = \left(\frac{r^*}{r^* - \delta\alpha}\right)^{\frac{\sigma}{\sigma+\phi}}\left[\frac{w^{*\frac{1+\phi}{\sigma+\phi}}}{(1-\alpha)^{\frac{\phi}{\sigma+\phi}}}\right].$$

4. The capital level in steady state (11.56):
$$K^* = \alpha Y^*/r^*; \tag{11.73}$$

5. The investment level in steady state (11.31):
$$I^* = \delta K^*; \tag{11.74}$$

6. The consumption level in steady state (11.29):
$$C^* = Y^* - I^*; \tag{11.75}$$

7. The labor level in steady state (11.44):
$$L^{*\phi} = C^{*-\sigma} w^*; \tag{11.76}$$

8. The productivity level in steady state (11.55):
$$A^* = 1. \tag{11.77}$$

Linearization and Calibration

We note that the model presented in Table 11.3 is difficult to solve due to its nonlinear structure. It is easier to solve the model and observe the dynamics of the variables when the model is presented in a linear form. Hence, we linearize the system of equations in Table 11.3 around the steady state. We define $\hat{x} = \ln x - \ln x^*$, which presents the logged deviation of x from its steady state value x^*, and note that $e^{\ln x} = x$.

We start with the Euler equation (11.43) by dividing $C_i^{*\sigma}$ on both sides:

$$\frac{E_t C_{it+1}^{\sigma}}{C_i^{*\sigma}} = \beta \left[(1-\delta) + r^* \frac{E_t r_{t+1}}{r^*} \right] \frac{C_{it}^{\sigma}}{C_i^{*\sigma}}$$

$$\Rightarrow e^{\ln\left(\frac{E_t C_{it+1}^{\sigma}}{C_i^{*\sigma}}\right)} = \beta \left[(1-\delta) + r^* e^{\ln\left(\frac{E_t r_{t+1}}{r^*}\right)} \right] e^{\ln\left(\frac{C_{it}^{\sigma}}{C_i^{*\sigma}}\right)}$$

$$e^{\sigma \ln E_t C_{it+1} - \sigma \ln C_i^*} = \beta \left[(1-\delta) + r^* e^{\ln E_t r_{t+1} - \ln r^*} \right] e^{\sigma \ln C_{it} - \sigma \ln C_i^*}$$

$$e^{\sigma[(E_t \ln C_{it+1} - \ln C_i^*) - (\ln C_{it} - \ln C_i^*)]} = \beta \left[(1-\delta) + r^* e^{E_t \ln r_{t+1} - \ln r^*} \right]$$

$$e^{\sigma \left(E_t \hat{C}_{t+1} - \hat{C}_t \right)} = \beta (1-\delta) + \beta r^* e^{E_t \hat{r}_{t+1}}, \tag{11.78}$$

where $E_t \hat{C}_{it+1} = E_t \left(\ln C_{it+1} - \ln C_i^* \right)$, $\hat{C}_{it} = \ln C_{it} - \ln C_i^*$, and $E_t \hat{r}_{t+1} = E_t \left(\ln r_{it+1} - \ln r^* \right)$. We further simplify Eq. (11.78) using the following linear approximation:[17]

---

[17] Note that $\ln(1+x) \approx x$, for a small x. It implies that $e^{\ln(1+x)} \approx e^x$, and therefore $1 + x \approx e^x$.

Macro Political Economy

$$1 + \sigma \left(E_t \hat{C}_{it+1} - \hat{C}_{it} \right) = \beta (1 - \delta) + \beta r^* \left(1 + E_t \hat{r}_{t+1} \right)$$
$$\Rightarrow 1 + \sigma \left(E_t \hat{C}_{it+1} - \hat{C}_{it} \right) = \beta (1 - \delta) + \beta r^* + \beta r^* E_t \hat{r}_{t+1}. \quad (11.79)$$

Since $E_t \hat{C}_{it+1} = \hat{C}_{it} = 0$ and $E_t \hat{r}_{t+1} = 0$ in steady state, we have:

$$1 = \beta (1 - \delta) + \beta r^*.$$

Finally, the linearized Euler equation can be presented as:

$$\sigma \left(E_t \hat{C}_{it+1} - \hat{C}_{it} \right) = \beta r^* E_t \hat{r}_{t+1}. \quad (11.80)$$

For the labor supply (11.41), we have:

$$L_{it}^{\phi} = C_{it}^{-\sigma} w_t,$$

and then take the logarithm on both sides:

$$\phi \ln L_{it} = -\sigma \ln C_{it} + \ln w_t. \quad (11.81)$$

The labor supply function in steady state is:

$$\phi \ln L_i^* = -\sigma \ln C_i^* + \ln w^*. \quad (11.82)$$

Now we subtract Eq. (11.81) from Eq. (11.82) to obtain the following linearized labor supply function:

$$\phi \ln L_{it} - \phi \ln L_i^* = -\sigma \ln C_{it} + \sigma \ln C_i^* + \ln w_t - \ln w^*$$
$$\Rightarrow \phi \hat{L}_{it} = -\sigma \hat{C}_{it} + \hat{w}_t. \quad (11.83)$$

For the income identity (11.29):

$$Y_{it} = C_{it} + I_{it},$$

we first rewrite the equation as follows:

$$Y_i^* \frac{Y_{it}}{Y_i^*} = C_i^* \frac{C_{it}}{C_i^*} + I_i^* \frac{I_{it}}{I_i^*}. \quad (11.84)$$

Using the property $e^{\ln x} = x$, we rewrite Eq. (11.84) as:

$$Y_i^* e^{\ln\left(\frac{Y_{it}}{Y_i^*}\right)} = C_i^* e^{\ln\left(\frac{C_{it}}{C_i^*}\right)} + I_i^* e^{\ln\left(\frac{I_{it}}{I_i^*}\right)}$$
$$\Rightarrow Y_i^* e^{\ln Y_{it} - \ln Y_i^*} = C_i^* e^{\ln C_{it} - \ln C_i^*} + I_i^* e^{\ln I_{it} - \ln I_i^*}. \quad (11.85)$$

We further simplify the equation by using the log-linear approximation (see FN 17):

$$Y_i^* \left(1 + \ln Y_{it} - \ln Y_i^*\right) = C_i^* \left(1 + \ln C_{it} - \ln C_i^*\right) + I_i^* \left(1 + \ln I_{it} - \ln I_i^*\right)$$
$$\Rightarrow Y_i^* + Y_i^* \left(\ln Y_{it} - \ln Y_i^*\right) = C_i^* + I_i^* + C_i^* \left(\ln C_{it} - \ln C_i^*\right) + I_i^* \left(\ln I_{it} - \ln I_i^*\right)$$
$$Y_i^* \left(\ln Y_{it} - \ln Y_i^*\right) = C_i^* \left(\ln C_{it} - \ln C_i^*\right) + I_i^* \left(\ln I_{it} - \ln I_i^*\right)$$
$$Y_i^* \hat{Y}_{it} = C_i^* \hat{C}_{it} + I_i^* \hat{I}_{it}, \tag{11.86}$$

where $Y_i^* = C_i^* + I_i^*$ in steady state.

Similarly, for the capital accumulation function (11.31):

$$K_{it+1} = (1 - \delta) K_{it} + I_{it},$$

we rewrite the equation as:

$$K_i^* \frac{K_{it+1}}{K_i^*} = (1 - \delta) K_i^* \frac{K_{it}}{K_i^*} + I_i^* \frac{I_{it}}{I_i^*}. \tag{11.87}$$

Again, we apply the rule $e^{\ln x} = x$ to obtain:

$$K_i^* e^{\ln\left(\frac{K_{it+1}}{K_i^*}\right)} = (1 - \delta) K_i^* e^{\ln\left(\frac{K_{it}}{K_i^*}\right)} + I_i^* e^{\ln\left(\frac{I_{it}}{I_i^*}\right)}$$
$$\Rightarrow K_i^* e^{\ln K_{it+1} - \ln K_i^*} = (1 - \delta) K_i^* e^{\ln K_{it} - \ln K_i^*} + I_i^* e^{\ln I_{it} - \ln I_i^*}. \tag{11.88}$$

Then, applying the log-linear approximation, we have:

$$K_i^* \left(1 + \hat{K}_{it+1}\right) = (1 - \delta) K_i^* \left(1 + \hat{K}_{it}\right) + I_i^* \left(1 + \hat{I}_{it}\right)$$
$$\Rightarrow K_i^* + K_i^* \hat{K}_{it+1} = (1 - \delta) K_i^* + I_i^* + (1 - \delta) K_i^* \hat{K}_{it} + I_i^* \hat{I}_{it}. \tag{11.89}$$

Since $\hat{K}_{it+1} = \hat{K}_{it} = \hat{I}_{it} = 0$ in steady state, we have:

$$K_i^* = (1 - \delta) K_i^* + I_i^*$$
$$\Rightarrow I_i^* = \delta K^*. \tag{11.90}$$

We insert Eq. (11.90) into Eq. (11.89):

$$K_i^* + K_i^* \hat{K}_{it+1} = (1 - \delta) K_i^* + I_i^* + (1 - \delta) K_i^* \hat{K}_{it} + \delta K^* \hat{I}_{it}$$
$$\Rightarrow K_i^* \hat{K}_{it+1} = (1 - \delta) K_i^* \hat{K}_{it} + \delta K^* \hat{I}_{it}$$
$$\hat{K}_{it+1} = (1 - \delta) \hat{K}_{it} + \delta \hat{I}_{it}. \tag{11.91}$$

Now we linearize the production function (11.54):

$$Y_{it} = A_t K_{it}^\alpha L_{it}^{1-\alpha}.$$

We first take the logarithm on both sides of the equation:

$$\ln Y_{it} = \ln A_t + \alpha \ln K_{it} + (1 - \alpha) \ln L_{it}. \tag{11.92}$$

In the steady state, the linearized production function is:

$$\ln Y_i^* = \ln A^* + \alpha \ln K_i^* + (1-\alpha) \ln L_i^*. \tag{11.93}$$

By subtracting Eq. (11.92) from Eq. (11.93), we have the linearized production function:

$$\ln Y_{it} - \ln Y_i^* = \ln A_t - \ln A^* + \alpha \left(\ln K_{it} - \ln K_i^*\right) + (1-\alpha)\left(\ln L_{it} - \ln L_i^*\right)$$
$$\Rightarrow \hat{Y}_{it} = \hat{A}_t + \alpha \hat{K}_{it} + (1-\alpha)\hat{L}_{it}. \tag{11.94}$$

The linearization of the productivity function (11.55) is straightforward. The steady state condition for the productivity function is:

$$\ln A^* = \rho \ln A^*. \tag{11.95}$$

We subtract Eq. (11.55) from Eq. (11.95), and the linearized productivity function becomes:

$$\ln A_t - \ln A^* = \rho \left(\ln A_{t-1} - \ln A^*\right) + \epsilon_t$$
$$\Rightarrow \hat{A}_t = \rho \hat{A}_{t-1} + \epsilon_t. \tag{11.96}$$

The labor demand (11.57) and capital demand (11.56) can be linearized in a similar way. The demand for labor is:

$$L_{it} = \frac{(1-\alpha) Y_{it}}{w_t}.$$

We take the logarithm on both sides:

$$\ln L_{it} = \ln(1-\alpha) + \ln Y_{it} - \ln w_t.$$

In steady state, we have:

$$\ln L_i^* = \ln(1-\alpha) + \ln Y_i^* - \ln w^*.$$

The linear function of labor demand deviated from the steady state can be presented as:

$$\ln L_{it} - \ln L_i^* = \left(\ln Y_{it} - \ln Y_i^*\right) - \left(\ln w_{it} - \ln w^*\right)$$
$$\Rightarrow \hat{L}_{it} = \hat{Y}_{it} - \hat{w}_{it}. \tag{11.97}$$

We also obtain the linear function of capital demand as:

$$\hat{K}_{it} = \hat{Y}_{it} - \hat{r}_{it}. \tag{11.98}$$

The complete linearized RBC model can be summarized in Table 11.4. Given the steady state conditions (11.63)–(11.77) and the linearized model in Table 11.4, we calibrate the model according to the parameter values presented in Table 11.5. We run the calibration with Dynare, a platform that performs

TABLE 11.4. *The linearized RBC model*

The demand side of the economy

Equation (11.80)	Euler Equation	$\sigma \left(E_t \hat{C}_{t+1} - \hat{C}_t \right) = \beta r^* E_t \hat{r}_{t+1}$
Equation (11.83)	Labor Supply Function	$\phi \hat{L}_t = -\sigma \hat{C}_{it} + \hat{w}_t$
Equation (11.86)	Income Identity	$Y^* \hat{Y}_{it} = C^* \hat{C}_{it} + I^* \hat{I}_{it}$
Equation (11.91)	Capital Accumulation Function	$\hat{K}_{it+1} = (1-\delta) \hat{K}_{it} + \delta \hat{I}_{it}$

The supply side of the economy

Equation (11.94)	Production Function	$\hat{Y}_{it} = \hat{A}_t + \alpha \hat{K}_{it} + (1-\alpha) \hat{L}_{it}$
Equation (11.96)	Productivity Function	$\hat{A}_t = \rho \hat{A}_{t-1} + \epsilon_t$
Equation (11.97)	Demand for Labor	$\hat{L}_{it} = \hat{Y}_{it} - \hat{w}_t$
Equation (11.98)	Demand for Capital	$\hat{K}_{it} = \hat{Y}_{it} - \hat{r}_t$

TABLE 11.5. *Parameter values*

Parameter	Value
σ	1.0
ϕ	1.5
β	0.99
δ	0.025
α	0.33
ρ	0.95
σ_ϵ	0.01

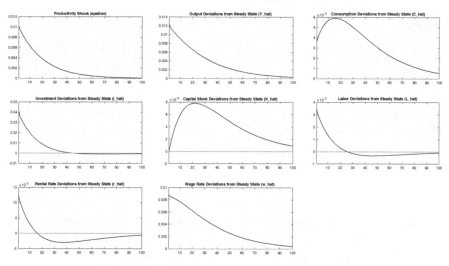

FIGURE 11.4. Calibration of the RBC model

simulation or calibration for economic models, particularly DSGE and overlapping generations (OLG) models. Figure 11.4 shows the movements of the endogenous variables over 100 periods when the productivity shock ϵ_t increases by one standard deviation σ_ϵ. A positive productivity shock shifts the production function upward and simulates the output level above its steady state $\hat{Y} > 0$. Given the initial levels of capital stock and labor, their marginal productivities increase, such that both rental rate $\hat{r}$ and wage rate $\hat{w}$ go up, according to Eqs. (11.45) and (11.46), respectively. As income increases, household i consumes more ($\hat{C} > 0$) and invests more ($\hat{I} > 0$) so that her capital stock also accumulates ($\hat{K} > 0$). When the wage rate increases initially, the household works more such that labor increases ($\hat{L} > 0$) initially.

However, due to the income increase, the household would desire more leisure. Therefore, L decreases over time such that $\hat{L}$ goes below zero, but gradually approaches its long run steady state, that is, $\hat{L} \to 0$ as $t \to \infty$. Similarly, as the initial productivity shock dies out in the long run, the rest of the variables also gradually approach their steady state levels as $t \to \infty$.

The Evolution of RBC Modeling: The DSGE Approach

Prescott (1986) summarizes the key results of the RBC model. Figure 11.5 compares the observed volatilities of major macroeconomic variables in the United States in the period 1947–1982 with the corresponding simulated volatilities. Similarly, Figure 11.6 compares the observed correlations of the variables with Gross National Product (GNP) and with the simulated data.[18] Both figures show that the simulated data match post-WWII data fairly well.

The great attraction of RBC theory is that it integrates both microeconomic and macroeconomic theories to explain how productivity shocks cause business cycles in an economy. Yet, initial acceptance was not forthcoming in the macroeconomic community. Many economists questioned the conclusion that recessions are caused by adverse productivity shocks and whether the output can always achieve full employment levels. Some critics also suggested shocks other than productivity shocks, such as military conflicts and the corresponding military expansions, have caused business cycles. Consequently, post-RBC economists allow for shocks other than productivity shocks included in a general equilibrium model. This modified theory is termed dynamic, stochastic, general equilibrium (DSGE).

The birth of DSGE models unified the classical and Keynesian theories in analyzing business cycle fluctuations (see Sbordone et al. 2010). Abel, Bernanke, and Croushore (2012, 435) state that:

One fundamental area of difference between classical and Keynesian economists had always been the degree to which a model incorporated microeconomic foundations. Many classical economists, especially after ideas about rational expectations came to the forefront in the early 1980s, believed that good models could be developed only

[18] The results are obtained from Prescott (1986).

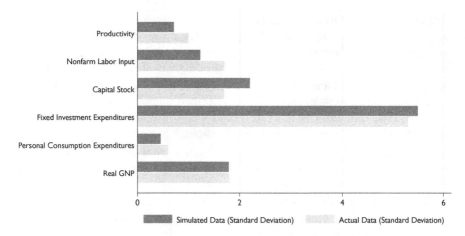

FIGURE 11.5. Actual versus simulated volatilities of macro-variables (Prescott 1986)

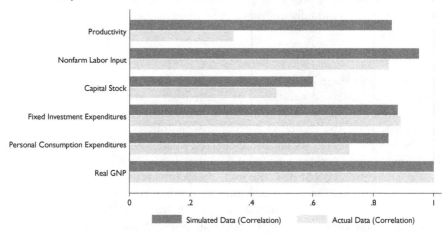

FIGURE 11.6. Actual versus simulated correlations of macro-variables with GNP (Prescott 1986)

by modeling microeconomic foundations, ... Keynesian economists, however, often believed that the attempt to find microeconomic foundations was unlikely to be fruitful, and instead they focused on large-scale macroeconomic models ... [S]ome researchers found ways to reconcile the two approaches. The basic idea was to show under what circumstances the Keynesian-type model with a few equations describing behavior was consistent with a classical model containing detailed microeconomic foundations. This [DSGE] research helped to reconcile the classical and Keynesian approaches, even though it did not convince everyone on both sides.

Indeed, Prescott foresaw this possibility. He wrote:

The models constructed within this theoretical framework are necessarily highly abstract. Consequently, they are necessarily false, and statistical hypothesis testing will reject them. This does not imply, however, that nothing can be learned from such quantitative theoretical exercises. I think much has already been learned and confidently predict that much more will be leaned as other features of the environment are introduced. Prime candidates for study are the effects of public finance elements, a foreign sector, and, of course, monetary factors. the research I review here is best viewed as a very promising beginning of a much larger research program. (Prescott 1986, 10)[19]

11.6.3 An introduction to Dynamic Optimization

A Simple Two-Period Consumption Model

Theoretical Setup

We assume there are two periods in the model. The first period $t = 1$ is "the present," and the second period $t = 2$ is "the future." We can write a two-period utility function, which is the sum for utility for present consumption and future consumption:

$$U = u(c_1) + \beta u(c_2), \tag{11.99}$$

where c_t represents the level of consumption at time t. Therefore, $u(c_t)$ is the utility of consumption at time t. We note that $u(c)$ is a well-defined concave utility function such that $du/dc = u'(\cdot) > 0$, and $d^2u/dc^2 = u''(c) < 0$. The term β is the discount factor (or a degree of patience). If an agent is more patient, she would put more weight on the utility of future consumption (i.e., a larger value of β).

The agent has budget constraints for periods 1 and 2. In period 1, her budget constraint can be written as:

$$y_1 + (1+r)s_0 = c_1 + s_1, \tag{11.100}$$

where y_t is the income level at time t, s_t represents the assets (or debt) the agent possesses at time t, and r is the rate of return on the assets (or the interest rate on debt). In this set up, s_0 represents the initial endowment for the agent. It can also be seen as either a bequest ($s_0 > 0$) or a debt burden ($s_0 < 0$) left from her parents. The individual's budget constraint for period 2 is then:

$$y_2 + (1+r)s_1 = c_2 + s_2. \tag{11.101}$$

---

[19] In addition to the basic component of households' and firms' optimal behavior in the basic RBC model, Keynesian economists allow for the possibility of price rigidity in the output market or wage rigidity in the labor market, and include policymakers' actions – fiscal policy or monetary policy – in the economy. The researchers then introduce different types of shocks in the model, for example, monetary policy shocks, to investigate the interaction between policymakers' decisions and agents' behaviors, and capture the dynamics of the endogenous variables of interest.

For simplicity, we assume the agent does not have any inheritance/debt at the beginning of period 1 and at the end of period 2, such that $s_0 = 0$ and $s_2 = 0$, respectively. Finally, by combining Eqs. (11.99)–(11.101), we have the following utility maximization problem:

$$\max_{c_1, c_2} U = u(c_1) + \beta u(c_2), \tag{11.102}$$

such that:

1. the first period budget constraint:

$$y_1 = c_1 + s_1, \tag{11.103}$$

2. the second period budget constraint:

$$y_2 + (1+r)s_1 = c_2. \tag{11.104}$$

Solving the Utility Maximization Problem

To determine the optimal consumption level over time, we solve the system of Eqs. (11.102)–(11.104). We present the following Lagrangian equation:

$$L = u(c_1) + \beta u(c_2) + \lambda_1 (y_1 - c_1 - s_1) + \lambda_2 (y_2 + (1+r)s_1 - c_2), \tag{11.105}$$

where λ_1 and λ_2 are Lagrangian multipliers. In this system, there are five choice variables: c_1, c_2, s_1, λ_1, and λ_2. We solve for those variables based on the following five first-order conditions (FOCs):

1. $\partial L / \partial c_1 = 0$:

$$u'(c_1) - \lambda_1 = 0; \tag{11.106}$$

2. $\partial L / \partial c_2 = 0$:

$$\beta u'(c_2) - \lambda_2 = 0; \tag{11.107}$$

3. $\partial L / \partial s_1 = 0$:

$$-\lambda_1 + (1+r)\lambda_2 = 0; \tag{11.108}$$

4. $\partial L / \partial \lambda_1 = 0$:

$$y_1 = c_1 + s_1; \tag{11.109}$$

5. $\partial L / \partial \lambda_2 = 0$:

$$y_2 + (1+r)s_1 = c_2. \tag{11.110}$$

Macro Political Economy

Using Eqs. (11.106)–(11.108), we have:

$$\lambda_1 = u'(c_1), \qquad (11.111)$$
$$\lambda_2 = \beta u'(c_2), \text{ and} \qquad (11.112)$$
$$-\lambda_1 + (1+r)\lambda_2 = 0. \qquad (11.113)$$

Next, we insert Eqs. (11.111) and (11.112) into Eq. (11.113), and we have the following equation:

$$u'(c_1) = \beta(1+r)u'(c_2). \qquad (11.114)$$

Equation (11.114) is called the Euler equation.[20] Combining Eqs. (11.109) and (11.110), we have the following lifetime budget constraint:

$$y_1 + \frac{y_2}{1+r} = c_1 + \frac{c_2}{1+r}. \qquad (11.115)$$

Now, given a certain functional form of $u(\cdot)$, we can use Eqs. (11.114) and (11.115) to obtain the optimal levels of c_1 and c_2, (i.e., c_1^* and c_2^*). To demonstrate the solution process for the utility maximization problem, we assume the utility function is in a simple functional form:

$$u(c_t) = \frac{1}{\alpha} c_t^\alpha,$$

where $\alpha \in (0, 1)$. For simplicity, let α be $1/2$, and we have:

$$u'(c) = c^{-1/2}. \qquad (11.116)$$

Inserting Eq. (11.116) into Eq. (11.114), we have:

$$c_1^{-1/2} = \beta(1+r) c_2^{-1/2}$$
$$\Rightarrow c_2 = [\beta(1+r)]^2 c_1. \qquad (11.117)$$

Then we plug Eq. (11.117) into Eq. (11.115) to solve for c_1^*:

$$y_1 + \frac{y_2}{1+r} = c_1 + \beta^2(1+r) c_1$$
$$y_1 + \frac{y_2}{1+r} = c_1 [1 + \beta^2(1+r)]$$
$$\Rightarrow c_1^* = [1 + \beta^2(1+r)]^{-1} \left(y_1 + \frac{y_2}{1+r}\right). \qquad (11.118)$$

Finally, we solve for c_2^* by inserting Eq. (11.118) into Eq. (11.117):

$$c_2^* = [\beta(1+r)]^2 [1 + \beta^2(1+r)]^{-1} \left(y_1 + \frac{y_2}{1+r}\right). \qquad (11.119)$$

---

[20] See Eq. (11.40) for the interpretation of the Euler equation.

Equations (11.118) and (11.119) represent the optimal levels of consumption for periods 1 and 2, respectively, in a two-period consumption model.

General Consumption Models in Discrete Time

We can also generalize the previous two-period model to a T-period model. To do so, we solve the following utility maximization problem, where a representative consumer lives for T periods:

$$\max_{c_t \forall t \in \{1,2,\ldots,T\}} U = U(c_1, c_2, \ldots, c_T), \quad (11.120)$$

such that:

$$y_t + (1+r)s_{t-1} = c_t + s_t. \quad (11.121)$$

Again, we assume that $s_0 = 0$ and $s_T = 0$ so that the individual does not receive any inheritance or debt from the previous generation ($t = 0$) and leave any bequest or debt for the next generation ($t = T$). Assuming that the functional form of utility is inter-temporally separable, we rewrite Eq. (11.120) as follows:

$$U = u(c_1) + \beta u(c_2) + \beta^2 u(c_3) + \cdots + \beta^{T-1} u(c_T),$$

$$\Rightarrow U = \sum_{t=1}^{T} \beta^{t-1} u(c_t). \quad (11.122)$$

As in the previous section, we present the following Lagrangian equation to solve the optimal level of consumption at time t:

$$L = \sum_{t=1}^{T} \beta^{t-1} u(c_t) + \sum_{t=1}^{T} \lambda_t [y_t + (1+r)s_{t-1} - s_t - c_t], \quad (11.123)$$

where $t = \{1, 2, \ldots, T\}$, and $s_0 = s_T = 0$. According to Eq. (11.123), we note that there are a total of $3T - 1$ choice variables: $c_1, c_2, \ldots, c_T, s_1, s_2, \ldots, s_{T-1}$, and $\lambda_1, \lambda_2, \ldots, \lambda_T$. As a result, we obtain the following $3T - 1$ first-order conditions:[21]

1. $\partial L / \partial c_t = 0$:

   $$\beta^{t-1} u'(c_t) - \lambda_t = 0, \quad (11.124)$$

   for $t = 1, \ldots, T$;

---

[21] In the two-period consumption model ($T = 2$) presented in the previous section, there are $3T - 1 = 3 \times 2 - 1 = 5$ choice variables. Hence, we obtain five first-order conditions (11.106)–(11.110).

2. $\partial L/\partial s_t = 0$:

$$-\lambda_t + (1+r)\lambda_{t+1} = 0, \tag{11.125}$$

for $t = 1, \ldots, T-1$;

3. $\partial L/\partial \lambda = 0$:

$$y_t + (1+r)s_{t-1} = c_t + s_t, \tag{11.126}$$

for $t = 1, \ldots, T$.

We can rewrite Eq. (11.124) in terms of t and $t+1$, respectively:

$$\beta^{t-1} u'(c_t) = \lambda_t, \tag{11.127}$$

and:

$$\beta^t u'(c_{t+1}) = \lambda_{t+1}. \tag{11.128}$$

Now, we insert Eqs. (11.127) and (11.128) into Eq. (11.125):

$$-\beta^{t-1} u'(c_t) + (1+r)\beta^t u'(c_{t+1}) = 0$$
$$\Rightarrow \beta^{t-1} u'(c_t) = [\beta^t (1+r)] u'(c_{t+1})$$
$$\Rightarrow u'(c_t) = \beta (1+r) u'(c_{t+1}), \tag{11.129}$$

for $t = 1, \ldots, T-1$. Therefore, Eq. (11.129) is the Euler equation for this finite horizon consumption model.

To derive the lifetime budget constraint, we first consider the budget constraint (11.126) at the last period ($t = T$), and we have:

$$y_T + (1+r)s_{T-1} = c_T + s_T. \tag{11.130}$$

Since $s_T = 0$, we simplify the previous equation as follows:

$$c_T = y_T + (1+r)s_{T-1}. \tag{11.131}$$

To derive the component s_{T-1} in Eq. (11.131), we revisit Eq. (11.130) and isolate s_T on the left-hand side:

$$s_T = y_T - c_T + (1+r)s_{T-1}, \tag{11.132}$$

then we move the equation one period backward:

$$s_{T-1} = y_{T-1} - c_{T-1} + (1+r)s_{T-2}. \tag{11.133}$$

Similarly, we move Eq. (11.133) backward for one more period:

$$s_{T-2} = y_{T-2} - c_{T-2} + (1+r)s_{T-3}. \tag{11.134}$$

We now substitute Eq. (11.133) into Eq. (11.131):

$$c_T = y_T + (1+r)\left[y_{T-1} - c_{T-1} + (1+r)s_{T-2}\right]$$
$$c_T = y_T + (1+r)y_{T-1} - (1+r)c_{T-1} + (1+r)^2 s_{T-2}$$
$$\Rightarrow c_T + (1+r)c_{T-1} = y_T + (1+r)y_{T-1} + (1+r)^2 s_{T-2}. \qquad (11.135)$$

By inserting Eq. (11.134) into Eq. (11.135), we have:

$$c_T + (1+r)c_{T-1} = y_T + (1+r)y_{T-1} + (1+r)^2$$
$$[y_{T-2} - c_{T-2} + (1+r)s_{T-3}]$$
$$\Rightarrow c_T + (1+r)c_{T-1} + (1+r)^2 c_{T-2} = y_T + (1+r)y_{T-1} + (1+r)^2 y_{T-2}$$
$$+ (1+r)^3 s_{T-3}.$$

Repeating this process for $T-1$ times, we obtain the following lifetime budget constraint:

$$\sum_{t=1}^{T}\left[(1+r)^{T-t} c_t\right] = \sum_{t=1}^{T}\left[(1+r)^{T-t} y_t\right], \qquad (11.136)$$

where $s_0 = 0$. Based on Eqs. (11.129) and (11.136), the complete system can be presented as follows:

$$u'(c_t) = \beta(1+r)u'(c_{t+1}) \qquad (11.137)$$

$$\sum_{t=1}^{T}\left[(1+r)^{T-t} c_t\right] = \sum_{t=1}^{T}\left[(1+r)^{T-t} y_t\right]. \qquad (11.138)$$

Finally, we can solve the system of Eqs. (11.137) and (11.138) for the optimal levels of consumption c_t^*, for $t = 1, \ldots, T$.[22]

---

[22] For the case of the two-period ($T = 2$) consumption model presented in the previous section, the Euler equation remains unchanged:

$$u'(c_t) = \beta(1+r)u'(c_{t+1}),$$

and the budget constraint is:

$$\sum_{t=1}^{T}\left[(1+r)^{T-t} c_t\right] = \sum_{t=1}^{T}\left[(1+r)^{T-t} y_t\right]$$

$$\sum_{t=1}^{T=2}\left[(1+r)^{T-t} c_t\right] = \sum_{t=1}^{T=2}\left[(1+r)^{T-t} y_t\right]$$

$$(1+r)^{2-1} c_1 + (1+r)^{2-2} c_2 = (1+r)^{2-1} y_1 + (1+r)^{2-2} y_2$$

$$(1+r)c_1 + c_2 = (1+r)y_1 + y_2$$

$$c_1 + \frac{c_2}{1+r} = y_1 + \frac{y_2}{1+r},$$

which is equivalent to Eq. (11.115). As a result, we can solve for the optimal levels of consumption at $t = 1$ and $t = 2$, presented in Eqs. (11.118) and (11.119), respectively.

Dynamic Programming: The Bellman Equation

In this section, we introduce an alternative method of optimization called dynamic programming, which has been widely used in the macroeconomic literature. This technique is based on a recursive representation of a value function called the Bellman equation – a value function in one period conditional on the value function in the next period. The maximization decision or the optimal path is determined by solving the optimal decision in the final period followed by those in previous periods using backward induction. The property of this optimal solution is also known as Bellman's optimality principle.

Consumption Dynamics
Consider the following maximization problem:

$$\max_{c_t \forall t \in \{1,2,\ldots,T\}} \left[U = \sum_{t=1}^{T} \beta^{t-1} u(c_t) \right], \qquad (11.139)$$

subject to the following budget constraint, which is similar to Eq. (11.121):

$$s_t = y_t - c_t + (1+r) s_{t-1}. \qquad (11.140)$$

According to the system of Eqs. (11.139) and (11.140), s_t is known as the state variable in each period t, and c_t is known as the control variable.[23] We note that the maximum value of utility not only depends on the level of consumption at time t but also depends on the resource level s_t left for future consumption. In other words, given the existing level of assets s_{t-1} available, the consumption level c_t decided at time t will affect the level of assets (s_t) available for time $t+1$.

We first define the value function $V_1(s_0)$ is the maximized value of the objective function from time $t = 1$ to the last period of $t = T$:

$$V_1(s_0) = \max_{c_t \forall t \in \{1,2,\ldots,T\}} \sum_{t=1}^{T} \beta^{t-1} u(c_t), \qquad (11.141)$$

$$V_1(s_0) = \max_{c_t \forall t \in \{1,2,\ldots,T\}} \left[u(c_1) + \beta u(c_2) + \beta^2 u(c_3) + \cdots + \beta^{T-1} u(c_T) \right],$$

$$V_1(s_0) = \max_{c_t \forall t \in \{1,2,\ldots,T\}} \left\{ u(c_1) + \beta \left[\sum_{t=2}^{T} \beta^{t-2} u(c_t) \right] \right\}, \qquad (11.142)$$

subject to:

$$s_t = y_t - c_t + (1+r) s_{t-1}. \qquad (11.143)$$

---

[23] For $T = 2$, this model is reduced to a two-period optimization problem presented in the previous section.

Equation (11.141) is the value function $V_1(s_0)$, which represents the maximized value of the objective function at time $t = 1$ given an initial stock of assets s_0. After solving the first-period maximization, the household repeats the utility maximization procedure for period $t = 2$ given the asset level left after $t = 1$ (that is, s_1):

$$V_2(s_1) = \max_{c_t \forall t \in \{2,\ldots,T\}} \sum_{t=2}^{T} \beta^{t-2} u(c_t), \tag{11.144}$$

subject to Eq. (11.143). Now we insert Eq. (11.144) into Eq. (11.142):

$$V_1(s_0) = \max_{c_1} \left[u(c_1) + \beta V_2(s_1) \right].$$

Assuming the household maximizes her utility in every period, the maximization problem can be written recursively. As a result, we obtain the following Bellman equation:[24]

$$V_t(s_{t-1}) = \max_{c_t} \left[u(c_t) + \beta V_{t+1}(s_t) \right],$$

where $s_t = y_t - c_t + (1+r)s_{t-1}$ as presented in Eq. (11.143). Since the utility function is time-invariant, we drop the time subscript from the value function:

$$V(s_{t-1}) = \max_{c_t} \left[u(c_t) + \beta V(s_t) \right]. \tag{11.145}$$

To solve the Bellman equation, we first take a derivative of Eq. (11.145) with respect to the choice variable c_t:

$$\frac{\partial V(s_{t-1})}{\partial c_t} = 0$$

$$\Rightarrow u'(c_t) + \beta V'(s_t) \frac{\partial s_t}{\partial c_t} = 0. \tag{11.146}$$

Then, according to the budget constraint (11.143), the derivation of the budget constraint with respect to consumption at time t is presented as:

$$\frac{\partial s_t}{\partial c_t} = -1. \tag{11.147}$$

---

[24] We assume there is a terminal time period T in the model. To solve an infinite horizon model where $t \to \infty$, we require a well-defined terminal condition (or transversality condition) as follows:

$$\lim_{t \to \infty} s_t V'(s_t) = 0.$$

This terminal condition suggests $t \to \infty$, and we assume that either $s_{t \to \infty}$ equals zero or the level of utility has been maximized, such that $\lim_{t \to \infty} V'(s_t) = 0$.

Macro Political Economy

Now we insert Eq. (11.147) into Eq. (11.146):

$$u'(c_t) - \beta V'(s_t) = 0. \tag{11.148}$$

Finally, we solve for $V'(s_t)$ to obtain the optimal solution. To do so, we take the derivative of the Bellman equation (11.145) with respect to the state variable s_{t-1}:

$$V'(s_{t-1}) = \beta V'(s_t) \frac{\partial s_t}{\partial s_{t-1}}.$$

According to Eq. (11.143), we find $\partial s_t / \partial s_{t-1} = 1 + r$, which is then inserted into the previous equation:

$$V'(s_{t-1}) = \beta (1+r) V'(s_t). \tag{11.149}$$

From Eq. (11.148), we can present $V'(s_t)$ as:

$$V'(s_t) = \frac{1}{\beta} u'(c_t). \tag{11.150}$$

By moving Eq. (11.150) one period backward, we have:

$$V'(s_{t-1}) = \frac{1}{\beta} u'(c_{t-1}). \tag{11.151}$$

Now we plug Eqs. (11.150) and (11.151) into Eq. (11.149):

$$\frac{1}{\beta} u'(c_{t-1}) = \beta (1+r) \frac{1}{\beta} u'(c_t)$$

$$u'(c_{t-1}) = \beta (1+r) u'(c_t).$$

Finally, we move the above equation one period forward to obtain the Euler equation, which is identical to the one derived by the method of Lagrangian multiplier (11.137).

An Example of Dynamic Optimization in Discrete Time: Pie Consumption

In order to understand the implications of dynamic optimization, we solve for a simple problem called "pie consumption." Suppose a person i consumes a pie with size $\Pi_0 = 1$ at the beginning of time $t = 1$, and her utility function at time t is $u(c_t) = 2c_t^{1/2}$, with a discount factor β. If the person consumes the whole pie at time T (that is, $\Pi_T = 0$), what is the optimal path of consumption? To solve this problem, we first write this optimization system as follows:

$$\max_{c_t \forall t \in \{1,2,\ldots,T\}} \sum_{t=1}^{T} \beta^{t-1} u(c_t), \tag{11.152}$$

subject to:

$$\Pi_t = \Pi_{t-1} - c_t,$$

for $t = 1, 2, \ldots, T$, and $\Pi_0 = 1$ and $\Pi_T = 0$. In this example, the choice variable is c_t and the state variable Π_t. We transform the dynamic problem into a Bellman equation:

$$V(\Pi_{t-1}) = \max_{c_t} [u(c_t) + \beta V(\Pi_t)], \tag{11.153}$$

where:

$$\Pi_t = \Pi_{t-1} - c_t. \tag{11.154}$$

Since the utility function is presented as $u(c_t) = 2c_t^{1/2}$, the Bellman equation can be presented as:

$$V(\Pi_{t-1}) = \max_{c_t} \left[2c_t^{1/2} + \beta V(\Pi_t) \right]. \tag{11.155}$$

Now we obtain a first-order condition by taking the derivative of Eq. (11.155) with respect to c_t:

$$\frac{\partial V}{\partial c_t} = 0$$

$$\Rightarrow c_t^{-1/2} + \beta V'(\Pi_t) \frac{\partial \Pi_t}{\partial c_t} = 0. \tag{11.156}$$

According to Eq. (11.154), we have: $\partial \Pi_t / \partial c_t = -1$. Therefore, Eq. (11.156) can be written as:

$$c_t^{-1/2} - \beta V'(\Pi_t) = 0. \tag{11.157}$$

By taking a derivative of Eq. (11.153) with respect to Π_{t-1}, we also obtain the following equation:

$$V'(\Pi_{t-1}) = \beta V'(\Pi_t) \frac{\partial \Pi_t}{\partial \Pi_{t-1}}$$

$$\Rightarrow V'(\Pi_{t-1}) = \beta V'(\Pi_t), \tag{11.158}$$

where $\partial \Pi_t / \partial \Pi_{t-1} = 1$ according to Eq. (11.154). By inserting Eq. (11.157) into Eq. (11.158), we derive the following Euler equation:

$$u'(c_{t-1}) = \beta u'(c_t) \tag{11.159}$$

$$c_{t-1}^{-1/2} = \beta c_t^{-1/2}$$

$$c_t^{1/2} = \beta c_{t-1}^{1/2}$$

$$\Rightarrow c_t = \beta^2 c_{t-1}. \tag{11.160}$$

Macro Political Economy 235

Equation (11.160) represents the optimal path of the consumption of a pie over time.

Given the terminal condition $\Pi_T = 0$, we can determine the optimal initial consumption c_1^* by performing the recursive substitution of (11.154) and (11.160).[25] The optimal initial consumption c_1^* can be presented as:

$$c_1^* = \frac{1-\theta}{1-\theta^T}\Pi_0, \tag{11.161}$$

---

[25] According to Eq. (11.154), we have:

$$\Pi_t = \Pi_{t-1} - c_t.$$

For $t = 1$, we have:

$$\Pi_1 = \Pi_0 - c_1, \tag{11.162}$$

and for $t = 2$, we have:

$$\Pi_2 = \Pi_1 - c_2. \tag{11.163}$$

Now we plug (11.162) into (11.163):

$$\Pi_2 = \Pi_0 - c_1 - c_2.$$

If we iterate the process T times, we have:

$$\Pi_T = \Pi_0 - c_1 - c_2 - \cdots - c_T. \tag{11.164}$$

Now we rewrite Eq. (11.160) as follows:

$$c_t = \theta c_{t-1},$$

where $\theta = \beta^2$. For $t = 2$, the equation can be written as:

$$c_2 = \theta c_1. \tag{11.165}$$

Similarly, for $t = 3$, we have:

$$c_3 = \theta c_2 = \theta(\theta c_1) = \theta^2 c_1. \tag{11.166}$$

Again after we iterate the process T times, we have:

$$c_T = \theta^{T-1} c_1. \tag{11.167}$$

Next, we plug Eqs. (11.165)–(11.167) into Eq. (11.164):

$$\Pi_T = \Pi_0 - c_1 - \theta c_1 - \cdots - \theta^{T-1} c_1$$
$$\Pi_T = \Pi_0 - (1 - \theta - \cdots - \theta^{T-1})c_1. \tag{11.168}$$

As the terminal condition is $\Pi_T = 0$, we express Eq. (11.168) as:

$$\Pi_T = \Pi_0 - (1 + \theta + \cdots + \theta^{T-1})c_1 = 0$$
$$\Rightarrow \Pi_0 = (1 + \theta + \cdots + \theta^{T-1})c_1. \tag{11.169}$$

TABLE 11.6. *The dynamic optimal consumption of a pie*

Time	Consumption (c_t)	Total consumption up to time t	Pie size (Π_t)
0	0	0	1
1	0.2039	0.2039	0.7961
2	0.1685	0.3723	0.6277
3	0.1392	0.5116	0.4884
4	0.1151	0.6266	0.3734
5	0.0951	0.7217	0.2783
6	0.0786	0.8003	0.1997
7	0.0650	0.8653	0.1347
8	0.0537	0.9190	0.0810
9	0.0444	0.9633	0.0367
10	0.0367	1	0

Notes: The initial size of the pie is $\Pi_0 = 1$, and the terminal size of the pie is $\Pi_{10} = 0$, for $t = 10$. The discount factor is $\beta = 1/1.1 = 0.9091$.

where $\theta = \beta^2$. Based on Eqs. (11.161) and (11.160) with the initial and terminal conditions of Π_0 and Π_T, we can derive the optimal path of pie consumption. We illustrate the model by assuming the following values of the parameters: $\Pi_0 = 1$, $\Pi_T = 0$, $\beta = 0.9091$, and $T = 10$. The optimal levels of consumption over time are presented in Table 11.6. We also present Figure 11.7, which graphically describes the optimal path of pie consumption.

Dynamic Optimization in Continuous Time

In the previous sections, we focused on the technique of dynamic optimization in discrete time.[26] In this section we consider the method of dynamic optimization in continuous time, where the values of the variables change when the change in time is assumed to be approaching zero (i.e., $\Delta t \to 0$). Commonly

---

Since $1 + \theta + \theta^2 + \cdots + \theta^T = \left(1 - \theta^{T+1}\right) / (1 - \theta)$, we rewrite the initial Π_0 as:

$$\Pi_0 = \frac{1 - \theta^T}{1 - \theta} c_1.$$

Finally, we can obtain the optimal level of initial consumption at $t = 1$:

$$c_1 = \frac{1 - \theta}{1 - \theta^T} \Pi_0,$$

which is presented in Eq. (11.161).

[26] A discrete time model describes the values of the variables of interest (for example, consumption c_t) in the model change as time moves from one time period to the next, where the change in time Δt is assumed to be finite. For example, if the time period follows the sequence of $\{0, 1, 2, 3, \ldots\}$, then $\Delta t = 1$ for all $t \geq 0$.

Macro Political Economy

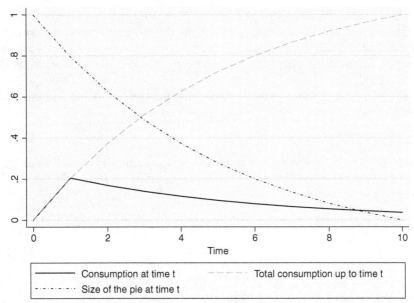

FIGURE 11.7. The optimal path of pie consumption

referred to as the Hamiltonian multiplier, this optimization method is more computationally convenient.

Let us consider a general continuous-time maximization problem, which can be written as follows:[27]

$$\max_{c_t} \int_0^T e^{-\rho t} f(c_t, s_t) \, dt, \tag{11.170}$$

subject to the constraint:

$$\dot{s}_t = h(c_t, s_t), \tag{11.171}$$

where $\dot{s}_t$ is a time derivative of s_t defined as ds_t/dt, and ρ is the discount rate in the model. If $\rho = 0$, then $e^{\rho t} = 1$. It implies that the household does not discount the values (utility) of the future activities. On the other hand, if ρ increases, then $e^{-\rho t}$ decreases, indicating the household becomes more impatient and the utility of the future activities is discounted. In the previous

---

[27] In a more general set up, the integration equation can also be written as:

$$\max \int_0^T e^{-\int_0^t r(\tau) d\tau} f(c_t, s_t) \, dt. \tag{11.172}$$

Comparing Eq. (11.172) with Eq. (11.170), we see that the similarity between the two equations is $\rho t \approx \int_0^t r(\tau) \, d\tau$, where the discount rate is changing over time in Eq. (11.172) while the discount rate remains constant in the entire horizon in Eq. (11.170).

sections we defined the discount factor as β, which is equivalent to $1/(1+\rho)$ in this section. For this model, c_t represents the choice variable, and s_t is the state variable. There are two functions: $f(\cdot)$ is the objective function – a utility function for most of our examples – and $h(\cdot)$ is the law of motion of the state variable.

To solve the dynamic problem, we set up the following Hamiltonian function:

$$H_t = e^{-\rho t}\left[f(c_t, s_t) + \lambda_t \dot{s}_t\right], \tag{11.173}$$

where $\lambda_t = \mu_t e^{\rho t}$ is known as the Hamiltonian multiplier. Now, we compute the following three conditions, which are required to obtain a solution for the system:

1. The first-order condition with respect to the choice variable (c_t):

$$\frac{\partial H_t}{\partial c_t} = 0; \tag{11.174}$$

2. The negative derivative of the Hamiltonian function with respect to the state variable s_t equals the time derivative of $\lambda_t e^{-\rho t}$:

$$-\frac{\partial H_t}{\partial s_t} = \frac{d\left(\lambda_t e^{-\rho t}\right)}{dt}; \tag{11.175}$$

3. The transversality condition:

$$\lim_{t \to \infty} \lambda_t e^{-\rho t} s_t = 0. \tag{11.176}$$

Pie Consumption Revisited

To understand the relation between the method of discrete time optimization and that of continuous time optimization, we solve the pie consumption problem in continuous time:

$$\max_{c_t} \int_0^T e^{-\rho t} u(c_t)\, dt, \tag{11.177}$$

subject to:[28]

$$\dot{\Pi}_t = -c_t. \tag{11.178}$$

---

[28] In Eq. (11.178), $\dot{\Pi}_t = d\Pi_t/dt$ is approximately $\Pi_t - \Pi_{t-1}$ in the discrete time model. Therefore, $\dot{\Pi}_t = -c_t$ can be approximate to $\Pi_t - \Pi_{t-1} = -c_t \Rightarrow \Pi_t = \Pi_{t-1} - c_t$, which is presented in Eq. (11.154) in the previous section.

Macro Political Economy

Now we set up the Hamiltonian equation as follows:

$$H_t = e^{-\rho t}\left(u(c_t) + \lambda_t \dot{\Pi}_t\right), \tag{11.179}$$

where λ_t is the Hamiltonian multiplier. We insert Eq. (11.178) into Eq. (11.179) and derive the final Hamiltonian equation:

$$H_t = e^{-\rho t}\left(u(c_t) - \lambda_t c_t\right). \tag{11.180}$$

Next we obtain the following three conditions:

1. The first-order condition with respect to c_t:

$$\frac{\partial H_t}{\partial c_t} = e^{-\rho t}\left(u'(c_t) - \lambda_t\right) = 0$$

$$\Rightarrow u'(c_t) = \lambda_t; \tag{11.181}$$

2. The negative derivative with respect to Π_t equals the time derivative of $\lambda_t e^{-\rho t}$:

$$-\frac{\partial H_t}{\partial \Pi_t} = \frac{d\left(\lambda_t e^{-\rho t}\right)}{dt}; \tag{11.182}$$

3. The transversality condition:

$$\lim_{t \to \infty} \lambda_t e^{-\rho t} \Pi_t = 0. \tag{11.183}$$

To solve for the system, we start with Eq. (11.182). We note that Π_t does not exist in the Hamiltonian equation (11.180). Therefore, the left hand of Eq. (11.182) is:

$$-\frac{\partial H_t}{\partial \Pi_t} = 0. \tag{11.184}$$

The right hand of Eq. (11.182) can be derived from Eq. (11.180):

$$\frac{d\left(\lambda_t e^{-\rho t}\right)}{dt} = \frac{d\lambda_t}{dt}e^{-\rho t} + \lambda_t\left(-\rho e^{-\rho t}\right)$$

$$\frac{d\left(\lambda_t e^{-\rho t}\right)}{dt} = \dot{\lambda}_t e^{-\rho t} - \lambda_t \rho e^{-\rho t}, \tag{11.185}$$

where $\dot{\lambda}_t = d\lambda_t/dt$. Now we equate Eq. (11.184) with Eq. (11.185), and we have:

$$-\frac{\partial H_t}{\partial \Pi_t} = \frac{d\left(\lambda_t e^{-\rho t}\right)}{dt}$$

$$0 = \dot{\lambda}_t e^{-\rho t} - \lambda_t \rho e^{-\rho t} \tag{11.186}$$

$$0 = \dot{\lambda}_t - \lambda_t \rho. \tag{11.187}$$

Now, we solve for $\dot{\lambda}_t$ in Eq. (11.187). According to Eq. (11.181), we know $\lambda_t = u'(c_t)$. Hence, we simply take a time derivative so that we have:

$$\dot{\lambda}_t = \frac{d\lambda_t}{dt} = \frac{du'(c_t)}{dc_t}\frac{dc_t}{dt}$$

$$\Rightarrow \dot{\lambda}_t = u''(c_t)\dot{c}_t, \qquad (11.188)$$

where $u''(c_t) = d^2u(c_t)/dc_t^2$ and $\dot{c}_t = dc_t/dt$. Now we plug Eqs. (11.181) and (11.188) into Eq. (11.187):

$$0 = \dot{\lambda}_t - \lambda_t \rho$$
$$0 = u''(c_t)\dot{c}_t - u'(c_t)\rho$$
$$\Rightarrow \dot{c}_t = \rho\left[\frac{u'(c_t)}{u''(c_t)}\right]. \qquad (11.189)$$

Equation (11.189) represents the Euler equation for the continuous-time pie consumption problem. The result is equivalent to the result derived from the discrete time model (11.159).[29]

---

[29] To show that Eq. (11.189) is equivalent to Eq. (11.159), we first rearrange Eq. (11.189) as follows:

$$\frac{\dot{c}_t u''(c_t)}{u'(c_t)} = \rho.$$

The left-hand side of the equation is basically the time derivative of $\ln(u'(c_t))$, that is, $d\ln(u'(c_t))/dt = \dot{c}_t u''(c_t)/u'(c_t)$. Therefore, we have:

$$\frac{d\ln[u'(c_t)]}{dt} = \rho. \qquad (11.190)$$

Equation (11.190) suggests that the optimal path of consumption is where the growth rate of marginal utility over time is equal to the discount rate ρ. As noted previously, the discount factor β is usually written as $1/(1+\rho)$. According to Eq. (11.159), in the discrete case we have:

$$u'(c_t) = \beta u'(c_{t+1})$$
$$\Rightarrow u'(c_t) = \frac{1}{1+\rho}u'(c_{t+1})$$
$$\Rightarrow u'(c_t)(1+\rho) = u'(c_{t+1})$$
$$\Rightarrow u'(c_t) + \rho u'(c_t) = u'(c_{t+1})$$
$$\Rightarrow \rho = \frac{u'(c_{t+1}) - u'(c_t)}{u'(c_t)},$$

where $[u'(c_{t+1}) - u'(c_t)]/u'(c_t)$ represents the growth rate of marginal utility over time in a discrete time model (see Chapter 3 FN 13 for details). Therefore, the results in both the discrete case and the continuous case are equivalent:

$$\frac{u'(c_{t+1}) - u'(c_t)}{u'(c_t)} \approx \frac{d\ln[u'(c_t)]}{dt}.$$

An Example of Dynamic Optimization in Continuous Time: The Ramsey Model

According to the Solow growth model (Solow 1956), households set a "fixed" or "exogenous" saving rate (s) to solve for the steady state (k^*, y^*) in the economy, where k^* and y^* represent the steady state levels of capital stock and income.[30] However, we observe the savings rate is not time-invariant. As a result, in this model we assume saving – $saving_t$ – is a function of income y_t and consumption c_t. A representative household maximizes her utility dynamically by choosing the levels of consumption c_t and saving $saving_t$ over time. This specified consumer behavior is a key element in the Ramsey growth model as suggested by Ramsey (1928) and refined by Cass (1965) and Koopmans (1965).

The Model Setup

To simplify the mathematical derivations as much as possible, we assume saving $saving_t$ is defined as:

$$saving_t = y_t - c_t,$$

where $y_t = f(k_t)$ is output (income) level, which depends on capital stock k_t, and c_t is the level of consumption at time t. The household maximizes her lifetime utility U_t:

$$U = \int_0^\infty e^{-\rho t} u(c_t) \, dt.$$

As a result, the complete model can be written as:

$$\max_{c_t} \int_0^\infty e^{-\rho t} u(c_t) \, dt, \qquad (11.191)$$

subject to:

$$\dot{k}_t = saving_t - \delta k_t$$
$$\Rightarrow \dot{k}_t = f(k_t) - c_t - \delta k_t, \qquad (11.192)$$

where $\dot{k}_t = dk/dt$, and $\delta =$ depreciation rate. We assume that the utility function is:

$$u(c_t) = 2c_t^{1/2}, \qquad (11.193)$$

and the Cobb–Douglas production function is:

$$f(k_t) = k_t^\alpha, \qquad (11.194)$$

---

[30] See Chapter 3 for a detailed discussion of the Solow model.

where $\alpha \in (0, 1)$. To maximize the utility function over time, we write this model as the following Hamiltonian equation H_t:

$$H_t = e^{-\rho t}[u(c_t) + \lambda_t \dot{k}_t]$$
$$= e^{-\rho t}\{u(c_t) + \lambda_t[f(k_t) - c_t - \delta k_t]\}, \quad (11.195)$$

where λ_t is known as the Hamiltonian multiplier, and the transversality (or terminal) condition is:

$$\lim_{t \to \infty} \lambda_t e^{-\rho t} k_t = 0.$$

To maximize Eq. (11.195), we obtain the following first order conditions (FOCs):

1. $\partial H_t / \partial c_t = 0$:

$$\frac{\partial H_t}{\partial c_t} = 0$$
$$\Rightarrow \frac{\partial H_t}{\partial c_t} = e^{-\rho t}[u'(c_t) - \lambda_t] = 0 \quad (11.196)$$
$$\Rightarrow \lambda_t = u'(c_t); \quad (11.197)$$

2. $-\partial H_t / \partial k_t = d(\lambda_t e^{-\rho t})/dt$:

$$-\frac{\partial H_t}{\partial k_t} = \frac{d(\lambda_t e^{-\rho t})}{dt}$$
$$\Rightarrow e^{-\rho t}(f'(k_t) - \delta)\lambda_t = \dot{\lambda}_t e^{-\rho t} - \lambda_t \rho e^{-\rho t} \quad (11.198)$$
$$\Rightarrow (f'(k_t) - \delta)\lambda_t = \dot{\lambda}_t - \lambda_t \rho. \quad (11.199)$$

From Eq. (11.197), we take a time derivative with respect to λ_t:

$$\dot{\lambda}_t = \frac{\partial u'(c_t)}{c_t} \frac{dc_t}{dt}$$
$$\dot{\lambda}_t = u''(c_t)\dot{c}_t, \quad (11.200)$$

where $\dot{\lambda} = d\lambda/dt$. Now, we insert Eqs. (11.197) and (11.200) into Eq. (11.199):

$$[f'(k_t) - \delta]\lambda_t = \rho \lambda_t - \dot{\lambda}_t$$
$$[f'(k_t) - \delta]u'(c_t) = \rho u'(c_t) - u''(c_t)\dot{c}_t \quad (11.201)$$
$$\Rightarrow u''(c_t)\dot{c}_t = [\rho + \delta - f'(k_t)]u'(c_t) \quad (11.202)$$
$$\frac{u''(c_t)\dot{c}_t}{u'(c_t)} = \rho + \delta - f'(k_t). \quad (11.203)$$

Macro Political Economy

Recall that $u(c_t) = 2c_t^{1/2}$. We have $u'(c_t) = c_t^{-1/2}$, and $u''(c_t) = -\frac{1}{2}c_t^{-3/2}$, and $f'(k) = \alpha k^{\alpha-1}$. We place these functional forms into Eq. (11.203):

$$\frac{u''(c_t)\dot{c}_t}{u'(c_t)} = \rho + \delta - f'(k_t)$$

$$\frac{\left(-\frac{1}{2}c_t^{-3/2}\right)\dot{c}_t}{c_t^{-1/2}} = \rho + \delta - \alpha k^{\alpha-1}$$

$$\frac{\dot{c}_t}{c_t} = 2(\alpha k_t^{\alpha-1} - \delta - \rho), \qquad (11.204)$$

where Eq. (11.204) is again known as the Euler equation.

Therefore, we have two differential equations (11.192) and (11.204) in this case:

$$\dot{k}_t = k_t^\alpha - c_t - \delta k_t, \qquad (11.205)$$

and:

$$\dot{c}_t = 2c_t(\alpha k_t^{\alpha-1} - \delta - \rho). \qquad (11.206)$$

From Eq. (11.206), if $\dot{c}_t = 0$, then:

$$\alpha k_t^{\alpha-1} - \delta - \rho = 0$$

$$\Rightarrow k_t = \left(\frac{\alpha}{\delta + \rho}\right)^{1/(1-\alpha)}.$$

If $\dot{c} > 0$ (i.e., c is increasing over time), this implies:

$$\dot{c}_t = 2c_t(\alpha k_t^{\alpha-1} - \delta - \rho) > 0$$

$$\Rightarrow \alpha k_t^{\alpha-1} - \delta - \rho > 0$$

$$\Rightarrow k_t^{\alpha-1} > \frac{\delta + \rho}{\alpha}$$

$$\Rightarrow k_t^{1-\alpha} < \frac{\delta + \rho}{\alpha} \text{ for } 0 < \alpha < 1$$

$$\Rightarrow k_t < \left(\frac{\delta + \rho}{\alpha}\right)^{1/(1-\alpha)}.$$

If $\dot{c} < 0$ (i.e., c is decreasing over time), this implies:

$$k_t > \left(\frac{\delta + \rho}{\alpha}\right)^{1/(1-\alpha)}.$$

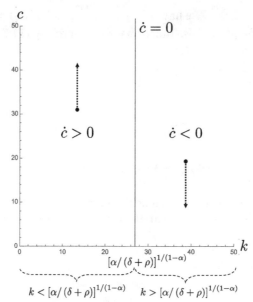

FIGURE 11.8. The function of $\dot{c}$

These conditions are illustrated in Figure 11.8.[31]

Next, let us consider Eq. (11.205):

$$\dot{k}_t = k_t^\alpha - c_t - \delta k_t.$$

If $\dot{k}_t = 0$, we have:

$$0 = k_t^\alpha - c_t - \delta k_t$$
$$c_t = k_t^\alpha - \delta k_t. \tag{11.207}$$

Therefore, when $c_t = 0$, from Eq. (11.207), we have:

$$k_t = 0 \text{ or } k_t = \left(\frac{1}{\delta}\right)^{1/(1-\alpha)}.$$

If $\dot{k} > 0$ (i.e., k is increasing over time), this implies:

$$k_t^\alpha - \delta k_t > c_t.$$

If $\dot{k} < 0$ (i.e., k is decreasing over time), this implies:

$$k_t^\alpha - \delta k_t < c_t.$$

---

[31] In Figure 11.8, the results are based on the following parameter values: $\alpha = 0.33$, $\delta = 0.025$, and $\rho = 0.01136$.

Macro Political Economy

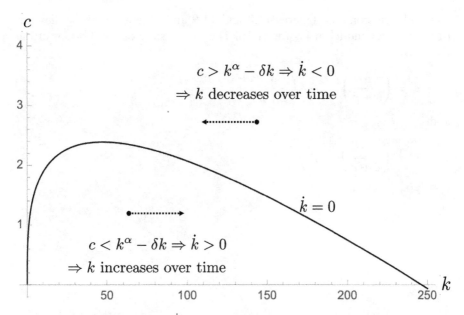

FIGURE 11.9. The function of $\dot{k}$

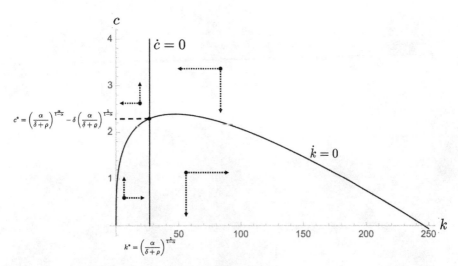

FIGURE 11.10. Phase diagram of the Ramsey Model

These results can be illustrated in Figure 11.9.[32]

---

[32] The set of parameters are the same as Figure 11.8.

Finally, we combine Figures 11.8 and 11.9 and obtain the phase diagram of the Ramsey model in Figure 11.10. The steady state or equilibrium of the model is:

$$c^* = \left(\frac{\alpha}{\delta+\rho}\right)^{\frac{\alpha}{1-\alpha}} - \delta\left(\frac{\alpha}{\delta+\rho}\right)^{\frac{1}{1-\alpha}}$$

and:

$$k^* = \left(\frac{\alpha}{\delta+\rho}\right)^{\frac{1}{1-\alpha}}.$$

12

Social Behavior and Evolutionary Dynamics

12.1 BACKGROUND

Chapter 11 introduces macro modeling and testing in the absence of closed form solutions. As an alternative, researchers generate dynamic patterns of the solutions by calibrating the model with different sets of parameter values. The estimated differences between simulated patterns from the model and those from actual data help us understand the reliability of the theoretical model. Notice also this modeling approach generally assumes there is only a representative agent (firm) making an optimal decision – maximizing their utility (profit). Heterogeneous agents' behavior are not considered in the model.

In this chapter, we turn our focus from mimicking observable macro-level political-economic structures to ones that imitate micro-level decisions via calibration and/or simulation – agent-based modeling (ABM). ABM is a "bottom-up" approach to modeling behavior of heterogeneous agents. Along with the emphasis on agent heterogeneity are less restrictive behavioral assumptions regarding information (e.g., imperfect information) and rationality (e.g., bounded rationality). ABM "tests" involve system simulation – linking agent responses to macro level outcomes – and comparing the simulated data with real-world data.[1]

One specific ABM approach that is commonly adopted to study economic behavior is the genetic algorithm (GA). The GA, developed by Holland (1970), is inspired by natural selection – "survival of the fittest." The GA describes the evolutionary process of a population of genetic individuals (chromosomes) with heterogeneous beliefs in response to the rules of nature (fitness function).

---

[1] Voinea (2016) offers a comprehensive survey of agent-based modeling in political science.

While the GA terminology we present below is atypical in the social sciences, the behavioral ramifications and applications for social science questions exist.[2]

We present two examples. The first example examines ABM work on voter turnout. The EITM linkage is the relation between the behavioral concepts of learning and decision making and the empirical concept of prediction. The second example focuses on firm price setting using GA. The EITM linkage in this second example is between the behavioral concept of social interaction (specifically imitation, invention, communication, and examination) and the empirical concept of prediction.

12.2 EXAMPLE 1: ABM AND VOTER TURNOUT

12.3 STEP 1: RELATING DECISION MAKING AND LEARNING TO PREDICTION

Recall from Chapter 9 that standard rational choice models derive a "paradoxical" result for voting turnout in large elections (e.g., Palfrey and Rosenthal 1985; Fiorina 1990; Myerson 1999).[3] Consider the instrumental view of rationality, where a voter decides to vote only if the net expected utility of voting is positive, that is, the benefits of voting exceed the costs (see Geys 2006). Unlike the EITM approach Achen takes using Bayesian updating (as described in Chapter 9), Bendor et al. (2003) and Fowler (2006) use ABM. Bendor et al. (2003) (hereafter BDT) set up a computational model assuming voters are adaptively rational: Voters learn to vote or to stay home, a form of trial-and-error. Voter actions are repeated (e.g., vote) in the future given a successful outcome today. The reverse also holds.

BDT find the turnout rate is substantially higher than the predictions in rational choice models. This result is observed even in electorates where voting is costly. Fowler (2006) revises the BDT model by removing the feedback in the probability adjustment mechanism and instead includes habitual voting behavior. Fowler finds his behavioral model is a better fit to the same data BDT use, but a point not to be lost is Fowler leverages the EITM approach to build on BDT's model and test.

---

[2] For example, Bullard and Duffy (1999) model the dynamic formation of heterogeneous expectations using GA. Chatterjee et al. (2017) solve the standard profit maximization problem with a meta-heuristic genetic algorithm approach. They show the algorithm is quite stable and adequate for solving an optimization problem.

[3] See Chapter 3, Section 3.3.2 for additional background on the turnout paradox.

12.4 STEP 2: ANALOGUES FOR DECISION MAKING, LEARNING, AND PREDICTION

BDT (2003) assume there are N citizens in society where n_d individuals support party d and the rest of them $n_r = N - n_d$ support party r. Each individual i can choose to vote V or abstain A at time t. They also assume citizens do not change their decisions from voting for one party to the other. In other words, if a voter decides to vote, they vote for their own party only. Finally, the winning party in the election is defined as the party with the most turnout. If the election ties, the winning party will be decided by a fair coin toss.

All members of the winning party in the society receive a fixed payoff b regardless of whether or not they voted. However, those individuals who choose to vote will pay c – a fixed cost. To account for voter heterogeneity, a stochastic shock (or uncertainty) θ_{it} is included in individual i's voting payoff at time t. The stochastic stock θ is uniformly distributed as $iid\,(0, \omega)$ across voters and time periods. Let there be four possible groups with the following payoffs:

1. Winning abstainers:
$$\pi_{it} = b + \theta_{it}; \tag{12.1}$$

2. Winning voters:
$$\pi_{it} = b - c + \theta_{it}; \tag{12.2}$$

3. Losing abstainers:
$$\pi_{it} = 0 + \theta_{it}; \text{ and} \tag{12.3}$$

4. Losing voters:
$$\pi_{it} = -c + \theta_{it}. \tag{12.4}$$

Each individual i in period t has the propensity to vote (V), with the probability of voting $p_{it}(V) \in [0, 1]$. However, if the individual decides to abstain (A), the probability of abstention can be written as $p_{it}(A) = 1 - p_{it}(V)$. Moreover, individual i has an aspiration level a_{it} identifying the payoff level they desire. After taking an action $I \in \{V, A\}$ based on her propensity, individual i realizes the election winner and is able to determine the resulting payoff π_{it} in the election at time t.

The Voting Rules

Recall BDT assume citizens are adaptively rational. They learn to vote or to stay home – a form of trial-and-error. BDT adopt the aspiration-based reinforcement learning rule suggested by Bush and Mosteller (1955). The law of motion is an individual's propensity to take an action at time $t + 1$ (i.e., $p_{it+1}(I)$) according to the realized payoff and the aspiration level at time t. Citizens increase their likelihood of taking the same action next time, which is known as reinforcement, if resulting payoffs are greater than or equal to aspirations ($\pi_{it} \geq a_{it}$) at time t. On the other hand, if resulting payoffs are less than their aspirations ($\pi_{it} < a_{it}$), citizens reduce their likelihood of taking the same action for time $t+1$, which is known as inhibition. Therefore, the propensity function (voting/abstaining) can be written as the following two cases:

$$p_{it+1}(I) = p_{it}(I) + \alpha\left(1 - p_{it}(I)\right), \text{ if } \pi_{it} \geq a_{it}, \tag{12.5}$$

and:

$$p_{it+1}(I) = p_{it}(I) - \alpha p_{it}(I), \text{ if } \pi_{it} < a_{it}, \tag{12.6}$$

where $I \in \{V, A\}$, and α represents the speed of learning, which determines the magnitude of the change in propensity to vote or abstain in response to reinforcement and inhibition.

From Eqs. (12.5) and (12.6), we can derive the following four cases for the propensities to vote and to abstain at $t+1$ if the individual i voted V or abstained A at time t:

1. VOTING REINFORCEMENT If an individual voted at time t and received a higher payoff than her aspiration level ($\pi_{it} \geq a_{it}$), her voting behavior will be reinforced. In other words, she will be more likely to vote again in the next period. The propensity to vote at time $t+1$ can be written as:

$$p_{it+1}(V) = p_{it}(V) + \alpha\left(1 - p_{it}(V)\right), \text{ if } \pi_{it} \geq a_{it}. \tag{12.7}$$

2. VOTING INHIBITION On the other hand, Eq. (12.8) shows that if an individual received a lower payoff than their aspiration level ($\pi_{it} < a_{it}$) after she voted at time t, she will be discouraged and less likely to vote again at time $t+1$:

$$p_{it+1}(V) = p_{it}(V) - \alpha p_{it}(V), \text{ if } \pi_{it} < a_{it}. \tag{12.8}$$

3. ABSTENTION REINFORCEMENT Similarly, we calculate the propensity to abstain for $t+1$ by comparing voter i's payoff π_{it} and her aspiration level a_{it} at time t. If individual i abstained A at time t and $\pi_{it} \geq a_{it}$, her propensity to abstain for $t+1$ is:

$$p_{it+1}(A) = p_{it}(A) + \alpha\left(1 - p_{it}(A)\right).$$

Since the propensity to abstain $p_{t+1}(A)$ is simply the propensity of not voting (i.e., $p_{t+1}(A) = 1 - p_{it+1}(V)$), we can rewrite the propensity to voting at time $t+1$ for an individual who did not vote in period t:

$$\begin{aligned} 1 - p_{it+1}(V) &= p_{it}(A) + \alpha\left(1 - p_{it}(A)\right) \\ p_{it+1}(V) &= 1 - p_{it}(A) - \alpha\left(1 - p_{it}(A)\right) \\ p_{it+1}(V) &= p_{it}(V) - \alpha p_{it}(V), \end{aligned} \tag{12.9}$$

Social Behavior and Evolutionary Dynamics

where $p_{it}(A) = 1 - p_{it}(V)$. Equation (12.9) shows that if the voter abstained A at time t and received a higher payoff than their aspiration level ($\pi_{it} \geq a_{it}$), the voter's abstention is reinforced and the propensity to vote at time $t+1$ falls. We can also see that the propensity to vote in this case (Eq. (12.9)) is equivalent to that in the case of voting inhibition (Eq. (12.8)).

4. ABSTENTION INHIBITION (I.E., VOTING AFTER ABSTENTION) In contrast, if an individual abstained at time t but her payoff is less than her aspiration ($\pi_{it} < a_{it}$), the individual's propensity to abstain at time $t+1$ (according to Eq. (12.6)) is written as:

$$p_{it+1}(A) = p_{it}(A) - \alpha p_{it}(A).$$

Again we can also derive the propensity to vote at time $t+1$ for an individual who did not vote at t:

$$1 - p_{it+1}(V) = p_{it}(A) - \alpha p_{it}(A)$$
$$p_{it+1}(V) = 1 - p_{it}(A) + \alpha p_{it}(A)$$
$$p_{it+1}(V) = p_{it}(V) + \alpha \left(1 - p_{it}(V)\right). \tag{12.10}$$

Equation (12.10) suggests that if the voter abstained A at time t but received a lower payoff than their aspiration level ($\pi_{it} < a_{it}$), they "adjust" their behavior and increase the likelihood of voting V at time $t+1$.

Aspiration Updating Function

When voters make their voting decisions for the next period $t+1$, they recall their payoff and aspiration levels at time t and compare them according to the four cases mentioned previously. BDT also assume citizens update their aspiration levels over time based on their current aspiration levels and payoffs. BDT follow the aspiration-updating function suggested by Cyert and March (1963):

$$a_{it+1} = \lambda a_{it} + (1-\lambda) \pi_{it}, \tag{12.11}$$

where $\lambda \in (0, 1)$. Equation (12.11) shows the aspiration level for individual i at time $t+1$ (a_{it+1}) is updated based on the weighed average of the aspiration level a_{it} and payoff π_{it} at time t.

If an individual i's current payoff and aspiration are equal ($\pi_{it} = a_{it}$), their aspiration level remains unchanged for the next period. If the current payoff is higher than the aspiration level ($\pi_{it} > a_{it}$), the aspiration level at $t+1$ will be adjusted upward ($a_{it+1} > a_{it}$). However, if the current payoff is lower than the aspiration level ($\pi_{it} < a_{it}$), the individual's aspiration level drops for the next period. Finally, BDT assume some citizens are inertial, meaning they do not update their propensity and aspiration levels with the probabilities of ϵ_p and ϵ_a, respectively.

12.5 STEP 3: UNIFYING AND EVALUATING THE ANALOGUES

BDT (2003) show that, in contrast to the prediction of the rational choice models, the turnout rate can be sufficiently high in large populations, although voting can be relatively costly. BDT's model has important empirical implications, but "tests" have been left to others. For internal consistency, one avenue is simulation. For example, Fowler (2006) simulates the BDT model – the payoff functions (Eqs. (12.1)–(12.4)), the propensity function (Eqs. (12.5) and (12.6)), and the aspiration function (Eq. (12.11)). The parameters are presented in Table 12.1. He simulates 50 elections in a society with 2,000 individuals for 1,000 times. After each simulation, Fowler stores the simulated data of individual voting turnout for the last six elections, which represent the final voting decisions after learning. Figure 12.1 represents the frequency

TABLE 12.1. *Adaptively rational voting model parameters*

Parameters	Description	Values
N	Number of individuals in the society	2,000
n_d	Number of individuals supporting Party d	1,000
n_r	Number of individuals supporting Party r	1,000
b	Benefit for an individual supporting the winning party	1
c	Cost for an individual who votes during the election	0.025
α	Speed of learning in the propensity equation	0.1
λ	Stickiness in the aspiration equation	0.95
ω	Noise in the payoff function	0.2
ϵ_p	Proportion of individuals who are not responsive to propensity adjustment	0.01
ϵ_a	Proportion of individuals who are not responsive to aspiration adjustment	0.01

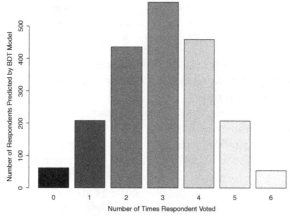

FIGURE 12.1. Simulations of adaptive rational model (BDT 2003)

distribution of voting turnout based on the simulated data. The x-axis in the figure indicates how many times an individual voted in the past six elections. The figure shows most of the individuals voted three times in the past six elections. The simulation also shows the average turnout rate is 51.23 percent. In contrast to the extremely low turnout rate predicted by rational voting theory, this predicted turnout rate is comparable with those found based on the actual data in previous studies.

12.6 SUMMARY

BDT (2003) introduce a theoretical model describing voting behavior fundamentals with testable voter turnout predictions. In forming the behavioral mechanism for decision making, BDT use payoffs, voting propensity, and aspiration. They then link these behavioral analogues with a measurable (empirical) analogue – prediction (the voter turnout rate). Still, there are some anomalies. One issue is the BDT (2003) model guarantees people vote in elections. For example, Fowler (2006) finds the expected propensity to vote is 0.5, given that the voter has an equal chance of being reinforced or inhibited to vote.[4]

Fowler then compares the BDT simulated data with the data in the South Bend Election Survey (Huckfeldt and Sprague 1985). He finds most people do not vote in both primary and general elections. Yet, there is a sizable group of people who always vote in general elections. Figure 12.2 represents the frequency distribution of voting turnout in South Bend, Indiana. We see that

---

[4] To illustrate this idea, we consider the propensity functions (12.5) and (12.6). If $\pi_{it} \geq a_{it}$, then $p_{it+1}(I) = p_{it}(I) + \alpha(1 - p_{it}(I))$. When $p_{it}(I) = 0$, $p_{it+1}(I)$ increases by α. When p_{it} reaches one, the propensity remains unchanged over time (i.e., $p_{it+1}(I) = p_{it}(I)$). As a result, the reinforcement effect diminishes as $p_{it}(I)$ increases over time. Similarly, if $\pi_{it} < a_{it}$, then $p_{it+1}(I) = p_{it}(I) - \alpha p_{it}(I)$. When $p_{it}(I) = 1$, p_{it+1} decreases by α. When p_{it} approaches zero, the propensity remains the same over time and $p_{it+1}(I) = p_{it}(I)$. Therefore, Eq. (12.6) shows the inhibition effect diminishes as $p_{it}(I)$ decreases. Finally, we compute the expected value of propensity as follows:

$$E(p_{it+1}) = Pr(\pi_{it} \geq a_{it})[p_{it} + \alpha(1 - p_{it})] + \\ Pr(\pi_{it} < a_{it})[p_{it} - \alpha p_{it}] \\ = p_{it} + \alpha Pr(\pi_{it} \geq a_{it})(1 - p_{it}) - \alpha Pr(\pi_{it} < a_{it})p_{it}.$$

We can show:

$$E(p_{it+1}) = p_{it}$$

if and only if:

$$Pr(\pi_{it} \geq a_{it}) = p_{it}.$$

This result suggests the propensity of voting $p_{it}(V)$ converges to 0.5 in the long run if the probability of reinforcement (or inhibition) is 50% (i.e., $Pr(\pi_{it} \geq a_{it}) = 0.5$).

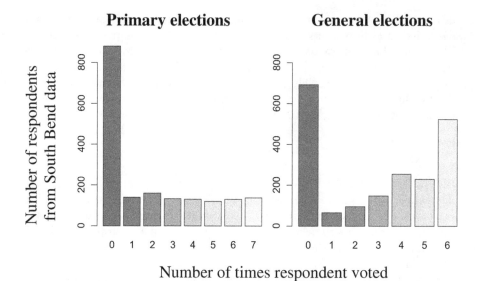

FIGURE 12.2. Frequency distribution of voting turnout in South Bend, Indiana (*Source*: Fowler 2006)

the distributions in Figure 12.2 are substantially different from Figure 12.1 generated by the BDT model. Hence, Fowler labels the voting pattern found in South Bend as habitual voting behavior, and argues this observed voting pattern is inconsistent with the casual voting behavior suggested in BDT (2003).

To develop the idea of habitual voting behavior, Fowler (2006) extends the BDT model by modifying the propensity functions as follows:

$$p_{it+1}(I) = \min\left(1, p_{it}(I) + \alpha\right), \text{ if } \pi_{it} \geq a_{it}, \tag{12.12}$$

and:

$$p_{it+1}(I) = \max\left(0, p_{it}(I) - \alpha\right), \text{ if } \pi_{it} < a_{it}. \tag{12.13}$$

The revised propensity functions (12.12) and (12.13) prevent the situation where the propensity of voting converges to a single value in the long run (as shown in BDT 2003). At any level of $p_{it} \in (0, 1)$, the change in p_{it} is either α (for $\pi_{it} \geq a_{it}$) or $-\alpha$ (for $\pi_{it} < a_{it}$). This set up supports a reinforcement effect – or the inhibition effect does not diminish as the propensity of voting increases or decreases over time. More importantly, some individuals can either have high or low propensities to make the same turnout decision for a longer period of time. This new prediction is consistent with habitual voting behavior.

Social Behavior and Evolutionary Dynamics

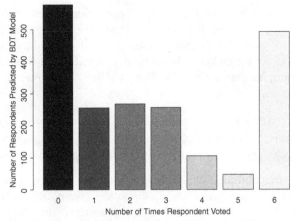

FIGURE 12.3. Simulations of habitual voting model (Fowler 2006)

Fowler (2006) simulates the modified BDT model with the alternative propensity functions.[5] The result is presented in Figure 12.3, which shows that most individuals either do not vote at all or always vote. This result closely matches the pattern of voting turnout observed in the South Bend election data.

12.7 EXAMPLE II: GA AND FIRM PRICE SETTING

Recall there are various approaches to ABM.[6] In this section we present the work of Arifovic (1994) on genetic algorithm (GA) learning. GA, developed by Holland (1970), has been recognized as an important method for computational optimization (Holland 1975; Goldberg 1989). It is used for solving optimal solutions numerically in mathematical systems when deriving closed-form solutions is technically difficult. The focus of this example is on how firms set prices.

Miller (1986) and Arifovic (1991) were early users of the GA approach to economic questions. Miller (1986), for instance, develops a model of adaptive economic behavior with applications to utility and profit maximization,

---

[5] Figures 12.1 and 12.3 are reproduced based on the codes written by James Fowler. The code can be downloaded from James Fowler's website: http://fowler.ucsd.edu/gbt.R. Note that the code available on Fowler's website is a stripped down version that needs several extended command lines for generating the figures similar to Figures 12.1 and 12.3. The extended code can be downloaded from uh.edu/hobby/eitm/eitmbook/. In addition, Jeremy Gilmore creates a web-based interactive simulation of Fowler's (2006) model. We refer interested readers to the following website for details: https://j-gilmore.shinyapps.io/fowlermodel/.

[6] See de Marchi (2005) for different computational modeling approaches.

technological innovation, and demographic transitions.[7] Arifovic's (1994) seminal work investigates whether macro-level stability conditions (the cobweb theorem) are necessary for a stable economy.[8] Arifovic simulates the cobweb model using GA and compares the simulated results with those based on an adaptive learning mechanism and Wellford's (1989) experiments.

12.8 STEP 1: RELATING ELEMENTS OF SOCIAL INTERACTION (IMITATION, INVENTION, COMMUNICATION, AND EXAMINATION) TO PREDICTION

In economics, the bounded rationality assumption is used with greater frequency. However, researchers often maintain the assumption of homogeneous agents due to the difficulty of obtaining closed-form solutions in heterogeneous settings. Using GA, we discuss how Arifovic (1991) demonstrates an alternative using both bounded rationality and heterogeneity.

In GA modeling, we assume individuals form different beliefs or take different actions based on various bounded rational behaviors observed in the society: trial-and-error decision making, learning from experience, and social interaction – imitation, invention, communication, and examination. If an individual performs "better" by creating new ideas or new actions based on those bounded rational behaviors, she is more likely to survive in the next generation through a process of natural selection (i.e., survival of the fittest).

Arifovic (1994) links these behavioral concepts with prediction and forecast error based on a simple cobweb-type supply–demand model (see Chapter 5 Section 5.6.4). Individuals (firms) are allowed to make heterogeneous production decisions by imitating peers' successful production strategies, and innovating new ideas on their own and with other firms.

12.9 STEP 2: ANALOGUES FOR SOCIAL INTERACTION AND PREDICTION

We now turn to how firms set prices in this model. Recall the cobweb model, presented in the Appendix of Chapter 5, is an example of a supply–demand

---

[7] Miller argues that the standard optimization approach and the adaptive approach are not mutually exclusive. Some studies adopt GA to determine selection criteria (i.e., determining stable solutions) when a model has multiple equilibria (Miller 1986; Arifovic 1996; Bullard and Duffy 1998b; Riechmann 1999, 2001; Geisendorf 2011).

[8] Other studies investigate the stability conditions of the model using different learning mechanisms. See, for example, Evans and Honkapohja (1995, 1996), Brock and Hommes (1997), Heinemann (2000), Branch and Evans (2006), Granato et al. (2008). There is also work involving lab experiments (Holt and Villamil 1986; Wellford 1989; Hommes et al. 2007).

model that demonstrates the dynamic process of a market economy. The cobweb model is summarized in Eq. (5.25):

$$p_t = A + Bp_t^e + \xi_t,$$

where $A = (\alpha - \gamma)/\beta$, $B = -\lambda/\beta$, and $\xi_t = \left(\epsilon_t^d - \epsilon_t^s\right)/\beta$. The equation shows the expected price level p_t^e at time t formed at $t-1$ *determines* the actual price level p_t at time t. Assuming that p_t^e is replaced with p_{t-1}, in the long run, the price level p_t is in a stationary equilibrium.[9]

Arifovic (1994) uses the cobweb model and assumes each firm i chooses a production level $q_{i,t}$ to maximize its expected profit $\pi_{i,t}^e$. This calculation is based on the production cost function $c_{it}(q_{it})$ and the expectations of the market price p_t^e that will prevail at time t. Formally, the market can be expressed in the following way.

First, the quadratic cost function for firm i is:

$$c_{it} = aq_{it} + \frac{1}{2}bmq_{it}^2, \tag{12.14}$$

where $a, b > 0$, c_{it} represents the cost of production given the level of output q_{it} at time t, and m is the number of firms in the market. Firm i's expected profit as the difference between expected total revenue and total cost:

$$\begin{aligned}\pi_{it}^e &= p_t^e q_{it} - c_{it}(q_{it}) \\ &= p_t^e q_{it} - aq_{it} - \frac{1}{2}bmq_{it}^2,\end{aligned} \tag{12.15}$$

where p_t^e is the expected price of the good in the market at time t. Each firm maximizes the expected profit function by setting the level of production q_{it}. The first-order condition can be written as:

$$\frac{\partial \pi_{it}^e}{\partial q_{it}} = 0$$

$$\Rightarrow p_t^e - a - bmq_{it} = 0.$$

The following optimal production level for firm i based on the first-order condition is:

$$q_{it} = \frac{p_t^e - a}{bm}. \tag{12.16}$$

---

[9] p_t converges to p^* as $t \to \infty$, provided the ratio of supply and demand slopes are less than one (i.e., $\lambda < \beta$). However, if the ratio is larger than one, the price level diverges from its long run equilibrium. This process is known as the *cobweb theorem* (Ezekiel 1938).

Assuming all firms are identical in the market, such that $q_{it} = q_t$, we have $y_t^s = \sum_{i=1}^{m} q_{it} = mq_t$. We can derive the market supply curve by summing up m firms' optimal output level from Eq. (12.16):

$$y_t^s = \sum_{i=1}^{m} q_{it} = mq_t$$

$$y_t^s = \frac{(p_t^e - a)}{b} \tag{12.17}$$

$$y_t^s = \gamma + \lambda p_t^e, \tag{12.18}$$

where $\gamma = -a/b$ and $\lambda = 1/b$. To determine the price level in the economy, we assume a linear market demand curve:

$$y_t^d = \alpha - \beta p_t, \tag{12.19}$$

where $y_t^d = \sum_{i=1}^{m} q_{it}^d$ is the total output demanded in the market. Finally, one can derive the market equilibrium of price level by equating market demand (12.19) and market supply (12.17):

$$\alpha - \beta p_t = \gamma + \lambda p_t^e$$
$$\Rightarrow p_t = \frac{\alpha - \gamma}{\beta} - \frac{\lambda}{\beta} p_t^e. \tag{12.20}$$

Equation (12.20) represents the cobweb model in Arifovic (1994). This expression is equivalent to Eq. (5.25). According to the Cobweb theorem, the price level in the model converges to the REE in the long run (i.e., $p_t^e = p_t$) only if λ/β is less than 1. If $\lambda/\beta > 1$, the model will be unstable and the sequence of market prices diverge away from the equilibrium.

Arifovic (1994) simulates price setting in the cobweb model based on three *basic* genetic operators in the GA simulations: (1) reproduction, (2) mutation, and (3) crossover. She also introduces a new operator, election, in the simulations. We describe the genetic operators and the GA procedure in the Appendix of this chapter.[10]

Reproduction is a genetic operator in which an individual chromosome is copied from the previous population to a new population. This operator mimics the behavior where agents *imitate* the strategies from better-performing agents.

Mutation is a genetic operator in which one or more genes within an individual chromosome changes value randomly. This operator mimics the condition where agents may change their strategies suddenly through *invention*.

---
[10] The Appendix in this chapter presents the basic GA approach. The election operator, suggested by Arifovic (1991, 1994), is not illustrated in the Appendix. We refer readers to Arifovic (1994) for the implementation of an election operator in the GA.

Social Behavior and Evolutionary Dynamics   259

Crossover is the third basic genetic operator. Crossover occurs when two randomly drawn chromosomes exchange parts of their genes. This operator imitates the action where agents *communicate* with others to innovate or develop a new strategy.

Election operator *examines* the fitness of newly generated (or offspring) chromosomes and then compares them with their parent chromosomes (the pair of chromosomes before crossover). Both offspring chromosomes *are elected* to be in the new population at time $t + 1$ if their potential fitness values evaluated at time t are higher than their parents' fitness values. However, if only one new chromosome possesses a higher fitness value than their parents, the one with the lower value will not enter the new population, but one of the parents with a higher value stays in the new population. If both new chromosomes have lower values than their parents, they cannot enter but their parents stay in the new population.

12.10 STEP 3: UNIFYING AND EVALUATING THE ANALOGUES

To investigate whether the Cobweb theorem is a necessary stability condition for convergence to the REE,[11] Arifovic (1994) compares the GA with three additional learning algorithms as well as cobweb lab experiments (Wellford 1989). The three learning algorithms are:[12]

- Static expectations (i.e., $p_t^e = p_{t-1}$),
- Simple adaptive expectations by averaging the past prices (i.e., $p_t^e = t^{-1} \sum_{s=0}^{t-1} p_s$) from the initial period up to time t,[13] and
- Expectations formed by a least squares updating mechanism.[14]

We simulate the model (i.e., Eq. (12.20)) using the basic GA approach (i.e., without the election operator) and the augmented GA approach (that is, with the election operator) according to the values of parameters suggested in

---

[11] From FN 9, the cobweb theorem suggests that if $\lambda/\beta < 1$, then the model is stable such that the price level will converge in the long run (i.e., $\lim_{t \to \infty} p_t = p^*$). However, if $\lambda/\beta > 1$, then the model is unstable and the price will diverge in the long run (see Section 5.6.4 for the detailed discussion on the cobweb model.)

[12] The following stability conditions hold:

- Static expectations: The model is stable only if $\lambda/\beta < 1$.
- Simple adaptive expectations: The model is stable if $\lambda/\beta < 1$ *and* $\lambda/\beta > 1$ (see Carlson 1968).
- Least squares learning: The model is stable only if $\lambda/\beta < 1$ (see Bray and Savin 1986).

[13] This expression is similar to Eq. (5.36) where the current price level is an average of all price levels observed in the past with an equal weight.

[14] See the Appendix in Chapter 6 for details.

TABLE 12.2. *Cobweb model parameters*

Parameters	Stable case ($\lambda/\beta < 1$)	Unstable case ($\lambda/\beta > 1$)
α	143.684	136.667
β	65.789	59.524
a	0	0
b	0.016	0.016
$\gamma = -a/b$	0	0
$\lambda = 1/b$	62.5	62.5
m	6	6
p^*	1.12	1.12
$y^* = mq^*$	70	70

TABLE 12.3. *Crossover and mutation rates*

Set	1	2	3	4	5	6	7	8
Crossover rate: κ	0.6	0.6	0.75	0.75	0.9	0.9	0.3	0.3
Mutation rate: μ	0.0033	0.033	0.0033	0.033	0.0033	0.033	0.0033	0.033

Arifovic (1994). In particular, we focus on two cases: (1) the parameter values of a stable cobweb model, and (2) those of an unstable cobweb model used in Wellford's (1989) experiments.

Table 12.2 presents the numerical parameters for the simulations. For the case of the stable cobweb model, we assign $\lambda = 62.5$ and $\beta = 65.789$, such that $\lambda/\beta = 0.95 < 1$. On the other hand, for the unstable case, the ratio of supply and demand slopes is $\lambda/\beta = 62.5/59.524 = 1.05 > 1$. Table 12.2 indicates both cases have an identical equilibrium price of 1.12. We also vary the crossover and mutation rates in the simulations (see Table 12.3).

The GA results are now compared to the three expectations/learning mechanisms (i.e, static expectations, adaptive expectations, and least squares learning) and experiments (Wellford 1989). Figure 12.4 presents simulations of the stable cobweb model with eight sets of crossover and mutation parameters corresponding to Table 12.3. We simulate the model 500 iterations (generations)

Social Behavior and Evolutionary Dynamics 261

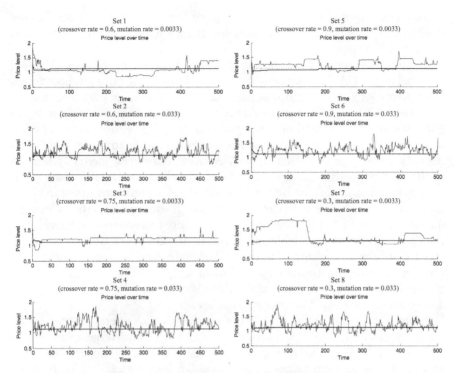

FIGURE 12.4. GA simulations (Stable case: $\lambda/\beta = 0.95 < 1$)

using both basic GA and augmented GA approaches.[15] The simulations show that the price level is more volatile when the basic GA is applied. Its movement is bounded around the REE, ranging between 0.6 and 1.8 for all simulations. The intuition behind this result is based on the following dynamic: The reproduction operator attempts to replicate the better performing strategies to reduce the variance in the population (i.e., prices), but crossover and mutation operators allow creation of new strategies, which increases the degree of variance. Hence,

[15] The number of periods in a simulated model is less relevant in the linkage between theory and empirics. One might be concerned that longer-span time-series data generated by a simulated model are incompatible with relatively shorter-span real data. While this is a valid concern, this limitation is typical and common for testing any theoretical model. As discussed in Chapter 11, calibration and simulation are numerical solution procedures. The purpose of this approach is to identify equilibrium conditions of a stochastic model when solving closed-form solutions are infeasible analytically (see FN 21 for the discussion of determining the simulation duration). Furthermore, some studies systematically discuss how simulation outputs can be compared to real-world data (Kleijnen 1995a,b; Sargent 2013). Gatti et al. (2011) describe an iterative validation procedure of matching and comparing simulated outputs with actual data. We refer interested readers to Gatti et al. (2011) for further discussion about the iterative validation procedure.

according to basic GA simulations, the price level cannot be stabilized at the equilibrium since crossover and mutation shocks happen in every generation (as shown in Figure 12.4).

On the other hand, if the election operator suggested by Arifovic (1994) is included in the GA (i.e., augmented-GA) simulations, the price level converges faster to the REE. The intuition behind this dynamic is as follows: The election operator "pre-screens" the performance of off-spring strategies (i.e., strategies after crossover and mutation). Off-spring strategies are either elected or eliminated (i.e., either enter or do not enter a new generation) via the previous period's fitness function. This "quality control" reinforces "better" strategies in the new population, and, therefore, reduces the variance at a faster pace. This dynamic is confirmed by the augmented GA simulations in Figure 12.4. Interestingly, when we compare GA learning to other expectations/learning mechanisms (see FN 12), we find alternative convergence results. Specifically, the convergence to an equilibrium exists under GA when all chromosomes (agents' strategies) become identical so that there is no strategy in the genetic population deviating from the optimal quantity q^*, which maximizes profit at an equilibrium price p^*. After equilibrium is achieved, the variance of prices and quantities in the population approaches zero.

More importantly, Arifovic (1994) finds that the GA operators produce an interesting result for the unstable case (i.e., $\lambda/\beta > 1$): The divergent patterns do not occur under GA learning (Figure 12.5). Instead, price and quantity fluctuate around the equilibrium values (under basic GA learning). Interestingly, if the election operator is imposed in the algorithm, the unstable model also converges to the REE.

Recall Arifovic's tests, in this example, also involve comparing the simulated data with the data generated in experiments in Wellford (1989). She finds the features of the GA are consistent with characteristics of human behavior as observed in the experiments. The findings imply that, in reality, agents might not rely on sophisticated forms of learning for solving their decision problems. Rather an alternative or more expansive view of human adaptation and change should consider how agents generate new beliefs and how these best beliefs and strategies survive.

12.11 SUMMARY

Arifovic (1994) introduces the GA procedure as an alternative learning mechanism, a mechanism that is used to determine convergence to an equilibrium. More importantly, this mechanism mimics social behavior, namely (trial-and-error) decision making, learning (from experience), and social interaction. These behavioral concepts can be transformed into an expanded and richer set of computationally generated analogues (genetic operators) – reproduction, crossover, mutation, and election, respectively.

Social Behavior and Evolutionary Dynamics

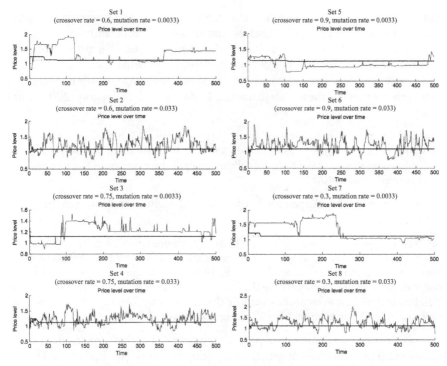

FIGURE 12.5. GA simulations (Unstable case: $\lambda/\beta = 1.05 > 1$)

While this example makes comparisons to experiments and other learning algorithms, GA simulation can be contrasted with "real world data" as well. An example is Arifovic and Maschek's (2006) data-based simulation on an agent-based currency crisis model. They find that the simulated data share similar properties with human-subject experimental data and empirical data from emerging markets. Along these lines, Gawrońska-Nowak and Grabowski (2016) investigate the dynamic process of speculative currency attacks and conclude that the simulated results are consistent with the theory and actual data (see also Chen and Yeh 1997).

12.12 APPENDIX

ABM introduces an important way to unify formal and empirical analysis for understanding complex economic and social systems. It also has sufficient analytic power that goes beyond traditional modeling practice assumptions. In economics, for example, the assumptions of utility maximization, perfect information, and market clearing are firmly rooted mainstream micro-foundations.

Furthermore, traditional practice also makes use of the representative-agent assumption since it allows for greater ease in solution procedures.[16]

Yet, these modeling assumptions and practices come at a price. Consider that fully rational agents are not bounded by any information limitation, heterogeneity becomes irrelevant, and interaction among agents are unnecessary. When they examine these shortcomings, LeBaron and Tesfatsion (2008) state that:

> [p]otentially important real-world factors such as subsistence needs, incomplete markets, imperfect competition, inside money, strategic behavioral interactions, and open-ended learning that tremendously complicate analytical formulations are typically not incorporated. (page 246)[17],[18]

Our focus in this Appendix is on a related technique – the GA. Arifovic (1991, 2) states:

> [a] genetic algorithm describes the evolution of a population of rules, representing different possible beliefs, in response to experience. ... Rules whose application has been more successful are more likely to become more frequently represented in the population, through a process similar to natural selection in population genetics. Random mutations also create new rules by changing certain features of rules previously represented in the population, thus allowing new ideas to be tried.

In sum, these rules allow scholars to examine whether agents obtain an equilibrium under a series of genetic processing scenarios (see Bullard and Duffy 1998a, 1998b, 1999; Arifovic 1994, 1995, 1996, 1998; Arifovic et al. 1997).

12.12.1 The Derivation of Optimal Firm Behavior

To explain how the basic GA works,[19] we consider a simple profit maximization problem where there exists a group of sellers who sell distinctive products in the market.[20] Assume each seller faces the same individual market demand curve:

$$p = p(q), \tag{12.21}$$

---

[16] We note that the ABM approach has been increasingly popular in political science and other social science disciplines. For example, Laver and Sergenti (2012) examine political party competition dynamics. Raub et al. (2011), on the other hand, discuss how micro-foundational ABM connects micro-level characteristics with macro-level observations in the field of sociology. Wilensky and Rand (2015) apply ABM to the natural, social, and engineering network systems with a specific simulation software called NetLogo. See also Namatame and Chen (2016) and Chen and Venkatachalam (2017) for a detailed discussion on the broader development of ABM.

[17] Miller and Page (2007) point out the importance of ABM for macro-level research.

[18] Along this line of argument, and after the financial crisis in 2007–2008, Farmer and Foley (2009) assert ABM helps "assemble the pieces and understand the behavior of the whole economic system" (page 685).

[19] See Goldberg (1989) and Riechmann (2001) for further analytical details.

[20] For simplicity, we assume each seller is a monopolist.

Social Behavior and Evolutionary Dynamics

where p is the price the seller receives, q is the level of production, and $p'(q) = dp/dq < 0$. Every seller also obtains the same production technology so that the cost function is identical for all sellers:

$$c = c(q), \qquad (12.22)$$

where $c(\cdot)$ represents the cost function and $c'(q) = dc/dq > 0$. Assume further that each seller attempts to maximize profit by choosing an optimal level of output q^* (based on the following profit function):

$$\max_q \pi = pq - c(q), \qquad (12.23)$$

where π is the profit level for a seller.

We derive the first-order condition from Eq. (12.23), and solve for the optimal level of output q^* by equating marginal revenue and marginal cost:

$$\left. \frac{d\pi}{dq} \right|_{q=q^*} = 0$$

$$\Rightarrow p'(q^*) q^* + p(q^*) = c'(q^*). \qquad (12.24)$$

To simplify the GA simulation, the demand and cost functions are assumed to be linear:

$$p = a - bq, \qquad (12.25)$$

and:

$$c = d + eq, \qquad (12.26)$$

where $a, b, d, e > 0$. Thus, the maximization of the profit function can be written as:

$$\max_q \pi = (a - bq) q - (d + eq). \qquad (12.27)$$

The optimal level of output q for each seller is:

$$q^* = \frac{a - e}{2b}, \qquad (12.28)$$

where $a > e$. Given q^* (presented in Eq. (12.28)), we obtain the optimal levels of price p^* and profit $\pi(q^*)$ from Eqs. (12.25) and (12.27), respectively.

In theory, sellers can determine the optimal level of output immediately and obtain the maximum level of profit. However, we relax this strong form of "rationality" and instead assume sellers go through a process of trial and error, and learn from experience to obtain the optimal solution in the model.

12.12.2 Formal Analogues: GA Operations

GENES, CHROMOSOMES, AND POPULATIONS To link the GA process with profit maximization, we first describe some fundamental operations. To begin, assume an initial population with M chromosomes (i.e., there are M individuals in a society or in an economy) is first generated at time $t = 0$. Each chromosome C_i consists of L genes formed in a binary structure with either '0' or '1.' For example, a production strategy followed by a representative chromosome (agent) i with length $L = 10$ can be written as: $C_i =$ 0100101110. Each chromosome is read as a binary number with a maximum number of possible strategies $B^{max} = 2^L - 1$. Given $L = 10$, the maximum value of a chromosome is: $B(C_i^{max}) = B^{max} = B(1111111111) = 2^{10} - 1 = 1023$, where $B(\cdot)$ is a binary operator for converting a binary number into a decimal number.

To understand the binary operator $B(\cdot)$, we consider a binary number $C_i =$ 0100101110. The corresponding decimal number is represented as:

$$\begin{aligned} B(0100101110) &= 0 \times 2^9 + 1 \times 2^8 + 0 \times 2^7 + 0 \times 2^6 \\ &\quad + 1 \times 2^5 + 0 \times 2^4 + 1 \times 2^3 + 1 \times 2^2 \\ &\quad + 1 \times 2^1 + 0 \times 2^0 \\ &= 302. \end{aligned}$$

This chromosome B(0100101110) can be interpreted as the 302nd strategy out of a possibility of 1023 strategies. Since there are m chromosomes with length of L in the population, the initial population P_0 can be represented as an $m \times L$ matrix where every gene in each chromosome coded either 0 or 1 with equal probability. Assuming there are eight genetic individuals (i.e., $M = 8$) in a society or economy at $t = 0$, a possible population P_0 can be written as:

$$P_0 = \begin{matrix} 0100101110 \\ 1110101010 \\ 0101110100 \\ 0100001010 \\ 1110101000 \\ 0101101101 \\ 1100101010 \\ 0100011100 \end{matrix}$$

Recall from above, a chromosome with $L = 10$ can have a possible value between zero and 1023. Its maximum value might be either too large or too small for an economic variable of interest (i.e., the output level). For the profit maximization example, suppose the parameters in the demand and cost functions are: $a = 200$, $b = 4$, and $e = 40$ in Eq. (12.28), and the optimal output level q^* is 20. If we are interested in the output level evolution in this genetic economy, we might restrict the output level range between zero and U^{max}, where U^{max} is an upper bound. We can also interpret U^{max} as the production capacity for all sellers in the society or economy. Under these conditions, the possible value of an economic variable of interest (i.e., the output level) can be written as:

$$V(C_i) = U^{\max} \times \frac{B(C_i)}{B^{\max}}, \qquad (12.29)$$

where $V(C_i) \in [0, U^{\max}]$ for $B(C_i) \in [0, B^{\max}]$. Therefore, given a chromosome $C_i = \texttt{0100101110}$, the genetic individual i produces an output level q_i:

$$q_i = V(C_i) = 100 \times \frac{302}{1023} = 29.52 \approx 30,$$

where $U^{\max}$ is assumed to be 100 in this example.

On the other hand, if the upper bound of the economic variable of interest (i.e., the output level) is larger than the maximum value of the binary number, one can increase the maximum value of the binary number by increasing the length of the chromosomes L in the population, and then apply Eq. (12.29) to restrict a possible range of the economic variable of interest. To sum up, since the population contains a total of m individuals with different production strategies, the GA procedure demonstrates the evolution of production strategies when heterogeneity, social interaction, and learning are assumed in the behavioral theory.

FITNESS FUNCTION To determine if a genetic "individual" is more likely to "survive" or be reproduced in the next period, we need to evaluate performance based on the fitness function. In our profit maximization example, the profit function (Eq. (12.27)) can be considered the fitness function $F(C_i)$:

$$\begin{aligned} F(C_i) &= \pi\left(V(C_i)\right) \\ &= \pi\left(q_i\right) = (a - bq_i)\,q_i - (d + eq_i). \end{aligned} \qquad (12.30)$$

For instance, with the values of $a = 200$, $b = 4$, $d = 50$, and $e = 40$, the fitness value of $C_i = \texttt{0100101110}$ is:

$$\begin{aligned} F(C_i) &= \pi\left(V(C_i)\right) \\ &= [200 - 4(29.52)]\,29.52 - [50 + 40(29.52)] = 1187.48. \end{aligned}$$

If the optimal level of output is $q^* = 20$, the maximum fitness level is:

$$F^{\max} = [200 - 4(20)]\,20 - [50 + 40(20)] = 1550. \qquad (12.31)$$

Note that the fitness function does not apply to minimization problems (i.e., cost minimization problems). For minimization problems an appropriate transformation of the economic values is needed for generating fitness values.

REPRODUCTION   Reproduction is a genetic operator where an individual chromosome is copied from the previous population to a new population. Given a probability of being drawn from each chromosome based on the fitness value, chromosomes are repeatedly drawn with replacement from the pool of the previous population. They are then put into the new population until the size of the new population equals that of the previous population (i.e., $M_t = M_{t+1}$).

Now, let the probability of reproduction be determined by the relative fitness function:

$$R(C_{i,t}) = \frac{F(C_{i,t})}{\sum_{m=1}^{M} F(C_{m,t})}, \qquad (12.32)$$

where $\sum_{i \in M} R(C_{i,t}) = 1$. For $F(C_{i,t}) \geq 0$ and for all i, $R(C_{i,t})$ is bounded between zero and one for all i. The relative fitness value $R(C_{i,t})$ gives us the probability chromosome i is copied to the new population at time $t + 1$. The larger the fitness value $F(C_{i,t})$, the higher likelihood the chromosome survives $R(C_{i,t})$ in the next period. One potential limitation in Eq. (12.32) is that $R(C_{i,t})$ can be negative if the fitness value $F(C_{i,t})$ is negative (see Eq. (12.30)). If the probability value is bounded between zero and one, then this limitation is not a threat.

To address this issue, Goldberg (1989) proposes a scaled relative fitness function:

$$\begin{aligned} S(C_{i,t}) &= \frac{F(C_{i,t}) + A}{\sum_{m=1}^{M} [F(C_{m,t}) + A]} \\ &= \frac{F(C_{i,t}) + A}{\sum_{m=1}^{M} F(C_{m,t}) + MA}, \end{aligned} \qquad (12.33)$$

where some $F(C_{i,t}) < 0$, and A is a constant such that $A > -\min_{C_i \in P_t} F(C_{i,t})$. Introducing A into the relative fitness function prevents negative probability values of being drawn for some chromosomes in the population (i.e., $S(C_{i,t}) > 0$ for all i.).

The reproduction operator is important for a class of topics in the social sciences. Since well-performed genetic agents are likely to be reproduced or survive in the next period, reproduction can be considered imitation. Agents are more likely to imitate or learn from their peers who have done better in a given setting or market.

CROSSOVER   Crossover occurs when two randomly drawn chromosomes exchange parts of their genes. This is known as the inter-chromosome recombination. In the GA environment, crossover is a process where parents are replaced by their children in the population. To explain the complete crossover procedure, assume there are two "parent" chromosomes, which are randomly selected (without replacement) from the population. A crossover point will be

Social Behavior and Evolutionary Dynamics

randomly chosen to separate each chromosome into two substrings. Finally, two "offspring" chromosomes will be formed by swapping the right-sided parents' substrings with probability κ. Figure 12.6 shows the crossover procedure where the crossover point is the seventh position from the right.

In the social sciences, crossover is a process of communication. Agents obtain new strategies by exchanging information from each other. Note that crossover may not improve fitness values. The lack of improvement can be interpreted as agents making mistakes in communication.

MUTATION Mutation is a genetic operator in which one or more gene within an individual chromosome changes value randomly. Every gene within a chromosome has a small probability μ of changing in value, independent of other positions. It is an intra-chromosome recombination. Figure 12.7 illustrates an example of the mutation process. In Figure 12.7, mutation occurs on the fifth gene from the right.

Mutation can be interpreted as invention or an experiment in new strategies. Firms may not improve their performance by merely imitating other firms. Instead, they may need to invent new products or experiment with new production processes. In a political science context the analogy could extend to any topic involving strategic messages, including campaigns, negotiations between rival nations, and the like.

Application: GA Simulation for Production Decisions

The GA simulation is based on the example of production decisions presented in Section 12.11.1. Figure 12.8 represents a standard structure for the GA

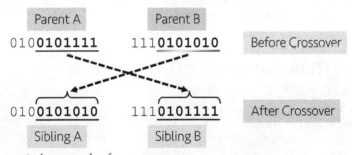

FIGURE 12.6. An example of crossover

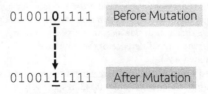

FIGURE 12.7. An example of mutation

operation.[21] Again, assume the parameters in the demand function are: $a = 200$ and $b = 400$, and those in cost functions are: $d = 50$ and $e = 40$. The optimal level of output is $q^* = 20$.

To investigate if agents in the GA environment are able to choose the optimal production level in the long run, we assume that there are 200 genetic agents ($M = 200$) in the economy with the length of 16 genes ($L = 16$). The maximum production capacity for each seller is $U^{max} = 50$. We also assume the fitness value for each agent is determined by the profit level presented in Eq. (12.30).[22] We simulate the GA economy with 500 iterations (generations) using MATLAB.[23] The output and code of the MATLAB program for the simulation is included at the end of the chapter.

Figure 12.9 presents the movement of average output levels over time. We obtain the figure by taking an average of the output levels from 200 agents in each generation, and then plotting the averages over 500 generations. Figure 12.9 shows there is a large production level adjustment, on average, in the first 60 generations ranging between 18 and 27. After the first 60 generations, the production level becomes more stable and is set around the optimal level of $q^* = 20$. In this simulation, the average output level over the whole time period is 19.93. This all-time average is very close to the optimal level q^*. It implies that, on average, genetic agents are able to learn and determine the optimal output level over time.

We further investigate the distribution of production levels in each generation. Figure 12.10 demonstrates the standard deviation of output levels within each generation over time. Not surprisingly, there are larger variations of output levels in the early generations. After the process of imitation, experiment, and communication, agents have a similar production pattern, with the standard deviations becoming smaller in latter generations.

12.12.3 MATLAB Simulations

MATLAB Output

```
This is a Genetic Algorithm Simulation.
The simple profit function is: profit = (a-bq)q - (d+eq).
Given the parameters: a=200, b=4, d=50, and e=40,
the optimal level of output is: q*=20
```

---

[21] To obtain the equilibrium, researchers simulate the model over a period of (notional) time (Evans and Honkapohja 2001, 2003b). Researchers commonly choose an ad-hoc duration for the simulation; however, they can decide an alternative convergence condition, also known as the stopping condition, where the difference of the simulated results between two time periods is less than a predetermined level.

[22] The simulation is based on the scaled relative fitness function (12.33). The probabilities for crossover (κ) and mutation (μ) are 0.3 and 0.0033, respectively.

[23] We set the stopping condition at 500 iterations.

Social Behavior and Evolutionary Dynamics

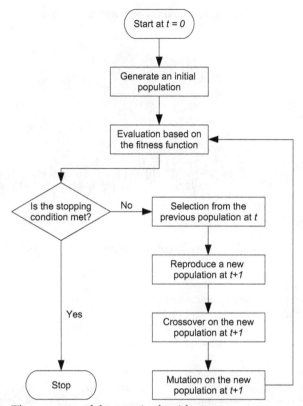

FIGURE 12.8. The structure of the genetic algorithm process

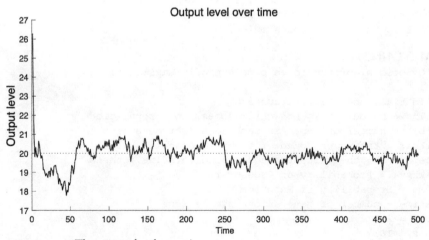

FIGURE 12.9. The output level over time

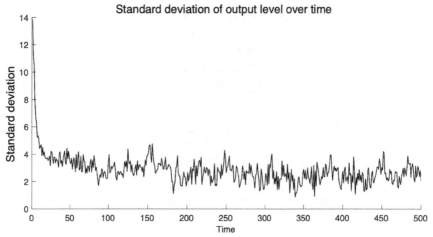

FIGURE 12.10. The standard deviation of the output level over time

```
In this simulation, you have:
a) 200 agents in each population;
b) 16 genes for each agent;
c) 50 as the maximum economic value;
d) 0.3 as the probability of crossover;
e) 0.0033 as the probability of mutation;
f) 500 generations in this simulation.
Hit any key to start running the simulation.
The simulation is now running…
Thank you for waiting. The process of simulation is over.
Please hit any key to get the results.
The mean of the output level in all generations is 19.931.
The variance of the output level is 0.38739.
This is the end of the simulation.
```

MATLAB Code

```
%Genetic algorithm for a simple profit maximization
%
%Initial Population Parameters:
%ind = number of agents(chromosomes) in a population
%bit = number of genes in each agent(chromosome)
%Lmax = the upper bound of the real economic values
%epsilon = the value for the scaled relative fitness
%kappa = Probability of Crossover
%mu = Probability of Mutation
%time = number of generations(simulations)
ind = 200;
bit = 16;
Umax = 50;
epsilon = .1;
```

Social Behavior and Evolutionary Dynamics 273

```
kappa = 0.3;
mu = 0.0033;
time = 500;
%
%Profit function parameters
% Demand function: p = a - bq
% Cost function: c = d + eq
% Profit function: profit = (a-bq)q - (d+eq)
% Optimal level of output: q* = (a-e)/2b
a = 200;
b = 4;
d = 50;
e = 40;
qstar = (a-e)/(2*b);
disp(' ')
disp(' ')
%
disp('This is a Genetic Algorithm Simulation.')
disp(' ')
disp('The simple profit function is: profit = (a-bq)q - (d+eq).')
disp(' ')
stra = ['Given the parameters: a=' num2str(a) ', b=' num2str(b) ',
d=' num2str(d) ', and e=' num2str(e) ','];
strb = ['the optimal level of output is: q*=' num2str(qstar)];
disp(stra);
disp(strb);
disp(' ');
disp(' ');
%
disp('In this simulation, you have:')
disp(' ')
str1 = ['a) ' num2str(Ind) ' agents in each population;'];
str2 = ['b) ' num2str(bit) ' genes for each agent;'];
str3 = ['c) ' num2str(Umax) ' as the maximum economic value;'];
str4 = ['d) ' num2str(kappa) ' as the probability of crossover;'];
str5 = ['e) ' num2str(mu) ' as the probability of mutation;'];
str6 = ['f) ' num2str(time) ' generations in this simulation.'];
disp(str1);
disp(str2);
disp(str3);
disp(str4);
disp(str5);
disp(str6);
disp(' ')
%
disp('Hit any key to start running the simulation.')
disp(' ')
pause
```

```
disp('The simulation is now running…')
disp(' ')
%
%Value Function and Definitions
Bmax = (2 .^ bit) - 1;
m = ind;
n = bit;
%Generate the Initial Population: "gen"
gen = rand(m,n);
for i=1:m
for j=1:n
if gen(i,j)<.5;
gen(i,j)=0;
else
gen(i,j)=1;
end
end
end
%
%Calculate the real value of each chromosome: "BC"
m2 = 2 * ones(n,1);
for i=1:n
m2(i,1)=m2(i,1).^(n-i);
end
%
%Starting the Genetic Simulation Here!
for t=1:time
BC = ones(m,1);
for i=1:m
BC(i,1)=gen(i,:) * m2;
end
%
%Calculate the real economic value of each chromosome: "VC"
VC = (Umax ./ Bmax) * BC;
%
%Calculate the real value from the objective function: "FC"
%This is the fitness function (The Most Important Function)
FC = (a - b .* VC) .* VC - d - e .* VC;
%Calcuate the relative fitness of each chromosome: "RC"
RC = FC ./ sum(FC);
%Calculate the scaled relative fitness of each chromosome: "SC"
A = abs(min(FC)) + epsilon;
FCA = FC + A;
SC = FCA ./ (sum(FC) + (m .* A));
genresult = [gen,VC,SC];
%
%Reproduction code
norm_fit = SC;
```

```
selected = rand(size(SC));
sum_fit = 0;
for i=1:length(SC),
sum_fit = sum_fit + norm_fit(i);
index = find(selected<sum_fit);
selected(index) = i*ones(size(index));
end
gen = gen(selected,:);
%
%This is the code for Crossover (Point & Pairwise)
%size(gen,1) = ind = number of individual
%size(gen,2) = bit = number of genes
sites = ceil(rand(size(gen,1)/2,1)*(size(gen,2)-1));
sites = sites.*(rand(size(sites))<kappa);
for i = 1:length(sites)
newgen([2*i-1 2*i],:) = [gen([2*i-1 2*i],1:sites(i)) gen([2*i 2*i-1],
sites(i)+1:size(gen,2))];
end
gen=newgen;
%
%This is the code for mutation
mutated = find(rand(size(gen))<mu);
newgen = gen;
newgen(mutated) = 1-gen(mutated);
gen=newgen;
%
%Collecting solutions of interest
%output(t) = the mean output level in each generation
%variance(t) = the variance of output level in each generation
output(t)=mean(VC);
stddev(t)=var(VC)^.5;
optq(t) = qstar;
tt(t) = t;
end
%
%Reporting results
%mean_output = the average of the mean output level in all
generations
%var_mean_output = the variance of the mean output level in
all generations
%t_stat_mean_output = the t-statistics of mean_output away from the
true parameter
disp(' ')
disp(' ')
disp('Thank you for waiting. The process of simulation is over.')
disp('Please hit any key to get the results. ')
pause
disp(' ')
```

```
disp(' ')
mean_output=mean(output);
var_mean_output=var(output);
str_output = ['The mean of the output level in all generations is
' num2str(mean_output) '.'];
str_varout = ['The variance of the output level is '
num2str(var_mean_output) '.'];
disp(str_output);
disp(str_varout);
%
figure(1)
subplot(2,1,1)
hold on
gop=plot(tt,output);
goptq = plot(tt,optq,'k:');
hold off
title('Output level over time')
set(gop,'Color','black','LineWidth',1.1)
xlabel('Time')
ylabel('Output level')
subplot(2,1,2)
gv=plot(stddev);
title('Standard deviation of output level over time')
set(gv,'Color','black','LineWidth',1)
xlabel('Time')
ylabel('Standard deviation of output level')
disp(' ')
disp(' ')
disp('This is the end of the simulation.')
disp(' ')
```

13

Competition and Reward Valuation

13.1 BACKGROUND

Studying human behavior is a central concern in the social sciences. As we have demonstrated in previous chapters, social scientists develop internally logical (or mathematical) relations with predictive capacity, and then link them with statistical regularities. Due to complex structures, some traditional empirical approaches fall short in establishing robust causal relations with data. List et al. (2011, 40) point out that "the literature [of economics] is replete with criticisms of their identifying assumptions, many times based on restrictiveness or implausibility."

The lab experiment is one way to address this challenge. Laboratory experiments serve this purpose because they use restrictions to minimize the influence of potential confounding factors. In this way researchers allow – with less "noise" – independent variable adjustment, known as a treatment or an intervention.[1] Furthermore, we can view experiments as an alternative simulation approach, one driven by human subjects in a laboratory, rather than by a representative agent (Chapter 11) or heterogeneous agents (Chapter 12) in a computational world. A laboratory experiment is simply a simulated world with a set of restrictive conditions, which are comparable to the assumptions imposed in a theoretical model. Unlike other computational approaches, researchers study human subjects' reactions when they allow for an exogenous event – a treatment – in the experiment.

Experimental studies in the social sciences can be traced back to the late nineteenth century. Physiologist and Nobel laureate Ivan Pavlov (1897) conducted experiments on the digestive systems of dogs. Political scientists followed suit,

---

[1] This treatment effect is defined as the causal effect of a treatment on the outcome variable in an experiment. Szmatka and Lovaglia (1996, 412) state that experiments using random assignment produce more convincing evidence than other observational research methods.

conducting experiments as early as the 1920s. For example, Gosnell (1926) used an experiment to see how direct mail of postcards influenced voter turnout.[2] In economics, Smith (1962) conducted an experiment to study equilibrium dynamics in a competitive market.[3]

Experimental research in the social sciences, especially in the field of political science, has seen wider usage in the past two decades (see Druckman et al. 2011). One research area is voter turnout. For example, Ansolabehere et al. (1994) conducted an innovative experiment to examine the effects of negative advertising on voter turnout. They found that subjects' voting intention dropped by five percent when exposed to negative campaign advertisements. This "demobilizing" effect of negative campaign advertising is also confirmed by aggregate and survey data in Ansolabehere et al. (1999). On the other hand, Levine and Palfrey (2007) apply experimental methods to the rational choice theory of turnout. They find that the comparative statics in a standard Bayesian Nash equilibrium model (i.e., the size effect, the competition effect, and the underdog effect) are supported by laboratory experiments (see Levine and Palfrey (2007) for details).

Experimental methods have also been applied to questions on partisanship and voting – recall from Chapter 5, retrospective (electoral sanctioning) (Key, 1966) and prospective (electoral selection) (Fiorina, 1981) theories.

To compare the two theories, Fox and Shotts (2009) set up a two-period policy choice model describing electoral sanctioning and electoral selection behavior. They show a perfect Bayesian equilibrium (describing a voter's optimal strategic voting behavior) exists. However, the authors do not test their model. Subsequently, Woon (2012) examine the validity of Fox and Shotts (2009) results via laboratory experiment. He concludes that "even in the absence of partisan motivations, learning may fail to be fully rational or Bayesian because citizens make inferential mistakes and are unable to correctly utilize the information at their disposal" (page 928).

In this chapter, we select Chaudoin and Woon (2018). The authors introduce an asymmetric contest model where two players have different subjective prize values. They derive a Nash equilibrium where both players optimally choose their effort levels to maximize their payoff functions.

Based on the Nash equilibrium, Chaudoin and Woon establish three testable hypotheses. First, the authors find players are willing to put in more effort if they perceive a higher prize value in the contest. This is known as the own-value effect. Second, the authors also find the opponent's subjective prize values matter in influencing a player's behavior. When the opponent's value is lower than the player's, an increase in the opponent's value will encourage the player to put more effort into the contest. This second result is known as the doing-

---

[2] See McDermott (2014) for a detailed discussion on the development of experimental political science.

[3] We refer readers to Roth (1993) for a discussion on the early history of experimental economics.

Competition and Reward Valuation

the-deterring effect. However, when the opponent's value is sufficiently high enough and surpasses the player's value, an increase in the opponent's value will discourage the player to put more effort into the contest. This negative relation (i.e., the third result) between the opponent's value and the player's effort level is known as the getting-deterred effect. Chaudoin and Woon's (2018) laboratory experiment mimics the theoretical model. They then evaluate the consistency of the Nash equilibrium predicted by the theory with the data generated by the experiment. The authors conclude that "[w]e find strong support for two comparative static predictions and mixed support for [the doing-the-deterring effect]" (page 587).

The EITM linkage in this example is the relation between the behavioral concept of strategic decision making and the empirical concept of prediction. The formal tools in this chapter include the method of optimization. The empirical tool is the experimental design. Basic experimental design elements and various sources are discussed in the Appendix.

13.2 STEP 1: RELATING DECISION MAKING AND PREDICTION

Chaudoin and Woon (2018) introduce a theoretical model consisting of a pair of representative players who compete with each other to win a prize. Both players are assumed to have different perceived prize values. They are required to make optimal decisions on how much effort they put into the game in order to maximize the expected payoffs. The authors then conduct a laboratory experiment, where subjects play a similar contest, closely described in the theoretical model, to test the consistency between the theoretical predictions and the behavioral patterns.

13.3 STEP 2: ANALOGUES FOR DECISION MAKING AND PREDICTION

Consider a two-player contest model in which two contestants, i and j, compete with each other in a one-time, nonrepeated contest. Both players choose their effort levels (with costs) to maximize their expected payoffs, given their subjective values of the prize and knowledge of the opponent's effort level. The subjective values (or utility) of winning the prize for contestants i and j are defined as $V_i > 0$ and $V_j > 0$, respectively, where $V_i \neq V_j$. Each contestant chooses an effort level, namely e_i and e_j, where their marginal costs of effort are assumed to be constant and equal to one, that is, $c_k = c(e_k) = e_k$, for $k \in \{i,j\}$.

Chaudoin and Woon (2018) adopt Tullock's (1967) contest success function: Each player's probability of winning the contest depends on her effort level relative to the total effort level in the contest. Therefore, the probability of player i winning the contest is $\phi_i(e_i, e_j) = e_i/(e_i + e_j)$, and that player j wins is

$\phi_j(e_i, e_j) = e_j/(e_i + e_j)$. If both players do not make any effort in the contest $(e_i = e_j = 0)$, then neither player i nor j wins the contest $(\phi_i = \phi_j = 0)$.

Let the expected payoffs for players i and j be written as follows:

$$\pi_i(e_i, e_j) = \phi_i(e_i, e_j) V_i - c(e_i), \tag{13.1}$$

and:

$$\pi_j(e_i, e_j) = \phi_j(e_i, e_j) V_j - c(e_j), \tag{13.2}$$

where π_i and π_j are the expected payoffs for players i and j, respectively.

Now, assume both players behave optimally in responding to the opponent's effort level. Thus, the best response function of choosing an effort level for player i is simply the first-order condition of Eq. (13.1):

$$\frac{\partial \pi_i}{\partial e_i} = 0$$

$$\left[\frac{V_i}{e_i + e_j} - \frac{e_i V_i}{(e_i + e_j)^2}\right] - 1 = 0$$

$$\Rightarrow e_i^* = (e_j V_i)^{1/2} - e_j. \tag{13.3}$$

Similarly, the best response function for player j is:

$$\frac{\partial \pi_j}{\partial e_j} = 0$$

$$\Rightarrow e_j^* = (e_i V_j)^{1/2} - e_i. \tag{13.4}$$

When both players choose their optimal effort levels with knowledge of the opponent's level in the contest, we can then obtain the Nash equilibrium effort levels. Solving the system of Eqs. (13.3) and (13.4), we have:[4]

$$e_i^* = \frac{V_i^2 V_j}{(V_i + V_j)^2}, \tag{13.5}$$

---

[4] To solve for the Nash equilibrium, we can rewrite Eqs. (13.3) and (13.4), respectively, as follows:

$$\frac{V_i e_j}{(e_i + e_j)^2} = 1, \text{ and} \tag{13.6}$$

$$\frac{V_j e_i}{(e_i + e_j)^2} = 1. \tag{13.7}$$

Now we set Eq. (13.6) equal to Eq. (13.7):

$$\frac{V_i e_j}{(e_i + e_j)^2} = \frac{V_j e_i}{(e_i + e_j)^2}$$

$$e_j V_i = e_i V_j$$

$$\Rightarrow e_j = e_i V_j / V_i. \tag{13.8}$$

Competition and Reward Valuation

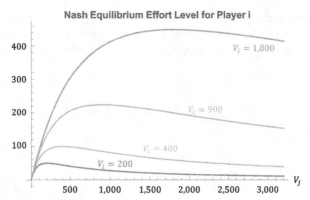

FIGURE 13.1. Nash equilibrium effort level for player i

and:

$$e_j^* = \frac{V_i V_j^2}{(V_i + V_j)^2}. \tag{13.9}$$

Figure 13.1 numerically represents the Nash equilibrium effort level (y-axis) for player i, given the subjective prize values for both players i and j. Interestingly, we see player i is willing to put more effort into the contest if she perceives a higher value for the prize, holding her opponent's perceived value constant. This monotonically positive relation between e_i^* and V_i is verified by showing the first derivative of Eq. (13.5) with respect to V_i is positive:

$$\frac{\partial e_i^*}{\partial V_i} = \frac{2 V_i V_j^2}{(V_i + V_j)^3} > 0, \tag{13.10}$$

for all $V_i, V_j > 0$. Chaudoin and Woon (2018) call this result the "own value" (OV) effect.

Then we insert Eq. (13.8) into Eq. (13.3):

$$e_i^* = (e_j V_i)^{1/2} - e_j$$
$$e_i^* = [(e_i^* V_j / V_i) V_i]^{1/2} - (e_i^* V_j / V_i)$$
$$e_i^* = (e_i^* V_j)^{1/2} - (e_i^* V_j / V_i)$$
$$(1 + V_j / V_i) e_i^* = (e_i^* V_j)^{1/2}$$
$$(1 + V_j / V_i)^2 e_i^* = V_j$$
$$(V_i^2 + 2 V_j + V_j^2) e_i^* = V_j V_i^2$$
$$e_i^* = V_j V_i^2 / (V_i + V_j)^2.$$

More importantly, Figure 13.1 describes how opponent's j's perceived value of the prize (x-axis) has a nonlinear effect on player i's effort. By taking the derivative of Eq. (13.5) with respect to player j's perceived prize value V_j, we have:

$$\frac{\partial e_i^*}{\partial V_j} = \frac{V_i^2 (V_i - V_j)}{(V_i + V_j)^3}. \tag{13.11}$$

Equation (13.11) shows the positive relation between e_i^* and V_j $(\partial e_i^*/\partial V_j > 0)$ if $V_i > V_j$. This result implies that if player i values the prize more highly than player j does $(V_i > V_j)$, player i's optimal effort level increases if player j's value of the prize increases. The authors call this result the "doing the deterring" (DD) effect. However, when player j's subjective value on the prize is higher than player i's $(V_i < V_j)$, an increase in player j's value (V_j) has a negative effect on player i's optimal effort $(\partial e_i^*/\partial V_j < 0)$. This result is known as the "getting deterred" (GD) effect.

Figure 13.2 depicts the joint effects of V_i and V_j on the optimal effort level for player i. As V_i increases, we observe the "own value" effect where player i increases her optimal effort in the contest. On the other hand, the "doing the deterring" (DD) and "getting deterred" (GD) effects on the optimal effort level

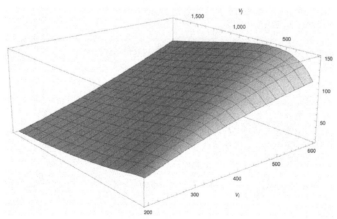

FIGURE 13.2. Nash equilibrium effort level for player i by varying V_i and V_j

Competition and Reward Valuation

for player i can be observed by varying the values of V_j, holding the value of V_i constant. The value of e_i^* increases as V_j is increasing from a small value (i.e., the DD effect) and $V_j < V_i$. Lastly, when opponent j's subjective value is above player i's value $(V_j > V_i)$, player i is discouraged and puts less effort into the contest as V_j increases (i.e., the GD effect).

These results are summarized in the following three testable hypotheses:

Hypothesis 1 (the own-value effect): An increase in player i's perceived prize value (V_i) raises her optimal level of effort (e_i^*), holding other factors constant.

Hypothesis 2 (the doing-the-deterring effect): Assuming that player i's perceived prize value is larger than player j's (i.e., $V_i > V_j$), an increase in player j's value increases player i's optimal effort level (e_i^*), holding other factors constant.

Hypothesis 3 (the getting-deterred effect): Assuming that player i's perceived prize value is less than player j's (i.e., $V_i < V_j$), an increase in player j's value reduces player i's optimal effort level (e_i^*), holding other factors constant.

With player i's and j's optimal strategies in place, Figure 13.3 plots player i's expected payoff level (y-axis) against player j's perceived value V_j, by varying player i's perceived value V_i. We see that as player i's perceived value of the prize V_i increases, her expected payoff level goes up and her expected payoff curve shifts away from the origin. More importantly, the expected payoff of player i decreases and asymptotically approaches zero as the opponent's perceived value of prize V_j increases. Figure 13.4 represents a three-dimensional diagram showing player i's expected payoff by varying V_i and V_j.

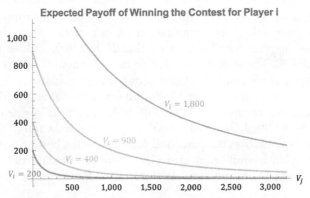

FIGURE 13.3. Player i's expected payoff level in Nash equilibrium

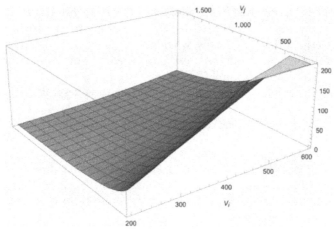

FIGURE 13.4. Player i's expected payoff value by varying V_i and V_j

13.4 STEP 3: UNIFYING AND EVALUATING THE ANALOGUES

The asymmetric contest model describes players' rational behavior based on their own perceived values and the opponent's value of the prize. To investigate whether human subjects would behave in the way comparable to the Nash equilibrium, Chaudoin and Woon (2018) conduct a "Lottery Contest Game" experiment, where two subjects play against each other to win a prize that would be worth different values to each subject in the game. There are 150 subjects participating in a multiple round experiment. Each subject is endowed 1,000 points for purchasing "contest tickets" in each round of the game. Each ticket is worth one point. The probability of winning the prize is equal to the number of tickets purchased by the subject relative to the total number of tickets purchased in each round. Lastly, all unused points can be kept by the subject.[5]

Subject i and j are assigned alternative prize values. The authors consider two sets of prize values. For the first set of valuations, single valuations S, the values of the prize for player i are either 200 or 900, and for player j are either 300 or 800. The authors also double the valuations for players i and j in the experiment. The second set of valuations, double valuations D, defines the values for player i as either 400 or 1,800, and for player j as either 600 or 1,600. The authors therefore categorize 200, 300, 400, and 600 as low perceived prize values, and 800, 900, 1,600, and 1,800 as high perceived values.

Table 13.1 summarizes the perceived prize values for both players and their corresponding Nash equilibrium effort levels and expected payoffs. The effects of OV, GD, and DD are presented in Table 13.1. For example, the OV effect

---

[5] Purchasing contest tickets represents effort level in the experiment. For further experimental details, see Chaudoin and Woon (2018).

Competition and Reward Valuation

TABLE 13.1. *Subjective values, equilibrium effort levels and expected payoffs*

	Perceived values of the prize		Nash equilibrium effort		Expected payoffs	
	V_i	V_j	e_i^*	e_j^*	π_i	π_j
Single valuations (S)	200	300	48	72	32	108
	200	800	32	128	8	512
	900	300	169	56	507	19
	900	800	224	199	253	177
Double valuations (D)	400	600	96	144	64	216
	400	1,600	64	256	16	1,024
	1,800	600	338	112	1,014	38
	1,800	1,600	448	398	506	354

occurs when an increase in V_i from 200 to 900 encourages player i to raise her effort level from 48 to 169 (given $V_j = 300$). Moreover, we also observe the GD effect from the table: When $V_i = 200 < V_j = 300$, player j's perceived value increases from 300 to 800 which lowers player i's effort level from 48 to 32. On the other hand, when $V_i = 900 > V_j = 300$, the increase in player j's perceived value from 300 to 800 motivates player i to increase her effort level from 169 to 224. This is the DD effect.

Chaudoin and Woon (2018) subject their model to two information availability treatments. The first treatment is known as the "Feedback" treatment, where respondents obtain information including the effort level of each player and the probabilities of winning the prize (given the effort levels that both players choose in previous rounds of the game). The second treatment is where subjects are provided an interactive graphical interface where they can obtain the probability of winning and expected payoff values under different effort scenarios for themselves and their opponent. This treatment effect is known as the "Calculator" treatment.

Chaudoin and Woon (2018) establish the EITM connection by linking the three hypotheses with the following regression model:

$$Effort_i = \sum_{t \in T} \beta_t High_{it} + \sum_{t \in T} \gamma_t GD_{it} + \sum_{t \in T} \delta_t DD_{it} + \sum_{t \in T} \alpha_t + \epsilon_i, \quad (13.12)$$

where $Effort_i$ represents the effort level for subject i in a certain round of the game, and $t \in T$ represents a specific treatment condition that a subject faces (from the entire set of treatments intersected with the valuations set, $T = \{BN, BF, CN, CF\} \times \{S, D\}$). We note that BN is the baseline condition where subjects do not get any information scenarios, BF is the situation where subjects receive the "Feedback" treatment only, CN is the situation where subjects receive the "Calculator" treatment only, and CF is the condition where subjects receive both "Feedback" and "Calculator." Finally, the authors define $S = \{200, 300, 800, 900\}$ and $D = \{400, 600, 1,600, 1,800\}$ as the single valuations and double valuations of the prize, respectively.

Regarding the independent variables of interest, *High* is a dummy variable that equals one if the subject's perceived value of the prize is high, and zero otherwise. The variable $High_{it}$ directly links to hypothesis 1 (the own-value effect), which represents the partial derivative of e_i^* with respect to V_i in Eq. (13.10). This relation suggests that an increase in player i's perceived value of the prize V_i has a positive effect on her equilibrium effort level e_i^*. Therefore, we expect $\beta_t > 0$ in Eq. (13.12).

On the other hand, according to Eq. (13.11), an increase in opponent j's perceived value of the prize V_j has either positive or negative effects on player i's equilibrium effort level e_i^*. The authors link Eq. (13.11) with two variables – GD_{it} and DD_{it} – in the regression model (13.12). The variable DD in the regression is associated with hypothesis 2 (the doing-the-deterring (DD) effect) in the model. According to Eq. (13.11), the DD effect exists when an increase in V_j motivates player i to make a higher level of effort in equilibrium e_i^* (given $V_i > V_j$). The variable DD in regression (13.12) is defined as a dummy variable equal to one if both subjects' values are high, and zero otherwise. Based on hypothesis 2, we expect the coefficient on DD_{it} to be positive, that is, $\delta_t > 0$.

Similarly, hypothesis 3 – the getting-deterred (GD) effect – is tested via the coefficient on the variable GD_{it} in regression (13.12), where GD is a dummy variable equal to one if the subject's value is low and the opponent's value is high, and zero otherwise. Hypothesis 3 shows that an increase in V_j discourages player i and reduces her equilibrium effort level e_i^* (when $V_i < V_j$). Therefore, we expect $\gamma_t < 0$. Finally, α_t represents the constant term for various treatment t.

Chaudoin and Woon (2018) estimate the model with ordinary least squares. Figure 13.5 presents the empirical results graphically. The estimated coefficients on $High_{it}$, GD_{it}, and DD_{it} are reported in the left, middle, and right panels of Figure 13.5, respectively. We see the coefficients on *High*, representing the "own value" (OV) effect, are positive and significant across different treatments in the experiment. This result supports hypothesis 1 that an increase in player i's perceived prize value V_i raises her optimal level of effort e_i^*. We also observe a clear pattern that subjects raise their effort level systematically during the rounds of double valuations.

The estimated getting-deterred (GD) effect in the experiment is also in line with hypothesis 3 that an increase in player j's value reduces player i's optimal effort level e_i^* when player i's perceived prize value is less than player j's. The estimated coefficients on GD are negative and significant in different types of treatments (i.e., BN and CF) at the conventional levels, except in the rounds of BF and CN treatments (intersected with single valuations). More importantly, the coefficients are more negative in the rounds with double valuations, meaning that subjects are more likely to be discouraged and make

Competition and Reward Valuation

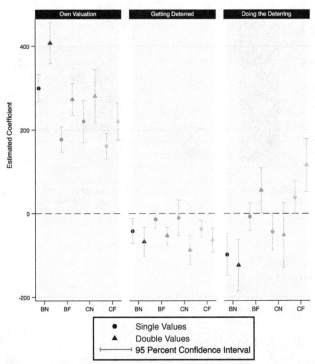

FIGURE 13.5. Estimated effects of own-value, getting-deterred, and doing-the-deterring on efforts in the asymmetric information contest experiment

less effort to win the game if their own valuation of the prize is low but the opponent has a double valuation of the prize.

Chaudoin and Woon (2018) find mixed results in supporting hypothesis 2 of the doing-the-deterring effect. More importantly, the authors observe the availability of information matters. In the rounds of BF and CF, where subjects receive Feedback treatment, subjects tend to raise their effort when they observe that their opponent's valuations are high. This pattern supports hypothesis 2. This positive effect is significant when both subjects have double valuations of the prize. However, when subjects do not obtain information about previous rounds of the game, they tend to lower their effort in response to their opponent's higher valuations. This result is inconsistent with hypothesis 2.

The results presented in Figure 13.5 suggest that subjects make decisions differently depending on how much information is available in the competition. Chaudoin and Woon (2018) further investigate the effects of information availability on subjects' decision making. They measure the average deviation of observed effort levels from the Nash prediction (in percent) across four

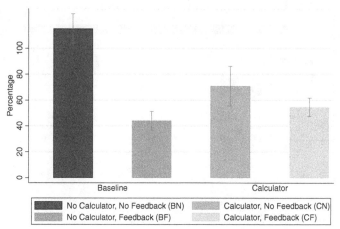

FIGURE 13.6. Percentage difference across treatments

different treatments. They name the deviation as Percentage Difference, which is formally defined as:

$$Percentage\ Difference_s = \frac{\hat{e}_s - e^*}{e^*} \times 100,$$

for $s \in \{BN, BF, CN, CF\}$, where $\hat{e}_s = \sum_{i \in s} Effort_i/n_s$, e^* is the Nash equilibrium effort level, and n_s is the number of observations where subjects are involved in the game with treatment s.[6] A smaller value of Percentage Difference implies that subjects' decisions are closer to the Nash prediction in the theoretical model.

Figure 13.6 presents a bar chart showing the Percentage Difference across four different treatments. The first bar (reading from left to right) shows the average deviation of subjects' effort levels from the Nash equilibrium level without feedback treatment (BN). The next two bars present the rounds with Feedback treatments (BF) and those with Calculator treatments (CN), respectively. Finally, the last bar represents the value for rounds with Feedback and Calculator treatments (CF).

Figure 13.6 shows information matters. When subjects do not obtain any historical information regarding the previous rounds of the experiment, that is, those rounds without Feedback treatments (BN and CN), they tend to overly compete with their opponents by making extra effort in the contest. However, when subjects have more information about their own and opponents' condition in past contests (the rounds with BF and CF treatments), their decisions are closer to the theoretical predictions.

---

[6] The observations in the rounds with zero valuations are excluded from this analysis. See Chaudoin and Woon (2018) for details.

Competition and Reward Valuation

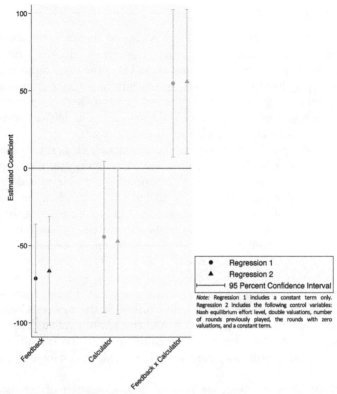

FIGURE 13.7. Estimated effects of information treatments

As a robustness check on the role of information availability, the authors estimate the effects of the Feedback and Calculator treatments on the deviations of the subject's effort level from the Nash prediction. They find that both Feedback and Calculator treatments reduce the subject's effort deviations. Figure 13.7 summarizes the estimated coefficients on Feedback treatment, Calculator treatment, and the interaction term between Feedback and Calculator (CF) treatments. Regression 1 represents a basic regression model with three variables of interest and a constant term, whereas regression 2 is an extended model controlling for other external factors: the Nash equilibrium effort level predicted by the theoretical model, double valuations, number of rounds that a subject has played previously, and rounds with zero valuations.

The regression results show the coefficients on Feedback and Calculator treatments are negative and significant at the 95% level. Subjects are less likely to overly compete with their opponents. On the other hand, the significantly positive coefficients on the interaction term show that subjects would raise their effort levels if they have both Feedback and Calculator treatments. However, this result is not in line with the predictions derived from the theoretical model.

13.5 SUMMARY AND EXTENSION

Chaudoin and Woon (2018) introduce an elegant theoretical model showing how asymmetric prize rewards can affect contestants' decisions on choosing their effort levels in the game. When players value the prize more highly, they are willing to play harder against their opponents. More interestingly, a player's degree of competitiveness also strategically depends on her own perceived value relative to the opponent's. The theoretical results are generally supported by the data obtained from a controlled laboratory experiment.

To discuss the possibility of leveraging the model, we first observe that the authors vary the degree of information availability in the extended experiment. They find subjects receiving historical information are able to make decisions closer to the Nash equilibrium. One possibility for extending the model is to introduce the cost of information acquisition. Instead of assuming the function of effort cost is perfectly linear and its marginal cost is constant, one can consider the effort cost $c(e)$ is a nonlinear function, where the degree of nonlinearity, albeit indirectly, represents the difficulty of obtaining information in the competition. In other words, if information is not readily available, the contestants are required to play harder and pay higher costs to obtain information (or to compute the optimal strategy) in the contest. Consequently, the marginal cost of effort increases as the contestant expends more effort in the competition. On the other hand, when the information is readily available and can be obtained with ease, an increase in effort level can lower the marginal cost.

With these ideas in mind, we propose a modification of the asymmetric contest model. As with Eqs. (13.1) and (13.2), the objective functions for subjects i and j are, respectively:

$$\pi_i(e_i, e_j) = \phi_i(e_i, e_j) V_i - c(e_i), \qquad (13.13)$$

and:

$$\pi_j(e_i, e_j) = \phi_j(e_i, e_j) V_j - c(e_j). \qquad (13.14)$$

In Chaudoin and Woon (2018), the effort costs for subjects i and j are $c(e_i) = e_i$ and $c(e_j) = e_j$, respectively, where the marginal cost of effort $c'(e_k) = dc(e_k)/de_k = 1$, for $k \in \{i, j\}$. Here we relax the linear cost assumption and introduce a simple nonlinear cost function:

$$c(e_k) = e_k^{\beta_k}, \qquad (13.15)$$

where $k \in \{i,j\}$, and the parameter $\beta_k > 0$ represents the rate of change in marginal cost with respect to the change in effort level.

Equation (13.15) captures the flexibility of the effort cost structure for players i and j. Intuitively, β_i and β_j are interpreted as the characteristics of information availability suggested previously. If an increase in the difficulty of obtaining information raises the marginal cost of player i's effort in the competition, we would expect that $\beta_i > 1$, ceteris paribus. On the other hand, if information is more readily available and easy to obtain, then player i's marginal cost of effort decreases as her effort level increases, that is, $0 < \beta_i < 1$, ceteris paribus. In other words, the value of β_i indicates the level of information availability in the contest. If information is less available in the contest, we have $\beta_i > 1$. However, if information is more available, then $\beta_i < 1$. Finally, if $\beta_i = \beta_j = 1$, then information availability does not affect the effort costs for players, which is equivalent to Chaudoin and Woon (2018).

To solve the Nash equilibrium for the modified contest model, we obtain the first-order conditions (FOCs) from the systems of Eqs. (13.13)–(13.15):

$$c'(e_i) = \frac{V_i e_j}{(e_i + e_j)^2},$$

and:

$$c'(e_j) = \frac{V_j e_i}{(e_i + e_j)^2},$$

where $c'(e_k) = \beta_k e_k^{\beta_k - 1}$, for $k \in \{i,j\}$.

Given the nonlinearity of the cost functions, we are unable to derive a general form for the Nash equilibrium. Instead, we investigate the equilibrium condition by assuming that player i faces two different types of information constraints with two particular sets of numeric parameters in the cost function. For the first type of information constraint, we assume $\beta_i = 2$ and $\beta_j = 1$. This situation implies that player i has less information available relative to player j in the contest so that player i's marginal cost increases as her effort level increases (holding player j's marginal cost constant). For the second type of information constraint, we set $\beta_i = 0.5$. Due to the higher degree of information availability, player i is assumed to pay less relative to player j as player i's effort increases (holding player j's marginal cost unchanged).[7]

---

[7] The marginal cost of player i relative to that of player j, given $\beta_i = 2$ and $\beta_j = 1$, is $2e_i$. For the case of $\beta_i = 0.5$ and $\beta_j = 1$, the relative marginal cost of player i is $0.5 e_i^{-1/2}$.

With the first set of parameter values $\{\beta_i, \beta_j\} = \{2, 1\}$, we can derive the best response function of effort for subject i as follows:

$$e^*_{i,\beta_i=2} = \frac{(-V_i V_j + \Theta)^2}{6 V_j^2 \Theta}, \tag{13.16}$$

where $\Theta \equiv \{V_i^2 V_j^3 (V_i + 27 V_j^2) + 3^{3/2} [V_i^4 V_j^8 (2V_i + 27 V_j^2)]^{1/2}\}^{1/3}$. Similarly, with the second set of parameter values $\{\beta_i, \beta_j\} = \{0.5, 1\}$, the best response function of effort for subject i is:

$$e^*_{i,\beta_i=0.5} = \frac{\left(V_i^2 - V_i V_j^{1/2} + 0.25 V_j\right) V_j}{V_i^2}. \tag{13.17}$$

To see how the nonlinearity of the cost function can affect players' optimal decisions, we plot player i's optimal effort level (e^*_i) against player j's perceived value of the prize (V_j) across four distinct perceived prize values for player i (V_i). The values of V_i are $\{200, 400, 900, 1800\}$, and V_j is in the range of $[0, 1600]$. The results are presented in Figure 13.8. The sub-figure on the left in Figure 13.8 illustrates the optimal level of effort for player i presented by Eq. (13.16), whereas the one on the right shows the optimal effort level described by Eq. (13.17).

Both sub-figures in Figure 13.8 show the existence of the "own value" effect (similar to Figure 13.1): An increase in player i's prize value makes her put

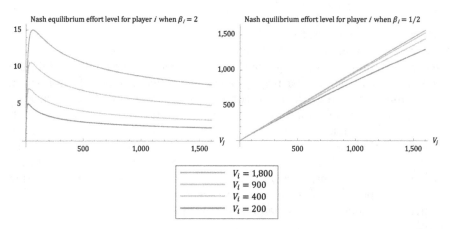

FIGURE 13.8. Optimal effort levels for player i in a modified asymmetric contest model

more effort into the game. However, we observe two dissimilar patterns in how player i responds to player j's perceived prize value when player i faces two different information availability scenarios.

According to the sub-figure on the left in Figure 13.8, we observe the "doing the deterring" (DD) effect where player i's optimal effort $e^*_{1,\beta_i=2}$ increases as V_j increases. However, the effect is significantly smaller than in the linear case (see Figure 13.1).[8] More importantly, since player i has less information available and it is more difficult to make optimal decisions, player i is discouraged more easily and tends to reduce her effort level even when V_j increases at a sufficiently low level. For example, the top curve in the sub-graph on the left indicates the optimal effort level for player i when $\beta_i = 2$ and $V_i = 1,800$. Player i is willing to raise her effort level if player j's perceived value of the award is below $V_j = [2(1800)]^{1/2} = 60$. However, as V_j increases above 60, the "getting deterred" (GD) effect dominates, and player i lowers her effort level in the contest.

This result may serve as an explanation on the negative effect of the "doing the deterring" found in the rounds without information treatments (BN) in the laboratory experiment presented in Figure 13.5. On the other hand, more information available for player i can help lower her marginal cost of making effort (i.e., $\beta_i = 0.5$). Hence, the sub-figure on the right shows that player i is willing to expend more effort in respond to player j's higher values of the prize. The DD effect dominates in this case.[9] This pattern is consistent with the positive "doing the deterring" effect shown in the rounds with information treatments (CF) illustrated in Figure 13.5.

13.6 APPENDIX

This appendix provides a brief discussion noting that experiments, in well-controlled environments, can serve as a tool to link formal and empirical analyses. Ideally, formal models, empirical tests, and experiments have different strengths and weaknesses, and evidence from all three should be used collectively, when possible (see Poteete et al. 2010). Note, an extensive description of experimental design is beyond the scope of this book, but we recommend the following texts (see Kagel and Roth 1995, 2015; Morton and Williams 2010; Kittel et al. 2012; McDermott 2014; Wilson 2014). Here we provide a nontechnical illustration on a couple of key social science topics.

---

[8] The turning point from the "doing the deterring" (DD) effect to the "getting deterred" (GD) effect is $V_j = (2V_i)^{1/2}$.

[9] The GD effect is also observed in this model. The turning point from the DD effect to the GD effect is $V_j = V_i^2$.

Experiments in the Social Sciences: Examples in Economics and Political Science

Experimental economics is a branch of economics that studies human behavior in a controlled laboratory setting. It uses scientific experiments to examine the choices people make under specific circumstances in order to identify possible alternative market mechanisms and economics theories. The field of experimental economics was pioneered by Vernon Smith, who was awarded the Nobel Prize in Economics in 2002. In summarizing Smith's contribution, the Nobel award committee stressed how experimental designs support a dialogue between theory and test:

[e]conomics has been widely considered a non-experimental science, relying on observation of real-world economies rather than controlled laboratory experiments. Nowadays, however, a growing body of research is devoted to modifying and testing basic economic assumptions; moreover, economic research relies increasing on data collected on the lab rather than in the field. (The Royal Swedish Academy of Sciences 2002)[10]

Initially, experiments were used to understand how and why markets and other exchange systems function as they do. In 1955, Vernon Smith initiated a market experiment in his Principles of Economics classroom to examine how and why any market approximates a competitive equilibrium (see Smith 1962). The experiment provided students with an opportunity to experience an actual market and how the market prices and quantities converge to their theoretical competitive equilibrium values. It has become a common practice to include this market experiment in economics classes to enhance students' understanding of the crucial concepts of modern economic theory.

Economics is concerned in making predictions of behavior in market settings, whereas political science is concerned in predicting behaviors in non-market settings (e.g., elections, committees, and juries). In economics, the unit of account for decisions involving allocations is commonly monetary, whereas in political science it is typically but not solely measured by votes. Ultimately, both disciplines are interested in human interactions and optimal outcomes. In the 1970s, Charles Plott collaborated with Vernon Smith and pioneered experiments in political science (see Plott and Smith 2008). In what follows, we discuss two popular types of experiments in economics and political science. The examples provided here represent the most basic designs, and variations to each example can be used to study different research questions.

PUBLIC GOOD EXPERIMENTS[11] Public good experiments are also known as social dilemma experiments and they are designed to study the tension between self-interest and social interest. A public good possesses two essential characteristics – it is nonexcludable and nonrival. As a consequence, individuals

---

[10] See www.nobelprize.org/prizes/economic-sciences/2002/press-release/
[11] See also the discussion on Ostrom's Social Dilemma Research in Chapter 3.

Competition and Reward Valuation

cannot be excluded from having access to the good (the use by one individual does not reduce availability to others), and the good can be effectively consumed simultaneously by more than one person. Examples of public goods would be sewer systems, public parks, clean air, national security, and the like. While public goods are important for a well-functioning society, the "free-rider" problem arises, because a perfectly rational individual will not have an incentive to contribute to the public good when everyone will receive the benefit of consuming it regardless of whether they contributed or not. However, if every individual uses this type of reasoning, standard economic theory predicts the public good will no longer be produced, making society worse-off.

To answer this question effectively, public goods experiments have been conducted since the 1970s to observe the behavior of real people when they are placed under various empirically informed conditions. For the purpose of illustration, we use a traditional public goods experiment discussed in Guala (2005). In this experimental environment, there are four players, each of whom is given an endowment of twenty points/tokens. These tokens can be spent either on private leisure or invested in the production of a public good. Each player can split the endowment between private leisure and a public good in many different combinations (twenty and zero, fifteen and five, ten and ten, and so on). Every player is aware that the others are simultaneously making a decision on how to anonymously allocate their 20 tokens. The total sum of the points invested in the production of the public good will be multiplied by two and divided equally among the players. The payoff function for each player is:

$$p_i = (20 - g_i) + 0.5 \sum_{j=1}^{4} g_j, \qquad (13.18)$$

where 20 is the total number of points/tokens to be shared between a private account $(20 - g)$ and a public account (g). The parameter 0.5 is the production factor and it specifies how much of the public good is enjoyed by each individual for each point invested by the group as a whole. Notice that this function is characterized by a linear relation between total payoff and total contribution to the public good. The payoff is identical for every player, resulting in complete symmetry. In this linear environment, standard economy theory predicts that the best move by an individual player is to not contribute anything to the public good. The intuition is straightforward: Given that each player would get back only half of each token they contribute, why would anyone spend any of their own tokens on the public good? Theory predicts that when everyone is perfectly rational (in the sense of Nash rationality) no public good will be produced.

For a "one-shot" linear environment experiment, an average contribution level of roughly 50 percent of the individual endowment to a public good is commonly observed. Moreover, if this experiment is played in multiple rounds – with the payoffs and average contributions from each round being released to every player – the high initial contributions (of 50 percent) tend to decrease over time and start to converge to a Nash equilibrium (zero contribution). This finding – where contributions decrease over time – is referred to as "overcontribution" and "decay" in the literature. Still, what is interesting is that even with a long series of repeated play (e.g., 50 or more rounds) some contributions to the public good continue. This finding suggests that at least some players hold values of altruism and fairness regardless of the actions of others (see McDermott 2002).

To summarize, the results from public goods experiments are typically in the middle between the aforementioned economic theory and alternative theory. In revising the payoff function and conducting different experiments accordingly, political scientists can examine the effects of public policies on human behavior as to how the role of political institutions would interact with the role of volunteering, and this direction of examination can help solve a variety of social issues, including designing more efficient ways to finance the production of public goods and to maximize welfare.

MARKET CLEARING EXPERIMENTS Market clearing experiments are used to illustrate the process of market convergence where prices adjust to the equilibrium. This process is also known as market clearing. Since they are pedagogical in nature, they are commonly conducted in classrooms; however, as long as agents can freely interact with one another they can be implemented in any environment. During different timed rounds, agents will be randomly divided into two halves. One half will be assigned the role of "seller," where each of them will be given one unit of a good and a minimum price to sell it. The other half will be assigned the role of "buyer," where each of them will be given a maximum purchasing price for the good the "sellers" offer. It is explained to sellers and buyers that their goal is to make as much producer and consumer surplus as possible, respectively – sellers get to sell at the highest price possible and buyers get to buy at the lowest price possible. All agents are left to freely negotiate with one another after receiving the basic instructions.

The experimenter provides the price information for each round. When an initial round ends, the experimenter shows the agents what happened to the final price and quantity, which is likely to be highly variant. Throughout the rounds, agents will be alternating between the roles (i.e., the roles of sellers and buyers will switch in each successive round). After a number of rounds, the price typically converges to an equilibrium.

Note that in political markets agents also interact and negotiate to attain as much surplus as possible. They compete for resources by lobbying and voting, given that the government allocates the resources. As a result, the market clearing experiment is useful for political scientists who are studying convergence conditions in the political arena. For example, market clearing experiments have been adopted to answer questions surrounding market effects of government regulations and presidential election forecasts (see Forsythe et al. 1992).

14

An Alternative Unification Framework

14.1 BACKGROUND

An important alternative framework for methodological unification is Guillermina Jasso's *Tripartite Structure of Social Science Analysis* (Jasso 2004).[1] Like the EITM framework, she seeks to unify formal and empirical analysis. What is also interesting is Jasso's framework can be used for measurement and data creation purposes – that are behaviorally and theoretically driven. The motivation for Jasso's (2004) tripartite structure:

> acknowledges the critical importance of the research activities that precede theoretical and empirical analysis – developing the framework out of which theoretical and empirical analysis emerge...it acknowledges the part played by nondeductive theories and links them to deductive theories, and it recognizes the extratheoretical empirical work...[it] represents more faithfully the varied kind of scientific work we do and their varied interrelationships. It invites to the table, so to speak, activities that in the old world of deductive theory and testing of predictions were slighted, even as they made their own fundamental contributions to the growth of knowledge. (pages 401–402)

This chapter has three parts. First, we provide a brief background into Jasso's tripartite framework. Second, we apply Jasso's framework to a measurement question: the creation and use of an index for justice. Specifically, our application uses Jasso's justice evaluation function and aggregates it to justice indexes.

Jasso's justice index sheds further light on thinking about different ways to characterize how people decide. Up to this point, the research we have highlighted, to the extent it involves decision making and decision theory, focuses on cost–benefit calculations or other "economic" motivations. However, people make decisions based on other factors. *Justice* is one such factor. In a series

---

[1] We use the term "framework" as a substitute for Jasso's term – "structure." However, note that a component of Jasso's "structure" contains the term "framework."

An Alternative Unification Framework 299

of papers, Jasso (1999, 2002, 2004, 2008, 2010) applies her measurement of justice to a variety of social science issues. Her measure has important behavioral properties: (1) *scale-invariance* and (2) *additivity*. These properties are "thought desirable on substantive grounds in a justice evaluation function" (Jasso 2004, 408).

Third, and not surprisingly, the use of formal and empirical analysis to construct indexes is also done in other disciplines. The final component of this chapter is an example from economics. We show in the appendix how monetary aggregates are constructed and – like Jasso – they are based on the linkage between theory and data.

14.2 JASSO'S TRIPARTITE STRUCTURE: A SUMMARY

The tools required to implement the tripartite structure are broad. Jasso incorporates a framework centering on various research design activities – ranging from the research questions to the way we characterize the relations – which add to the process of linking formal and empirical analysis.

Jasso's (2004) tripartite structure is represented in Figure 14.1. To maintain fidelity to the concepts and definitions she describes, we use Jasso's voice, summarize the key elements, and (where possible) follow the order in which she describes her tripartite structure:

Element 1: The Framework
Element 2: Theoretical Analysis
Element 3: Empirical Analysis

Social Science Analysis

Theoretical Analysis	Framework	Empirical Analysis
Deductive	Questions	Measure/ estimate terms/relations
Postulates	Actors	
Predictions	Quantities	
---------	Functions	Test deduced predictions
Hierarchical	Distributions	
Postulates	Matrices	---------
Propositions	Contexts	Test propositions

FIGURE 14.1. Jasso's tripartite structure

14.2.1 Element I: The Framework

The middle column of Figure 14.1 lists the framework elements. In the case of justice analysis we have the following considerations.

Fundamental Questions: For *justice analysis* fundamental questions can include (page 405):

1. What do individuals and collectivities think is just, and why?
2. How do ideas of justice shape determination of actual situations?
3. What is the magnitude of the perceived injustice associated with given departures from perfect justice?
4. What are the behavioral and social consequences of perceived injustice?

Fundamental Actors: Jasso argues there are two fundamental actors in justice analysis: the observer and the rewardee. "The observer forms ideas of the just reward for particular rewardees and judges the justice or injustice of the actual rewards received by rewardees (where the observer may be among the rewardees)" (page 404).

Fundamental Quantities: For justice analysis, Jasso presents three fundamental quantities: the actual reward, the just reward, and the justice evaluation.

Fundamental Functions: Fundamental functions "become critical building blocks both for theoretical work, where they often appear as assumptions, and for empirical work, where they appear as relations to be estimated" (page 408). Each of the central questions are addressed by a function (or family of functions) that combines some of the fundamental quantities. "For justice analysis, the first central question is addressed by the just reward function, the third central question by the justice evaluation function, and so on". (page 406)

Jasso characterizes an agent's decision on what is just and not just (actual reward and just reward) with a particular functional form. The justice evaluation function's functional form reflects losses being given greater weight than gains: While the justice evaluation increases with the actual reward it does so at a decreasing marginal rate. A functional form characterizing these behavioral traits is the logarithm of the ratio of the actual reward to the just reward:

$$J = \theta \ln\left(\frac{A}{C}\right), \tag{14.1}$$

An Alternative Unification Framework

where J is the justice evaluation (the assessment by an observer that a rewardee is rewarded justly or unjustly); A is the rewardee's actual reward; C is the observer's idea of the just reward for the rewardee; and θ is the signature constant.

Jasso calls the sign of θ the *framing coefficient*. The reason is this coefficient "embodies the observer's framing of the reward as a good or as a bad (negative for a bad, positive for a good), and the absolute value of it called the expressiveness coefficient since it transforms the observer's experience of justice into the expression thereof" (page 408).

A critical matter in linking the theory and the nature of how people decide what is just resides in the log-ratio specification. Jasso notes that this particular specification of the justice evaluation function has been shown to be the only specification that satisfies both *scale-invariance and additivity*. These two conditions are desirable on substantive grounds in a justice evaluation function.

Fundamental Distributions

For the case of justice many distributions are available. Jasso explains:

> In the case of cardinal goods, the actual reward distribution and the just reward distribution can assume a variety of shapes, usually modeled by variates specified on the positive support, such as the lognormal and Pareto. And the justice evaluation distribution, reflecting the operation of both actual reward and just reward in the production of the justice evaluation, can assume a large variety of shapes as well. (page 410)

Jasso notes the distribution or distributions used will depend on how the justice evaluation is modeled. Many distributions fit, including "the negative exponential, the positive exponential, the Erlang, the normal, the logistic, the quasi-logistic, the Laplace, and the asymmetrical Laplace" (page 410).

Fundamental Matrices

Jasso shows the fundamental actors can be arrayed in matrix form and, therefore, applicable to applied statistical analysis. In the justice analysis example the three fundamental quantities are represented by "three fundamental matrices: the just reward matrix, the actual reward matrix (which in the absence of perception error collapses to a vector), and the justice evaluation matrix" (page 409).

In applying Eq. (14.1) to these matrices, Jasso provides the following notation (page 409). Let the observers be indexed by $i = 1, \ldots, N$ and rewardees by $r = 1, \ldots R$. Consequently, c_{ir}, a_{ir}, and j_{ir} represent the observer-specific and rewardee-specific just reward, actual reward, and justice evaluation, respectively. With these details we have the following matrices or vector.

1. The **just reward matrix**

$$C = \begin{bmatrix} c_{11} & c_{12} & c_{13} & \cdots & c_{1R} \\ c_{21} & c_{22} & c_{23} & \cdots & c_{2R} \\ c_{31} & c_{32} & c_{33} & \cdots & c_{3R} \\ \cdot & \cdot & \cdot & \cdots & \cdot \\ \cdot & \cdot & \cdot & \cdots & \cdot \\ \cdot & \cdot & \cdot & \cdots & \cdot \\ c_{N1} & c_{N2} & c_{N3} & \cdots & c_{NR} \end{bmatrix}$$

2. The **actual reward matrix**[2]

$$A = \begin{bmatrix} a_{11} & a_{12} & a_{13} & \cdots & a_{1R} \\ a_{21} & a_{22} & a_{23} & \cdots & a_{2R} \\ a_{31} & a_{32} & a_{33} & \cdots & a_{3R} \\ \cdot & \cdot & \cdot & \cdots & \cdot \\ \cdot & \cdot & \cdot & \cdots & \cdot \\ \cdot & \cdot & \cdot & \cdots & \cdot \\ a_{N1} & a_{N2} & a_{N3} & \cdots & a_{NR} \end{bmatrix}$$

3. The **justice evaluation matrix** is

$$J = \begin{bmatrix} j_{11} & j_{12} & j_{13} & \cdots & j_{1R} \\ j_{21} & j_{22} & j_{23} & \cdots & j_{2R} \\ j_{31} & j_{32} & j_{33} & \cdots & j_{3R} \\ \cdot & \cdot & \cdot & \cdots & \cdot \\ \cdot & \cdot & \cdot & \cdots & \cdot \\ \cdot & \cdot & \cdot & \cdots & \cdot \\ j_{N1} & j_{N2} & j_{N3} & \cdots & j_{NR} \end{bmatrix}.$$

Fundamental Contexts

The use of context is also a consideration. In justice analysis context-specific variation occurs in a variety of areas. Formalization of context considerations include: "b for the benefit under consideration, r for the type or identity of the rewardee, o for the observer, t for the time period, and s for the society" (page 410).

---

[2] Jasso indicates that "if there are no perception errors, the actual reward matrix collapses to a vector" (page 409).

$$a_{.r} = \begin{bmatrix} a_{.1} & a_{.2} & a_{.3} & \cdots & a_{.R} \end{bmatrix}$$

14.2.2 Element II: Theoretical Analysis

As shown in the left column of Figure 14.1 (the theoretical panel), Jasso distinguishes between two main kinds of theories – deductive theories and hierarchical (nondeductive) theories:

both deductive and hierarchical theories have a two-part structure, the first part containing an assumption or a set of assumptions – also called postulates... the assumption set should be as short as possible, and the second part [predictions and propositions] should be as large as possible and, indeed, always growing ... (page 411)

> **Deductive Theory:** Jasso argues deductive theory possesses "the starting assumption, perhaps in combination with other assumptions, is used as the starting point from which to deduce new implications. These implications (predictions) show the link of the process described by the starting assumption. They are observable, testable implications; as well. They are ceteris paribus implications, given the multifactor world in which we live" (page 411).

Deductive theories are assessed on both theoretical and empirical criteria.

Theoretical criteria focus on the structure of the theory. A good theory has a minimum of assumptions and a maximum of predictions... Moreover, in a good theory, the predictions constitute a mix of intuitive and nonintuitive predictions, and at least some of them are novel predictions... Empirical criteria for evaluating deductive theories focus, of course, on tests of the predictions. It may happen that early in the life of a theory, the assumption set grows. It may come to be seen that the single starting assumption is not sufficient by itself to yield many predictions but that the introduction of one or two additional assumptions produces unexpected synergies and an explosion of new predictions. Often, work with a particular set of assumptions leads to codification of special methods for deriving predictions. These special methods may focus on special representations of the assumptions or special kinds of tools. (page 412)

> **Hierarchical Theory:** Hierarchical theory differs from deductive theory. Even though "both kinds of theories begin with an assumption, in a hierarchical theory there is no deduction; instead, propositions are constructed by linking a term from the assumption with an observable term" (page 414). For justice analysis:

[A] hierarchical theory in which the justice evaluation function is an assumption might be used to construct propositions linking observables to the justice evaluation or to the proportion overrewarded or to the average underreward among the underrewarded. (page 414)

14.2.3 Element III: Empirical Analysis

Three forms of empirical analysis are identified in Figure 14.1.[3] Two involve testing the predictions deduced in deductive theories and the propositions constructed in hierarchical theories. "A third kind of empirical work, and sometimes the only empirical activity – especially in the early stages of development of a particular topical subfield – consists of basic measurement and estimation operations. The quantities identified in the framework are measured, the functions and distributions estimated, and the matrices populated" (page 422).

Testing the Predictions of Deductive Theories vs. Testing Propositions Construed in Hierarchical Theories
Jasso argues there are similarities and differences between tests for deductive and hierarchical theories. Deductive theories test predictions based on a well defined "path," but in the case of hierarchical theories tests focus on the propositions. "Testing the propositions constructed in hierarchical theories is less demanding in part because the proposition is already at least half observable, given that it was crafted by linking a term from a postulate to an observable term" (page 423).

On the other hand, when designing the specification and estimation procedures, both types of theories are equally demanding. Because many causal factors are in play, similar specification challenges exist, and both the nature of the specification and the quality of the data lead to similar estimation challenges.

A final aspect is interpreting the results. "Because in the construction of propositions in hierarchical theories no pathways have been specified, the knowledge gained from empirical tests is less informative in some sense than the results of tests of predictions, though nonetheless important" (page 424).

Extratheoretical Measurement and Estimation:
In Figure 14.1, this type of work is represented in the top row of the empirical analysis column. Jasso characterizes extratheoretical research as consisting "mainly of measurement and estimation of quantities and relations in the

---

[3] When it comes to determining the usefulness of a model, Jasso asserts:

> There is widespread agreement that rejecting a prediction is not a sufficient condition for rejecting a theory. Moreover, rejecting a prediction is not a necessary condition for rejecting a theory; even if all of a theory's predictions survive test unrejected, one may still reject the theory – in favor of a better theory, one with "excess corroborated content" (Lakatos 1970). Indeed, the view known as sophisticated falsificationism holds that it is not possible to judge the empirical merits of a theory in isolation; falsification requires comparison of the relative merits of two theories (Lakatos 1970, 116). (page 423)

framework" (page 424). Extratheoretical research activities are quite numerous and informative in justice analysis. They include (but are not limited to):

- Measuring the true and disclosed just rewards.
- Measuring the experienced and expressed justice evaluations.
- Estimating the just reward function and the principles of microjustice.
- Assessing the extent of interindividual disagreement on the principles of justice.
- Ascertaining whether individuals frame particular things as goods or as bads.
- Estimating the observer's expressiveness, comparing the just inequality with the actual inequality.
- Assessing just gender gaps and their underlying mechanisms.
- Measuring trends in overall injustice.
- Estimating the poverty and the inequality components of overall injustice.[4]

14.3 AN ILLUSTRATION OF EXTRATHEORETICAL RESEARCH: THE JUSTICE INDEX AND GENDER GAPS

In this illustration we apply aspects of Jasso's *tripartite structure* to extratheoretical research, and creating a justice measurement. Jasso examines justice indexes and gender gaps in the United States. The data are from the 1991 International Social Justice Project (ISJP). Respondents state their actual earnings and the earnings they think just for themselves (Jasso 1999).[5] Some *fundamental questions* pertain to the experience of injustice.

1. How pervasive is the experience of unjust underreward?
2. Does the experience of injustice vary systematically by gender?
3. Is the experience of injustice driven by poverty or by inequality?

To measure the individual's justice evaluation, the justice evaluation function introduced previously is used (Eq. (14.2)). It calculates the personal justice evaluation from the information provided on actual and just earnings. Jasso call this experienced justice evaluation. This type of evaluation omits the signature constant θ:

$$J = \ln\left(\frac{A}{C}\right). \tag{14.2}$$

---

[4] This list can be found in Jasso (2004, 424).
[5] The complete dataset of International Social Justice Project, 1991 and 1996, can be obtained from Inter-university Consortium for Political and Social Research (ICPSR) at the University of Michigan. The data of the US sample are available from the following website: uh.edu/hobby/eitm/eitmbook/. Interested readers can also download the STATA do-file to compute the results in Table 14.1 (Jasso 2004, 426).

This *fundamental function* includes the following implications:

1. In the state of perfect justice, the rewardee's actual reward A equals the perceived just reward C, such that the justice index $J = \ln(A/C) = \ln(1) = 0$.
2. The justice index is positive (i.e., $J > 0$) when the actual reward A is greater than the previous just reward C.
3. Implication 2 suggests that the rewardee perceives herself that she is over-benefit or under-burden in terms of her actual earnings. However, a rewardee would consider herself as under-benefit or over-burden when her actual reward A is less than her perceived just reward. It indicates that $J < 0$.

14.3.1 Justice Indexes

Two justice indexes are suggested by Jasso, but one is a special case of the other. The "main" justice index – $JI1$ – is defined as the arithmetic mean of the experienced justice evaluation: $JI1 = E(J) = E(\ln(A/C))$. "It can assume positive, negative, and zero values. A positive value has the interpretation that the center of gravity of the distribution of justice evaluations lies in the over-reward region, and a negative value indicates that the center of gravity lies in the under-reward region" (page 245).

Decomposition Methods

Along with these distributional characteristics, Jasso (1999) also presents two decomposition methods:

- *Mean-inequality decomposition*
- *Reality-ideology decomposition.*

Mean-Inequality Decomposition

For the method of mean-inequality decomposition, the argument is that the justice index $JI1$ can be calculated as the sum of justice evaluation about the mean $JI1_{Mean}$ and the justice evaluation about the inequality $JI1_{Ineq}$.

Note that the formula of justice index can be rewritten as the log of the ratio of geometric mean of actual reward to geometric mean of just reward:

$$JI1 = E[\ln(A/C)] = \ln[G(A)/G(C)], \tag{14.3}$$

where $E(\cdot)$ represents the operator of computing arithmetic means (or expected values), that is, $E(X) = \left(\sum_{n=1}^{N} x_n\right)/N$. $G(\cdot)$ is the geometric mean operator where $G(X) = \left(\Pi_{n=1}^{N} x_n\right)^{1/N}$.

An Alternative Unification Framework

To calculate the component of inequality in the justice index, Jasso considers Atkinson's (1975) measure I, which is defined as:

$$I(X) = 1 - [G(X)/E(X)]. \tag{14.4}$$

According to Eq. (14.4), if the geometric mean equals the arithmetic mean in a dataset, that is, $G(X) = E(X)$, then Atkinson's measure $I(X)$ equals zero. This result indicates there is no inequality observed in the data.

However, the value of Atkinson's measure increases as the distribution of the observations becomes more unequal. We obtain the geometric mean from Eq. (14.4):

$$G(X) = E(X)[1 - I(X)], \tag{14.5}$$

where the geometric mean can be written as a function of arithmetic mean and Atkinson's measure.

Finally, expressing the geometric means for actual reward $G(A)$ and just reward $G(C)$ – according to Eq. (14.5) – we can rewrite the justice index $JI1$ as follows:

$$JI1 = \ln\left\{\frac{E(A)[1-I(A)]}{E(C)[1-I(C)]}\right\}. \tag{14.6}$$

As a result, Eq. (14.6) can be expressed as the sum of two components:

$$\begin{aligned}JI1 &= \ln\left[\frac{E(A)}{E(C)}\right] + \ln\left[\frac{1-I(A)}{1-I(C)}\right] \\ &= JI1_{Mean} + JI1_{Ineq},\end{aligned} \tag{14.7}$$

where $JI1_{Mean} \equiv \ln[E(A)/E(C)]$, and $JI1_{Ineq} \equiv \ln\{[1-I(A)]/[1-I(C)]\}$.

The justice index, about the mean $JI1_{Mean}$, represents an (arithmetic) average value of the actual rewards relative to that of the perceived just rewards in the sample. On the other hand, the justice index about the inequality $JI1_{Ineq}$ indicates the difference between the inequality of the actual rewards and the inequality of the just rewards in the sample.[6]

Reality-Ideology Decomposition

While inequality measures portray factual inequality, they do not include knowledge of individual-specific ideas of justice. Jasso, therefore, suggests the justice index $JI1$ can be interpreted in an alternative way. She distinguishes between injustice due to reality $JI1_{Reality}$ and injustice due to ideology

---

[6] Jasso (1999) argues that the justice index about the mean $JI1_{Mean}$ is the perceived injustice driven by scarcity or poverty, while the second component of justice is due to inequality in the distribution of income.

$JI1_{Ideology}$. Injustice due to reality is based on how a person observes their actual income in relation to the mean and the inequality of the income distribution. Injustice due to ideology is based on what a person perceives to be just income in terms of the mean and inequality distribution.

Hence, the justice index can be rewritten as follows:

$$JI1 = \ln\{E(A)[1 - I(A)]\} - \ln\{E(A)[1 - I(A)]\}$$
$$= JI1_{Reality} - JI1_{Ideology}, \qquad (14.8)$$

where $JI1_{Reality} \equiv \ln\{E(A)[1 - I(A)]\}$ and $JI1_{Ideology} \equiv \ln\{E(A)[1 - I(A)]\}$. Equation (14.8) shows that $JI1$ is equal to the reality component minus the ideology component (as also shown in the formula in Table 14.1).

An Alternative Index

The second index – $JI1^*$ – is a special case of $JI1$ in which the just rewards (i.e., C) equal the mean rewards (i.e., $E(A)$). Intuitively, this measure arises when justice is equality. Hence, we can express $JI1^*$ as follows:

$$JI1^* = JI1\big|_{C=E(A)} = E\left[\ln\left(\frac{A}{E(A)}\right)\right].$$

Jasso (2004, 425) argues this measure is consistent with other sociological interpretations in the literature (Blau 1960, 1964; Blalock 1967). It can be applied to small homogeneous groups or utopian communities.

14.3.2 Results

The results, presented as five components, are in Table 14.1. The component are:

BASE DATA This includes the average actual earnings, the average just earnings, and the sample size, both for the US sample as a whole and for gender-specific subsamples.

JUSTICE INDEX $JI1$ ITS DECOMPOSITIONS The results indicate there is four percent more injustice for women (-0.236) than men (-0.207). Recall from Eq. 14.7, $JI1$ is the sum of the mean component and the inequality component: this "first decomposition of $JI1$ makes it possible to distinguish between two components of overall injustice, injustice due to the mean, and injustice due to inequality" (page 425).

Jasso notes these results have rival interpretations. "Depending on the context, the mean component may be interpreted as a scarcity component or a poverty component. The mean component is larger than the inequality component for both men and women; however, the relative magnitudes differ

TABLE 14.1. *Justice indexes and gender gaps: US sample, ISJP 1991 (Jasso 2004, 426)*

	Men	Women	All
Base Data			
Average actual earning ($)	36,950	20,084	28,847
Average just earning ($)	43,137	25,106	34,474
Number of obs	438	405	843
Justice Index $JI1$ and Its Decompositions[a]			
$JI1$	−0.207	−0.236	−0.221
Decomposition into Mean and Inequality Components			
$JI1 = JI1_{Mean} + JI1_{Ineq}$			
Mean component $JI1_{Mean}$	−0.155	−0.223	−0.178
Inequality component $JI1_{Ineq}$	−0.052	−0.013	−0.043
Decomposition into Reality and Ideology Components			
$JI1 = JI1_{Reality} - JI1_{Ideology}$			
Reality component	10.178	9.637	9.918
Ideology component	10.385	9.873	10.139
Justice Index $JI1^*$ and Its Gender Decomposition[b]			
$JI1^*$	−0.34	−0.271	−0.352
Decomposition into Within-Gender and Between-Gender Components			
Within-gender component			−0.307
Between-gender component			−0.0453
Gender Gaps in Actual and Just Earnings			
Actual gender gap			0.544
Just gender gap			0.582
Special Relation between Mean Component of $JI1$ and Ratio of Gender Gaps			
$JI1_{Female,Mean} - JI1_{Male,Mean} = \ln$ (Actual Gender Gap/Just Gender Gap)			−0.0684

Notes:
[a] Justice index $JI1$ is defined as $JI1 = E(J) = E[\ln(A/C)]$, where A = the rewardee's actual reward, and C = the observer's idea of the just reward fro the rewardee (Jasso 2004).
[b] Justice index $JI1^*$ is defined as $JI1^* = E(J^*) = E\{\ln[A/E(A)]\}$, where A = the rewardee's actual reward (Jasso 2004).

considerably" (page 425). Seventy-five percent (i.e., −0.155/−0.207) of overall injustice for men is due to scarcity, but for women it is a higher proportion, 94 percent (i.e., −0.223/ − 0.236). Note, too, nearly all of injustice for women is due to scarcity.

The reality-ideology decomposition, as defined in Eq. 14.8 show there are differences between reality and ideology. "Among both women and men, the ideology component exceeds the reality component, producing the negative $JI1$. As already known from the magnitudes of $JI1$, the discrepancy is larger among women than among men" (page 425).

Justice Index JI1 and Its Gender Decomposition

Jasso notes that "if equality was used as the standard for just earnings, experienced injustice would be greater, substantially so among men (−0.207 versus −0.340 among men and −0.236 versus −0.271 among women)" (page 426). Within-group (gender) and between-group (gender) decompositions add further information. Recall that $JI1^*$ is equal to the sum of the two components. The within-group (gender) component is "the weighted sum of the group-specific values of $JI1^*$, where the weights represent the fraction of the population in each group" (page 426). The calculation for the between-group (gender) component is "the weighted sum of the log of the ratio of the group mean to the overall mean." The results in Table 14.1 show the within-gender component is much larger than the between-gender component, constituting 87 percent of the overall $JI1^*$: There is more variability within genders than between genders.

Gender Gaps in Actual and Just Earnings

On page 426, Jasso finds the "gender gaps, defined as the ratio of the women's average to the men's average, includes both actual earnings and just earnings. As shown, and as evident from the base data the gender gap is greater for actual earnings than for just earnings." (i.e., 0.544 vs. 0.582 according to Table 14.1.)

Special Relation between Mean Component of JI1 and Ratio of Gender Gaps

An important finding was "the usual way of measuring gender gaps is completely inattentive to within-gender inequality" (page 427). The reason for this conclusion is found in Table 14.1. This gender gap ratio "provides a numerical approximation to an exact relation between aspects of the justice index and aspects of the gender gap. The signed difference between the women's mean component of $JI1$ and the men's mean component of $JI1$ is equal to the log of the ratio of the actual gender gap to the just gender gap" (page 427). The just gender gap exceeds the actual gender gap and it is the just gender gap that captures the higher variation in within-gender inequality.

To sum up, some highlights from the justice index analysis include the following:

1. In a 1991 United States sample women experienced more injustice, on average, than men.
2. For both genders, scarcity (poverty) is a more important factor in perceiving injustice than inequality. Women, however, reveal the factor of scarcity is more important to them than to men.
3. Average "just" earnings exceed average actual earnings. Women have a greater gap than men.

14.4 SUMMARY

Due to its unifying properties there are several ways to build on the justice index. To begin, this index should be used in a comparative setting over time. The sample used here is only for the United States in 1991, but expanding the sample to many countries and many years is a logical next step. A second extension would be to sample the same individuals over time to see if their views on justice evolve and what the context was for the changes in their justice evaluation. A third consideration is to continue with other subgroup breakdowns. Gender is important but factors such as age and education, amongst other factors, can also provide new insights on how people judge something to be just. A fourth issue would be to determine the relation between the justice index and indicators of societal and political stability and the overall legitimacy of a political, social, and economic system. A final consideration is a determination of whether a justice index based on "equality" can be extended to include a justice index based on an individual's sense of freedom and liberty.

14.5 APPENDIX

The use of theory to create valid indices can be found in other social science disciplines as well. Here we demonstrate – using a totally unrelated topic and measurement challenge – how theory plays a role in the construction of measures of the money supply – monetary aggregates. We relate the process and the tools involved and the challenges that are faced.

The tools introduced in this process are: (1) Aggregation Theory and (2) Index Number Theory.

14.5.1 Linking Instruments to Outcomes: The Case of Monetary Aggregates

Monetary aggregate measures are as straightforward as adding the components together: so-called simple-sum aggregates. But components can also be aggregated applying microeconomic reasoning to aggregation theory and index number theory. These "Divisia aggregates" possess important policy implications. They provide a more accurate reading on changes and the expected consequences of monetary policy than the rival simple-sum aggregates.

An example where inaccurate measurement affected the conduct of monetary policy occurred during the recession in the early 1980s. Policy, it could be argued, prolonged the recession. In reviewing the behavior of these rival monetary aggregate measures, William Barnett (1984) concluded:

> Monetary policy during the sample period induced slower and more volatile monetary growth than was indicated by the official simple sum aggregates... Because monetary policy, as indicated by Divisia monetary aggregates, was tighter than indicated by

the official aggregates, our results provide an illustration of how inattention to well-established statistical theory can lead to policymaking that may be less effective than it might be. (page 171)

A decoupling between instruments and the money stock has, at times, had tragic consequences, including the Great Depression.[7] One reason for the discrepancy is the public reduces its demand deposits but holds more currency. This contracts the money stock and the supply of loanable funds. At the same time, however, the shift from demand deposits to currency increases the level of the monetary base (provided reserves do not decline by a commensurate proportion, the currency increases).

Measurement and Spurious Outcomes: Aggregation Error
While it is well known to students of monetary policy that the official monetary aggregates are based on simple sums of the component quantities, a valid simple sum aggregate requires the components be perfect substitutes. We cannot add apples to oranges to get an aggregate of oranges; it simply makes no sense to say a dollar in currency provides the same monetary services as a dollar in Series E bonds. They are not perfect substitutes.[8] The impact of aggregation error grows as the number of components increases.[9]

In sum, the effect aggregation error fostered by imperfect substitution cannot be overemphasized. Simply combining components in a monetary aggregate can contain so much aggregation error that it gives the appearance of endogeneity (responding to business cycle conditions or interest rates). A more correct aggregation index accounting for internal substitution effects reduces the potential for a spurious diagnosis on endogeneity.[10]

---

[7] It is possible for monetary instruments, such as the monetary base (high powered money) to exhibit behavior that is inversely related (or not related at all) to the money stock (MlB for example). Indeed, this occurred during the Great Depression (1929–1933). Friedman and Schwartz (1963, 332–333) document that deposit reserve and deposit-currency ratios fell during this period while the monetary base exhibited an increase. Up until that period, however, Friedman and Schwartz assert the relation between the money stock and the monetary base was strong.

[8] Taken to its logical extreme, a government that used simple sum monetary aggregates could monetize its entire debt holdings and have no change in the money stock as government securities and currency would be considered substitutes for each other.

[9] The problem of imperfect substitution is less severe for the narrower monetary aggregate because the respective components tend to be more closely related. In comparative analysis, one would expect that since both simple sum and Divisia aggregates are constructed differently they should exhibit different behavior. This suspicion is confirmed (see Barnett 1982; Barnett et al. 1984). There are exceptions, however. Barnett et al. (1984) have found that at lower levels of aggregation, simple sum aggregates can, under certain tests, outperform Divisia aggregates.

[10] By way of example, consider an increase in interest rates (which do correspond to the business cycle). This would have an impact on user costs between various monetary assets (components of a monetary aggregate) that are either rate regulated or not.

14.5.2 Relating Theory to Measurement

In an effort to address these challenges, William Barnett derived the theoretical link between monetary theory and economic aggregation theory (Barnett 1980). Barnett's aggregates, known as Divisia aggregates, have microeconomic foundations.[11] In effect, he replaced the ad-hoc component summation and weighting schemes with a monetary aggregation method that relates component quantities to their *user costs* (e.g., the rental price of holding an asset at some point in time).

The result is Divisia monetary aggregates change under certain circumstances, but the dynamics are linked to agent (public) behavior. For example, the aggregate responds when the change in the interest rate has a microeconomic effect (in this case an income effect); otherwise, all changes in interest rates will lead to pure substitution effects along the indifference curve. The implication then is the Divisia aggregate is not dependent on interest rate or business cycle fluctuations.[12] The effects are accounted for by internal substitution.[13]

Defining User Costs

Recall the fundamental measurement problem resides in the simple-sum data being constructed in such a way as to make it vulnerable to external shocks, which undoubtedly leads to spurious inferences. To account for these distinct component values, Barnett (1980) derived a user cost formula for monetary assets (components):

$$\Pi_{i,t} = \frac{P_t^*(R_t - r_{i,t})(1 - \tau_t)}{1 + R_t(1 - \tau_t)},$$

---

[11] Divisia aggregates "dominate" simple sum aggregates in comparative statistical tests (Barnett 1982). The results, to date, show that Divisia aggregates not only give different qualitative results but they also have superior properties for statistical inference.

[12] In more technical language, the weights of components should show increasing dispersion, which would also have a commensurate affect on the Divisia quantity variance. However, the dependence of the monetary aggregate on interest rate fluctuations (or business cycle fluctuations) will be greater or less depending on the difference between the dispersion in weights (shares) of components and the user cost price variance. If increases in dispersion of the weights (shares) of components are matched by an increase (of roughly equal proportion) in the user cost price variance, then the Divisia aggregate quantity disturbance should be relatively undisturbed. These products are expenditures on the respective components. The expenditures on each component are then divided by the total expenditures on all components of the aggregate to determine the share of a given component. These shares are then averaged between the current and preceding month. Each individual share is used in "weighting" the growth rate for each appropriate individual component, which are then summed up to determine the growth rate of the aggregate. On the other hand, simple sum aggregates, because the components are assumed to be perfect substitutes, fail to internally substitute relative user cost changes (decisions made by agents). This weakness creates spurious findings.

[13] In an empirical test on Divisia second moments, Barnett et al. (1984) found exactly this result. Divisia aggregates are not endogenous to business cycle fluctuations or interest rate fluctuations.

where $\Pi_{i,t}$ is the user cost for monetary asset i during period t; R_t represents the expected yield on bonds during period t; $r_{i,t}$ is the expected nominal holding period yield on monetary asset i during period t; P_t^* is cost of living index for period t; and τ_t denotes the marginal tax rate on earnings for period t. This user cost formula represents the rental price for holding a monetary asset for period t. User costs are crucial because as prices they are readily applicable for statistical index number theory. Statistical index number theory is important since it can be used to account for component dispersion.

Statistical index numbers are functions of component prices and quantities for a respective aggregate. Let q_t represent a vector of quantities consumed of the component goods and p_t represent a vector of component prices. To derive correct price and quantity aggregates we simply make the aggregate a function $f(p_t, q_t, p_{t-1}, q_{t-1})$, which is based on values at period t and $t-1$. This gives quotients for rates of change in prices and quantities during period t.

Since we now have respective component prices and quantities, it is appropriate to determine the approximate growth rate for the monetary aggregate. Let $m_{i,t}$ be the quantity of monetary asset i during period t, and $s_{i,t} = (\Pi_{i,t} m_{i,t}) / \left(\sum_{k=1}^{N} \Pi_{k,t} m_{k,t}\right)$ be the user cost "weighted average" (rental price) of the component i during period t. Finally, let Q_t^D be the monetary aggregate itself.

With these identities we now derive the Divisia index p for monetary aggregate Q_t^D:

$$\ln Q_t^D - \ln Q_{t-1}^D = \sum_{i=1}^{N} s_{i,t}^* (\ln m_{i,t} - \ln m_{i,t-1}),$$

where:

$$s_{i,t}^* = \frac{1}{2}(s_{i,t} + s_{i,t-1}).$$

This Divisia aggregate is now the user cost weighted average of component quantities. Its form approximates Diewert's (1976) superlative index number class, which is extremely accurate, up to a third-order error term. Divisia aggregates, by virtue of their construction, yield findings qualitatively different and statistically superior to simple sum aggregates.

14.5.3 Aggregation Theory

Aggregation theory is a branch of economic theory that creates macroeconomic data from microeconomic data. Aggregation theory's virtue is that it ensures that aggregated (macroeconomic) data will behave exactly *as if* it were elementary, disaggregated data. From aggregation theory we can derive a well-specified utility function. And from this utility function we can specify marginal

An Alternative Unification Framework

utilities from each component, which is vital in the construction of an economic aggregate. We can also aggregate up, given certain assumptions about utility functions. In short, aggregation theory derives aggregates from an optimization procedure that maximizes a utility function subject to a budget constraint.

To get a monetary aggregate to behave as an elementary good we derive a utility function. For ease of discussion we must introduce the following notation and conventions. Let the consumption space be represented by the nonnegative Euclidean-orthant:

$$\Lambda^n = \{(x_1, \ldots, x_n) = X, R^n; X > 0^n\},$$

where R^n is Euclidean space and 0^n is an n-dimensional null vector. The constraint $X > 0^n$ implies at least one of the components in $X : x_i > 0$. Let $S = \{1, 2, \ldots, n\}$ is a set of integers and $S_1, \ldots, S_q$ is a partition of the set S into q subsets. Therefore:

$$S_1 \cup S_2 \cup \ldots S_q = S,$$

$$S_i \cap S_j = \emptyset,$$

for $i \neq j$, where $i, j = 1, \ldots, q$, and:

$$S_i \neq \emptyset,$$

for $i = 1, \ldots, q$. Now partition the consumption space Λ^n as a Cartesian product with a subspace corresponding to a given partition:

$$\Lambda^n = \Lambda^{n_1} \times \Lambda^{n_2} \times \ldots \times \Lambda^{n_q}.$$

Thus, a component vector $X \in \Lambda^n$ and a strictly positive price vector can be broken down into:

$$X = (x_{n_1}, x_{n_2}, \ldots, x_{n_q}),$$

and:

$$P = (p_{n_1}, p_{n_2}, \ldots, p_{n_q}).$$

The preference relations of the price and component vectors are represented by utility functions $U: \Lambda^n \to R$. Utility functions are quadratic and as such we further assume that U is continuously twice differentiable and quasi-concave with a strictly positive marginal utility. For a utility function to exist, a change in the consumption of one component must not induce a change in consumption in another component. That is, the marginal rates of substitution (cross elasticities) of each component are independent of each other.

With these conventions in place we can now proceed to a two-stage budgetary decision. The purpose here is to establish a real-world disaggregated utility function and aggregate up to a shadow world, which behaves *as if* it were a consumer maximizing utility subject to a budget constraint.

A two-stage budgeting decision takes the following form:

$$\max U(x),$$

subject to:

$$px = m,$$

where $x \in \Lambda$, p is is a strictly positive price vector, and m is total income. With this simple optimization function we represent the consumer budget in two stages.

Stage One:

$$\max U = F\left(U^1, U^2, \ldots, U^q\right),$$

subject to:

$$\sum_i^q p^i x^i = m.$$

Stage Two:

$$\max U^i\left(x_{n_i}\right),$$

subject to:

$$p_{n_i} X_{n_i} = p^i u^i\left(X_{n_i}\right),$$

for $i = 1, 2, \ldots, q$.

In the first stage the consumer allocates the total income m to the component groups (blocks) $\{U^i(X_{n_i})\}$; this establishes a budget constraint. The second stage involves the specific expenditure on each component that makes up a given block. If the results in the utility function are the same as the in the two-stage budgeting decision, then the solution is consistent or exact and we have a well-defined utility function.

Consistency is a necessary and sufficient condition for establishing an equivalent relation from the real (disaggregated) world to the shadow (aggregated) world. Green (1964) set out the conditions by which consistency (or exactness) could hold:

Theorem 4. *Green's Theorem 4: A two stage budgeting decision is exact and* $\exists U^i(X_{n_i})$ *and* p^i *iff* $U(x)$ *is weakly separable in the partition* $S_1, \ldots, S_q$ *and the functions* U^i *are linearly homogeneous with respect to* X^n.

Formally, this "blockwise weak separability" condition is defined as:

Definition 5. $U(x)$ is weakly separable with respect to the partition $S_1, \ldots, S_q$ if $\frac{\partial [U_i(x)/U_j(x)]}{\partial X_k} = 0$, $\forall i, j \in S_q$ and $K \notin S_q$.

The existence of weak separability is derived from Gorman (1953):

Theorem 6. *Gorman's Theorem:* $U(x)$ *is weakly, separable with respect to the partition* $S_1, \ldots, S_q$ *iff* $\exists F : R^n \to R$ *and* $U^i : \Lambda^{n_i} \to R$ *such that* $U(x) = F[U^1(x_{n_1}), U^2(x_{n_2}), \ldots, U^q(x_{n_q})]$.

From Green's Theorem 4 the weak separability condition allows for the establishment of a well-defined utility function. In addition to the weak separability condition, Green's theorem imposes one more condition – linear homogeneity.[14] Linear homogeneity (homotheticity) is a necessary and sufficient condition for the existence of aggregate prices. It ensures that exact expenditure values feed into the second stage budgeting decision from the first stage.

However, linear homogeneity is a severe assumption, which cannot be justified empirically. Linear homogeneity violates Engel's law because it produces income elasticities for every good that must be unity. The implication then is expenditure shares of all goods are independent of income and only dependent on relative prices: Poor people spend the same proportion of income on food as rich people. This is clearly implausible.

There are many ways to get around this problem. The key is to devise a method that will allow for aggregation across consumers but will not also imply unitary price and income elasticities. Affine transformations present such an accommodation.[15] An Affine transformation has the simple form:

$$T(p) = A(p) + B,$$

where A is a linear function and B is a fixed vector. The difference between a linearly homogeneous transformation and the Affine transformation is the fixed vector B. In Figure 14.2 the difference is demonstrated by the fact the homothetic transformation passes through the origin. The Affine transformation, in contrast, begins at some fixed point in the northeast quadrant (b_i). This difference has important qualitative implications. A vector passing through the origin means consumers have zero consumption.

On the other hand, a vector beginning at some fixed point indicates consumers have a survival set, which they cannot consume less than. Yet, the

---

[14] Linear homogeneity means that when all components are increased k-fold, the aggregate itself also increases k-fold.
[15] If the quantity aggregator function is not linearly homogeneous (i.e., nonlinear Engel curves) then we cannot use two-stage budgeting for the purposes of finding quantity aggregator functions. Distance functions are used in this case (see Barnett 1987, 145–149).

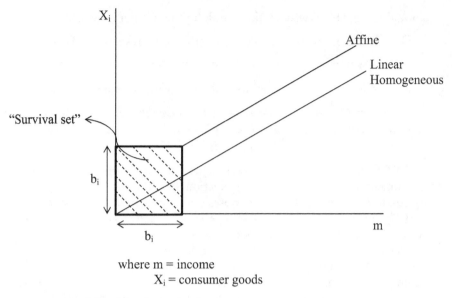

FIGURE 14.2. Affine transformation

Affine transformation still allows for linear homogeneity beyond b_i so that we can aggregate across consumers. Of no less importance is the fixed vector b_i. It represents a region where price and income elasticities are indeterminate; therefore, price and income elasticities are not unitary.

The Affine transformation introduces a new stage in the budgeting process. The constraint, $px = m$, must now be transformed to $\hat{m}$, where $\hat{m} = m - p'b$. The variable m represents supernumerary income, which the consumer uses as a budget constraint.

With the two (three) stage budget procedure and Green's Theorem 4, corrected for homotheticity, an aggregator function (or economic aggregate) is said to be "exact." Consumers treat the aggregate *as if* it were made up of elementary goods. At this stage, however, we only know how to block components comprising an aggregate function. To estimate an aggregate (or aggregator) function we must use index number theory.

14.5.4 Index Number Theory

Recall Barnett's Divisia aggregates are considered superlative index numbers. The specific properties they hold for accuracy require a brief discussion of index number theory. Index number theory is used to approximate aggregator functions. Index numbers come in two different forms: functional and statistical. Functional index numbers estimate aggregator functions using empirical

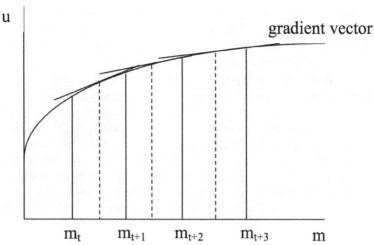

FIGURE 14.3. Gradient

estimates for unknown parameters. On the other hand, statistical index numbers are parameter free; they depend on component prices and quantities.[16]

For many years there was controversy as to which index numbers provided a better approximation to an economic aggregate (aggregator function). The two index numbers are necessarily competing with different strengths and weaknesses. Because functional forms are dependent on parameter specification, they are necessarily ad-hoc and data dependent approximations.

Conversely, statistical index numbers are dependent on prices and quantities to reveal a current point on an aggregator function. Yet statistical index numbers, because they are contingent on prices and quantities, they cannot provide a valid second-order approximation to track an aggregate function. They are useful in the local sense only.

However, in 1976 Diewert proved that statistical index numbers were linked to functional index numbers. To prove this, Diewert utilized a modified Taylor expansion of the following form:

$$\nabla f(m^1) - \nabla f(m^0) = \frac{1}{2} \left[\nabla f(m^1) + \nabla f(m^0) \right]^T (M^1 - M^0),$$

where $\nabla f(m^n)$ is a gradient vector of function f estimated at m^n.

---

[16] Functional index numbers $= F(x, \theta)$ and statistical index numbers $= F(x, p)$, where $x =$ quantities of commodities, $\theta =$ unknown parameter(s), and $p =$ prices. By their construction, functional index numbers require data for one period only; whereas, statistical index numbers require data for more than one period.

Diewert's contribution was to seek many local approximations in small neighborhoods. From a graphical standpoint (Figure 14.3), we see how Diewert's index numbers could then track an aggregator function. Intervals were set to cover some average distance between two points $(m_t + m_{t-1})/2$, where this approximation was across a sufficiently small neighborhood $(m_t - m_{t-1})$ yielding a third-order remainder. In short, it is extremely accurate.[17]

In sum, index number theory and, in particular, superlative index numbers, are means of estimating (given prices and quantities) specific points of an aggregator function (economic aggregate). We know these estimates are exact in the Diewert sense. A flexible aggregator function can obtain first and second order derivatives. Marginal utilities can be considered as quasi-weights, which implies that these weights are theoretically and empirically driven and not ad-hoc. They must be blockwise weakly separable and Affine linearly homogeneous.

---

[17] Diewert's method has a residual $(m_t - m_{t-1})$ smaller than rounding error, which speaks favorably about its accuracy. Quantity indices of the Diewert variety that are exact over a second-order approximation to a homothetic function are known as superlative. Superlative index numbers, therefore, can always attain the current value of a flexible aggregator function.

15

Conclusion

We believe significant scientific progress can be made by unifying formal and empirical modeling. This advancement will require ending existing barriers between formal modelers and empirical modelers. As the 2002 NSF EITM Report concluded, practices must change:

> formal modelers must subject their theories to closely related tests while, at the same time, empirical modelers must formalize their models prior to conducting any of the available statistical tests. The point is not to sacrifice logically coherent and mathematical models. Breakthroughs in theory can be enhanced with the assistance of empirical models in experimental and non-experimental settings. (page 13)

This methodological unification will also lead to more rigorous representations of behavioral concepts: Application of the EITM framework means new and better ways will be discovered to model human behavior. And the repeated application of competing analogues raises the possibility of building a cumulative process in thinking how humans act, but now with a sense there is a rigor in putting these new behavioral developments to the test.[1] The "new" developments in bounded rationality, learning, and evolutionary modeling are indeed important in EITM, but they are by no means the only ones.

Recall the EITM framework is a response to current and on going methodological practices. Some methodological practices inhibit the cumulation of knowledge due, in part, to the ongoing disconnect between formal and empirical modelers. The status quo is one where isolation of fields and subfields is dominant. Such compartmentalization exacerbates the separation between theoretical and empirical models impairing the potential for scientific advancement.

---

[1] A key challenge is to improve upon step 3 in the EITM framework. New strategies with greater specificity in linking formal and empirical analogues are no doubt necessary.

Along these lines, it is also important to avoid the trap of conducting current debates using our past and current training as the basis for the debate. Straight jacketed thinking translates to an evasion in dealing with known weaknesses in our current practices. Instead, what is needed is the belief that unifying modeling practices and tools can be pushed further and new ideas survive – for a limited time – if they improve upon past and current practice.

These new innovations are certain to possess properties we know to enhance understanding, whether it involves measurement, better ways to characterize human behavior, sampling, and more. But bear in mind that the new ways of analyzing important and numerous social science research questions must also be designed to preserve and enhance the dialogue between the inner workings of a system and tests.

15.1 CURRENT AND FUTURE IMPLEMENTATION CHALLENGES

As we noted – at its most elementary level – EITM is a framework for unifying formal and empirical analysis. Even though methodological unification of this kind is not new in social-behavioral science, barriers exist concerning the purpose and application of EITM (e.g., "that is what we are doing anyway"). Short-term barriers for adopting EITM include a basic misunderstanding of what EITM means. Longer term barriers include rigid training traditions within and across social and behavioral science disciplines. The sources of resistance are not surprising and we referred to them earlier. They include (1) the intellectual investment one has made and the additional investment that would have to be made; (2) training differences; and (3) research practice.

15.1.1 Instruction: A Reorientation

A direct way and means to execute generational changes requires establishing new ways to instill formal and empirical modeling competency. Without that foundation any substantial progress in the use of EITM in social sciences research is limited. Ideally, reorientation in training involves two parts:

1. Adding courses to ensure sufficient coverage of both formal and empirical tools – and appropriate competency testing.
2. Coherent sequencing of the courses so that skills increase over time.

There are various ways to fulfill these requirements. A first step is requiring graduate students to take one full year (usually) of mathematics for social scientists. However, what is not typically done is to continue reinforcement of this training. To that end, mathematical (quantitative) competency in these graduate courses can be demonstrated not only in these foundational courses but also in qualifying examinations in the summer after the first year of coursework. Students must clear this hurdle before being allowed to proceed with their Ph.D. It is safe to say this latter component would be novel in most social science disciplines.

This mathematical (and quantitative) approach would also be reinforced in revised substantive courses, where examples of methodological unification are used. Not only substantive survey courses but methodological capstone courses integrating formal and empirical modeling can serve this purpose. These capstone courses could include a data gathering component in EITM. Since new technologies have an impact on theoretical implications, the curricula must reflect the fact that theory guides data collection. Further momentum would be reflected in these new syllabi, reflecting the use of EITM.

15.1.2 Supporting Science, Policy, and Society

In assessing metrics to evaluate whether EITM was making a meaningful contribution to improving social science practices, the 2002 NSF EITM Report stated the following:

How will progress be measured? There are several performance indicators, including the number of articles that use formal and empirical analysis in the major professional journals. Another measurable indicator is the number of NSF grant proposal submissions by faculty and graduate students (doctoral dissertations) that use both approaches. (page 13)

This increasing presence can be evident in the increasing number of journal articles, dissertation proposals, books, and research grants. While these metrics represent "inputs," they still have ramifications since they represent how merging formal and empirical analysis contributes to transforming how researchers think about problems and undertake intellectual risks in synthesizing the two. The work and achievements of Elinor Ostrom do, however, illustrate the payoffs in "reaching outside your comfort zone" and partnering with others who have skill sets you would like to learn and build on.

Ultimately, the most important metric is improving our stock of knowledge. Measuring improvement in our quality of knowledge is not straightforward. EITM – methodological unification – is a bridge for establishing transparency and undertaking a dialogue, but a scholars ability to see and describe the patterns and puzzles in new and more accurate ways is still the driving force. To put it another way, this dialogue provides a coherent way to take every idea further, where something new is shown to be better than what has been established.

Earlier we asserted EITM can improve current methodological practice. But, what about the policy value and social value? Consider the research in macro political economy since the 1930s. Beginning with the work of Jan Tinbergen, efforts were made to assist policymakers in devising ways to stabilize business cycles.[2] The result was the volatility of business cycles has been reduced in the past 50 years – even when we take current economic conditions into consideration. In addition, the duration of economic expansions has increased in the United States (Granato and Wong 2006) and around the world (Sheffrin 1988f). In retrospect these:

> salutary economic events occurred at approximately the same time that quantitative political economic methodologies emphasized and were judged on their ability to produce identified and invariant predictions. Is this relation a coincidence? A good case can be made that the guidelines of the Cowles Commission and successor methodologies has contributed to changes in business cycle behavior (since World War II). And while they have received their share of criticism, these quantitative tools have assisted policymakers by providing useful knowledge and creating a systematic scientific justification for their actions. (Granato 2005, 13)

EITM-inspired efforts that lead to greater cooperation between the various sciences can enhance policy acumen and aid society. Prior ways of conducting policy research – where integration between the social sciences, natural sciences, and engineering is rare – can lead to misleading predictions and policy failure. In particular, downplaying or ignoring behavioral responses to various phenomena and new technologies may have negative ramifications for public policies regarding energy (i.e., the smart grid), education, health, and numerous other important policy areas where human behavior and human response are factors.

Because it places an emphasis on modeling and testing analogues of human behavior, EITM translates at a technical level understood by the natural sciences, the physical sciences, and engineering. This potential for enhanced understanding and cooperation can be key in policy success. Among the most important broader impacts of EITM – and one with the most lasting consequences – will be simply raising awareness of the complexities and challenges involved with the linkage of models and tests to the study of social, behavioral, and economic processes.

---

[2] The study of business cycles – a public policy and societal concern – was the impetus for the development of econometrics. Economic historian Mary Morgan (1990) points out that econometrician Jan Tinbergen's first:

> ... macrodynamic model was built in response to a request from the Dutch Economic Association to present a paper in October 1936 on policies to relieve the depression... His model is a remarkable piece of work, involving not only building and estimating a model of the whole economy but also using the model to simulate the likely impact of various policies. (page 102)

Bibliography

Abel, Andrew B., Ben S. Bernanke, and Dean Croushore. 2012. *Macroeconomics*. Boston, MA: Pearson.

Achen, Christopher H. 2002. "Toward a New Political Methodology: Microfoundations and ART." *Annual Review of Political Science* 5 (1): 423–450.

——— 2005. "Let's Put Garbage-Can Regressions and Garbage-Can Probits Where They Belong." *Conflict Management and Peace Science* 22 (4): 327–339.

——— 2006. "Expressive Bayesian Voters, Their Turnout Decisions, and Double Probit: Empirical Implications of a Theoretical Model." Working Paper. Princeton University, Typescript.

——— 2012. "When Is Myopic Retrospection Rational?" Typescript. Princeton University.

Achen, Christopher H., and W. Phillips Shively. 1995. *Cross-Level Inference*. University of Chicago Press.

Adams, James, and Samuel Merrill. 2006. "Why Small, Centrist Third Parties Motivate Policy Divergence by Major Parties." *The American Political Science Review* 100 (3): 403–417.

Aidt, Toke S. 2000. "Economic Voting and Information." *Electoral Studies* 19 (2): 349–362.

Akerlof, George A. 2002. "Behavioral Macroeconomics and Macroeconomic Behavior." The *American Economic Review* 92 (3): 411–433.

Alcañiz, Isabella, and Timothy Hellwig. 2011. "Who's to Blame? The Distribution of Responsibility in Developing Democracies." *British Journal of Political Science* 41 (2): 389–411.

Aldrich, John H. 1980. *Before the Convention: Strategies and Choices in Presidential Nomination Campaigns*. Chicago: University of Chicago Press.

——— 1993. "Rational Choice and Turnout." *American Journal of Political Science* 37 (1): 246–278.

Aldrich, John H., James E. Alt, and Arthur Lupia. 2008. "The EITM Approach: Origins and Interpretations." In *The Oxford Handbook of Political Methodology*, edited by J. M. Box-Steffensmeier, H. E. Brady, and D. Collier, 828–843. New York: Oxford University Press.

Alesina, Alberto, and Howard Rosenthal. 1995. *Partisan Politics, Divided Government, and the Economy*. Cambridge, MA: Cambridge University Press.

Amadae, Sm, and Bruce Bueno de Mesquita. 1999. "The Rochester School: The Origins of Positive Political Theory." *Annual Review of Political Science* 2: 269–295.

Andreasen, Eugenia, Guido Sandleris, and Alejandro Van der Ghote. 2018. "The Political Economy of Sovereign Defaults." *Journal of Monetary Economics*, September.

Ansolabehere, Stephen D., Shanto Iyengar, and Adam Simon. 1999. "Replicating Experiments Using Aggregate and Survey Data: The Case of Negative Advertising and Turnout." *The American Political Science Review* 93 (4): 901–909.

Ansolabehere, Stephen D., Shanto Iyengar, Adam Simon, and Nicholas Valentino. 1994. "Does Attack Advertising Demobilize the Electorate?" *The American Political Science Review* 88 (4): 829–838.

Arifovic, Jasmina. 1991. "Learning by Genetic Algorithms in Economic Environments." Doctoral Dissertation. Department of Economics, University of Arizona.

———. 1994. "Genetic Algorithm Learning and the Cobweb Model." *Journal of Economic Dynamics and Control*, Special Issue on Computer Science and Economics, 18 (1): 3–28.

———. 1995. "Genetic Algorithms and Inflationary Economies." *Journal of Monetary Economics* 36 (1): 219–243.

———. 1996. "The Behavior of the Exchange Rate in the Genetic Algorithm and Experimental Economies." *Journal of Political Economy* 104 (3): 510–541.

———. 1998. "Stability of Equilibria under Genetic Algorithm Adaption: An Analysis." *Macroeconomic Dynamics* 2 (1): 1–21.

Arifovic, Jasmina, James Bullard, and John Duffy. 1997. "The Transition from Stagnation to Growth: An Adaptive Learning Approach." *Journal of Economic Growth* 2 (2): 185–209.

Arifovic, Jasmina, and Michael K. Maschek. 2006. "Currency Crisis: Evolution of Beliefs, Experiments with Human Subjects and Real World Data." Working Paper.

Arnason, Ragnar, Fridrik M. Baldursson, and Jon Thor Sturluson. 2006. "Experiments in Natural Resource Economics." *Journal of Economic Behavior & Organization* 61 (2): 145–148.

Arrow, Kenneth J. 1948. "Mathematical Models in the Social Sciences." In *Advances in Experimental Psychology*, edited by D. Lerner and H. D. Lasswell. Stanford, CA: Stanford University Press.

———. 1951. *Social Choice and Individual Values*. New York: John Wiley.

Aytaç, Selim Erdem. 2018. "Relative Economic Performance and the Incumbent Vote: A Reference Point Theory." *The Journal of Politics* 80 (1): 16–29.

Bamber, Donald, and Jan P. H. van Santen. 1985. "How Many Parameters Can a Model Have and Still Be Testable." *Journal of Mathematical Psychology* 29 (4): 443–473.

———. 2000. "How to Assess a Model's Testability and Identifiability." *Journal of Mathematical Psychology* 44 (1): 20–40.

Bapat, Navin A., and Bo Ram Kwon. 2015. "When Are Sanctions Effective? A Bargaining and Enforcement Framework." *International Organization* 69 (1): 131–162.

Bargsted, Matias A., and Orit Kedar. 2009. "Coalition-Targeted Duvergerian Voting: How Expectations Affect Voter Choice under Proportional Representation." *American Journal of Political Science* 53 (2): 307–323.

Barnett, William A. 1980. "Economic Monetary Aggregates an Application of Index Number and Aggregation Theory." *Journal of Econometrics* 14 (1): 11–48.

　1982. "The Optimal Level of Monetary Aggregation." *Journal of Money, Credit and Banking* 14 (4): 687–710.

　1984. "Recent Monetary Policy and the Divisia Monetary Aggregates." *The American Statistician* 38 (3): 165–172.

　1987. "The Microeconomic Theory of Monetary Aggregation." In *New Approaches to Monetary Economics*, edited by William A. Barnett and Kenneth J. Singleton, 115–168. New York: Cambridge University Press.

Barnett, William A., Edward K. Offenbacher, and Paul A. Spindt. 1984. "The New Divisia Monetary Aggregates." *Journal of Political Economy* 92 (6): 1049–1085.

Barro, Robert J., and Xavier Sala-i-Martin. 1992. "Convergence." *Journal of Political Economy* 100 (2): 223–251.

Bartels, Larry M., and Henry E. Brady. 1993. "The State of Quantitative Political Methodology." In *Political Science: The State of the Discipline II*, edited by A. W. Finifter, 121–159. Washington, DC: American Political Science Association.

Bas, Muhammet A., Curtis S. Signorino, and Robert W. Walker. 2008. "Statistical Backwards Induction: A Simple Method for Estimating Recursive Strategic Models." *Political Analysis* 16 (December): 21–40.

Basak, Gopal K., Mrinal K. Ghosh, and Diganta Mukherjee. 2019. "A Stochastic Model with Inflation, Growth and Technology for the Political Business Cycle." *Computational Economics* 53 (1): 125–140.

Bendor, Jonathan, Daniel Diermeier, and Michael Ting. 2003. "A Behavioral Model of Turnout." *American Political Science Review* 97 (2): 261–280.

Bernanke, Ben S., and Michael Woodford. 1997. "Inflation Forecasts and Monetary Policy." *Journal of Money, Credit and Banking* 29 (4): 653–684.

Bernanke, Ben S., Thomas Laubach, Frederic S. Mishkin, and Adam S. Posen. 2001. *Inflation Targeting: Lessons from the International Experience*. Princeton, NJ: Princeton University Press.

Black, Duncan. 1948. "On the Rationale of Group Decision-Making." *Journal of Political Economy* 56 (1): 23–34.

　1958. *The Theory of Committees and Elections*. Cambridge: Cambridge University Press.

Blais, André. 2000. *To Vote or Not to Vote: The Merits and Limits of Rational Choice Theory*. Pittsburgh: University of Pittsburgh Press.

　2006. "What Affects Voter Turnout?" *Annual Review of Political Science* 9: 111–125.

Blalock, Hubert M. 1967. "Status Inconsistency, Social Mobility, Status Integration and Structural Effects." *American Sociological Review* 32 (5): 790–801.

Blau, Peter M. 1960. "Structural Effects." *American Sociological Review* 25 (2): 178–193.

　1964. *Exchange and Power in Social Life*. New Brunswick: Transaction Publishers.

Blomberg, S. Brock, and Gregory D. Hess. 2003. "Is the Political Business Cycle for Real?" *Journal of Public Economics* 87 (5): 1091–1121.

Blonigen, Bruce, and Miao Wang. 2005. "Inappropriate Pooling of Wealthy and Poor Countries in Empirical FDI Studies." In *Does Foreign Direct Investment Promote Development?* Institute for International Economics, 221–244. Washington, DC: Peterson Institute.

Blydenburgh, John C. 1971. "The Closed Rule and the Paradox of Voting." *The Journal of Politics* 33 (1): 57–71.

Bolton, Gary E., and Axel Ockenfels. 2000. "ERC: A Theory of Equity, Reciprocity, and Competition." *The American Economic Review* 90 (1): 166–193.

Boussard, Jean-Marc. 1971. "A Model of the Behavior of Farmers and Its Application to Agricultural Policies." *European Economic Review* 2 (4): 436–461.

Bowles, Samuel. 2008. "Policies Designed for Self-Interested Citizens May Undermine 'The Moral Sentiments': Evidence from Economic Experiments." *Science* 320 (5883): 1605–1609.

Box, George E. P., and Gwilym M. Jenkins. 1970. *Time Series Analysis: Forecasting and Control*. San Francisco: Holden-Day.

Box-Steffensmeier, Janet M., Henry E. Brady, and David Collier. 2008. *The Oxford Handbook of Political Methodology*. Oxford University Press.

Boyd, Richard N. 1973. "Realism, Underdetermination, and a Causal Theory of Evidence." *Noûs* 7 (1): 1–12.

Brady, Henry E. 2008. "Causation and Explanation in the Social Science." In *The Oxford Handbook of Political Methodology*, edited by J. M. Box-Steffensmeier, H. E. Brady, and D. Collier. New York: Oxford University Press.

Brady, Henry E., and David Collier. 2004. *Rethinking Social Inquiry: Diverse Tools, Shared Standards*. Second edition. Lanham, MD: Rowman & Littlefield Publishers.

Branch, William A., and George W. Evans. 2006. "A Simple Recursive Forecasting Model." *Economics Letters* 91 (2): 158–166.

Brandt, Patrick T., and John R. Freeman. 2009. "Modeling Macro-Political Dynamics." *Political Analysis* 17 (2): 113–142.

Bray, Margaret M. 1982. "Learning, Estimation, and the Stability of Rational Expectations." *Journal of Economic Theory* 26 (2): 318–339.

Bray, Margaret M., and Nathan E. Savin. 1986. "Rational Expectations Equilibria, Learning, and Model Specification." *Econometrica* 54 (5): 1129–1160.

Brians, Craig Leonard, and Bernard Grofman. 1999. "When Registration Barriers Fall, Who Votes?: An Empirical Test of a Rational Choice Model." *Public Choice* 99 (1): 161–176.

Brock, William A., and Cars H. Hommes. 1997. "A Rational Route to Randomness." *Econometrica* 65 (5): 1059–1160.

Bronowski, Jacob. 1978. *The Common Sense of Science*. Cambridge, MA: Harvard University Press.

Bullard, James, and John Duffy. 1998a. "Learning and the Stability Of Cycles." *Macroeconomic Dynamics* 2 (1): 22–48.

———. 1998b. "A Model of Learning and Emulation With Artificial Adaptive Agents." *Journal of Economic Dynamics and Control* 22 (2): 179–207.

———. 1999. "Using Genetic Algorithms to Model the Evolution of Heterogeneous Beliefs." *Computational Economics* 13 (1): 41–60.

Bullard, James, and Kaushik Mitra. 2002. "Learning about Monetary Policy Rules." *Journal of Monetary Economics* 49 (6): 1105–1129.

———. 2007. "Determinacy, Learnability, and Monetary Policy Inertia." *Journal of Money, Credit and Banking* 39 (5): 1177–1212.

Bush, Robert R., and Frederick Mosteller. 1955. *Stochastic Models for Learning*. New York: John Wiley & Sons.

Cagan, Phillip. 1956. "The Monetary Dynamics of Hyperinflation." In *Studies in the Quantity Theory of Money*, edited by Friedman Milton, 25–117. Chicago: University of Chicago Press.

Calvo, Ernesto, and Timothy Hellwig. 2011. "Centripetal and Centrifugal Incentives under Different Electoral Systems." *American Journal of Political Science* 55 (1): 27–41.

Camerer, Colin F. 2003. *Behavioral Game Theory: Experiments in Strategic Interaction*. First Edition edition. New York: Princeton, NJ: Princeton University Press.

Camerer, Colin F., and Ernst Fehr. 2006. "When Does 'Economic Man' Dominate Social Behavior?" *Science* 311 (5757): 47–52.

Campbell, Angus, Philip E. Converse, Warren E. Miller, and Donald E. Stokes. 1960. *The American Voter*. New York: John Wiley & Sons, Inc.

Campello, Daniela. 2018. "Retrospective Voting and Democratic Accountability." In *Routledge Handbook of Brazilian Politics*, Ed. Ames, Barry. New York: Routledge.

Campello, Daniela, and Cesar Zucco. 2015. "Presidential Success and the World Economy." *The Journal of Politics* 78 (2): 589–602.

Carlson, John A. 1968. "An Invariably Stable Cobweb Model." *The Review of Economic Studies* 35 (3): 360–362.

Carlson, John A., and Neven Valev. 2001. "Credibility of a New Monetary Regime: The Currency Board in Bulgaria." *Journal of Monetary Economics* 47 (June): 581–594.

Carson, Jamie L. 2003. "Strategic Interaction and Candidate Competition in U.S. House Elections: Empirical Applications of Probit and Strategic Probit Models." *Political Analysis* 11 (4): 368–380.

Carter, David B. 2010. "The Strategy of Territorial Conflict." *American Journal of Political Science* 54 (4): 969–987.

Carter, David B., and Randall W. Stone. 2015. "Democracy and Multilateralism: The Case of Vote Buying in the UN General Assembly." *International Organization* 69 (1): 1–33.

Cass, David. 1965. "Optimum Growth in an Aggregative Model of Capital Accumulation." *Review of Economic Studies* 32 (3): 233–240.

Chakravartty, Anjan. 2017. "Scientific Realism." In *The Stanford Encyclopedia of Philosophy*, edited by Edward N. Zalta, Summer 2017. Metaphysics Research Lab, Stanford University.

Chamley, Christophe P. 2004. *Rational Herds: Economic Models of Social Learning*. Cambridge: Cambridge University Press.

Chappell, Henry W., and William R. Keech. 1983. "Welfare Consequences of the Six-Year Presidential Term Evaluated in the Context of a Model of the U.S. Economy." *American Political Science Review* 77 (1): 75–91.

Chatterjee, Sankhadeep, Rhitaban Nag, Nilanjan Dey, and Amira S. Ashour. 2017. "Efficient Economic Profit Maximization: Genetic Algorithm Based Approach." In *Smart Trends in Systems, Security and Sustainability*, 307. London: Springer Proceedings Book.

Chaudoin, Stephen, and Jonathan Woon. 2018. "How Hard to Fight? Cross-Player Effects and Strategic Sophistication in an Asymmetric Contest Experiment." *The Journal of Politics* 80 (2): 585–600.

Chen, Shu-Heng, and Ragupathy Venkatachalam. 2017. "Agent-Based Models and Their Development through the Lens of Networks." In *Economic Foundations*

for Social Complexity Science: Theory, Sentiments, and Empirical Laws, 89–106. Singapore: Springer.
Chen, Shu-Heng, and Chia-Hsuan Yeh. 1997. "Modeling Speculators with Genetic Programming." In *Lecture Notes in Computer Science*, 1213: 137–147. Berlin: Springer.
Cheung, Yin-Wong, and Kon S. Lai. 1995. "Lag Order and Critical Values of the Augmented Dickey-Fuller Test." *Journal of Business & Economic Statistics* 13 (3): 277–280.
Christ, Carl F. 1951. "A Test of an Econometric Model for the United States, 1921–1947." In *Proceedings of the Conference on Business Cycles*. New York: National Bureau of Economic Research.
⎯⎯⎯. 1952. "Economic Theory and Measurement: A Twenty Year Research Report 1932–1952." *Cowles Commission for Research in Economics*. Baltimore, MD: The University of Chicago.
⎯⎯⎯. 1994. "The Cowles Commission's Contributions to Econometrics at Chicago, 1939–1955." *Journal of Economic Literature* 32 (1): 30–59.
Clarida, Richard, Jordi Gali, and Mark Gertler. 2000. "Monetary Policy Rules and Macroeconomic Stability: Evidence and Some Theory." *The Quarterly Journal of Economics* 115 (1): 147–180.
Clarke, Harold D., and Jim Granato. 2004. "Time Series Analysis in Political Science." In *Encyclopedia of Social Measurement*, edited by Kimberly Kempf-Leonard, 829–837. New York: Elsevier.
Clarke, Harold D., David Sanders, Marianne C. Stewart, and Paul Whiteley. 2004. *Political Choice in Britain*. Oxford University Press.
Clarke, Kevin A., and David M. Primo. 2007. "Modernizing Political Science: A Model-Based Approach." *Perspectives on Politics* 5 (4): 741–753.
⎯⎯⎯. 2012. *A Model Discipline: Political Science and the Logic of Representations*. New York: Oxford University Press.
Coase, Ronald H. 1994. "How Should Economists Choose." In *Essays on Economics and Economists*, edited by Ronald H. Coase. Chicago: University of Chicago Press.
Cobb, Charles W., and Paul H. Douglas. 1928. "A Theory of Production." *The American Economic Review* 18 (1): 139–165.
Colucci, Domenico, and Vincenzo Valori. 2011. "Adaptive Expectations and Cobweb Phenomena: Does Heterogeneity Matter?" *Journal of Economic Dynamics and Control* 35 (8): 1307–1321.
Converse, Philip E. 1964. "The Nature of Belief Systems in Mass Publics." In *Ideology and Discontent*, edited by D. E. Apter, 206–261. New York: The Free Press of Glencoe.
⎯⎯⎯. 1969. "Of Time and Partisan Stability." *Comparative Political Studies* 2 (2): 139–171.
⎯⎯⎯. 1970. "Attitudes and Non-Attitudes: Continuation of a Dialogue." In *The Quantitative Analysis of Social Problems*, edited by E. R. Tufte. Reading, MA: Addison-Wesley.
⎯⎯⎯. 2000. "Assessing the Capacity of Mass Electorates." *Annual Review of Political Science* 3 (January): 331–353.
Cooper, Gershon. 1948. "The Role of Econometric Models in Economic Research." *American Journal of Agricultural Economics* 30 (1): 101–116.
Cox, Gary W. 1984. "Strategic Electoral Choice in Multi-Member Districts: Approval Voting in Practice?" *American Journal of Political Science* 28 (4): 722–738.

1997. *Making Votes Count: Strategic Coordination in the World's Electoral Systems.* Cambridge: Cambridge University Press.

2004. "Lies, Damned Lies, and Rational Choice Analyses." In *Problems and Methods in the Study of Politics*, edited by Ian Shapiro, 167–185. Cambridge; New York: Cambridge University Press.

Cox, James C., and Cary A. Deck. 2005. "On the Nature of Reciprocal Motives." *Economic Inquiry* 43 (3): 623–635.

Cox, James C., Daniel Friedman, and Steven Gjerstad. 2007. "A Tractable Model of Reciprocity and Fairness." *Games and Economic Behavior* 59 (1): 17–45.

Crawford, Sue E. S., and Elinor Ostrom. 1995. "A Grammar of Institutions." *The American Political Science Review* 89 (3): 582–600.

Cyert, Richard M., and James G. March. 1963. *A Behavioral Theory of the Firm.* Englewood Cliffs, NJ: Prentice-Hall.

Deaton, Angus. 1985. "Panel Data from Time Series of Cross-Sections." *Journal of Econometrics* 30 (1): 109–126.

Devenow, Andrea, and Ivo Welch. 1996. "Rational Herding in Financial Economics." *European Economic Review, Papers and Proceedings of the Tenth Annual Congress of the European Economic Association*, 40 (3): 603–615.

Devitt, Michael. 2008. "Realism/Anti-Realism." In *The Routledge Companion to Philosophy of Science*, edited by Stathis Psillos and Martin Curd, 224–235. London: Routledge.

Dickey, David A., and Wayne A. Fuller. 1979. "Distribution of the Estimators for Autoregressive Time Series with a Unit Root." *Journal of the American Statistical Association* 74 (366): 427–431.

Diewert, Walter E. 1976. "Exact and Superlative Index Numbers." *Journal of Econometrics* 4 (2): 115–145.

Downs, Anthony. 1957. *An Economic Theory of Democracy.* New York: Harper.

Drazen, Allan. 2000a. *Political Economy in Macroeconomics.* Princeton, NJ: Princeton University Press.

2000b. "Interest-Rate and Borrowing Defense against Speculative Attack." *Carnegie-Rochester Conference Series on Public Policy* 53 (1): 303–348.

Druckman, James N., Donald P. Green, James H. Kuklinski, and Arthur Lupia, eds. 2011. *Cambridge Handbook of Experimental Political Science.* Cambridge: Cambridge University Press.

Duch, Raymond M., and Randolph T. Stevenson. 2008. *The Economic Vote: How Political and Economic Institutions Condition Election Results.* New York: Cambridge University Press.

Duch, Raymond M., and Randy Stevenson. 2010. "The Global Economy, Competency, and the Economic Vote." *The Journal of Politics* 72 (1): 105–123.

Duhem, Pierre Maurice Marie. 1954. *The Aim and Structure of Physical Theory.* Princeton, NJ: Princeton University Press.

Duo, Qin. 1993. *The Formation of Econometrics: A Historical Perspective.* New York: Oxford University Press.

Eichengreen, Barry, Andrew Rose, and Charles Wyplosz. 1996. "Contagious Currency Crises: First Tests." *The Scandinavian Journal of Economics* 98 (4): 463–484.

Elliott, Graham, Thomas J. Rothenberg, and James H. Stock. 1996. "Efficient Tests for an Autoregressive Unit Root." *Econometrica* 64 (4): 813–836.

Enders, Walter. 2014. *Applied Econometric Time Series.* Hoboken, NJ: Wiley.

Engle, Robert F., and Clive W. J. Granger. 1987. "Co-Integration and Error Correction: Representation, Estimation, and Testing." *Econometrica* 55 (2): 251–276.

Engle, Robert F., David F. Hendry, and Jean-Francois Richard. 1983. "Exogeneity." *Econometrica* 51 (2): 277–304.

Erikson, Robert S., Michael B. MacKuen, and James A. Stimson. 2002. *The Macro Polity*. Cambridge: Cambridge University Press.

Evans, George W. 1985. "Expectational Stability and the Multiple Equilibria Problem in Linear Rational Expectations Models." *The Quarterly Journal of Economics* 100 (4): 1217–1233.

———. 1989. "The Fragility of Sunspots and Bubbles." *Journal of Monetary Economics* 23 (2): 297–317.

Evans, George W., and Seppo Honkapohja. 1992. "On the Robustness of Bubbles in Linear RE Models." *International Economic Review* 33 (1): 1–14.

———. 1995. "Adaptive Learning and Expectational Stability: An Introduction." In *Learning and Rationality in Economics*, edited by A. Kirman and M. Salmon. Oxford: Blackwell Pub.

———. 1996. "Least Squares Learning with Heterogeneous Expectations." *Economics Letters* 53 (2): 197–201.

———. 2001. *Learning and Expectations in Macroeconomics*. Princeton, NJ: Princeton University Press.

———. 2003a. "Adaptive Learning and Monetary Policy Design." *Journal of Money, Credit and Banking* 35 (6): 1045–1072.

———. 2003b. "Expectations and the Stability Problem for Optimal Monetary Policies." *The Review of Economic Studies* 70 (4): 807–824.

Evans, George W., and Bruce McGough. 2018. "Interest-Rate Pegs in New Keynesian Models." *Journal of Money, Credit and Banking* 50 (5): 939–965.

Ezekiel, Mordecai. 1938. "The Cobweb Theorem." *The Quarterly Journal of Economics* 52 (2): 255–280.

Farmer, J. Doyne, and Duncan Foley. 2009. "The Economy Needs Agent-Based Modeling." *Nature* 460 (August): 685–686.

Fehr, Ernst, Usr Fischbacher, and Michael Kosfeld. 2005. "Neuroeconomic Foundations of Trust and Social Preferences: Initial Evidence." *The American Economic Review* 95 (2): 346–351.

Fehr, Ernst, and Klaus M. Schmidt. 1999. "A Theory of Fairness, Competition, and Cooperation." *The Quarterly Journal of Economics* 114 (3): 817–868.

Femenia, Fabienne, and Alexandre Gohin. 2011. "Dynamic Modelling of Agricultural Policies: The Role of Expectation Schemes." *Economic Modelling* 28 (4): 1950–1958.

Fiorina, Morris P. 1978. "Economic Retrospective Voting in American National Elections: A Micro-Analysis." *American Journal of Political Science* 22 (2): 426–443.

———. 1981. *Retrospective Voting in American National Elections*. New Haven, CT: Yale University Press.

———. 1990. "Information and Rationality in Elections." In *Information and Democratic Processes*, edited by John A. Ferejohn, James H Kuklinski, 329–342. Chicago: University of Illinois Press.

Fisher, Franklin M. 1966. *The Identification Problem in Econometrics*. New York: McGraw-Hill.

Fisher, Ronald A. 1922. "The Goodness of Fit of Regression Formulae, and the Distribution of Regression Coefficients." *Journal of the Royal Statistical Society* 85 (4): 597–612.
Forsythe, Robert, Forrest Nelson, George R. Neumann, and Jack Wright. 1992. "Anatomy of an Experimental Political Stock Market." *The American Economic Review* 82 (5): 1142–1161.
Fowler, James H. 2006. "Habitual Voting and Behavioral Turnout." *Journal of Politics* 68 (2): 335–344.
Fox, Justin, and Kenneth W. Shotts. 2009. "Delegates or Trustees? A Theory of Political Accountability." *The Journal of Politics* 71 (4): 1225–1237.
Franklin, Charles H., and John E. Jackson. 1983. "The Dynamics of Party Identification." *The American Political Science Review* 77 (4): 957–973.
Freedman, David, Robert Pisani, and Roger Purves. 1998. *Statistics*. New York: W.W. Norton & Company.
Freeman, John R. 1983. "Granger Causality and the Times Series Analysis of Political Relationships." *American Journal of Political Science* 27 (2): 327–358.
Freeman, John R., and Daniel Houser. 1998. "A Computable Equilibrium Model for the Study of Political Economy." *American Journal of Political Science* 42 (2): 628–660.
Freeman, John R., Tse-Min Lin, and John T. Williams. 1989. "Vector Autoregression and the Study of Politics." *American Journal of Political Science* 33 (4): 842–877.
Friedman, Milton. 1953. *Essays in Positive Economics*. Chicago: University of Chicago Press.
  1957a. *A Theory of the Consumption Function*. Princeton, NJ: Princeton University Press.
  1957b. "The Permanent Income Hypothesis." *NBER Chapters*. National Bureau of Economic Research, Inc.
Friedman, Milton, and Anna J. Schwartz. 1963. *A Monetary History of the United States, 1867–1960*. Princeton, NJ: Princeton University Press.
  1991. "Alternative Approaches Analyzing Economic Data." *American Economic Review* 81 (February): 39–49.
Fuller, Wayne A. 1976. *Introduction to Statistical Time Series*. New York: Wiley-Interscience.
  1987. *Measurement Error Models*. New York: John Wiley & Sons.
Gabaix, Xavier, and David Laibson. 2008. "The Seven Properties of Good Models." In *The Foundations of Positive and Normative Economics: A Handbook*, edited by A. Caplin and A. Schotter. New York: Oxford University Press.
Gatti, Domenico Delli, Saul Desiderio, Edoardo Gaffeo, Pasquale Cirillo, and Mauro Gallegati. 2011. *Macroeconomics from the Bottom-Up*. Milan: Springer Science & Business Media.
Gawrońska-Nowak, Bogna, and Wojciech Grabowski. 2016. "Using Genetic Algorithm in Dynamic Model of Speculative Attack." *Equilibrium. Quarterly Journal of Economics and Economic Policy* 11 (2): 287–306.
Geisendorf, Sylvie. 2011. "Internal Selection and Market Selection in Economic Genetic Algorithms." *Journal of Evolutionary Economics* 21 (5): 817–841.
Gerber, Elizabeth. 2003. "What Is Political Economy?" *The Political Economist* 11: 1–4.
Geys, Benny. 2006. "'Rational' Theories of Voter Turnout: A Review." *Political Studies Review* 4 (1): 16–35.

Goldberg, David E. 1989. *Genetic Algorithms in Search, Optimization, and Machine Learning*. Boston: Addison Wesley.
Gorman, William M. 1953. "Community Preference Fields." *Econometrica* 21 (1): 63–80.
Gosnell, Harold F. 1926. "An Experiment in the Stimulation of Voting." *The American Political Science Review* 20 (4): 869–874.
Gow, David J. 1985. "Quantification and Statistics in the Early Years of American Political Science, 1880–1922." *Political Methodology* 11 (1/2): 1–18.
Grafstein, Robert. 2002. "The Political Economy of Postmaterialism: Material Explanations of Changing Values." *Economics & Politics* 14 (2): 163–190.
Granato, Jim. 2005. "Scientific Progress in Quantitative Political Economy." *The Political Economist* 12 (4): 11–13.
Granato, Jim, Eran A. Guse, and M. C. Sunny Wong. 2008. "Learning from the Expectations of Others." *Macroeconomic Dynamics* 12 (3): 345–377.
Granato, Jim, Cong Huang, Kwok Wai Wan, Ching-Hsing Wang, and M. C. Sunny Wong. 2015. "EITM: An Assessment with an Application to Economic Voting." *Electoral Studies* 40 (December): 372–393.
Granato, Jim, and George A. Krause. 2000. "Information Diffusion within the Electorate: The Asymmetric Transmission of Political–Economic Information." *Electoral Studies* 19 (4): 519–537.
Granato, Jim, Melody Lo, and M. C. Sunny Wong. 2010a. "A Framework for Unifying Formal and Empirical Analysis." *American Journal of Political Science* 54 (3): 783–797.
   2010b. "The Empirical Implications of Theoretical Models (EITM): A Framework for Methodological Unification." *Politica y Gobierno* 17 (1): 25–57.
   2011. "Modeling and Testing the Diffusion of Expectations: An EITM Approach." *Electoral Studies, Special Symposium on the Politics of Economic Crisis* 30 (3): 389–398.
Granato, Jim, and Frank Scioli. 2004. "Puzzles, Proverbs, and Omega Matrices: The Scientific and Social Significance of Empirical Implications of Theoretical Models (EITM)." *Perspectives on Politics* 2 (2): 313–323.
Granato, Jim, and M. C. Sunny Wong. 2004. "Political Campaign Advertising Dynamics." *Political Research Quarterly* 57 (September): 349–361.
   2006. *The Role of Policymakers in Business Cycle Fluctuations*. New York: Cambridge University Press.
Granger, Clive W. J. 1969. "Investigating Causal Relations by Econometric Models and Cross-Spectral Methods." *Econometrica* 37 (3): 424–438.
Green, H. A. John. 1964. *Aggregation in Economic Analysis*. Princeton, NJ: Princeton University Press.
Greene, William H. 2011. *Econometric Analysis*. Upper Saddle River: Prentice Hall.
Grier, Kevin, and Shu Lin. 2010. "Do High Interest Rates Deter Speculative Attacks? – Evidence and Some Theory." *Journal of International Money and Finance* 29 (5): 938–950.
Guala, Francesco. 2005. *The Methodology of Experimental Economics*. New York: Cambridge University Press.
Guse, Eran A. 2005. "Stability Properties for Learning with Heterogeneous Expectations and Multiple Equilibria." *Journal of Economic Dynamics and Control* 29 (10): 1623–1642.

2010. "Heterogeneous Expectations, Adaptive Learning, and Evolutionary Dynamics." *Journal of Economic Behavior & Organization* 74 (1): 42–57.

2014. "Adaptive Learning, Endogenous Uncertainty, and Asymmetric Dynamics." *Journal of Economic Dynamics and Control* 40 (March): 355–373.

Haavelmo, Trygve. 1943. "The Statistical Implications of a System of Simultaneous Equations." *Econometrica* 11 (1): 1–12.

1944. "The Probability Approach in Econometrics." *Econometrica* 12: 3–115.

Hamilton, James D. 1994. *Time Series Analysis*. 1st edition. Princeton, NJ: Princeton University Press.

Hardin, Russell. 1982. *Collective Action*. First Edition. Baltimore: Johns Hopkins University Press.

Hausman, Daniel M. 1998. "Problems with Realism in Economics." *Economics & Philosophy* 14 (2): 185–213. https://doi.org/10.1017/S0266267100003837.

Hausman, Jerry. 2001. "Mismeasured Variables in Econometric Analysis: Problems from the Right and Problems from the Left." *The Journal of Economic Perspectives* 15 (4): 57–67.

Heckman, James J. 2000. "Causal Parameters and Policy Analysis in Economics: A Twentieth Century Retrospective." *The Quarterly Journal of Economics* 115 (1): 45–97.

Heinemann, Maik. 2000. "Adaptive Learning of Rational Expectations Using Neural Networks." *Journal of Economic Dynamics and Control* 24 (5): 1007–1026.

Helmke, Gretchen. 2010. "The Origins of Institutional Crises in Latin America." *American Journal of Political Science* 54 (3): 737–750.

Hendry, David F. 1995. *Dynamic Econometrics*. New York: Oxford University Press.

Hibbs, Douglas A. 1977. "Political Parties and Macroeconomic Policy." *American Political Science Review* 71 (4): 1467–1487.

Highton, Benjamin. 2004. "Voter Registration and Turnout in the United States." *Perspectives on Politics* 2 (3): 507–515.

Hildreth, Clifford. 1986. *The Cowles Commission in Chicago, 1939–1955. Lecture Notes in Economics and Mathematical Systems*. Berlin; Heidelberg: Springer-Verlag.

Hinich, Melvin J. 1981. "Voting as an Act of Contribution." *Public Choice* 36 (1): 135–140.

Hodrick, Robert, and Edward C. Prescott. 1981. "Postwar U.S. Business Cycles: An Empirical Investigation." Working Paper, Northwestern University.

1997. "Postwar U.S. Business Cycles: An Empirical Investigation." *Journal of Money, Credit and Banking* 29 (1): 1–16.

Holland, John H. 1970. "Robust Algorithms for Adaptation Set in a General Formal Framework." In *1970 IEEE Symposium on Adaptive Processes* (9th) Decision and Control, 175.

1975. *Adaptation in Natural and Artificial Systems: An Introductory Analysis with Applications to Biology, Control, and Artificial Intelligence*. Ann Arbor, MI: University of Michigan Press.

Holt, Charles, and Anne Villamil. 1986. "A Laboratory Experiment with a Single-Person Cobweb." *Atlantic Economic Journal* 14 (July): 51–54.

Hommes, Cars, Joep Sonnemans, Jan Tuinstra, and Henk van de Velden. 2007. "Learning in Cobweb Experiments." *Macroeconomic Dynamics* 11 (November): 8–33.

Hood, William C., and Tjalling C. Koopmans. 1953. "Studies in Econometric Method." In *Cowles Commission Monograph No. 14*. New York: John Wiley and Sons.

Hoover, Kevin D. 2001a. *Causality in Macroeconomics*. New York: Cambridge University Press.

2001b. *The Methodology of Empirical Macroeconomics*. New York: Cambridge University Press.

Hotelling, Harold. 1929. "Stability in Competition." *The Economic Journal* 39 (153): 41–57.

Houser, Daniel, and John Freeman. 2001. "Economic Consequences of Political Approval Management in Comparative Perspective." *Journal of Comparative Economics* 29 (4): 692–721.

Huckfeldt, Robert, and John Sprague. 1985. *Presidential Election Campaign Study, 1984*. South Bend, IN: Indiana University, Center for Survey Research.

Jasso, Guillermina. 1999. "How Much Injustice Is There in the World? Two New Justice Indexes." *American Sociological Review* 64 (1): 133–168.

2002. "Formal Theory." In *Handbook of Sociological Theory*, edited by Jonathan H. Turner, 37–68. New York: Springer Science & Business Media.

2004. "The Tripartite Structure of Social Science Analysis." *Sociological Theory* 22 (3): 401–431.

2008. "A New Unified Theory of Sociobehavioral Forces." *European Sociological Review* 24 (4): 411–434.

2010. "Linking Individuals and SocietiesJournal of Mathematical Sociology." *Journal of Mathematical Sociology* 34 (1): 1–158.

Johansen, Søren. 1988. "Statistical Analysis of Cointegration Vectors." *Journal of Economic Dynamics and Control* 12 (2): 231–254.

1992. "Determination of Cointegration Rank in the Presence of a Linear Trend." *Oxford Bulletin of Economics and Statistics* 54 (February): 383–397.

1995. *Likelihood-Based Inference in Cointegrated Vector Autoregressive Models*. New York: Oxford University Press.

Johansen, Søren, and Katarina Juselius. 1990. "Maximum Likelihood Estimation and Inference on Cointegration–with Applications to the Demand for Money." *Oxford Bulletin of Economics and Statistics* 52 (May): 169–210.

Johnston, Jack, and John DiNardo. 1997. *Econometric Methods*. New York: McGraw Hill Higher Education.

Kagel, John H., and Alvin E. Roth. 1995. *The Handbook of Experimental Economics*. Princeton, NJ: Princeton University Press.

2015. *The Handbook of Experimental Economics*, Volume 2. Princeton, NJ: Princeton University Press.

Kaldor, Nicholas. 1934. "A Classificatory Note on the Determinateness of Equilibrium." *The Review of Economic Studies* 1 (2): 122–136.

Kandel, Eugene, and Ben-Zion Zilberfarb. 1999. "Differential Interpretation of Information in Inflation Forecasts." *The Review of Economics and Statistics* 81 (2): 217–226.

Kedar, Orit. 2005. "When Moderate Voters Prefer Extreme Parties: Policy Balancing in Parliamentary Elections." *The American Political Science Review* 99 (2): 185–199.

Keister, Todd. 2009. "Expectations and Contagion in Self-Fulfilling Currency Attacks." *International Economic Review* 50 (3): 991–1012.

Kellstedt, Paul M., and Guy D. Whitten. 2009. *The Fundamentals of Political Science Research*. New York: Cambridge University Press.

Kenkel, Brenton, and Curtis S. Signorino. 2014. "Estimating Extensive Form Games in R." *Journal of Statistical Software* 56 (8): 1–27.

Key, Valdimer O., Jr. 1966. *The Responsible Electorate: Rationality in Presidential Voting, 1936–1960*. Cambridge, MA: Belknap Press.

Keynes, John M. 1939. "Professor Tinbergen's Method." *Economic Journal* 49: 558–577.

 1940. "On a Method of Statistical Business-Cycle Research. A Comment." *The Economic Journal* 50 (197): 154–156.

Kiewiet, D. Roderick, and Douglas Rivers. 1984. "A Retrospective on Retrospective Voting." *Political Behavior* 6 (4): 369–393.

Kinder, Donald R., and D. Roderick Kiewiet. 1979. "Economic Discontent and Political Behavior: The Role of Personal Grievances and Collective Economic Judgments in Congressional Voting." *American Journal of Political Science* 23 (3): 495–527.

 1981. "Sociotropic Politics: The American Case." *British Journal of Political Science* 11 (2): 129–161.

Kitcher, Philip. 2001. "Real Realism: The Galilean Strategy." *The Philosophical Review* 110 (2): 151–197.

Kittel, Bernhard, Wolfgang J. Luhan, and Rebecca B. Morton. 2012. *Experimental Political Science: Principles and Practices*. Basingstoke: Palgrave Macmillan.

Kleijnen, Jack P. C. 1995a. "Verification and Validation of Simulation Models." *European Journal of Operational Research* 82 (1): 145–162.

 1995b. "Statistical Validation of Simulation Models." *European Journal of Operational Research* 87 (1): 21–34.

Klein, Lawrence R. 1947. "The Use of Econometric Models as a Guide to Economic Policy." *Econometrica* 15 (2): 111–151.

Koopmans, Tjalling C. 1945. "Statistical Estimation of Simultaneous Economic Relations." *Journal of the American Statistical Association* 40 (232): 448–466.

 1949a. "Identification Problems in Economic Model Construction." *Econometrica* 17 (2): 125–44.

 1949b. "Koopmans on the Choice of Variables to Be Studies and the Methods of Measurement: A Reply." *The Review of Economics and Statistics* 31 (2): 86–91.

 1950. *Statistical Inference in Dynamic Economic Models*. New York: Wiley.

 1965. "On the Concept of Optimal Economic Growth." In *The Econometric Approach to Development Planning*, 225–287. Chicago: Rand McNally College Pub. Co.

Koopmans, Tjalling C., and Olav Reiersol. 1950. "The Identification of Structural Characteristics." *The Annals of Mathematical Statistics* 21 (2): 165–181.

Kramer, Gerald H. 1983. "The Ecological Fallacy Revisited: Aggregate-versus Individual-Level Findings on Economics and Elections, and Sociotropic Voting." *The American Political Science Review* 77 (1): 92–111.

Kremer, Jana, Giovanni Lombardo, Leopold von Thadden, and Thomas Werner. 2006. "Dynamic Stochastic General Equilibrium Models as a Tool for Policy Analysis." *CESifo Economic Studies* 52 (4): 640–665.

Krugman, Paul. 1979. "A Model of Balance-of-Payments Crises." *Journal of Money, Credit and Banking* 11 (3): 311–325.

1994. "The Rise and Fall of Development Economics." In *Rethinking The Development Experience: Essays Provoked by the Work of Albert O. Hirschman*, edited by L. Rodwin and D. A. Schön. Washington, DC: The Brookings Institution and Cambridge: The Lincoln Institute of Land Policy.

1998. "Two Cheers for Formalism." *The Economic Journal* 108 (451): 1829–1836.

Kuhn, Thomas S. 1979. *The Essential Tension: Selected Studies in Scientific Tradition and Change*. Chicago: University of Chicago Press.

Kyburg, Henry E. 1988. "The Justification of Deduction in Science." In *The Limitations of Deductivism*, edited by Adolf Grünbaum and Wesley C. Salmon, 61–94. Berkeley, CA: University of California Press.

Kydland, Finn E., and Edward C. Prescott. 1982. "Time to Build and Aggregate Fluctuations." *Econometrica* 50 (6): 1345–1370.

1990. "Business Cycles: Real Facts and a Monetary Myth." *Quarterly Review*, no. Spring: 3–18.

1996. "The Computational Experiment: An Econometric Tool." *Journal of Economic Perspectives* 10 (February): 69–85.

Ladyman, James, and Don Ross, with David Spurrett and John Collier. 2007. *Every Thing Must Go: Metaphysics Naturalized*. New York: Clarendon Press.

Lakatos, Imre. 1970. "Falsification and the Methodology of Scientific Research Programme." In *Criticism and the Growth of Knowledge*, edited by Imre Lakatos and Alan Musgrave, 1:91–196. Cambridge: Cambridge University Press.

Landreth, Harry, and David C. Colander. 2002. *History of Economic Thought*. Boston: Houghton Mifflin.

Laver, Michael, and Ernest Sergenti. 2012. *Party Competition: An Agent-Based Model*. Princeton, NJ: Princeton University Press.

Lazarsfeld, Paul F., Bernard Berelson, and Hazel Gaudet. 1944. *The People's Choice: How the Voter Makes Up His Mind in a Presidential Campaign*. New York: Columbia University Press.

Leamer, Edward E. 1983. "Let's Take the Con Out of Econometrics." *The American Economic Review* 73 (1): 31–43.

2010. "Tantalus on the Road to Asymptopia." *Journal of Economic Perspectives* 24 (2): 31–46.

LeBaron, Blake, and Leigh Tesfatsion. 2008. "Modeling Macroeconomies As Open-Ended Dynamic Systems of Interacting Agents." *The American Economic Review* 98 (2): 246–250.

Leblang, David. 2003. "To Devalue or to Defend? The Political Economy of Exchange Rate Policy." *International Studies Quarterly* 47 (4): 533–559.

Levine, David K., and Thomas R. Palfrey. 2007. "The Paradox of Voter Participation? A Laboratory Study." *The American Political Science Review* 101 (1): 143–158.

Lewis, Jeffrey B., and Kenneth A. Schultz. 2003. "Revealing Preferences: Empirical Estimation of a Crisis Bargaining Game with Incomplete Information." *Political Analysis* 11 (4): 345–367.

Lewis-Beck, Michael S. 2008. "Forty Years of Publishing in Quantitative Methodology." *The Oxford Handbook of Political Methodology*, August.

Lijphart, Arend. 1984. *Democracies: Patterns of Majoritarian and Consensus Government in Twenty-One Countries*. New Haven, CT: Yale University Press.

Lin, Tse-Min. 1999. "The Historical Significance of Economic Voting, 1872–1996." *Social Science History* 23 (4): 561–591.

Bibliography

List, John, Sally Sadoff, and Mathis Wagner. 2011. "So You Want to Run an Experiment, Now What? Some Simple Rules of Thumb for Optimal Experimental Design." *Experimental Economics* 14 (4): 439–457.

Lopez, Maria C., James J. Murphy, John M. Spraggon, and John K. Stranlund. 2009. "Comparing the Effectiveness of Regulation and Pro-Social Emotions to Enhance Cooperation: Experimental Evidence from Fishing Communities in Colombia." Typescript. University of Massachusetts Amherst Dept. of Resource Economics.

Lovell, Michael C. 1983. "Data Mining." *Review of Economics and Statistics* 65 (1): 1–12.

Lubik, Thomas A., and Christian Matthes. 2016. "Indeterminacy and Learning: An Analysis of Monetary Policy in the Great Inflation." *Journal of Monetary Economics* 82 (September): 85–106.

Lucas, Robert E. 1972. "Expectations and the Neutrality of Money." *Journal of Economic Theory* 4 (2): 103–124.

———. 1973. "Some International Evidence on Output-Inflation Tradeoffs." *American Economic Review* 63 (3): 326–334.

———. 1976. "Econometric Policy Evaluation: A Critique." *Carnegie-Rochester Conference Series on Public Policy* 1 (January): 19–46.

———. 1988. "On the Mechanics of Economic Development." *Journal of Monetary Economics* 22 (1): 3–42.

Lupia, Arthur, and Mathew D. McCubbins. 1998. *The Democratic Dilemma*. Cambridge: Cambridge University Press.

MacKinnon, James. 1991. "Critical Values for Cointegration Tests." In *Long-Run Economic Relationships*, edited by R. F. Engle and C. W. J. Granger. New York: Oxford University Press.

Mankiw, N. Gregory, David Romer, and David N. Weil. 1992. "A Contribution to the Empirics of Economic Growth." *The Quarterly Journal of Economics* 107 (2): 407–437.

Manski, Charles F. 1995. *Identification Problems in the Social Sciences*. Cambridge, MA: Harvard University Press.

———. 2001. "Daniel McFadden and the Econometric Analysis of Discrete Choice." *The Scandinavian Journal of Economics* 103 (2): 217–229.

Marcet, Albert, and Thomas J. Sargent. 1989a. "Convergence of Least-Squares Learning in Environments with Hidden State Variables and Private Information." *Journal of Political Economy* 97 (6): 1306–1322.

———. 1989b. "Convergence of Least Squares Learning Mechanisms in Self-Referential Linear Stochastic Models." *Journal of Economic Theory* 48 (2): 337–368.

Marchi, Scott de. 2005. *Computational and Mathematical Modeling in the Social Sciences*. New York: Cambridge University Press.

Marschak, Jacob. 1947. "Economic Structure, Path, Policy, and Prediction." *The American Economic Review* 37 (2): 81–84.

———. 1953. "Economic Measurements for Policy and Prediction." In *Studies in Econometric Method*, edited by W. C. Hood and T. C. Koopmans, 293–322. Theory and Decision Library. New York: John Wiley and Sons.

Mayo-Smith, Richmond. 1890. "On Census Methods." *Political Science Quarterly* 5 (2): 259–268.

McCabe, Kevin A., and Vernon L. Smith. 2001. "Goodwill Accounting and the Process of Exchange." In *Bounded Rationality: The Adaptive Toolbox*, edited by Gerd Gigerenzer and Reinhard Selten. Cambridge, MA: MIT Press.

McCall, John J. 1965. "The Economics of Information and Optimal Stopping Rules." *The Journal of Business* 38 (3): 300–317.

McCallum, Bennett T. 1983. "On Non-Uniqueness in Rational Expectations Models: An Attempt at Perspective." *Journal of Monetary Economics* 11 (2): 134–168.

———. 1989. *Monetary Economics: Theory and Policy*. Facsimile edition. New York: Macmillan Pub Co.

———. 2003. "Multiple-Solution Indeterminacies in Monetary Policy Analysis." *Journal of Monetary Economics* 50 (5): 1153–1175.

McCallum, Bennett T., and Edward Nelson. 1999. "An Optimizing IS-LM Specification for Monetary Policy and Business Cycle Analysis." *Journal of Money, Credit and Banking* 31 (3): 296–316.

McDermott, Rose. 2002. "Experimental Methodology in Political Science." *Political Analysis* 10 (4): 325–342.

———. 2014. "Experimental Political Science." In *Laboratory Experiments in the Social Sciences*, edited by Murray Webster and Jane Sell, 295–309. Amsterdam: Academic Press/Elsevier.

McFadden, Daniel L. 1973. "Conditional Logit Analysis of Qualitative Choice Behavior." In *Frontiers in Econometrics*, edited by Zarembka, P. New York: Wiley.

———. 1974. "The Measurement of Urban Travel Demand." *Journal of Public Economics* 3 (4): 303–328.

McKelvey, Richard D., and Peter C. Ordeshook. 1976. "Symmetric Spatial Games without Majority Rule Equilibria*." *American Political Science Review* 70 (4): 1172–1184.

McKelvey, Richard D., and Thomas R. Palfrey. 1995. "Quantal Response Equilibria for Normal Form Games." *Games and Economic Behavior* 10 (1): 6–38.

———. 1996. "A Statistical Theory of Equilibrium in Games*." *The Japanese Economic Review* 47 (2): 186–209.

———. 1998. "Quantal Response Equilibria for Extensive Form Games." *Experimental Economics* 1 (1): 9–41.

McLean, Elena V., and Taehee Whang. 2010. "Friends or Foes? Major Trading Partners and the Success of Economic Sanctions." *International Studies Quarterly* 54 (2): 427–447.

Mebane, Walter R. 2000. "Coordination, Moderation, and Institutional Balancing in American Presidential and House Elections." *American Political Science Review* 94 (1): 37–57.

Meredith, Marc. 2009. "Persistence in Political Participation." *Quarterly Journal of Political Science* 4 (3): 187–209.

Merriam, Charles E. 1921. "The Present State of the Study of Politics." *The American Political Science Review* 15 (2): 173–185.

———. 1923. "I. Recent Advances in Political Methods." *American Political Science Review* 17 (2): 275–295.

———. 1924. "Round Table I. Psychology and Political Science." *American Political Science Review* 18 (1): 122–125.

Merriam, Charles E., Robert T. Crane, John A. Fairlie, and Clyde L. King. 1923. "III. Recommendations." *The American Political Science Review* 17 (2): 311–312.

Merriam, Charles E., and Harold F. Gosnell. 1924. *Non-Voting: Causes and Methods of Control*. Chicago: The University of Chicago Press.
Milani, Fabio. 2007. "Expectations, Learning and Macroeconomic Persistence." *Journal of Monetary Economics* 54 (7): 2065–2082.
Milbrath, Lester W. 1965. *Political Participation: How and Why Do People Get Involved in Politics?* Chicago: Rand McNally College Pub. Co.
Miller, John H. 1986. "A Genetic Model of Adaptive Economic Behavior." Working Paper. University of Michigan.
Miller, John H., and Scott E. Page. 2007. *Complex Adaptive Systems: An Introduction to Computational Models of Social Life*. Princeton, NJ: Princeton University Press.
Minford, Patrick. 1992. *Rational Expectations Macroeconomics: An Introductory Handbook*. Subsequent edition. Oxford; Cambridge, MA: Blackwell Pub.
Mitchell, Wesley C. 1930. *The Backward Art of Spending Money*. New Brunswick, NJ: Transaction Publishers.
 1937. "Institutes for Research in the Social Sciences." In *The Backward Art of Spending*. New York: McGraw-Hill Book Co.
Mitra, Sophie, and Jean-Marc Boussard. 2012. "A Simple Model of Endogenous Agricultural Commodity Price Fluctuations with Storage." *Agricultural Economics* 43 (1): 1–15.
Mizon, Grayham E. 1995. "Progressive Modelling of Macroeconomic Time Series: The LSE Methodology." In *Macroeconometrics: Developments, Tensions, and Prospects*, edited by K. D. Hoover, 107–170. The Netherlands: Kluwer Publications.
Monton, Bradley, and Chad Mohler. 2017. "Constructive Empiricism." In *The Stanford Encyclopedia of Philosophy*, edited by Edward N. Zalta, Summer 2017. Metaphysics Research Lab, Stanford University.
Morgan, Mary S. 1990. *The History of Econometric Ideas*. New York: Cambridge University Press.
Morgan, Stephen L., and Christopher Winship. 2007. *Counterfactuals and Causal Inference*. New York: Cambridge University Press.
Morton, Rebecca B. 1991. "Groups in Rational Turnout Models." *American Journal of Political Science* 35 (3): 758–776.
 1999. *Methods and Models: A Guide to the Empirical Analysis of Formal Models in Political Science*. New York: Cambridge University Press.
Morton, Rebecca B., and Kenneth C. Williams. 2010. *Experimental Political Science and the Study of Causality: From Nature to the Lab*. New York: Cambridge University Press.
Musgrave, Alan. 1988. "The Ultimate Argument for Scientific Realism." In *Relativism and Realism in Science*, edited by Robert Nola, 229–252. Australasian Studies in History and Philosophy of Science. Dordrecht: Springer Netherlands.
Muth, John F. 1961. "Rational Expectations and the Theory of Price Movements." *Econometrica* 29 (3): 315–335.
Myerson, Roger B. 1999. "Theoretical Comparisons of Electoral Systems." *European Economic Review* 43 (4): 671–697.
Nakosteen, Robert A., and Michael Zimmer. 1980. "Migration and Income: The Question of Self-Selection." *Southern Economic Journal* 46 (3): 840–851.
Namatame, Akira, and Shu-Heng Chen. 2016. *Agent-Based Modeling and Network Dynamics*. Oxford: Oxford University Press.

National Science Foundation. 2001. "Transcripts (7/9/01 & 7/10/01) of the Empirical Implications of Theoretical Models (EITM) Workshop."
  2002. "Empirical Implications of Theoretical Models." Political Science Program, Directorate For Social, Behavioral and Economic Sciences.
Nelson, Phillip. 1970. "Information and Consumer Behavior." *Journal of Political Economy* 78 (2): 311–329.
Nerlove, Marc. 1958. "Adaptive Expectations and Cobweb Phenomena." *The Quarterly Journal of Economics* 72 (2): 227–240.
Niemi, Richard G. 1976. "Costs of Voting and Nonvoting." *Public Choice* 27: 115–119.
Niemi, Richard G., and Michael J. Hammer. 2010. "Voter Turnout among College Students: New Data and a Rethinking of Traditional Theories." *Social Science Quarterly* 91 (2): 301–323.
Oberschall, Anthony. 1980. "Loosely Structured Collective Conflict: A Theory and an Application." In *Research in Social Movements, Conflicts and Change*, edited by Kriesberg, Louis, 45–68.
Obstfeld, Maurice. 1994. "The Logic of Currency Crises." *Cahiers Economiques et Monetaires* 43 (October): 189–213.
Ogburn, William F., and Inez Goltra. 1919. "How Women Vote." *Political Science Quarterly* 34 (3): 413–433.
Ogburn, William F., and Delvin Peterson. 1916. "Political Thought of Social Classes." *Political Science Quarterly* 31 (2): 300–317.
Okasha, Samir. 2002. *Philosophy of Science: A Very Short Introduction*. Oxford: Oxford University Press.
Olson, Mancur. 1965. *The Logic of Collective Action: Public Goods and the Theory of Groups*. Cambridge, MA: Harvard University Press.
Osterwald-Lenum, Michael. 1992. "A Note with Quantiles of the Asymptotic Distribution of the Maximum Likelihood Cointegration Rank Test Statistics." *Oxford Bulletin of Economics and Statistics* 54: 461–472.
Ostrom, Elinor. 2009. "A General Framework for Analyzing Sustainability of Social-Ecological Systems." *Science* 325 (5939): 419–422.
  2010. "Revising Theory in Light of Experimental Findings." *Journal of Economic Behavior & Organization* 73 (1): 68–72.
Ostrom, Elinor, and James Walker. 1991. "Communication in a Commons: Cooperation without External Enforcement," January.
Ostrom, Elinor, James Walker, and Roy Garden. 1992. "Covenants with and without a Sword: Self-Governance Is Possible." *The American Political Science Review* 86 (2): 404–417.
Ostrom, Elinor, James Walker, and Roy Gardner. 1994. *Rules, Games, and Common-Pool Resources*. University of Michigan Press.
Pal, Manoranjan. 1980. "Consistent Moment Estimators of Regression Coefficients in the Presence of Errors in Variables." *Journal of Econometrics* 14 (3): 349–364.
Palfrey, Thomas R., and Howard Rosenthal. 1985. "Voter Participation and Strategic Uncertainty." *The American Political Science Review* 79 (1): 62–78.
Pavlov, Ivan. 1897. *The Work of the Digestive Glands*. London: Charles Griffin & Co.
Pearl, Judea. 2000. *Causality: Models, Reasoning and Inference*. Cambridge; New York: Cambridge University Press.
Pearson, Karl. 1957 (2004). *The Grammar of Science*. Mineola: Dover Publications.

Persson, Torsten, and Guido Enrico Tabellini. 2002. *Political Economics: Explaining Economic Policy*. Cambridge, MA: MIT Press.

Pfajfar, Damjan. 2013. "Formation of Rationally Heterogeneous Expectations." *Journal of Economic Dynamics and Control* 37 (8): 1434–1452.

Pfajfar, Damjan, and Blaž Žakelj. 2016. "Uncertainty in Forecasting Inflation and Monetary Policy Design: Evidence from the Laboratory." *International Journal of Forecasting* 32 (3): 849–864.

Pfleiderer, Paul. 2014. "Chameleons: The Misuse of Theoretical Models in Finance and Economics." *SSRN Electronic Journal* 16 (July).

Plott, Charles, and Vernon Smith, eds. 2008. *Handbook of Experimental Economics Results*. Vol. 1. Amsterdam: Elsevier/North Holland.

Poteete, Amy R., Marco A. Janssen, and Elinor Ostrom. 2010. *Working Together: Collective Action, the Commons, and Multiple Methods in Practice*. Princeton, NJ: Princeton University Press.

Powell, G. Bingham. 2000. *Elections as Instruments of Democracy: Majoritarian and Proportional Visions*. New Haven, CT: Yale University Press.

Prescott, Edward C. 1986. "Theory Ahead of Business-Cycle Measurement." *Carnegie-Rochester Conference Series on Public Policy* 25 (Fall): 11–44.

Preston, Bruce. 2005. "Learning about Monetary Policy Rules When Long-Horizon Expectations Matter." *International Journal of Central Banking* 1 (2).

Pruitt, Seth. 2012. "Uncertainty Over Models and Data: The Rise and Fall of American Inflation." *Journal of Money, Credit and Banking* 44 (2–4): 341–365.

Putnam, Hilary. 1975. *Philosophical Papers: Volume 2, Mind, Language and Reality*. Cambridge: Cambridge University Press.

Ramsey, Frank P. 1928. "A Mathematical Theory of Saving." *The Economic Journal* 38 (152): 543–559.

Raub, Werner, Vincent W. Buskens, and Marcel van Assen. 2011. "Micro-Macro Links and Microfoundations in Sociology." *Physiology & Behavior* 35 (January): 1–25.

Ravn, Morten O., and Harald Uhlig. 2002. "On Adjusting the Hodrick-Prescott Filter for the Frequency of Observations." *The Review of Economics and Statistics* 84 (2): 371–376.

Reichenbach, Hans. 1951. *The Rise of Scientific Philosophy*. Berkeley: University of California Press.

Riechmann, Thomas. 1999. "Learning and Behavioral Stability: An Economic Interpretation of Genetic Algorithms." *Journal of Evolutionary Economics* 9 (May): 225–242.

2001. *Learning in Economics: Analysis and Application of Genetic Algorithms*. Heldelberg: Physica-Verlag.

Rigden, John S. 2005. "The Mystique of Physics: Relumine the Enlightenment." *American Journal of Physics* 73 (12): 1094–1098.

Riker, William H. 1958. "The Paradox of Voting and Congressional Rules for Voting on Amendments." *The American Political Science Review* 52 (2): 349–366.

1986. *The Art of Political Manipulation*. New Haven, CT: Yale University Press.

Riker, William H., and Peter C. Ordeshook. 1968. "A Theory of the Calculus of Voting." *The American Political Science Review* 62 (1): 25–42.

Rilling, James K., David A. Gutman, Thorsten R. Zeh, Giuseppe Pagnoni, Gregory S. Berns, and Clinton D. Kilts. 2002. "A Neural Basis for Social Cooperation." *Neuron* 35 (2): 395–405.

Romer, David. 2019. *Advanced Macroeconomics*. New York: McGraw-Hill.
Roth, Alvin E. 1993. "The Early History of Experimental Economics." *Journal of the History of Economic Thought* 15 (2): 184–209.
Sally, David. 1995. "Conversation and Cooperation in Social Dilemmas: A Meta-Analysis of Experiments from 1958 to 1992." *Rationality and Society - RATION SOC* 7 (January): 58–92.
Salmon, Wesley C. 1988. "Introduction." In *The Limitations of Deductivism*, edited by A. Grünbaum and Wesley C. Salmon, 1–18. Berkeley, CA: University of California Press.
Sargent, Robert G. 2013. "Verification and Validation of Simulation Models." *Journal of Simulation* 7 (1): 12–24.
Sargent, Thomas J. 1976. "The Observational Equivalence of Natural and Unnatural Rate Theories of Macroeconomics." *Journal of Political Economy* 84 (3): 631–640.
   1979. *Macroeconomic Theory*. San Diego: Academic Press, Inc.
   1993. *Bounded Rationality in Macroeconomics: The Arne Ryde Memorial Lectures*. New York: Oxford University Press.
Sargent, Thomas J., and Neil Wallace. 1975. "'Rational' Expectations, the Optimal Monetary Instrument, and the Optimal Money Supply Rule." *Journal of Political Economy* 83 (2): 241–254.
Sbordone, Argia M., Andrea Tambalotti, Krishna Rao, and Kieran Walsh. 2010. "Policy Analysis Using DSGE Models: An Introduction - FEDERAL RESERVE BANK of NEW YORK." *FRBNY Economic Policy Review* 16 (2): 23–43.
Schmitt, Pamela, Kurtis Swope, and James Walker. 2000. "Collective Action with Incomplete Commitment: Experimental Evidence." *Southern Economic Journal* 66 (4): 829–854.
Schumpeter, Joseph A. 1954 (1994). *History of Economic Analysis*. London: Routledge.
Shachar, Ron. 2003. "Party Loyalty as Habit Formation." *Journal of Applied Econometrics* 18 (3): 251–269.
Shaw, Jamie. 2018. "Why the Realism Debate Matters for Science Policy: The Case of the Human Brain Project." *Spontaneous Generations: A Journal for the History and Philosophy of Science* 9 (1): 82–98.
Sheffrin, Steven M. 1988. "Have Economic Fluctuations Been Dampened? A Look at Evidence Outside the United States." *Journal of Monetary Economics* 21 (1): 73–83.
Shively, W. Phillips. 2017. *The Craft of Political Research*. Abingdon-on-Thames: Routledge.
Signorino, Curtis S. 1999. "Strategic Interaction and the Statistical Analysis of International Conflict." *The American Political Science Review* 93 (2): 279–297.
   2002. "Strategy and Selection in International Relations." *International Interactions* 28 (January): 93–115.
   2003. "Structure and Uncertainty in Discrete Choice Models." *Political Analysis* 11 (4): 316–344.
Signorino, Curtis S., and Ahmer Tarar. 2006. "A Unified Theory and Test of Extended Immediate Deterrence." *American Journal of Political Science* 50 (3): 586–605.
Signorino, Curtis S., and Kuzey Yilmaz. 2003. "Strategic Misspecification in Regression Models." *American Journal of Political Science* 47 (July): 551–566.
Sims, Christopher A. 1980. "Macroeconomics and Reality." *Econometrica* 48 (1): 1–48.
   1996. "Macroeconomics and Methodology." *The Journal of Economic Perspectives* 10 (1): 105–120.

Smith, Vernon L. 1962. "An Experimental Study of Competitive Market Behavior." *Journal of Political Economy* 70 (2): 111–137.

Solow, Robert M. 1956. "A Contribution to the Theory of Economic Growth." *The Quarterly Journal of Economics* 70 (1): 65–94.

Sowell, Thomas. 1974. *Classical Economics Reconsidered*. Princeton, NJ: Princeton University Press.

———. 2006. *On Classical Economics*. New Haven, CT: Yale University Press.

Stadler, George W. 1994. "Real Business Cycles." *Journal of Economic Literature* 32 (4): 1750–1783.

Stigler, George J. 1961. "The Economics of Information." *Journal of Political Economy* 69 (3): 213–225.

———. 1962. "Information in the Labor Market." *Journal of Political Economy* 70 (5): 94–105.

Stokes, Donald E. 1963. "Spatial Models of Party Competition." *The American Political Science Review* 57 (2): 368–377.

Suzuki, Motoshi, and Henry W. Chappell. 1996. "The Rationality of Economic Voting Revisited." *The Journal of Politics* 58 (1): 224–236.

Szmatka, Jacek, and Michael J. Lovaglia. 1996. "The Significance of Method." *Sociological Perspectives* 39 (3): 393–415.

Taylor, John B. 1993. "Discretion versus Policy Rules in Practice." *Carnegie-Rochester Conference Series on Public Policy* 39 (December): 195–214.

———, ed. 1999. *Monetary Policy Rules*. Chicago: University of Chicago Press.

Tullock, Gordon. 1967. "The Welfare Costs of Tariffs, Monopolies, and Theft." *Western Economic Journal* 5 (3): 224.

Turner, John. 1987. "Demand and Supply in the Political Market." *Studies in Economics and Finance* 11 (1): 3–17.

van Fraassen, Bas C. 1980. *The Scientific Image*. Oxford: Oxford University Press.

———. 2007. "From a View of Science to a New Empiricism." In *Images of Empiricism: Essays on Science and Stances, with a Reply From Bas C. Van Fraassen*, edited by Bradley John Monton. Oxford: Oxford University Press.

Viner, Jacob. 1958. *The Long View and the Short*. New York: The Free Press of Glencoe.

Vining, Rutledge. 1949. "Koopmans on the Choice of Variables to Be Studies and the Methods of Measurement." *The Review of Economics and Statistics* 31 (2): 77–86.

Voinea, Camelia F. 2016. *Political Attitudes: Computational and Simulation Modelling*. Chichester: John Wiley & Sons.

Von Neumann, John, Oskar Morgenstern, and Ariel Rubinstein. 1944. *Theory of Games and Economic Behavior* (60th Anniversary Commemorative Edition). Princeton, NJ: Princeton University Press.

Wagner, Markus. 2012. "When Do Parties Emphasise Extreme Positions? How Strategic Incentives for Policy Differentiation Influence Issue Importance?" *European Journal of Political Research* 51 (January): 64–88.

Wagner, R. Harrison. 2001. "Who's Afraid of 'Rational Choice Theory'?" Typescript. University of Texas at Austin.

———. 2007. *War and the State: The Theory of International Politics*. Ann Arbor: University of Michigan Press.

Wang, Miao, and M. C. Sunny Wong. 2005. "Learning Dynamics in Monetary Policy: The Robustness of an Aggressive Inflation Stabilizing Policy." *Journal of Macroeconomics* 27 (1): 143–151.

Weintraub, E. Roy. 2002. *How Economics Became a Mathematical Science*. Durham, NC; London: Duke University Press Books.
Wellford, Charissa P. 1989. "A Laboratory Analysis of Price Dynamics and Expectations in the Cobweb Model." Discussion Paper No. 89-15. Department of Economics, University of Arizona.
Weschle, Simon. 2014. "Two Types of Economic Voting: How Economic Conditions Jointly Affect Vote Choice and Turnout." *Electoral Studies* 34 (June): 39–53.
Whang, Taehee, Elena V. McLean, and Douglas W. Kuberski. 2013. "Coercion, Information, and the Success of Sanction Threats." *American Journal of Political Science* 57 (1): 65–81.
Whittle, Peter. 1963. *Prediction and Regulation by Linear Least-Square Methods*. London: English Universities Press.
    1983. *Prediction and Regulation by Linear Least-Square Methods*. Minneapolis: University of Minnesota Press.
Wilensky, Uri, and William Rand. 2015. *An Introduction to Agent-Based Modeling: Modeling Natural, Social, and Engineered Complex Systems with NetLogo*. Cambridge, MA: MIT Press.
Wilson, Rick K. 2014. "Voting and Agenda Setting in Political Science and Economics." In *Laboratory Experiments in the Social Sciences*, edited by Murray Webster and Jane Sell, 433–458. Amsterdam: Academic Press/Elsevier.
Wolpin, Kenneth I. 2013. *The Limits of Inference without Theory*. Cambridge, MA: MIT Press.
Wooldridge, Jeffrey M. 2015. *Introductory Econometrics: A Modern Approach*. 4th edition. Mason, OH: South Western Cengage Learning.
Woon, Jonathan. 2012. "Democratic Accountability and Retrospective Voting: A Laboratory Experiment." *American Journal of Political Science* 56 (4): 913–930.
Worcester, Kenton W. 2001. *Social Science Research Council, 1923–1998*. New York: Social Science Research Council.
Wray, K. Brad. 2008. "The Argument from Underconsideration as Grounds for Anti-realism: A Defence." *International Studies in the Philosophy of Science* 22 (3): 317–326.
    2013. "Success and Truth in the Realism/Anti-Realism Debate." *Synthese* 190 (9): 1719–1729.
Zellner, Arnold. 1984. *Basic Issues in Econometrics*. Chicago: University of Chicago Press.

Index

Abel, Andrew B., 223–225
abstention inhibition, 251
abstention reinforcement, voter turnout modeling, 250
abstract models, 4–5
   EITM and, 39–44
Achen, Christopher, 15–16, 43–44, 64–66
   cumulative distribution function application, 172
   voter turnout model, 166–168
actual reward matrix, tripartite unification framework, 301–302
Adams, James, 155–156
adaptive expectations
   genetic algorithm modeling, 259–262
   macropartisanship dynamics, 95–96
adaptive learning
   information diffusion and, 124, 129–131
   least squares learning and stochastic recursive algorithms, 119–120
   macroeconomics research, 110, 112–114
   overview of, 117–119
adaptively rational voting model, 252
additivity, tripartite unification framework, 301–302
Affine transformation, aggregation theory, 317–318
agent-based modeling (ABM)
   currency crisis model, 263
   decision making, learning, and prediction, 248
   genetic algorithm and firm price setting, 255–263

   overview, 247–248
   voter turnout, 248–255
agent error, strategic choice models, 184–189
agent knowledge
   information diffusion and, 128–129
   in macroeconomics policy, 114–115
   macroeconomics policy and, 108–109
   tripartite unification framework, 299–305
aggregate demand (AD)
   economic growth models, 62–63
   information diffusion and, 127–131
aggregate party identification, macropartisan dynamics, 80–81
aggregate supply (AS) shock
   economic growth models, 62–63
   information diffusion and, 127–131
   multiple expectations models, 105–107
aggregation error, monetary aggregates model, 312
aggregation theory
   basic principles, 314–318
   Gorman's theorem, 317–318
   Green's theorem, 316
   measurement and, 313–314
   tripartite unification framework, 311–312
Akaike information criterion (AIC), 143
   information diffusion analogues, 133–134
Akerlof, George, 43–44
Alcañiz, Isabella, 63–64
Alesina, Alberto, 58–62, 66, 76–77
The American Voter (Campbell), 78
American Voter model, 79

Index

analogues. *see also* specific analogues, e.g., behavioral analogues
　as aggregate supply (AS) shock, 62–63
　BDT voter turnout model, 252
　computational, 266–270
　decision making, 151–153, 197–201, 249–251
　economic voter model, unification and evaluation, 61–62
　in EITM unification, 30
　empirical analogues, 67–68, 87–89, 266–270
　for expectations, uncertainty and measurement error, 59–61
　genetic algorithm modeling, 259–262
　human behavior modeling, 279–285, 289
　in information diffusion, 127–138
　international political economy, 175–176
　learning, 151–153, 249–251
　least squares regression, formal analogues, 69
　linear projection, 69–71
　in macroeconomics research, 110–114
　in macropartisanship, 81–84
　macro political economy, unification of, 201–204
　nominal choice, 151–153
　prediction, 197–201, 249–251
　recursive projections, 71–73
　voter turnout models, 166–170, 249–251
　voting models and unification of, 151–155
Andreasen, Eugenia, 205–208
Annenberg presidential election study (2000), voter turnout models, 169–170
Ansolabehere, Stephen D., 277–279
applied statistics
　behavioral analogues in EITM and, 29
　economic voting model, 58–59
　expectations and persistence analysis, 80–81
　in political science, 10
　theory unification with, in EITM, 28–29
approval dynamics
　DSGE model, 204–206
　economic performance and, 196, 201–204
　macro political economy, 199–204, 204
　transition probabilities, 203
Arifovic, Jasmina, 255–263
Arrow, Kenneth, 4
aspiration-based reinforcement learning rule
　BDT voter turnout model, 249–251
　updating function, 251
asymmetric information contest
　behavior modeling and, 284–289
　modification of, 290–293
Atkinson's measure, justice index, 306
augmented aggregate supply curve, economic growth models, 59–61
augmented Dickey-Fuller test, information diffusion, 135–138, 142–144
autoregressive-moving-average (ARMA) structure, competence modeling and, 64–66
autoregressive processes
　augmented Dickey-Fuller test, 135–138, 142–144
　Cagan hyperinflation model, 104–105
　conditional expectations, macropartisanship dynamics, 90
　Dickey-Fuller test, 135–138, 140–142
　empirical analogues, macropartisanship, 87
　macroeconomics research, 108–109, 112–114
　multiple expectations models, 106–107
Aytaç, Selim Erdem, 66

bargaining, international political economy, 175–176
Bargsted, Matias A., 156
Barnett, William, 311, 313–314
Bartels, Larry M., 10
Basak, Gopal K., 205–208
Bayesian analysis
　human behavioral modeling, 277–279
　voter turnout models, 166–170, 172–173
BDT voter turnout model, 248
　abstention inhibition, 251
　abstention reinforcement, 250
　analogues in, 249–252
　aspiration updating function, 251
　behavioral analogues, 253–255
　voting inhibition in, 250
　voting reinforcement in, 250
　voting rules, 249–251
behavioral analogues
　applied statistics in EITM and, 29
　BDT voter turnout model, 253–255
　economic growth models, 60–61
　economic voting model, 57–59
　expectations and persistence analysis, 80–81
　speculative currency crises, 179–181
　unification of, in economic voter model, 61–62
　voter turnout models, 166–168

Index

Bellman equation
  dynamic programming and, 231–233
  pie consumption problem, 233–237
Bellman's optimality principle, 231–233
Bendor, Jonathan, 248
Bernanke, Ben, 223–225
Bernoulli distribution, estimation testing, 160–161
bias, regression model errors and, 67–68
binary choice models, political parties and representation and, 157–159
bivariate projections, 73
Blomberg, S. Brock, 196
boomerang effect, information diffusion and, 135–138
bounded rationality assumption, firm price setting model, 256
Box-Steffensmeier, Janet, 10
Brady, Henry E., 10
Bullard, James, 115
Bush, Robert R., 249–251

Cagan hyperinflation model, 102–105
  autoregressive policy or treatment, 104–105
  constant policy or treatment, 103–104
calibration, macro political economy model, 218–224
Calvo, Ernesto, 150–151
Campbell, Angus, 78
Campello, Daniela, 64
capital accumulation
  conditional convergence hypothesis, 32–34
  Solow economic growth model and, 30–31, 35
Carter, David B., 179–181
cause
  in abstract models, 4
  models of, 4–5
  non-cumulative research practices and, 14–19
  scientific definition of, 3
chance
  models of, 4–5
  scientific definition of, 3
Chappell, Henry W., 62–63, 196, 199–201
Chaudoin, Stephen, 278–285, 289
citizen expectations, aggregate party identification, 80–81
Clarke, Harold D., 79–81, 84–86
Clarke, Kevin A., 39–49
closed form solutions, structural modeling, 195–196

Cobb-Douglas production function
  firm profit maximization, 213–215
  Solow model, 30–31
  steady state equilibrium, 31–32
cobweb modeling
  adaptive learning and, 117–119
  analogue unification and evaluation, 259–262
  E-stability conditions derivation, 120–123
  genetic algorithm applications, 256
  information diffusion and, 124
  observable variables, 101–102
  rational expectations model, 100–101
  social interaction and prediction analogues, genetic algorithm and, 256–259
  speed of adjustment errors in expectations, 81–82
  static expectations, 90–91
cointegration testing
  Engle-Granger (EG) procedure, 144–145
  information diffusion, 135–138, 140–149
  Johansen procedure, 145–149
common-pool resources (CPRs), social dilemma research, 36–37
communication, firm price setting model, 256
compensational voting behavior
  analogue unification and evaluation, 154–155
  decision making and nominal choice, 151–153
competence
  economic growth rates and, 64–66
  in economic voter model, 59–60
  expectations of political responsibility and, 63–64
  incumbent competence, 64–66, 76–77
  international performance measurements, 66
  responsibility attribution, 63
  voter assessment of, 61–62
competitive equilibrium, experimental economics, 294
computational analogues, genetic algorithm modeling, 266–270
conditional convergence hypothesis
  derivation, 57
  GDP per capita and economic growth rate, 35
  Solow model, 30–34
conditional expectations, macropartisanship dynamics, 90
  Cobweb theorem observable variables, 101–102

conditional forecast, reduced forms problems with, 21–22
conditional logit model, party identification, 159–160
consumption models
  in discrete time, 228–230
  dynamic programming, Bellman equation, 231–233
  pie consumption problem, 233–240
  Ramsey consumption optimization growth model, 241–246
  two-period model, 225–228
contest success function, human behavior modeling, 279–285
context, social dilemma research, 38
contingency plan or rule, party identification and, 80
continuous time dynamic optimization
  basic principles, 236–238
  pie consumption problem, 238–240
Cournot, Antoine Augustin, 4
Cowles Commission
  EITM framework and, 5, 27–28
  establishment of, 7–9
  macroeconomics research, 110
  structural modeling, 195–196
cross-marginal products, firm profit maximization, 211–215
crossover operator, genetic algorithm modeling, 258–262, 268–269
Croushore, Dean, 223–225
cumulative distribution function (CDF)
  analogue unification and evaluation, voter turnout, 168–170
  international political economy, 176
  strategic choice models, 184–189
  voter turnout models, 166–168, 171–172
currency crises modeling
  agent-based modeling, 263
  analogue unification, 177–179
  behavioral analogues, 179–181
  decision making, bargaining, strategic interaction and nominal choice, 175–176
  QRE analysis, 174–175
Current Population Surveys (CPSs), voter turnout models, 169–170
Cyert, Richard M., 251

data mining, 15–16
  EITM criticism concerning, 40–41
decision making analogue
  genetic algorithm (GA) modeling, 264–265

human behavior modeling, 279–285
international political economy, 175–176
political parties and representation, 151–153
prediction and, 197
voter turnout models, 166–168, 249–251
decomposition methods, justice index and, 306
deductive inference, models and, 4–5
deductive theory
  testing predictions of, 304
  tripartite unification framework, 303
demobilizing effect of negative campaigning, 277–279
Dickey-Fuller test, information diffusion, 135–138, 140–142
Diewert, Walter E., 318–320
difference equations, macropartisanship dynamics, 92–94
differencing methods, nonstationary variables and, 140–149
diminishing marginal returns, firm profit maximization, 211–215
discounting voter choice model
  decision theory and discrete choice and, 151
  political parties and representation research, 150–151
discrete choice, voter turnout models, 166–168
discrete time, dynamic optimization in, 228–230
Divisa aggregates
  index number theory, 318–320
  measurement of, 313–314
  tripartite unification framework, 311–312
  user costs, 313–314
doing the deterring effect
  asymmetric information contest, 291–293
  behavior modeling, 281–285
  Lottery Contest Game, 284–289
Dorfman, Gerald, 10
Downs, Anthony, 46, 78, 151, 164–165
Duch, Raymond, 63
dynamic optimization
  in continuous time, 236–238
  in discrete time, 228–230
  macro political economy, 225–246
  pie consumption problem, 233–240
  Ramsey consumption optimization growth model, 241–246
  two-period consumption model, 225–228
dynamic programming, Bellman equation, 231–233

Index

Dynamic Stochastic General Equilibrium (DSGE) model, 196, 204–206, 208
   real business cycle (RBC) modeling and, 223–225

Econometrica (journal), 7–9
econometrics
   criticism of, 48
   nonstationary time series in, 140–149
Econometric Society, 7–9
An Economic Theory of Democracy (Downs), 78
economic growth models
   administration competence and fortuitous events in, 60–61
   expectations, uncertainty and measurement error in, 59–61
   Solow model of, 30–36
economic performance
   approval dynamics and, 196, 204–206
   information diffusion and, 124–126
economic shocks, in economic voter model, 59–60
economic voting model
   analogue unification in, 61–62
   EITM framework for, 57
   expectations, uncertainty and measurement error in, 59–61
   information assessment and, 66
   international comparisons, 66
   overview of research, 57–59
   responsibility attribution, 63
   retrospective judgments and, 64–66
   theory *vs.* test research and, 62–66
   uncertainty in, 59–63
education variable
   as information proxy, 128–129
   voter turnout models, 169–170
EITM
   agent-based modeling, 247–248
   analogue unification and evaluation, 30
   asymmetric information contest and, 290–293
   basis principles, 3
   behavioral and applied statistical analogues development, 29
   criticism of, 39–44
   economic voting model, 57
   framework for, 27–30, 45–49
   future research applications, 321–324
   human behavior modeling, 277–279
   hypothetico-deductive (H-D) method and, 44–49
   implementation challenges, 322–324
   information diffusion and, 126
   institutional developments in, 5–10
   international political economy analysis, 179–181
   limitations of, 49–50
   Lottery Contest Game, 284–289
   in macroeconomics policy, 114–115
   macroeconomics policy and, 108–109
   macropartisan dynamics and, 79, 84
   motivation criticisms of, 39–44
   persistence perspective in, 86–87
   political parties and representation, 155–156
   rational choice theory and, 47–49
   real business cycle modeling, 195–196
   research design and, 44–46
   scientific research methods and, 12–14
   social dilemma research, 36–38
   Solow model unification, 35–36
   theoretical concepts and applied statistics unification, 28–29
   voter turnout models, 165, 169–170
election operator, genetic algorithm modeling
   analogue unification and evaluation, 259–262
   genetic algorithm modeling, 258
electoral rule effect, political parties and representation research, 150–151
Elliott-Rothenberg-Stock test, information diffusion, 135–138
empirical analogues
   autoregressive processes, 87
   genetic algorithm modeling, 266–270
   macropartisanship dynamics, 87–89
   measurement error and error in variables regression, 67–68
   political parties and representation, 157–161
   random walk and random shock persistence, 88–89
   voter turnout models, 171–172
empirical modeling
   criticism of, 39–44
   EITM framework and, 45–49
   formal modeling *vs.*, 43–44
   future research applications, 321–324
   theory *vs.*, 12–14, 41–42
   tripartite unification framework, 304–305
endogeneity, Granger causality test for, information diffusion analogues, 133–134, 139

Engel's law, 317–318
Engle, Robert F., 140–149
Engle-Granger (EG) procedure, 144–145
equilibrium choice probabilities, international political economy, 176
Erikson, Robert S., 79
error weighting, Omega matrices, 16–18
E-stability conditions
  adaptive learning and, 118
  adaptive learning models, 110
  derivation of, 120–123
  least squares learning and stochastic recursive algorithms, 119–120
  macroeconomics analogue unification, 112–114
estimation testing, party identification, 160–161
Evans, George W., 108–109, 117–124, 129–131
evolution of the initiative, hypothetical-deductive method and, 44–46
examination, firm price setting model, 256
expectations modeling. *see also* specific types of expectations, e.g., rational expectations
  adaptive expectations, 95–96
  analogues in information diffusion, 127–131
  analogues in macroeconomics research, 110–112
  analogues in macropartisanship for, 81–82
  behavioral and applied statistical analysis of, 80–81
  competency as basis for, 63–64
  conditional expectations, macropartisanship dynamics, 90
  in economic voting model, 59–62
  information diffusion and, 126
  iterated expectations, 99
  macroeconomics research, 110
  macropartisan dynamics and, 79
  of political responsibility, competence based on, 63–64
  speed of adjustment errors, macropartisanship dynamics, 94
  static expectations, Cobweb theorem and, 90–91
  voting models and, 151–153
expected payoff value, behavior modeling, 281–285
experimental economics
  market clearing experiments, 296–297
  overview of, 294–297

  public goods experiments, 294–296
extensive-form game, international political economy, 176–177

face-to-face communication, social dilemma research, 36–37
favorability perceptions, party identification and, 80
Feynman, Richard, 12–14
Fiorina, Morris P., 78, 164–165
firm price setting model
  analogues for social interaction and prediction in, 256–259
  analogue unification and evaluation, 259–262
  genetic algorithm and, 255–263
  social interaction elements in, 256
firm profit maximization, 199, 211–215
first-order conditions (FOCs), asymmetric information contest, 291–293
fitness function, genetic algorithm modeling, 267
formal analogues
  conditional expectations, 90
  dynamic optimization, 225–246
  Dynamic Stochastic General Equilibrium (DSGE) model, 208
  genetic algorithm modeling, 264–265
  international political economy analysis, 181–194
  macro political economy, 208
  macroeconomics research, 116–117
  macropartisanship dynamics, 90–107
  party identification and, 161–163
  voter turnout models, 172–173
formal modeling
  empirical modeling *vs.*, 39–44
  future research applications, 321–324
  least squares regression, 69
  linear projection, 69–71
  recursive projections, 71–73
Fowler, James H., 248, 253–255
Fox, Justin, 277–279
framing coefficient, tripartite unification framework, 301–302
Franklin, Charles H., 78–79
free-rider problem, public goods experiments, 294–296
Freeman & Houser, 204–206
Freeman, John R., 139, 196, 199–201
frequency distribution of voting turnout, BDT model, 253–255

Index

Friedman, Milton, 15–16, 59
Fuller, Wayne A., 140–142

Gabaix, Xavier, 4–5
game theory
   agent error and private information in, 184–189
   human behavior modeling, 278
   international political economy, 176–177
   QRE applications, 179–181
   social dilemma research, 36–38
   strategic choice modeling, 181–182
   strategic probit model, 177–179
   STRAT program and, 189–194
garbage-can regression, 40–41
Gawrońska-Nowak, Bogna, 263
gender gap
   actual and just earnings, 310
   justice index and, 310
   ratio of, 310
   tripartite unification framework research, 305–310
generalization in models
   critique of, 4
   EITM and, 39–44
genes, chromosomes, and populations, genetic algorithm operation, 266–267
genetic algorithm (GA) modeling
   analogues for social interaction and prediction in, 256–259
   analogue unification and evaluation, 259–262
   computational and empirical analogues, 266–270
   crossover operator, 258, 268–269
   decision theory and, 264–265
   development of, 247–248
   election operator, 258
   firm price setting model, 255–263
   fitness function, 267
   formal analogues, 264–265
   genes, chromosomes, and populations, 266–267
   MATLAB simulation, 270–276
   mutation operator, 258, 269
   process overview, 271
   production decision application, 269–270
   real world data *vs.*, 263
   reproduction operator, 258, 268
   social interaction in, 256
getting deterred effect
   asymmetric information contest, 291–293
   behavior modeling, 281–285
   Lottery Contest Game, 284–289
good luck, in economic voter model, 59–60
Gorman's theorem, 317–318
government approval target deviation minimization
   macro political economy, 199–204
   transition probabilities, 203
Grabowski, Wojciech, 263
Grafstein, Robert, 196
Granato, Jim, 27, 39–46, 79–81, 84–86, 108–109, 124
Granger, Clive W. J., 140–149
Granger causality test, information diffusion, 133–134, 139
Greene, William H., 161–162
Green's theorem, aggregation theory, 316
Guala, Francesco, 295–296

habitual voting behavior, BDT voter turnout model, 253–255
Hausman, Daniel N., 67–68
Hellwig, Timothy, 63–64, 150–151
Hess, Gregory D., 196
hierarchical theory
   propositions construed in, 304
   tripartite unification framework, 303
higher approval target (HAT), approval dynamics, 203–204
Hodrick, Robert, 203
Holland, John H., 247–248, 255
Honkapohja, Seppo, 108–109, 117–124, 129–131
Hotelling, Harold, 151
household utility maximization, 197–199
   analogue unification and evaluation, 201–204
   behavioral analogues, 208–211
   derivation of, 205–208
Houser, Daniel, 196, 199–201
human behavior modeling
   analogue unification and evaluation, 284–289
   decision making and prediction analogues, 279–285
   overview, 277–279
   public goods experiments, 295–296
   tripartite unification framework for, 298–311
hypothesis testing, party identification, 161
hypothetico-deductive (H-D) method, EITM and, 44–49

identification
  EITM limitations concerning, 49–50
  probability approach and, 7–9
imitation, firm price setting model, 256
incumbent competence
  optimal forecasting of, 76–77
  voter retrospective judgment of, 64–66, 164–165
index function model, 157–158
index number theory, 318–320
individual behavior, social dilemma research, 37
inductive inference, models and, 4–5
inertia, in macroeconomics policy, 114–115
inflation and policy analysis
  inflation persistence, macroeconomics policy, 113
  non-cumulative research and, 20–21
information diffusion
  analogues in models of, 127–131
  analogue unification and evaluation, 132–138
  asymmetric information contest and, 290–293
  augmented Dickey-Fuller test, 135–138, 142–144
  cointegration testing, 135–138, 140–149
  Engle-Granger (EG) procedure, 144–145
  Granger causality test, 133–134, 139
  Johansen procedure, cointegration testing, 145–149
  Lottery Contest Game, 284–289
  overview, 124–126
  social interaction, expectation and learning, simultaneity and prediction error and, 126
  unit root testing, 134–138, 140–149
interest rate policy rule, non-cumulative research and, 19–24
international comparisons, economic voter model, 66
international political economy
  analogue unification, 177–179
  decision making, bargaining, strategic interaction and nominal choice, 175–176
  EITM framework and, 174–175
International Social Justice Project (ISJP), 305–310
invariance of relation, probability approach and, 7–9
invention, firm price setting model, 256
Iron Law of Econometrics, 67–68
IS curve, aggregate demand, 19–24

iterated expectations, macropartisanship dynamics, 99

Jackson, John E., 78–79
Jasso, Guillermina, 298–311
Johansen, Søren, 140–149
Johansen procedure, cointegration testing, 145–149
Jones, Richard, 4
just earnings, gender gap in, 310
justice analysis, tripartite unification framework, 299–305
justice evaluation matrix, tripartite unification framework, 301–302
justice index, 298–299
  alternative just rewards structure, 308
  decomposition methods, 306
  gender decomposition, 310
  gender gap and, 305–310
  methods for, 306–308
  results analysis, 308–309
just reward matrix
  justice index, 308
  tripartite unification framework, 301–302

Kaldor, Nicholas, 90–91
Kedar, Orit, 150–155, 161
Keech, William R., 196, 199–201
Kenkel, Brenton, 188
Key, 78
Keynes, John Maynard, 48
Keynesian economics
  DSGE model and, 223–225
  macroeconomics policy and, 108–109, 115
known reliability ratio, empirical analogue measurement errors, 68
Kramer, Gerald H., 58
Krause, George A., 124
Kydland, Finn E., 195–196

Lagrange multiplier (LM) test, information diffusion analogues, 133–134
Laibson, David, 4–5
larger approval shocks (LAS), approval dynamics, 203–204
laws of motion
  adaptive learning and, 118–120
  Cagan hyperinflation model, 103–104
  E-stability conditions derivation, 120–123
  information diffusion and, 129–131
  macroeconomics policy and, 108–109
  voting rules and, 249–251

Index

Lazarsfeld, Paul F., 124–126
learning analogues
  aspiration-based reinforcement learning rule, 249–251
  in information diffusion, 127–131
  information diffusion and, 124
  in macroeconomics research, 110–112
  simultaneity and prediction error and, 126
  voter turnout models, 166–168, 249–251
least squares learning, 119–120, 129–131
  genetic algorithm modeling, 259–262
least squares regression, formal analogues, 69
Leblang, David, 175–176, 189–194
Levine, David K., 277–279
Lijphart, Arend, 154–155
likelihood function, estimation testing, 160–161
linear environment, public goods experiments, 295–296
linear homogeneity, aggregation theory, 317–318
linearization, macro political economy model, 218–224
linear projection, formal analogues, 69–71
log-ratio specification, tripartite unification framework, 301–302
logit model, party preferences, 158
Lopez, Maria C., 36–37
Lottery Contest Game, behavior modeling and, 284–289
Lubik, Thomas A., 115
Lucas, Robert, 8, 46, 59, 74–76
Lucas relative-general uncertainty model, signal extraction problems, 74–76
Lucas supply model, information diffusion and, 127–131

MacKinnon, James, 140–142
macroeconomics research
  analogues for expectations, learning and persistence in, 110–112
  empirical *vs.* formal modeling, 43–44
  expectations, learning and persistence in, 110
  formal analogues in, 116–117
  overview of, 108–109
  RBC theory and DSGE model transition, 223–225
  unification and evaluation of analogues in, 112–114
macropartisanship. *see also* political parties and representation

adaptive expectations, 95–96
analogues for expectations and persistence and, 81–82
analogue unification and evaluation, 82–84
Cobweb theorem and, 90–91
difference equations, 92–94
EITM perspective on persistence in, 86–87
empirical analogues, 87–89
expectations and persistence analysis, 80–81
formal analogues, 90–107
overview of research, 78–79
random walk and random shock persistence, 88–89
rational expectations modeling, 90, 96–99
speed of adjustment errors in expectations, 94
macro political economy
  analogues, 197–201
  analogue unification and evaluation, 201–204
  consumption models in discrete time, 228–230
  continuous time dynamic optimization, 236–238
  decision making and prediction in, 197
  dynamic optimization, 225–246
  dynamic programming, Bellman equation, 231–233
  firm profit maximization, 199, 211–215
  formal analogues, 208, 225–246
  government approval target deviation minimization, 199–201
  household utility maximization, 197–199, 201–211
  international comparisons, 204–206
  linearization and calibration in model of, 218–224
  non-cumulative research practices and, 19–24
  pie consumption problem, 233–240
  Ramsey consumption optimization growth model, 241–246
  RBC theory and DSGE model transition, 223–225
  research background, 195–196
  steady state of model structure, 213–215
  two-period consumption model, 225–228
Malthus, Robert, 4
Mankiw, N. Gregory, 35
March, James G., 251
Marcus, George, 10

marginal decision rule, party identification and, 161–162
marginal product of capital (MPK), firm profit maximization, 211–215
marginal product of labor (MPL), firm profit maximization, 211–215
market clearing experiments, 296–297
Markov Chain process, macro political economy model, 201–204
mathematical models, 4–5
MATLAB simulation, genetic algorithm (GA) modeling, 270–276
Matthes, Christian, 115
maximum likelihood estimation (MLE)
  analogue unification, international political economy, 177–179
  party identification, 160–161
McCallum, Bennett T., 106–107
McFadden, Daniel L., 159–160, 162–163
McKelvey, Richard D., 174–175, 182–184, 189
mean-equality decomposition, justice index, 306
mean-inequality decomposition, justice index, 306
mean squared error (MSE), information diffusion analogue unification and evaluation, 132–138
measurement error
  in economic voting model, 59–62
  empirical analogues, 67–68
  signal extraction problems, 74
  voter uncertainty models and, 64–66
Mebane, Walter R., 66
Merriam, Charles, 6
Merrill, Samuel, 155–156
methodological unification
  alternative framework for, 298–311
  future research applications, 321–324
  Solow model, 30–36
Miller, John H., 255
Minford, Patrick, 49–50
minimum state variable (MSV) solution
  analogue unification and evaluation, 82–84
  Clark & Granato model, 84–86
  expectations and persistence analogues, 81–82
  inflation and policy analysis, 20–21
  macroeconomics analogues unification, 112–114
  macroeconomics formal analogues, 116–117
  multiple expectations models, 106–107
Mitra, Kaushik, 115

mixed expectations equilibrium (MEE), information diffusion and, 130–131
models and modeling
  methodological unification, 30–38
  utility of, 4–5
model testing practices, 45
monetary aggregates
  error in, 312
  theory $vs.$ measurement, 313–314
  tripartite unification framework, 311–312
  user costs, 313–314
Mosteller, Frederick, 249–251
motivation criticism of EITM, 39–44
moving average (MA(1)) process
  analogue unification, 61–62
  in economic voter model, 59–60
multinomial choice models, party preferences, 159–160
multinomial logit model (MNL), party preferences, 159
mutation operator, genetic algorithm modeling, 258, 269
Muth, John F., 86

Nash equilibrium
  asymmetric information contest, 291–293
  decision making and prediction analogues, behavior modeling, 279–285
  human behavior modeling, 277–279
  Lottery Contest Game, 284–289
  public goods experiments, 295–296
New Keynesian model, macroeconomics and, 115
nominal choice analogue
  international political economy, 175–176
  political parties and representation, 151–153
non-cumulative research practices
  overview of, 14–19
  problems with, 19–24
non-governmental actors, responsibility attribution and, 63
non-linear cost functions, asymmetric information contest, 291–293
nonstationary variables, cointegration testing and, 140–149

observational equivalence, EITM limitations and, 49–50
observational error, information diffusion and, 131, 134–138
observational validation, prediction and, 12–14

Index

Omega matrices, 16–18
  statistical patches and, 40–41
order
  in abstract models, 4
  models of, 4–5
  scientific definition of, 3
Ordeshook, Peter C., 78, 164–165
ordinary differential equation (ODE),
  E-stability conditions, 118
ordinary least squares (OLS)
  economic voting model, 57–59
  Omega matrices, 16–18
orthogonality principle
  least squares regression, 69
  linear projection, 69–71
  recursive projections, 71–73
  signal extraction measurement error, 74
Ostrom, Elinor, 36–38, 295–296
overparameterization, 16
  EITM criticism concerning, 40–41
own value effect
  asymmetric information contest, 291–293
  behavior modeling, 281–285
  Lottery Contest Game, 284–289

Palfrey, Thomas R., 174–175, 182–184, 189, 277–279
parameters
  macro political economy model, 201–204
  predictions and, 19–24
  real business cycle (RBC) linearization and calibration, 218–224
party identification
  analogue evaluation and unification, 154–155
  binary choice models, 157–159
  decision making and nominal choice analogues, 151–153
  decision theory and discrete choice in, 151
  EITM perspective on persistence in, 86–87
  empirical analogues, 157–161
  estimation testing, 160–161
  expectations and persistence analysis, 80–81
  formal analogues, 161–163
  hypothesis testing, 161
  logit model, 158
  marginal decision rule, 161–162
  multinomial choice models, 159–160
  overview of research, 78–79
  political parties and representation research, 150–151
  probit model, 157–158

Pearson, Karl, 3
persistence
  analogues in macroeconomics research, 110–112
  analogues in macropartisanship for, 81–82
  behavioral and applied statistical analysis of, 80–81
  EITM perspective on, 86–87
  inflation persistence, macroeconomics policy, 113
  macroeconomics research, 110
  macropartisan dynamics and, 79
  random shocks, macropartisanship empirical analogues, 88–89
Pfajfar, Damjan, 108–109, 115, 124–126
Phillips curve, 19–24
pie consumption problem
  continuous time optimization, 238–240
  discrete time optimization, 233–237
Plott, Charles, 294–296
policy and inflation analysis
  Cagan hyperinflation model, 103–104
  EITM applications in, 323–324
  non-cumulative research and, 20–21
  shift dummy variables and, 22–24
policy outcomes, voting models and, 151–153, 164–165
Political Analysis (journal), 10
political business cycle (PBC) model, 196
Political Methodology (journal), 10
political parties and representation. *see also* party identification
  analogue unification and evaluation and, 154–155
  binary choice models, 157–159
  decision making and nominal choice analogues, 151–153
  decision theory and discrete choice, 151
  EITM framework and, 155–156
  empirical analogues, 157–161
  formal analogues, 161–163
  research overview, 150–151
political science
  economics and, 294–296
  human behavior modeling, 277–279
  public goods experiments, 294–296
Political Science Department at the University of Rochester, 9–10
political science research
  applied statistics in, 10
  hypothetical-deductive method and, 44–46
  statistical methods in, 9–10

positive political theory, 9–10
prediction
  agent-based modeling, 248
  analogues in genetic algorithm modeling, 256–259
  decision making and, 197
  errors of, 127–131
  firm price setting model, 256
  genetic algorithm modeling, 256
  human behavior modeling, 279–285
  information diffusion and error in, 126
  observational validation and, 12–14
  parameters and, 19–24
  voter turnout models, 249–251
Prescott, Edward C., 195–196, 203, 223–225
Preston, Bruce, 108–109
p-restriction, Omega matrices, 18
pricing dynamics, stochastic difference equations, 92–94
Primo, David M., 39–49
private information, strategic choice models, 184–189
probability approach
  identification and invariance and, 7–9
  statistical inference, 4
probability density function (PDF), voter turnout models, 171–172
probit model
  voter turnout and, 168–170
  voting preferences and, 157–158
production decision, genetic algorithm modeling, 269–270
productivity shocks, RBC theory and DSGE model transition, 223–225
propensity function, voting rules and, 249–251
proximity model
  decision making and nominal choice analogues, 151–153
  decision theory and discrete choice and, 151
  political parties and representation research, 150–151
public approval seeking government, target deviation minimization, 199–201
public expectations, macroeconomic policy and, 108–109
public goods experiments, 294–296

quantal response equilibrium (QRE)
  international political economy, 174–175, 179–181
  rationality and perfect information, 182–189
quantitative economics, Cowles approach in, 7–9

Ramsey consumption optimization growth model, 241–246
random shocks, macropartisanship empirical analogues, 88–89
random utility model (RUM), party identification and, 159, 162–163
random walk, macropartisanship empirical analogues, 88–89
rational choice theory
  failure of models for, 47–49
  human behavior modeling, 277–279
rational expectations equilibrium (REE)
  adaptive learning and, 117–119
  Cobweb theorem, 100–102
  E-stability derivation, 120–123
  genetic algorithm modeling, 259–262
  information diffusion and, 127–131
  macroeconomics research, 110
  macropartisanship modeling, 81–82, 84, 86
  multiple expectations models, 106–107
  unification and evaluation of macroeconomics analogues, 112–114
rational expectations modeling
  Cagan hyperinflation model, 102–105
  Cobweb theorem observable variables, 100–102
  macroeconomics policy and, 108–109, 116–117
  macropartisanship dynamics, 90, 96–99
  multiple expectations models, 105–107
  solutions, 99–107
real business cycle (RBC) modeling
  approval dynamics and, 204–206
  development of, 8
  DSGE models and, 223–225
  fiscal policy outcomes and, 204–206
  formal analogues, 208
  linearization and calibration, 218–224
  macro political economy and, 195–196
reality-ideology decomposition, justice index, 306
recursive least squares (RLS), adaptive learning and, 119–120
recursive projections and equation analogue unification, 61–62
  formal analogues, 71–73

Index

incumbent competence, optimal forecasting of, 76–77
reduced form estimates
  inflation and policy analysis, 21–22
  limitations of, 49–50
  multiple expectations models, 105–107
regression models, empirical analogues and errors in, 67–68
representational voting behavior
  analogue unification and evaluation, 154–155
  decision making and nominal choice, 151–153
reproduction operator, genetic algorithm modeling, 258, 268
responsibility attribution, economic voter model, 63
retrospective judgment
  of incumbent competence, 64–66
  voter behavior and, 64–66
Revising Theory in Light of Experimental Findings (Ostrom), 36–38
Ricardo, David, 4
Riker, William, 9–10, 78, 164–165
Riker, William H., 78, 164–165
Rosenthal, Howard, 58–62, 66, 76–77

Sally, David, 36–37
Salmon, Wesley, 45–47
Sargent, Thomas, 49–50, 69
Sargent, Thomas J., 105–107
Say, Jean Baptiste, 4
scale-invariance, tripartite unification framework, 301–302
Schwartz, Anna J., 15–16
Schwarz Information Criterion (SIC), 143
scientific research methods
  EITM applications in, 323–324
  non-cumulative research practices, 14–19
  theory *vs.* empirics, 12–14
Scioli, Frank, 39–46
seat premium, political parties and representation research, 150–151
self-regarding model
  information diffusion and, 127–131
  social dilemma research, 36–37
shift dummy variables (SHIFT), policy and inflation analysis, 22–24
Shotts, Kenneth W., 277–279
signal extraction problems
  economic voting model, 59–60

Lucas model (relative-general uncertainty), 74–76
measurement error, 74
optimal forecast of political incumbent competence, 76–77
responsibility attribution, 63
Signorino, Curtis S., 174–176, 182–194
simple-sum aggregates, tripartite unification framework, 311–312
Sims, Christopher, 8
simulation results, policy and inflation analysis, 22–24
simultaneity
  analogues in information diffusion, 127–131
  Granger causality test, 133–134, 139
  information diffusion and, 126
Sismonde, J. C. L., 4
Smith, Adam, 296–297
Smith, Vernon, 294–297
social dilemma research, 36–38
  context and, 38
  individual behavior and, 37
social interaction
  analogues for, in genetic algorithm modeling, 256–259
  analogues for, in information diffusion, 127–131
  firm price setting model, 256
  information diffusion and, 124
  simultaneity and prediction error and, 126
Social Science Research Council (SSRC), 6, 132–138
social science, EITM applications in, 323–324
social sciences
  experimental economics and, 294–297
  human behavior modeling, 277–279
  non-cumulative research practices in, 14–19
  quantitative analysis in, 6
Society for Political Methodology, 10
Solow growth model, 30–36, 241–246
  conditional convergence hypothesis, 30–34
  steady state equilibrium and, 31–32
  unification in, 35–36
spatial theory, political parties and representation research, 150–151
speculative currency crises
  analogue unification, 177–179
  decision making, bargaining, strategic interaction and nominal choice, 175–176
  EITM framework and, 174–175
  QRE analysis, 174–175

speed of adjustment errors, macropartisanship dynamics, 94
  rational expectations modeling, 96–99
Stackelberg framework, information diffusion and, 124
static expectations
  Cobweb theorem and, 90–91
  genetic algorithm modeling, 259–262
statistical index numbers, 318–320
  monetary aggregates, 313–314
statistical inference, probability approach, 4
statistical methods, in political science, 9–10
statistical patching, EITM criticism concerning, 40–41
Statistical Research Group (Columbia University), 15–16
steady state equilibrium
  macro political economy, 213–215
  Solow model and, 31–32
Stevenson, Randolph T., 63
stochastic difference equations, macropartisanship dynamics, 92–94
stochastic recursive algorithm (SRA), adaptive learning and, 119–120
stochastic shocks
  party identification and, 80–81
  strategic choice models, 184–189
Stone, Randall W., 179–181
strategic coalition voting, 156
strategic interaction
  international political economy, 175–176
  in macroeconomics policy, 115
strategic probit model, international political economy, 177–179
strategic voting model, international comparisons, 179–181
STRAT program, statistical strategic models, 189–194
structural modeling, macro political economy, 110, 195–196
subgame perfect equilibrium (SPE), strategic choice modeling, 181–182
Sullivan, John, 10
Suzuki, Motoshi, 62–63
systemtime variable, voter turnout models, 169–170

Taylor rule/Taylor principle
  analogues in macroeconomics research, 111
  macroeconomics policy and, 108–109
theoretical models
  applied statistics and, 28–29
  data mining and, 15–16
  EITM framework, 27–30, 45–49
  empirics and, 12–14, 44–49
  rational choice theory, 47–49
  test $vs.$, 18–19
Threat and Imposition of Sanctions (TIES) database, 179–181
time series analysis, cointegration testing and, 140–149
T-mapping, E-stability conditions, 118, 120–123
transition probabilities, macro political economy and, 201–204
Tripartite Structure of Social Science Analysis (Jasso), 298–299
tripartite unification framework
  aggregation theory, 314–318
  deductive theory, 303
  elements of, 299–305
  empirical analysis, 304–305
  extratheoretical measurement and estimation, 304–310
  gender gap and justice index, 305–310
  hierarchical theory, 303
  index number theory, 318–320
  monetary aggregates, 311–312
  overview, 298–299
t-statistic
  non-cumulative research and, 15
  numerator influences on, 40
  Omega matrices and, 16–18
  overparameterization, 16
  statistical patches and, 40–41
Tullock, Gordon, 279–285
turnout paradox, rational choice theory, 47–49
two-period consumption model, 225–228
two-player, three-outcome game, strategic choice modeling, 181–182
two-player contest model
  analogue unification and evaluation, 284–289
  decision making and prediction analogues for, 279–285
  human behavior modeling, 278
two-stage least squares, economic voting model, 57–59
two-step communication model, information diffusion and, 124–126
Type I error, false rejection of null hypothesis, 40
Type II error, false acceptance of null hypothesis, 40

Index

uncertainty
  alternative measurement of, 62–63
  in economic voting model, 59–62
  Lucas model (relative-general uncertainty), 74–76
undetermined coefficients
  Cagan hyperinflation model, 104–105
  inflation and policy analysis, 20–21
unit root testing, information diffusion and, 134–138, 140–149
univariate projections, 73
unreality, theories of, 40
user costs, monetary aggregates, 313–314
utility maximization
  aggregation theory, 314–318
  continuous-time maximization problem, 236–238
  dynamic programming, Bellman equation, 231–233
  household, 197–199
  international political economy, 176–177
  party identification and, 150–151, 155–156, 162–163
  policy outcomes and, 151–153
  strategic choice models, 184–189
  two-period consumption model, 225–228
  voter turnout models, 166–168, 248

variables regression error, empirical analogues, 67–68
vector autoregression (VAR)
  information diffusion and, 124, 133–134
  Johansen procedure, cointegration testing, 145–149
vote-maximizing parties
  alternative theories concerning, 155–156
  political parties and representation research, 150–151
voter affiliation. *see* party identification
voter turnout modeling, *see* specific models, e.g., BDT voter turnout model
  abstention inhibition, 251
  adaptively rational parameters, 251
  agent-based modeling, 248–255
  analogue unification and evaluation, 168–170
  aspiration updating function, 251
  decision making analogue, 166–168, 248–251
  discrete choice analogue, 166–168
  empirical analogues, 171–172
  formal analogues, 172–173
  learning analogue, 166–168, 248–251
  overview of research on, 78, 164–165
  prediction analogue, 248–251
  turnout paradox, 47–49
  voting inhibition in, 250
  voting reinforcement in, 250
voter turnout models, voting rules in, 249–251
voting models. *see also* party identification
  human behavior modeling, 277–279
  logic and empirical truth in, 46
  rational choice theory, 47–49

Wallace, Neil, 105–107
weak separability, aggregation theory, 316
Wellford, Clarissa, 262
Whang, Taehee, 179–181
Wong, M. C. Sunny, 84, 108–109
Woon, Jonathan, 277–285, 289

Žakelj, Blaž, 108–109, 115
Zucco, Cesar, 64

CPSIA information can be obtained
at www.ICGtesting.com
Printed in the USA
LVHW092127070521
686799LV00001B/25